William L. Petersen, Dr. Theol. (Utrecht, 1984), is Associate Professor at the Pennsylvania State University.

Johan S. Vos, Ph. D. (1973), University of Utrecht, is Lecturer in New Testament studies at the Vrije Universiteit Amsterdam.

Henk Jan de Jonge, Ph. D. (1983), University of Leiden, is Professor of New Testament and Early Christian Literature at the University of Leiden.

SAYINGS OF JESUS:
CANONICAL AND NON-CANONICAL

SUPPLEMENTS TO
NOVUM TESTAMENTUM

VOLUME LXXXIX

SAYINGS OF JESUS:
CANONICAL AND NON-CANONICAL

Essays in Honour of
Tjitze Baarda

EDITED BY

WILLIAM L. PETERSEN
JOHAN S. VOS
HENK J. DE JONGE

BRILL
LEIDEN · NEW YORK · KÖLN
1997

This book is printed on acid-free paper.

The LaserHebrew, LaserSyriac, and LaserGreek fonts used to print this work are available from Linguist's Software, Inc., PO Box 580, Edmonds, WA 98020-0580 USA, tel. (206) 775-1130.

Library of Congress Cataloging-in-Publication Data

Sayings of Jesus : canonical and non-canonical : essays in honour of
    Tjitze Baarda / edited by William L. Petersen, Johan S. Vos, Henk J.
    de Jonge.
        p.   com. — (Supplements to Novum Testamentum, ISSN 0167-9732 ;
    v. 89)
        Includes bibliographical references and indexes.
        ISBN 9004103805 (cloth : alk. paper)
        1. Jesus Christ—Words.   I. Baarda, Tjitze.   II. Petersen,
    William Lawrence, 1950–   .   III. Vos, J. S.   IV. Jonge, H. J. de.
    V. Series.
    BT306.S335   1997   97–34258
                                                                            CIP

Die Deutsche Bibliothek – CIP-Einheitsaufnahme

[Novum testamentum / Supplements]
Supplements to Novum testamentum. – Leiden ; New York ; Köln :
Brill
        Früher Schriftenreihe
        Fortlaufende Beiheftreihe zu: Novum testamentum
Vol. 89. Sayings of Jesus: canonical and non-canonical. – 1997
Sayings of Jesus: canonical and non-canonical : essays in honour
of Tjitze Baarda / ed. William L. Petersen ... – Leiden ; New York ;
Köln : Brill, 1997
        (Supplements to Novum testamentum ; Vol. 89)
        ISBN 90–04–10380–5

                                ISSN   0167-9732
                                ISBN   90 04 10380 5

PRINTED IN THE NETHERLANDS

CONTENTS

INDICES

Hooggeleerde Baarda, beste Tjitze!

The *Festschrift* is certainly one of the happiest, noblest traditions of academe. It stands as a tangible monument, reflecting upon the past, celebrating the present, and pointing to the future.

This is a happy day for all of us, as we, your friends and colleagues from around the world, join together in celebrating with you a great milestone in your life: your retirement from your professional academic career, and your sixty-fifth birthday.

When you were a child, rather than attend the public school close to your humble home in Vogelenzang, you were enrolled in the *School met de Bijbel* in Bennebroek, a walk which took an hour on a little boy's short legs. Since then, that boy has traveled many more miles: to the Vrije Universiteit Amsterdam, where you first studied with, then assisted, and finally succeeded Rein Schippers as Professor of New Testament; to St. Andrews in Scotland, where you taught beside Matthew Black and your good friend Robin Wilson; to Utrecht University, where you held the chair of New Testament and Ancient Judaism, and continued its distinguished line of Diatessaronic scholarship, founded by Daniël Plooij; to The Divinity School of Harvard University, where you enjoyed the colleagueship of your friend Helmut Koester; and, finally, back to your *alma mater*, the Vrije Universiteit, where you now retire not only from the chair of New Testament, but also from the Deanship of the Faculty of Theology. Along the way we, who have observed you in so many states—weary from three conference papers in three weeks or editing or reading dissertations or another Atlantic crossing, honoured upon your election to the Royal Academy in 1982, elated after the success of your *notarikon* paper at the SNTS conference in Edinburgh in 1994, patiently helping a student understand a point in Syriac grammar—we have wondered not only at your boundless energy, your unflagging enthusiasm for your craft, your constant kindness, and your profound humanity, but also at the vastness of your erudition, the unfailing accuracy of your learning, the wisdom of your judgements, and the depth of your insight. It is we who have benefited from all of these for nearly forty years, and for them we are permanently in your debt. Future generations of scholars are in your debt as well for, as you well know, your learning and wisdom are at this very moment being transmitted to students who are your intellectual grandchildren and great-grandchildren. The chain of learning began in humanity's ancient past; it extends to some still-unknown point in the future. You have been a strong link in that chain, a link which—no matter how heavily burdened—never failed.

We offer you these studies as a token of our love, respect, and admiration. It is our hope they will not only give you pleasure, but also advance those areas of scholarship to which your studies have contributed so much. May you and your dear wife Hilda be blessed with good health and happiness in your retirement, and may you be given—at last!—the leisure to pursue projects postponed during the press of a professional career. *Ad multos annos!*

W. L. P., J. S. V., H. J. de J.
Amsterdam
10.X.1997

A BIBLIOGRAPHY OF THE WRITINGS OF TJITZE BAARDA

compiled by J. S. Vos

BOOKS

1. *De betrouwbaarheid van de Evangeliën*, Cahiers voor de gemeente 2 (Kampen 1967; 1969³), pp. 92.
2. *Kanttekeningen bij het lijdensverhaal naar Mattheüs* [edited text of seven broadcast lectures], Verken de bijbel 4 (Amsterdam/Driebergen 1969), pp. 63.
3. *Vier = Een. Enkele bladzijden uit de geschiedenis van de harmonistiek der Evangeliën* [inaugural address Amsterdam, 5 December 1969] (Kampen 1970), pp. 64.
4. *The Gospel Quotations of Aphrahat the Persian Sage, Part I: Aphrahat's Text of the Fourth Gospel* (dissertation, VUA; Meppel [the Netherlands] 1975), 2 vols., pp. 520.
5. *Early Transmission of Words of Jesus. Thomas, Tatian and the Text of the New Testament* [a collection of Baarda's articles, selected and edited by J. Helderman and S. J. Noorda] (Amsterdam 1983), pp. 333 [= *ETWJ*].
6. *Essays on the Diatessaron*, CBETh 11 (Kampen 1994), pp. 320 [= *ED*].

SCHOLARLY ARTICLES AND CHAPTERS IN MULTIPLE AUTHORED WORKS

7. "Mark IX,49," *NTS* 5 (1958/59), 318–321.
8. "The Gospel Text in the Biography of Rabbula," *VigChr* 14 (1960), 102–127 [= *ETWJ*, 11–36].
9. "Thomas en Tatianus," in R. Schippers (in cooperation with T. Baarda), *Het Evangelie van Thomas*, Boeketreeks 14 (Kampen 1960), 135–155 [English translation: "Thomas and Tatian," in *ETWJ*, 37–49].
10. "A Syriac Fragment of Mar Ephraem's Commentary on the Diatessaron," *NTS* 8 (1961/62), 287–300 [= *ETWJ*, 51–64].
11. "Op zoek naar de tekst van het Diatessaron," *VoxTh* 32 (1961/62), 107–119 [English translation: "In Search of the Diatessaron Text," in *ETWJ*, 65–78].
12. "Dionysios bar Salibi and the Text of Luke I.35," *VigChr* 17 (1963), 225–229 [= *ETWJ*, 79–83].

13. Contribution to: R. Schippers, "De Zoon des Mensen in Mt.
     12,32–Lk. 12,10, vergeleken met Mk. 3,28," in *Ex Auditu Verbi.*
     Theologische opstellen aangeboden aan prof. dr. G. C. Berkhouwer ...
     (Kampen 1965), 223–257.
14. "Het gezag van de Heilige Schrift. Vragen aan Dr. M. J. Arntzen,"
     GTT 66 (1966), 82–106.
15. "Gadarenes, Gerasenes, Gergesenes and the 'Diatessaron' Tradi-
     tions," in *Neotestamentica et Semitica. Studies in Honour of Matthew*
     Black (Edinburgh 1969), 181–197 [= *ETWJ*, 85–101].
16. "Het opstandingsverhaal in het Diatessaron van Tatianus volgens
     drie Syrische patristische getuigenissen," appendix to: T. Baarda,
     Vier = Een [= no. 3], 49–64 [English translation: "The Resurrection
     Narrative in Tatian's Diatessaron according to three Syrian
     Patristic Witnesses," in *ETWJ*, 103–115].
17. "Jes 45,23 in het Nieuwe Testament (Rm 14,11; Flp 2,10v.)," *GTT*
     71 (1971), 137–179.
18. Contribution to: M. Black, "The Syriac Versional Tradition," in
     Die alten Übersetzungen des Neuen Testaments, die Kirchenväterzitate
     und Lektionare, ed. K. Aland, ANTT 5 (Berlin/New York 1972),
     120–159, esp. 126, 145–150.
19. "Markus 14,11: ΕΠΗΓΓΕΙΛΑΝΤΟ: 'Bron' of 'Redactie'?," *GTT* 73
     (1973), 65–75.
20. "Het ontstaan van de vier Evangeliën volgens 'Abd al–Djabbar,"
     NTT 28 (1974), 215–238.
21. "De opgestane en de aardse Heer," in *Rondom het Woord* 16 (1974),
     21–45 [Reprinted in *Eigentijds verstaan van de bijbel*, edd. P. J.
     Roscam Abbing & A. S. van der Woude (Kampen 1974), 27–51].
22. "An Archaic Element in the Arabic Diatessaron (T^A 46:18 = John
     XV,2)," *NovT* 17 (1975), 151–155 [= *ETWJ*, 173–177].
23. "Luke 12,13–14, Text and Transmission from Marcion to
     Augustine," in *Christianity, Judaism and Other Graeco-Roman Cults.*
     Studies for Morton Smith at Sixty, ed. J. Neusner, SJLA 12 (Leiden
     1975), Vol. I, 107–162 [= *ETWJ*, 117–172].
24. "Jezus zeide: 'Weest passanten'. Over betekenis en oorsprong van
     logion 42 in het Evangelie van Thomas," in *Ad Interim. Opstellen* ...
     aangeboden aan Prof. Dr. R. Schippers, edd. T. Baarda *et alii*
     (Kampen 1975) [= no. 161], 113–140 [English translation: "Jesus
     said: 'Be Passers-by'. On the Meaning and Origin of Logion 42 of
     the Gospel of Thomas," in *ETWJ*, 179–205].
25. "'Het uitbreiden van mijn handen is zijn teken'. Enkele notities bij
     de gebedshouding in de Oden van Salomo," in *Loven en Geloven.*
     Opstellen ... *aangeboden aan Prof. Dr. Nic. H. Ridderbos*, edd. M.H.
     van Es *et alii* (Amsterdam 1975), 245–259.
26. "I Corinthe 10,1–13. Een schets," *GTT* 76 (1976), 1–14.
27. "The Author of the Arabic Diatessaron," in *Miscellanea Neotes-
     tamentica*, edd. T. Baarda *et alii*, NovT.S 47 (Leiden 1978) [= no.
     162], Vol. I, 61–103 [= *ETWJ* 207–250].

28. "Jezus in de mystiek van de Islam. Het beeld van Jezus in de werken van Abû Hamid Ibn Muhammad al Ghazzâlî," *GTT* 78 (1978), 157–186.

29. "'... Als hij die bedient' (Luc. 22:27). Marginalia bij een woord van Jezus in het verhaal van het avondmaal in het evangelie van Lucas," in *De Knechtsgestalte van Christus. Studies ... aangeboden aan Prof. Dr. H.N. Ridderbos*, ed. J. C. de Moor (Kampen 1978), 11–22.

30. "'Nunc dimittis ...'. Annotaties bij Lukas 2,29–30," in *Zending op weg naar de toekomst. Essays aangeboden aan Prof. Dr. J. Verkuyl*, edd. T. Baarda *et alii* (Kampen 1978) [= no. 163], 59–79.

31. "Op weg naar een standaardtekst van het Nieuwe Testament? Enkele opmerkingen bij de verschijning van de 26ste druk van 'Nestle'," *GTT* 80 (1980), 83–137.

32. "Het recht van de tekstemendatie bij Abraham Kuyper," in *In rapport met de tijd. 100 jaar theologie aan de Vrije Universiteit 1880–1980*, edd. C. Augustijn *et alii* (Kampen 1980), 13–42.

33. "Another Treatise of Aphrahat the Persian Sage in Ethiopic Translation," *NTS* 27 (1980/81), 632–640 [= *ETWJ*, 251–259].

34. "Spreuken van Pseudo-Menander. Vertaald, ingeleid en toegelicht," in *De pseudepigrafen, vol. 3*, edd. P. W. van der Horst & T. Baarda (Kampen 1982), 43–83.

35. "2 Clement 12 and the Sayings of Jesus," in *Logia. Les paroles de Jésus – The Sayings of Jesus. Mémorial Joseph Coppens*, ed. J. Delobel, BEThL 59 (Leuven 1982), 529–556 [= *ETWJ*, 261–288].

36. "Mar Ephraem's Commentary on the Diatessaron, Ch. XVII:10," in *ETWJ*, 1983, 289–317.

37. "Luther over een joods 'leven van Jezus' ('Vom Schem Hamphoras ...')," *THer* 11 (1983), 113–120.

38. *Daniël Plooij als Nieuwtestamenticus* [inaugural address Utrecht, 8 October 1984], 12 pp.

39. "'Maar de toorn is over hen gekomen ...' (1 Thess 2:16c)," in *Paulus en de andere joden*, edd. T. Baarda *et alii* (Delft 1984) [= no. 164], 15–74.

40. "Paulus en de andere joden: ter inleiding," in *Paulus en de andere joden*, edd. T. Baarda *et alii* [= no. 164], 9–15.

41. *Matthew 17:24–27 in the Eastern Diatessaron Tradition*. Lecture for the Seminar on New Testament Textual Criticism on 25 November 1985 at the SBL Conference Los Angeles, 1985, 38 pp. (80 copies in private circulation).

42. "1 Thess 2:14–16. Rodrigues in 'Nestle-Aland'," *NTT* 39 (1985), 186–193.

43. "The Sentences of the Syriac Menander. A New Translation and Introduction," in *The Old Testament Pseudepigrapha*, ed. J. H. Charlesworth, Vol. II (Garden City, N.Y. 1985), 583–606.

44. "ΑΝΟΙΞΑΣ–ΑΝΑΠΤΥΞΑΣ. Over de vaststelling van de tekst van Lukas 4,17 in het Diatessaron," *NTT* 40 (1986), 199–208 [English translation: " 'Ανοίξας – ἀναπτύξας. The text of Luke 4:17 in the Diatessaron," in *ED*, 49–58].

45. "The Flying Jesus. Luke 4:29–30 in the Syriac Diatessaron," *VigChr* 40 (1986), 313–341 [= *ED*, 59–85].

46. "Jesus and Mary (John 20 16f.) in the Second Epistle on Virginity Ascribed to Clement," in *Studien zum Text und zur Ethik des Neuen Testaments. Festschrift zum 80. Geburtstag von Heinrich Greeven*, ed. W. Schrage, BZNW 47 (Berlin 1986), 11–34 [= *ED*, 87–110].

47. "To the Roots of the Syriac Diatessaron Tradition (T^A 25:1–3)," *NovT* 28 (1986), 1–25 [= *ED*, 111–132].

48. "Een (a)ha–Erlebnis. Enkele opmerkingen bij een stelling gewijd aan een 'gedachte van rabbi Sjim'on ben Laqisj'," *THer* 14 (1986), 10–15.

49. "De aanwijzende voornaamwoorden in Romeinen 9:6 en 8 (οὗτοι–ταῦτα). Over de 'Semitische' achtergrond van Romeinen 9:6–9," *ACEBT* 7 (1986), 101–113.

50. "צידורא. A Graecism in Midrash Echa Rabba I,5," *JSJ* 18 (1987), 69–80.

51. "De namen van de kinderen van Levi. De duiding van de namen Gersjôn, Qehath, Merari en Jochebed in het Testament van Levi 11," *ACEBT* 8 (1987), 87–107.

52. "Openbaring-Traditie en Didachè. Paulus' zelfstandigheid in het licht van Galaten 1,11–12," in *Zelfstandig geloven. Studies voor Jaap Firet*, edd. F. H. Kuiper (Kampen 1987), 152–167.

53. "The Sabbath in the Parable of the Shepherd (Evangelium Veritatis 32 18–34)," *NTT* 41 (1987), 17–28 [= *ED*, 133–145].

54. "'She recognized Him'. Concerning the Origin of a Peculiar Textual Variation in John 20,16 Sy^s," in *Text and Testimony. Essays … in Honour of A. F. J. Klijn*, edd. T. Baarda et alii (Kampen 1988) [= no. 165], 24–38.

55. "Geven als vreemdeling. Over de herkomst van een merkwaardige variant van Ms. 713 in Mattheus 17,26," *NTT* 42 (1988), 99–113.

56. "Het einde van de wet is Christus. Rom 10:4–15, een Midrasj van Paulus over Deut 30:11–14," *GTT* 88 (1988), 208–248.

57. "Luke 22:42–47a. The Emperor Julian as a Witness to the Text of Luke," *NovT* 30 (1988), 289–296.

58. "Marcion's Text of Gal 1:1. Concerning the Reconstruction of the First Verse of the Marcionite Corpus Paulinum," *VigChr* 42 (1988), 236–256.

59. "'If you do not sabbatize the Sabbath …'. The Sabbath as God or World in Gnostic Understanding (Ev. Thom. Log. 27)," in *Knowledge of God in the Graeco-Roman World*, edd. R. van den Broek et alii, EPRO 112 (Leiden 1988) [= no. 166], 178–201 [= *ED*, 147–171].

60. "Qehath–'What's in a Name?'. Concerning the Interpretation of the Name 'Qehath' in the Testament of Levi 11:4–6," *JSJ* 19 (1988), 215–229.

61. "'A Staff only, not a Stick'. Disharmony of the Gospels and the Harmony of Tatian (Matthew 10,9f.; Mark 6,8f.; Luke 9,3 and 10,4)," in *The New Testament in Early Christianity*, ed. J.-M. Sevrin, BEThL 86 (Leuven 1989), 311–333 [= *ED*, 173–196].

62. "ΔΙΑΦΩΝΙΑ-ΣΥΜΦΩΝΙΑ: Factors in the Harmonization of the Gospels, especially in the Diatessaron of Tatian," in *Gospel Traditions in the Second Century*, ed. W. L. Petersen, CJA 3 (Notre Dame/London 1989), 133–154 [= *ED*, 29–47].

63. "De korte tekst van het Onze Vader in Lucas 11:2–4: een Marcionitische corruptie?," *NTT* 44 (1990), 273–287.

64. "Het Martyrium van Marcus. Het martelaarschap van de evangelist Marcus, volgens het Leidse handschrift," *BenT* 52 (1991), 168–177.

65. "'Als Christus niet is opgewekt ...'. Het Nieuwe Testament in het 'Geding'," *KeTh* 42 (1991), 305–316.

66. "De opstanding en de opstandingsverhalen," in *Terwijl zij onderweg daarover spraken ...*, P. N. Holtrop & A. J. Jelsma, edd., Kamper Cahiers 73 (Kampen 1991), 14–40.

67. "'Chose' or 'Collected': Concerning an Aramaism in Logion 8 of the Gospel of Thomas and the Question of Independence," *HThR* 84 (1991), 373–397 [= *ED*, 241–262].

68. "Gal 5:1a: ᾗ ἐλευθερίᾳ ... Over de 'Westerse Tekst' en de Tekst van Marcion," in *Christologische Perspectieven. Exegetische en hermeneutische studies. Artikelen van en voor Prof. Dr. Heinrich Baarlink* (Kampen 1992), 173–193.

69. "'He holds the Fan in his Hand ...' (Mt 3:12, Lk 3:17) and Philoxenus. Or, how to reconstruct the original Diatessaron text of the Saying of John the Baptist?," *Muséon* 105 (1992), 63–86 [= *ED*, 197–218].

70. "The Etymology of the Name of the Evangelist Mark in the *Legenda Aurea* of Jacobus a Voragine," *NAKG* 72 (1992), 1–12.

71. "Philoxenus and the Parable of the Fisherman. Concerning the Diatessaron text of Mt 13:47–50, in *The Four Gospels 1992, Festschrift Frans Neirynck*, edd. F. Van Segbroeck *et alii*, BEThL 100 (Leuven 1992), Vol. II, 1403–1423 [= *ED*, 219–239].

72. "TI ETI ΔΙΩΚΟΜΑΙ in Gal. 5:11, Apodosis or Parenthesis ?," *NovT* 34 (1992), 250–256.

73. "The Parable of the Fisherman in the Heliand. The Old Saxon Version of Matthew 13:47–50," in *Amsterdamer Beiträge zur älteren Germanistik* 36 (1992), 39–58 [= *ED*, 263–281].

74. "The Shechem Episode in the Testament of Levi. A Comparison with other Traditions," in *Sacred History and Sacred Texts in Early Judaism. A Symposium in Honour of A.S. van der Woude*, edd. J. N. Bremmer & F. García Martínez, CBETh 5 (Kampen 1992), 11–73.

75. "Clement of Alexandria and the Parable of the Fisherman. Matthew 13,47–48 or Independent Tradition," in *The Synoptic Gospels*, ed. C. Focant, BEThL 110 (Leuven 1993), 582–598 [= *ED*, 283–298].

76. "Syriac Menander," in *The Anchor Bible Dictionary*, edd. D. N. Freedman *et alii* (New York 1992), Vol. VI, 281–282.

77. "Van 'stof' tot 'zout'. Een motief in de Verhandelingen van Afrahat," *KeTh* 44 (1993), 211–218.

78. "John 1:5 in the *Oration* and *Diatessaron* of Tatian. Concerning the Reading καταλαμβάνει," *VigChr* 47 (1993), 209–225 [= *ED*, 299–314).

79. "'Signore Dio Nostro'. Over de aanhef van het gebed van Jezus in het 'Evangelie van Barnabas'," *KeTh* 44 (1993), 276–280.

80. "The Diatessaron of Tatian and its Influence on the Vernacular Versions. The case of John 19:30," English translation [by Th. Korteweg] of a lecture delivered in French in Montpellier, June 1992, in *ED* (1994), 11–28.

81. "Matthew 18:14c. An 'Extra-canonical' Addition in the Arabic Diatessaron?," *Muséon* 107 (1994), 135–149

82. "What Critical Apparatus of the New Testament do we need? – demonstrated in Luke 23:48," in *New Testament Textual Criticism, Exegesis and Early Church History*, edd. B. Aland & J. Delobel, CBETh 7 (Kampen 1994), 37–97.

83. "'Over wie Mozes schreef, èn de Profeten ...' (Johannes 1,45). De belijdenis van Filippus in het licht van Johannes 1,51," in *Broeder Jehosjoea. Opstellen voor Ben Hemelsoet*, edd. D. Akerboom *et alii* (Kampen 1994), 63–76.

84. "The Syriac Versions of the New Testament," in *The Text of the New Testament in Contemporary Research. A Volume in Honor of Bruce M. Metzger*, edd. B. D. Ehrman & M. W. Holmes, StD 46 (Grand Rapids 1995), 97–112.

85. "Sabbath, Σάββατον, Sabbatum," in *Dictionary of Deities and Demons in the Bible*, edd. K. van der Toorn *et alii* (Leiden 1995), 1353–1355.

86. "'Ge zijt nog geen vijftig jaar, en ge hebt Abraham gezien?' De vraag van Jezus' tegenstanders in Johannes 8:57," in *Een boek heeft een rug. Studies voor Ferenc Postma ...*, ed. M. Gosker (Zoetermeer 1995), 23–31.

87. "'The Cornerstone'. An Aramaism in the Diatessaron and the Gospel of Thomas?," *NovT* 37 (1995), 285–300.

88. "Nathanael, 'the Scribe of Israel'. John 1,47 in Ephraem's Commentary on the Diatessaron," *EThL* 71 (1995), 321–336.

89. "An Unexpected Reading in the West-Saxon Gospel Text of Mark 16,11," *NTS* 41 (1995), 458–465.

90. "'Mogen de zondaren van de aarde vergaan'. Psalm 104:35, een andere manier van lezen?," *KeTh* 46 (1995), 90–92.

91. "John 8:57B. The Contribution of the Diatessaron of Tatian,"
     NovT 38 (1996), 336–343.
91a. "'Vader–Zoon–Heilige Geest.' Logion 44 van 'Thomas'," *NTT* 51
     (1997), 13–30.

A SELECTION OF POPULARIZING AND
NON-SPECIALIST ARTICLES

92. Contribution to: M. Giliam, "Brachten de Arabieren Elia het
     vlees?," *Christelijk Schoolblad. Onze Vacatures* 52/49 (29.9.1961), 9.
93. "De aard van het gezag van de Schrift," *Opdracht en Dienst* 42
     (1967), 20–23.
94. "De zon die stilstond ...," *Regelrecht* 5 (1968), 33–49.
95. "Een snoer van kralen (Markus)," *De Bazuin* 51 (1968), 2–4.
96. Contribution to: G. Puchinger, "Gesprek over de Bijbel," *Gaande-
     weg* 3 (1968), 221–244 (with H. M. Kuitert and G. P. Hartvelt).
97. "Heilige Humor?," *Merite* 2 (1968), 10–11.
98. "Over exegese gesproken," *VoxTh* 39 (1969), 146–154.
99. "... als engelen ...," *Voorlopig* 1 (1969), 238–241.
100. "Kerygma en historie," *Ministerium* 3 (1969), 154–160.
101. "Niet zoals vroeger. De antithesen in de Bergrede, Mt 5:21–48,"
     Schrift 12 (1970), 219–223.
102. "Kort antwoord aan Dominee Hegger," *Waarheid en Eenheid* 22/
     13 (7.4.1970), 6.
103. "... 'want Hij heeft omgezien'..." (Lc 1:48a). Nieuwtestamentische
     notities n.a.v. het thema 'The Good News of Salvation Today',"
     De Heerbaan 23 (1970), 418–426.
104. "Geen ander evangelie!" in *VU-visies op mens en maatschappij*
     (Amsterdam n.d. [1971]), 17–24.
105. "Het verhaal van de zon die stilstond ...," *De Bijbel* II/17 (Haar-
     lem 1971), 541.
106. "Onnodige sensatie rondom Markus," *Trouw/Kwartet* 30, no.8589
     (29.4.1972), 2.
107. "De Synoptische Evangeliën I. Van Marcus 10:17–18 naar
     Matteüs 19:16–17," *De Bijbel* II/74 (Haarlem 1972), 2366.
108. "De Synoptische Evangeliën II. Van Palestina (Marcus 10:11)
     naar Rome (Marcus 10:12)," *De Bijbel* II/75 (Haarlem 1972), 2406.
109. "De Synoptische Evangeliën III. De rok is nader dan het hemd:
     van Matteüs 5:40 naar Lucas 6:29b," *De Bijbel* II/78 (Haarlem
     1972), 2470.
110. "De Synoptische Evangeliën IV. Wat er gezegd is over de
     duisternis," *De Bijbel* II/80 (Haarlem 1972), 2535.
111. "Zijn bloed kome over ons en onze kinderen," *De Bijbel* II/72
     (Haarlem 1972), 2374.
112. "Namen geven aan Jezus ...," *Voorlopig* 4 (1972), 83–87 [unauthor-
     ized reprint in *Open Deur. Goede Tijding* 6/7 (1982)].

113. "Daar kwamen twaalf koningen met een ster ...," *Trouw/Kwartet* 30 no. 9109 (5.1.1974), 2.

114. Contribution to: C.P. van Andel *et alii*, "Een geschil over de uitleg van het Oude Testament," *KeTh* 27 (1976), 89–101.

115. "Bij het afscheid van Prof. Dr. R. Schippers," *GTT* 77 (1977), 221–223.

116. "Tussen dogma en exegese," *Kosmos + Oekumene* 11 (1977), 239–242.

117. "Bij het afscheid van Prof. Dr. H.N. Ridderbos," *Gereformeerd Weekblad* 34 (1978/79), 198–201.

118. "Mattheüs en het Passie-verhaal," *Preludium.* Blad van het Concertgebouw Amsterdam 39/8 (1981), 9–11.

119. "De vier evangeliën en het éne evangelie," *Schrift* 135 (1991), 105–109.

120. "Het boek dat er niet meer is ...," *Kabats.* Blad van de Theologische Faculteit aan de VU 5/1 (1991), 11–12.

121. "Berkouwer en Bultmann," *Kabats.* Blad van de Theologische Faculteit aan de VU 6/5 (1993), 46–47.

122. "De betrouwbaarheid van de bijbel," in *Lijnrecht of Richtlijn?* Over de normativiteit van bijbel en belijdenis, Themadag VUSA–Centrum/Faculteit der Godgeleerdheid (Amsterdam 1993), 16–22 [23–24].

123. "Kurt Aland. Levensbericht," in *Levensberichten en herdenkingen 1995,* Koninklijke Nederlandse Akademie van Wetenschappen (Amsterdam, November 1995), 7–11.

124. "Individueel onderzoek en onderzoek in programma's," *Nieuwsbrief NOSTER* 5/4, 1995, 2–5.

125. "Welke commentaar las Mr. Parker van Scotland Yard?," *Kabats.* Blad van de Theologische Faculteit aan de VU 8/3 (1995), 18–20.

126. "Over de Ierse non Fidelma," *Kabats.* Blad van de Theologische Faculteit aan de VU 9/1 (1995), 12–13.

127. "Abba, Vader," *KeTh* 48 (1997), 3–8.

127a. "Drs. J. Slavenburg en de 'Zaligspreking van de armen'," *GTT* 97 (1997), 28–32.

A SELECTION OF BOOK REVIEWS

128. B. M. Metzger, *Chapters in the History of New Testament Textual Criticism* (Leiden 1963), in *GTT* 64 (1964), 258–259.

129. J. H. Greenlee, *Introduction to New Testament Textual Criticism* (Grand Rapids 1964), in *GTT* 64 (1964), 259–261.

130. B. Jongeling, *Le rouleau de la guerre des manuscrits de Qumrân* (Assen 1962), in *GTT* 64 (1964), 59–60.

131. G. M. Lamsa, *Die Evangelien in aramäischer Sicht* (Gossau/St.Gallen 1963), in *GTT* 65 (1965), 189–190.

132. H. Goedhart, *De slothymne van het Manual of Discipline* (Rotterdam 1965), in *GTT* 66 (1966), 219–220.

133. E. D. Freed, *Old Testament Quotations in the Gospel of John* (Leiden 1965), in *GTT* 66 (1966), 221–222.

134. J. de Waard, *A Comparative Study of the Old Testament Text in the Dead Sea Scrolls and in the New Testament* (Leiden 1965), in *GTT* 67 (1967), 65–66.

135. E. Nellesen, *Untersuchungen zur altlateinischen Überlieferung des ersten Thessalonicherbriefes* (Bonn 1965), in *GTT* 67 (1967), 67–68.

136. H. P. Rüger, *Text und Textform im hebräischen Sirach* (Berlin 1970), in *GTT* 71 (1971), 105.

137. F. Christ, *Jesus Sophia* (Zürich 1970), in *GTT* 71 (1971), 106–107.

138. M. E. Schild, *Abendländische Bibelvorreden bis zur Lutherbibel* (Gütersloh 1970), in *GTT* 71 (1971), 110–111.

139. R. Schnackenburg, *Das Johannesevangelium*, II (Freiburg etc. 1971), in *GTT* 72 (1972), 112–113.

140. M. H. Bolkestein, *De Brieven van Petrus en Judas* (Nijkerk 1972²), in *GTT* 73 (1973), 51.

141. C. C. de Bruin, *De Zuidnederlandse vertaling van het Nieuwe Testament* (Leiden 1971), in *GTT* 73 (1973), 239–240.

142. Ch. de Beus, *Johannes' getuigschrift van het Woord* (Nijkerk 1973) in *GTT* 74 (1974), 123–125.

143. *Als vijf hetzelfde zeggen* ..., het evangelie van Markus en de brief aan de Efeziërs in vijf Nederlandse vertalingen (Amsterdam/Boxtel 1975), in *GTT* 76 (1976), 108–109.

144. *Het Evangelie van Mattheüs in het Grieks en vier vertalingen* (Amsterdam/Boxtel 1975), in *GTT* 76 (1976), 109–110.

145. R. J. Swanson, *The Horizontal Line Synopsis of the Gospels* (Dillsboro [North Carolina] 1975), in *GTT* 76 (1976), 110–112.

146. Ch. de Beus, *Komst en toekomst van het Koninkrijk* (Heemstede 1979), in *GTT* 82 (1982), 45.

147. "Een nieuwe publicatie van Hans Jansen. Enkele opmerkingen bij het eerste deel van de monografie over *de nieuwtestamentische wortels van het antisemitisme*," in *THer* 13 (1985), 73–79.

148. F. Siegert, *Drei hellenistisch-jüdische Predigten*, I (Tübingen 1980), in *JSJ* 16 (1985), 157–159.

149. D. A. Koch, *Die Schrift als Zeuge des Evangeliums* (Tübingen 1986), in *Tijdschrift voor Theologie* 27 (1987), 406–407.

150. M. Hengel, *Die Evangelienüberschriften* (Heidelberg 1984), in *NTT* 41 (1987), 315–316.

151. J. van Bruggen, *Het lezen van de Bijbel* (Kampen 1986²), and idem, *Wie maakte de Bijbel?* (Kampen 1986), in *NTT* 42 (1988), 261–262.

152. Emil Schürer, *The History of the Jewish People in the Age of Jesus Christ*, edd. G. Vermes *et alii*, III/I (revised edition: Edinburgh 1986), in *NTT* 42 (1988), 158–159.

153. *The New Testament Apocrypha and Pseudepigrapha*, edd. J. H. Charlesworth and J. R. Mueller (Metuchen [New Jersey]/London 1987), in *NTT* 44 (1990), 165–166.

154. A.-M. Denis, *Concordance grecque des pseudépigraphes d'Ancien Testament* (Louvain-la-Neuve 1988), in *NTT* 44 (1990), 261–262.
155. G. Rouwhorst, *Efrem de Syriër. Hymnen voor de viering van het kerkelijk jaar* (Kampen 1991), in *KeTh* 43 (1992), 258.
156. D. A. Verhey, *De Geest wijst wegen in de tijd* (Kampen 1991), in *KeTh* 43 (1992), 258–259.
157. E. de Vries, *De Brief van Jacobus. Dispositie en theologie* (Kampen 1991), in *KeTh* 43 (1992), 167.
158. G. Mussies, *De autobiografie van de joodse historicus Flavius Josephus, vertaald, ingeleid en toegelicht* (Kampen 1991), in *KeTh* 43 (1992), 165–166.
159. H. Merkel, *Die Pastoralbriefe* (Göttingen 1991), and A. Strobel, *Der Brief an die Hebräer* (Göttingen 1991), in *KeTh* 43 (1992), 166.
160. "The Textual Apparatus in the Greek New Testament, Fourth Edition," in Review Symposium on GNT⁴, *BiTr* 45 (1994), 353–356 [Dutch Translation: "Het kritisch apparaat van de vierde editie van The Greek New Testament," *Met andere woorden* 14 (1995), 14–17].
161   W. I. Petersen, *Tatian's Diatessaron. Its Creation, Dissemination, Significance, and History in Scholarship* (Leiden 1994), in *Bib.* 77 (1996), 577–580.

EDITORIAL RESPONSIBILITIES

Collections of essays

162. *Ad Interim. Opstellen over eschatologie, apocalyptiek en ethiek, aangeboden aan Prof. Dr. R. Schippers*, with J. Firet and G. Th. Rothuizen (Kampen 1975).
163. *Miscellanea Neotestamentica*, with A. F. J. Klijn and W. C. van Unnik, 2 vols., NovT.S 47/48 (Leiden 1978).
164. *Zending op weg naar de toekomst. Essays aangeboden aan Prof. Dr. J. Verkuyl*, with J. van den Berg *et alii* (Kampen 1978).
165. *Paulus en de andere joden. Exegetische bijdragen en discussie*, with H. Jansen, S. J. Noorda, and J. S. Vos (Delft 1984).
166. *Text and Testimony. Essays on New Testament and Apocryphal Literature in Honour of A. F. J. Klijn*, with A. Hilhorst, G. P. Luttikhuizen, and A. S. van der Woude (Kampen 1988).
167. *Knowledge of God in the Graeco-Roman World*, with R. van den Broek and J. Mansfeld, EPRO 112 (Leiden 1988).
168. *Jodendom en vroeg christendom: continuïteit en discontinuïteit*, with H. J. de Jonge and M. J. J. Menken (Kampen 1991).

Serial publications

169. *Segmenten. Studies op het gebied van de theologie,* with H. M. Kuitert, G. N. Lammens, and P. L. Schram, 2 vols. (Amsterdam 1978–1981).
170. *Contributions to Biblical Exegesis & Theology,* with A. van der Kooij and A. S. van der Woude, 18 vols. to date (Kampen 1990 –).
171. *Compendia rerum Iudaicarum ad Novum Testamentum,* with S. Safrai, M. Stern *et alii,* vols. III/1–4 (Assen/Philadelphia 1990 –).

Periodicals

172. *Kerk en Theologie* [= KeTh], vol. 42 (1991) – .

Tjitze Baarda

Curriculum vitae

Born	Vogelenzang, the Netherlands, 8 July 1932
Married	Hilda Juliana Giliam, 23 February 1958; five children

Education

1958	B.A. in Semitic Languages (*kandidaatsexamen*), Vrije Universiteit Amsterdam (= VUA)
1061	B.A. in Theology (*kandidaatsexamen*), VUA
1962	M.A. in Theology (*doctoraal examen*), VUA
1975	Dr.theol. (*promotie*), VUA (Promotor: R. Schippers)

Appointments

1958–64	Hebrew teacher in various secondary schools
1958–69	Assistant Professor (*medewerker*) of New Testament Studies, Faculty of Theology, VUA
1967	Visiting Lecturer in New Testament and Textual Criticism, St. Mary's College, St. Andrews University, Scotland
1969–75	Associate Professor (*hoofdmedewerker*) of New Testament Studies, Faculty of Theology, VUA
1975–83	Professor of New Testament Studies, Faculty of Theology, VUA
1981–90	Professor of New Testament Studies and of Early Judaism, Faculty of Theology, Utrecht University
1989	Visiting Professor of New Testament and Early Christian History, The Divinity School, Harvard University, Cambridge, Massachusetts
1990–97	Professor of New Testament Studies, Faculty of Theology, VUA

1979–81 & 1992–97	Dean, Faculty of Theology, VUA
1982–	Member, Royal Netherlands Academy of Arts and Sciences

ABBREVIATIONS

(adapted from S. Schwertner, *Abkürzungsverzeichnis*[2] [TRE])

AAA.H	Acta Academiae Aboensis, Humaniora (Abo)
AASF	Annales Academiae Scientiarum Fennicae, Dissertationes humanarum litterarum (Helsinki)
AAWG	Abhandlungen der Akademie der Wissenschaften, Göttingen (Göttingen)
ACEBT	Amsterdamse cahiers voor exegese en bijbelse theologie (Kampen)
AGJU	Arbeiten zur Geschichte des Antiken Judentums und Urchristentums (Leiden)
AncSoc	Ancient Society (Louvain)
ANRW	Aufstieg und Niedergang der römischen Welt (Berlin)
ANTT	Arbeiten zur neutestamentlichen Textforschung (Berlin)
AOAT	Alter Orient und Altes Testament (Kevelaer/Neukirchen)
APF	Archiv für Papyrusforschung und verwandte Gebiete (Berlin)
ASP	American Studies in Papyrology (New Haven [Connecticut], Atlanta [Georgia])
AVTR	Aufsätze und Vorträge zur Theologie und Religionswissenschaft (Berlin)
B/D/R	Blass-Debrunner-Rehkopf, *Grammatik des neutestamentlichen Griechisch* (Göttingen)
BenT	Benedictijns tijdschrift (Egmond-Binnen)
BEThL	Bibliotheca Ephemeridum theologicarum Lovaniensium (Louvain)
BGrL	Bibliothek der Griechischen Literatur (Stuttgart)
BiAuPr	Bibelauslegung für die Praxis (Stuttgart)
Bib.	Biblica (Roma)
BiblInt	Biblical Interpretation (Leiden)
BibOr	Biblica et Orientalia (Rome)
BiKi	Bibel und Kirche (Stuttgart)
BiTr	The Bible Translator (London)
BK	Biblischer Kommentar (Neukirchen)
BoBKG	Bonner Beiträge zur Kirchengeschichte (Köln)
BS	Bibliotheca sacra (Dallas [Texas])
BZ	Biblische Zeitschrift (Paderborn)
BZNW	Beihefte zur Zeitschrift für die neutestamentliche Wissenschaft (Berlin)
CBETh	Contributions to Biblical Exegesis and Theology (Kampen)

CBQ   Catholic Biblical Quarterly (Washington, D.C.)
CGTC   Cambridge Greek Testament Commentaries (Cambridge [U.K.])
CJA   Christianity and Judaism in Antiquity (Notre Dame [Ind.])
CPJ   Corpus papyrorum Judaicarum (Cambridge [Mass.])
CRI   Compendia rerum Iudaicarum ad Novum Testamentum (Assen)
CSCO   Corpus scriptorum christianorum orientalium (Louvain)
CSEL   Corpus scriptorum ecclesiasticorum Latinorum (Pragae/ Vindobonae/Lipsiae)
DBS   Dictionnaire de la bible, Supplément (Paris)
ED   *Essays on the Diatessaron* (no. 6 in Baarda's bibliography)
EdF   Erträge der Forschung (Darmstadt)
EHS   Europäische Hochschulschriften (Bern/New York)
EJL   Early Judaism and its Literature (Atlanta [Georgia])
EKK   Evangelisch-katholischer Kommentar zum Neuen Testament (Zürich)
ELW   Empirische Literaturwissenschaft (Tübingen)
EPRO   Études préliminaires aux religions orientales dans l'empire romain (Leiden)
ET   Expository Times (Edinburgh)
EtB   Études bibliques (Paris)
EThL   Ephemerides theologicae Lovanienses (Louvain)
ETWJ   *Early Transmission of Words of Jesus* (no. 5 in Baarda's bibliography)
EvTh   Evangelische Theologie (München)
EWNT   *Exegetisches Wörterbuch zum NT* (Stuttgart)
Exp   The Expositor (Edinburgh)
FC   Fontes christiani (Freiburg im Br.)
FilNeo Filología Neotestamentaria (Córdoba)
FRLANT Forschungen zur Religion und Literatur des Alten und Neuen Testaments (Göttingen)
fzb   Forschungen zur Bibel (Würzburg)
GBS.NTS Guides to Biblical Scholarship, NT series (Philadelphia [Pennsylvania])
GCS   Die griechischen christlichen Schriftsteller... (Berlin)
GNT   see TGNT
Gr   Gregorianum (Roma)
GTT   Gereformeerd Theologisch Tijdschrift (Kampen)
HC   Hand-Commentar zum Neuen Testament (Freiburg, etc.)
Hen   Henoch (Torino)
HNT   Handbuch zum NT (Tübingen)

HSem	Horae Semiticae (London)
HThK	Herders theologischer Kommentar zum NT (Freiburg im Br.)
HThR	Harvard Theological Review (Cambridge [Massachusetts])
ICC	International Critical Commentary (Edinburgh)
Int.	Interpretation (Richmond [Virginia])
IZBG	Internationale Zeitschriftenschau für Bibelwissenschaft und Grenzgebiete (Düsseldorf)
JAC	Jahrbuch für Antike und Christentum (Münster)
JBL	Journal of Biblical Literature (Atlanta)
JEA	Journal of Egyptian Archaeology (London)
JJS.S	Journal of Jewish Studies, Supplements (Oxford)
JR	Journal of Religion (Chicago)
JSHRZ	Jüdische Schriften aus hellenistisch-römischer Zeit (Gütersloh)
JSJ	Journal for the Study of Judaism (Leiden)
JSJ.S	Journal for the Study of Judaism, Supplements (Leiden)
JSNT	Journal for the Study of the New Testament (Sheffield)
JSNT.S	Journal for the Study of the New Testament, Supplements (Sheffield)
JSPE.S	Journal for the Study of the Pseudepigrapha, Supplements (Sheffield)
JSS.S	Journal of Semitic Studies, Supplements (Oxford)
JThS	Journal of Theological Studies (Oxford)
KAV	Kommentar zu den apostolischen Vätern (Göttingen)
KEH	Kurzgefaßtes exegetisches Handbuch (Leipzig)
KEK	Kritisch-exegetischer Kommentar über das NT (Göttingen)
KeTh	Kerk en Theologie (Wageningen)
KP	*Der Kleine Pauly. Lexikon der Antike* (Stuttgart)
LAB	*Liber Antiquitatum Biblicarum*
LCL	Loeb Classical Library (London/Cambridge [Mass.])
LeDiv	Lectio Divina (Paris)
LingBibl	Linguistica biblica (Bonn)
ML.T	Museum Lessianum, section théologique (Bruxelles)
Muséon	Muséon. Revue d'études orientales (Louvain)
N-A	Nestle-Aland, *Novum Testamentum Graece* (Stuttgart)
NAKG	Nederlands archief voor kerkgeschiedenis ('s-Gravenhage)
NEB	Die Neue Echter Bibel (Würzburg)
NedThT	Nederlands Theologisch Tijdschrift ('s-Gravenhage)
NHS	Nag Hammadi Studies (Leiden)
NIGTC	New International Greek Testament Commentary (Exeter)
NovT	Novum Testamentum (Leiden)

NovT.S Novum Testamentum, Supplements (Leiden)
NTA   Neutestamentliche Abhandlungen (Münster)
NTD   Das Neue Testament Deutsch (Göttingen)
NTS   New Testament Studies (Cambridge)
NTT   Nederlands Theologisch Tijdschrift ('s-Gravenhage)
NTTS   New Testament Tools and Studies (Leiden)
OCD   *Oxford Classical Dictionary* (Oxford)
OLBT   Old Latin Biblical Texts (Oxford)
OrChr   Oriens Christianus (Roma)
OrChrA Orientalia Christiana analecta (Roma)
OrChrP Orientalia Christiana periodica (Roma)
ÖTK   Ökumenischer Taschenbuchkommentar zum Neuen Testa-
     ment (Gütersloh/Würzburg)
OTP   *Old Testament Pseudepigrapha*, 2 vols., ed. J. H. Charlesworth
     (New York/London 1985)
OTS   Oudtestamentische studiën (Leiden)
PaThSt   Paderborner Theologische Studien (Paderborn)
PG   *Patrologia Graeca*, ed. Migne (Paris)
PGM   *Papyri Graecae Magicae*, ed. K. Preisendanz et al. (Leipzig/
     Berlin)
PL   *Patrologia Latina*, ed. Migne (Paris)
PNTC   Pelican NT Commentaries (London)
PO   *Patrologia Orientalis* (Paris)
PRE   see PW
PS   *Patrologia Syriaca*, ed. Parisot (Paris)
PTA   Papyrologische Texte und Abhandlungen (Bonn)
PTS   Patristische Texte und Abhandlungen (Bonn)
PW   *Real-Encyclopädie der classischen Altertumswissenschaft*, edd. A.
     Pauly and G. Wissowa (Stuttgart)
RAC   *Reallexikon für Antike und Christentum* (Stuttgart)
REG   Revue des études grecques (Paris)
RHE   Revue d'histoire ecclésiastique (Louvain)
RMP   Rheinisches Museum für Philologie (Bonn)
RNT   Regensburger Neues Testament (Regensburg)
RVV   Religionsgeschichtliche Versuche und Vorarbeiten (Gießen)
SBAW Sitzungsberichte der (k.) Bayerischen Akademie der Wissen-
     schaften (München)
SBB   Stuttgarter biblische Beiträge (Stuttgart)
SBL.DS Society of Biblical Literature, Dissertation Series (Missoula
     [Montana], Atlanta [Georgia], etc.)
SBS   Stuttgarter Bibelstudien (Stuttgart)
SC   Sources chrétiennes (Paris)

SH	Subsidia Hagiographica (Bruxelles)
SJC	Studies in Judaism and Christianity (London)
SJLA	Studies in Judaism in Late Antiquity (Leiden)
SKC	Serie Kamper Cahiers (Kampen)
SNT	Schriften des Neuen Testaments (Göttingen)
SNTS.MS	Studiorum Novi Testamenti Societas, monograph series (Cambridge [U.K.])
SPB	Studia Post-Biblica (Leiden)
SQAW	Schriften und Quellen der Alten Welt (Berlin)
StAns	Studia Anselmiana (Roma)
StD	Studies and Documents (London, etc.)
StPatr	Studia Patristica (Berlin, Louvain, etc.)
StUNT	Studien zum Umwelt des Neuen Testaments (Göttingen)
SUC	Schriften des Urchristentums (Darmstadt)
TaS	Texts and Studies (Cambridge)
TB	Theologische Bücherei. Neudrucke und Berichte aus dem 20. Jahrhundert (München)
TGNT	*The Greek New Testament* (United Bible Societies edition [Stuttgart])
ThA	Theologische Arbeiten (Berlin)
THAT	Theologisches Handwörterbuch z. AT (München)
THer	Ter Herkenning ('s-Gravenhage)
ThHK	Theologischer Handkommentar z. NT (Berlin)
ThLZ	Theologische Literaturzeitung (Leipzig)
ThR	Theologische Rundschau (Tübingen)
ThStKr	Theologische Studien und Kritiken (Hamburg)
ThWbAT	*Theologisches Wörterbuch zum Alten Testament* (Stuttgart)
ThWbNT	*Theologisches Wörterbuch zum Neuen Testament* (Stuttgart)
ThZ	Theologische Zeitschrift (Basel)
TRE	*Theologische Realenzyklopädie* (Berlin)
TT	Texts and Translations (Atlanta [Georgia])
TT.PS	Texts and Translations, Pseudepigrapha Series (Atlanta)
TU	Texte und Untersuchungen (Berlin)
TZ(W)	Theologische Zeitschrift (Wien)
UBS	see TGNT
UTB	Uni-Taschenbücher (Heidelberg)
VigChr	Vigiliae Christianae (Leiden)
VigChr.S	Vigiliae Christianae, Supplements (Leiden)
VNAW	Verhandelingen der (K.) Nederlands(ch)e Akademie van Wetenschappen, Afdeling Letterkunde (Amsterdam)
VoxTh	Vox Theologica (Assen)
VUA	Vrije Universiteit Amsterdam (Baarda's *alma mater*)

WBC	Word Biblical Commentary (Dallas [Texas])
WMANT	Wissenschaftliche Monographien zum Alten und Neuen Testament (Neukirchen)
WUNT	Wissenschaftliche Untersuchungen zum Neuen Testament (Tübingen)
ZKTh	Zeitschrift für katholische Theologie (Wien, etc.)
ZKWL	Zeitschrift für kirchliche Wissenschaft und kirchliches Leben (Leipzig)
ZNW	Zeitschrift für die neutestamentliche Wissenschaft (Berlin)
ZPE	Zeitschrift für Papyrologie und Epigraphik (Bonn)
ZThK	Zeitschrift für Theologie und Kirche (Tübingen)

THE MARCOSIANS' TEXT OF JESUS' CRY OF JUBILATION (MATT 11:26 ‖ LUKE 10:21) IN IRENAEUS *ADV. HAER.* I.20.2

J. Neville Birdsall
University of Birmingham
(Birmingham, England)

In his study of Aramaic as a cause of textual variants, the late Matthew Black[1] laid stress upon a variant found in a patristic quotation. He placed such reliance upon it as to claim that it admitted no doubt. This we may elucidate to imply that without doubt the source of variation at this point lay in a mistranslation. The patristic quotation gives us the original text, one word transliterated in the Aramaic of Jesus' own speech. This word in the text transmitted in the manuscripts is a mistranslation.

The dominical saying in question is the Cry of Jubilation (Matt 11:26 ‖ Luke 10:21b) in the form transmitted by Irenaeus of Lyons in the first book of *Adversus haereses*. The passage is numbered 1.13.2 by Harvey[2]; recent editors[3] have returned to an alternative capitation originating with Massuet, giving 1.20.2. The form of the saying is attributed by the heresiologist to the Valentinian group known as the Marcosians. The text has been preserved by Epiphanius. Within it the Synoptic words numbered as verse 26 in Matthew and part of verse 21 in Luke have been transmitted in the following form.

οὐὰ ὁ πατήρ μου ὅτι ἔμπροσθέν σου εὐδοκία μοι ἐγένετο.

(The first person pronouns, genitive and dative cases, are placed in brackets by editors in view of their absence in the Latin version of Irenaeus.)

---

[1] M. Black, *An Aramaic Approach to the Gospels and Acts* (Oxford 1967³), p. 246.

[2] *Sancti Irenaei Libros quinque adversus haereses*, ed. W. Wigan Harvey, 2 vols. (Cambridge 1857), Vol. 1, p. 180.

[3] *Irénée de Lyon. Contre les hérésies,* Livre I, tome 2, ed. A. Rousseau and L. Doutreleau, SC 264 (Paris 1979), p. 292.

This is in contrast with the generally transmitted Greek which runs

ναὶ ὁ πατήρ, ὅτι οὕτως εὐδοκία ἐγένετο ἔμπροσθέν σου.

There are many variations of the saying of Jesus as a whole in patristic and versional sources of the text of the gospels, but this alone is in point here. Black discussed none other of them, even from this verse, but concentrated on the introductory interjection. It is uniquely attested in this one patristic place, against the whole manuscript and other evidence in both gospels.

Black claims that οὐά is an Aramaic word הו. It expresses joy, and an explanation of its meaning is to be found in Midrash Ekah. The Greek source of the form in canonical Matthew and Luke has misunderstood הו and translated it as if it were אי or איז, ναί.

Black makes no acknowledgement of any source for his identification of the language of οὐά. It goes back, in fact, to Harvey's comment. It must have been known to Black from Adalbert Merx's study of the Sinaitic Syriac[4] in which its source is given with a marginal reference. It is from Merx that Black, with due acknowledgement, derives his conjectural reconstruction of the origin of ναί in an error of translation.

Merx believed that this reading was not only that of the Marcosians but that of the text accepted by Irenaeus himself. Otherwise he would have castigated the Gnostics for their corruption of the text in this particular. In making this point, he has failed, however, to note the context in which this father introduces the quotation used by his opponents. He has just expounded their exegesis of the doctrine that knowledge previously secret has been revealed by Jesus. He then continues, ἀπόδειξιν δὲ τὴν τῶν ἀνωτάτω καὶ οἱονεὶ κορωνίδα τῆς ὑποθέσεως αὐτῶν φέρουσι ταῦτα. He is clearly quoting from his source, and since the word οὐά does not bear upon the argument, he does not dwell upon it. The text is clearly that of the Marcosians, but we cannot know the text of Irenaeus. He makes no other reference to this verse, and the Latin has rendered οὐά by "*ita*," the regular Old Latin rendering here. Merx was clearly over-enthusiastic in this point, but Black did not follow him.

---

[4] A. Merx, *Die vier kanonischen Evangelien nach ihrem ältesten bekannten Texte*, Teil II/1 (*Das Evangelium Matthaeus*) (Berlin 1902), pp. 198–203.

It was never absolutely certain that the quotation could be assumed to be derived from the canonical text of Matthew or Luke. Since the variant οὐά is not attested elsewhere, we may be dealing with a source parallel to those from which the synoptic tradition was formed. This possibility would be particularly strong if the hypothesis espoused by Black were correct, that it is to be understood as an Aramaic word. Since the discussions referred to took place, the Nag Hammadi text of the *Gospel of Thomas* has come to light, and much recent research has suggested that forms of the sayings of Jesus there found may be nearer to their putative Aramaic originals than the Synoptists' wording. The interpretation that the Marcosian form under discussion comes from such a source may be strengthened by this recent discovery. We observe that an *agraphon* is part of the argument summarized by Irenaeus. It runs: Πολλάκις ἐπεθύμη-σαν ἀκοῦσαι ἕνα τῶν λόγων τούτων καὶ οὐκ ἔσχον τὸν ἐροῦντα. A variant form of this is now known from the Coptic gospel as Saying 38: "Many times you have desired to hear these words which I speak to you, and you have no one else from whom to hear them."[5] The second person plural in this version adds weight to the suggested emendation by Resch. Purely on grounds of the logic of the argument as recorded, he corrected the first person singular of the first verb, as transmitted, into the third person plural to accord with the second verb. We give his emended form, adopted by the editors in *Sources chrétiennes*. The form of the whole of this saying in Irenaeus will have been transposed into the third person either within the tradition, or as reporting the Marcosian document in *oratio obliqua*.

Were the form of the parallel to the synoptic texts to be from a non-canonical source, it would have its place in the search for the original form of the sayings of Jesus. If it were to be seen, however, as coming from a canonical text, we should have to ask whether it is likely that two Aramaic expressions, not evidently close phonetically, would have been so confused in the original translation process. This is a question which must be addressed, if the interjection οὐά here continues to be considered part of the Aramaic lexicon.

But is the word οὐά, in this occurrence, Aramaic in Greek dress? Would this word have been retained in Greek, unless it had a *Sitz im Leben* in the life of the early Christian community?

---

[5] *The Nag Hammadi Library in English*, ed. J. M. Robinson, revised edition (Leiden 1988), p. 130.

There seems to be a total lack of any evidence that it had. Nor, so far as I can trace, is a *Sitz im Leben* for Aramaic loans to be demonstrated in the Marcosian community.

In spite of the series of eminent scholars who have sought the Aramaic explanation, I suggest that we might profitably examine the alternative possibility that the word is to be considered as Greek. Its presence, unremarked, in a Greek document suggests in fact that this may prove to be the foremost probability. The failure to perceive it as such may lie in the manner of its usage in its one appearance elsewhere in the New Testament. The word occurs in the passion scene, used in an address to Jesus on the cross, mocking his impotence to set himself free, in spite of his words of seeming threat to the Temple (Mark 15:29). It might seem from this to be a word of mockery. But checking on other occurrences, readily available in standard grammars and lexica, shows that the artistry of the evangelist is the source of this impression. In his account, the word is used with heavy irony by those who mock Jesus.

The basic emotion expressed by this interjection is "Verwunderung," to quote Blass in his revision of Kühner, "amazement."[6] The occurrences given by the latest edition of Bauer's *Wörterbuch* and its English version are instructive. Its potential for use in acclamation is best seen in Cassius Dio,[7] where the emperor is addressed in the words: ὀλυμπιονῖκα οὐᾶ πυθιονῖκα οὐᾶ αὔγουστε αὔγουστε. νέρωνι τῶι ἡρακλεῖ νέρωνι τῶι ἀπόλλωνι. ὡς εἷς περιοδονίκης εἷς ἀπ' αἰῶνος αὔγουστε αὔγουστε ἱερὰ φωνή. μακάριοι οἳ σου ἀκούοντες.

Three examples are given from Epictetus.[8] Two of the passages use the word (one along with θαυμαστῶς), of the praise of a philosopher by his pupils. The third gives the phrase οὐᾶ βασιλεὺς καὶ τὸ τοῦ Διὸς σκῆπτρον ἔχων. Another instance has come to light fairly recently in an Oxyrhynchus fragment identi-

---

[6] *Ausführliche Grammatik der griechischen Sprache v. Dr. R. Kühner in neuer Bearbeitung v. Dr. Fr. Blass* (Hannover 1892), Teil 1, Band 2, p. 252 (¶ 326.2); cp. E. Schwyzer, *Griechische Grammatik*, Band 2 (*Syntax u. syntaktische Stilistik*) (München 1959), p. 601 (οὐά, "Staunen").

[7] Book 63.20 (*Roman History*, ed. U. P. Boissevain [Berlin 1895–1931], Vol. 3, pp. 82f.).

[8] Ed. H. Schenkl (Leipzig 1916). References in order as given above: 3.23.24; 3.23.32; 3.22.34.

fied as belonging to the category of Acta Alexandrinorum. The phrase οὐὰ κύρι occurs.[9]

The word might thus properly be used in a cry of praise and acclamation of the deity. It is not inappropriate in the context in which the Marcosians used it. It is doubtful whether it could be original, if we understand it as a Greek word, as I believe that we undoubtedly should do. It is a substitution for ναί. It was probably regarded as a more proper word for its context. The quotation has other marks of secondary redaction in the verse, namely the addition of μου after πατήρ and μοι after εὐδοκία. Both emphasise sonship rather than fatherhood, and the latter addition seems to have echoes of the *Bath Qol* at Jesus' baptism.

Tjitze Baarda has been a good friend and colleague for many years. We have frequently met and our wives are well acquainted. We have shared our triumphs, I by attending his defence of his dissertation on Afrahat, he by travelling to be present at my inaugural lecture. We have participated in the Text-critical Seminar of Studiorum Novi Testamenti Societas, each under the other's chairmanship. For most of that time our debates and discussions have been on the Diatessaron of Tatian, and latterly on the text of the New Testament in general.

At the last meeting at which we were both present, he presented criticisms of the choice and presentation of the evidence in the edition of the critical apparatus of St. Luke by the American and British Committees of the International Greek New Testament Project.[10] I was executive editor of that Apparatus from 1970 to 1977. Present for that discussion were also Dr. J. Keith Elliott who was my immediate successor and brought the work through the Press, and Dr. David Parker, who, with Dr. W. J. Elliott, is now joint editor of the volumes to be devoted to the gospel according to St. John. We were able to debate the issues he raised, and we were largely in agreement with him. Our problems of the past are known to such friends as he. For the most part, we may now look to the future.

It is regrettable, then, that attention must be drawn, before this article comes to its close, to a blemish of that apparatus. This was undetected by Baarda and played no part in his remarks on that

---

[9] *Oxyrhynchus Papyri*, Vol. XXV, edd. E. Lobel and E. G. Turner (London 1959), p. 107 (no. 2435, *recto* lines 4f.).

[10] *The New Testament in Greek. The Gospel according to St. Luke*, ed. by the American and British Committees of the International Greek New Testament Project, Part I, Chaps. 1–12 (Oxford 1984), Part II, Chaps. 13–24 (Oxford 1987).

discussion, but accuracy must now record it. The apparatus was allowed to go to press with the uncorrected lemma to chapter 10, verse 21 reading: ναι: ουαι. This totally erroneous statement probably goes back to some very junior collator, whose name is buried forever in the archives of the edition. Failure in oversight at several successive stages alone can explain the printing of this piece of egregious nonsense. As one associated with the edition, I must express regret. For what it is worth, we may observe that it is probably an instance of the kind of transcriptional error for which A. C. Clark gave us the useful term ὁμ. As I look at the preliminary work which has been recently published on the succeeding edition of the gospel according to St. John, I believe that we may entertain hopes of better prospects for the accuracy of the record.

Meanwhile, I salute Tjitze Baarda by this note for two things without blemish and worthy of record: his immense and sure scholarship, and his sterling qualities of encouragement and human kindness.

THE GATES/BARS OF SHEOL REVISITED

Sebastian P. Brock
The Oriental Institute, University of Oxford
(Oxford, England)

The interpretation of the "gates of Hades" in Matt 16:18 has played a comparatively minor role in the discussion of Jesus' reply to Peter's confession (Matt 16:16–19); while a survey of the considerable variety of opinions, both ancient and modern, concerning the phrase would no doubt be instructive, the present contribution is deliberately confined to one particular strand of interpretation in early Christianity, first witnessed (it would seem) in the Diatessaron.

Some thirty five years before Dom Louis Leloir published the Syriac original of the *Commentary on the Diatessaron (CD)*[1] under Ephrem's name,[2] Sebastian Euringer (among others) had perceived[3] that the Syriac Diatessaron must have read "bars of Sheol" at Matt 16:18, even though the Armenian translation of the Commentary on the Diatessaron provided "gates,"[4] in common with the Old Syriac (so Syr^{cur}; Syr^{sin} is missing), Peshitta and the entire

---

[1] *Saint Éphrem. Commentaire de l'Évangile concordant. Texte syriaque (Manuscrit Chester Beatty 709)*, ed. L. Leloir (Dublin 1963). A number of further folios of the same manuscript subsequently turned up and were fortunately bought by the Chester Beatty Library; these were edited by Leloir in a volume of the same title, but published at Leuven (by Peeters) in 1990.

[2] E. Beck, in a series of articles in *OrChr* over the years 1989–1993, has argued that the *Commentary* cannot be by Ephrem himself. For the purpose of the present contribution the matter is not of direct concern, and the author will, for convenience, be cited as Ephrem.

[3] S. Euringer, "Der locus classicus des Primates (Mt. 16,18) und der Diatessarontext des hl. Ephräm," in *Beiträge zur Geschichte des christlichen Altertums und der byzantinischen Literatur: Festgabe A. Ehrhard*, ed. A. M. Koeniger (Bonn/Leipzig 1922), pp. 141–172.

[4] L. Leloir, *Saint Éphrem. Commentaire de l'Évangile concordant, version arménienne*, CSCO 137 [Arm. 1] (Louvain 1953). There is no trace of the reading "bars" left in the Arabic or Persian Diatessarons either (the Persian paraphrases by "le mani del demonio" [see G. Messina, *Diatessaron Persiano*, BibOr 14 (Rome 1951), p. 133]).

Greek and Latin manuscript tradition. The publication of the Syriac original revealed that the Syriac text at *CD* XIV.1 did indeed read "bars":

ܘܐܢܬܘܢ ܠܡ ܡܢܐ. ܫܡܥܘܢ ܕܝܢ ܪܫܐ. ܒܘܟܪܐ ܡܠܠ ܕܐܢܬ
ܗܘ ܒܪܐ ܡܫܝܚܐ. ܒܪܗ ܕܐܠܗܐ ܚܝܐ. ܘܛܘܒܝܟ ܠܟ ܫܡܥܘܢ.
ܘܡܘܟܠܐ ܕܫܝܘܠ ܠܐ ܢܚܣܢܘܢܟ.

> And (as for) you, what (do you say that I am). Now Simon the head uttered the firstfruit: You are the Son, the Messiah, the Son of the living God. And Blessed are you, Simon; and *The bars of Sheol* will not overpower you.

In his Latin translation Leloir puts the whole of this passage in italics (indicating a direct biblical quotation), with the sole exception of "the head" and "the firstfruit," and in this judgement he was followed by Carmel McCarthy, in her translation.[5] Whether consciously or not, Leloir was in fact following the much earlier view of von Harnack, who considered[6] that the Armenian translation of *CD* XIV.1 implied the omission of καὶ ἐπὶ ταύτῃ τῇ πέτρᾳ οἰκοδομήσω μου τὴν ἐκκλησίαν, and that the Diatessaron commented upon in *CD* had read "will not overpower you" (rather than "it"). Euringer, after a careful exposition of the passage and its context in *CD*,[7] plausibly argued that Ephrem was simply compressing elements from verses 15–18, adapting the syntax accordingly: thus, it is illegitimate, not only to claim the passage as evidence for the omission, but also to use it as supporting the reading "you" instead of "it"; accordingly, to italicise "you" in translations is misleading. That Euringer is probably[8] correct in this is indicated by the fact that, while there is (as will be seen) massive evidence in later Syriac writers for ܡܘܟܠܐ (*mukle*: "bars"), there is none in Syriac in support of a supposed variant "will not overpower *you*."[9]

---

[5] *Saint Ephrem's Commentary on Tatian's Diatessaron*, trans. C. McCarthy, JSS.S 2 (Oxford 1993).

[6] A. von Harnack, "Der Spruch über Petrus als den Felsen der Kirche, Mat 16,17f.," *SBAW* 1918, pp. 637–654.

[7] Euringer, "Der locus classicus," pp. 144–153.

[8] Slight hesitation arises from the fact that the Stuttgart and The Hague manuscripts of the medieval Dutch harmony also attest "you": see *The Liège Diatessaron*, edd. D. Plooij, C. A. Phillips, VNAW 31.3 (Amsterdam 1933), p. 259.

[9] Von Harnack had adduced two passages from the *Commentary on Isaiah* which circulates under Ephrem's name, published by Lamy: as Euringer was

The appearance of "bars of Sheol" in the Syriac Diatessaron text commented upon by Ephrem has certain implications for the early history of the Diatessaron, since there seems to be absolutely no support for such a reading in any western Diatessaron witness, whether in Greek, Latin or medieval vernacular language. If we accept for the moment that the compiler of the Diatessaron was Tatian, it is important to know in which language he composed it[10]: if Greek, and the Syriac is a translation, why is there no trace of this distinctive alteration in the western Diatessaron tradition? The implication must be that "bars" is an innovation on the part of the Syriac translator, who would thus need to be seen as carrying further the sort of interpretative process initiated by Tatian. Alternatively, one might suppose that Tatian himself made the translation and in the process introduced further interpretative elements.[11] If, on the other hand, the Diatessaron was first composed in Syriac,[12] then there is still the puzzle of why no trace of it has been left in the western Diatessaron tradition, for it is not very likely that a Greek translation of an original Syriac Diatessaron would just ignore "the bars" and revert to "the gates."

We are in fact not dealing with an isolated phenomenon, for there exist a few other distinctive Syriac Diatessaron readings which have no parallels in any of the western Diatessaron witnesses: notable among these are the choice of the verb *aggen*, which has its background in the Palestinian Targum tradition, to render

---

easily able to show (pp. 171, 176–178), he had been misled by the Latin translation "...*te*," taking it as masculine; in fact the Syriac has -*ek(y)* (fem.), not -*ak* (masc.), and the antecedent is therefore "Sion": the author of these passages has, in fact, treated Matt 16:18 in the same way as Ephrem in *CD*.

[10] On this debated question, see W. L. Petersen, "New Evidence for the Question of the Original Language of the Diatessaron," in *Studien zum Text und zur Ethik des Neuen Testaments. Festschrift zum 80. Geburtstag von H. Greeven*, ed. W. Schrage, BZNW 47 (Berlin 1986), pp. 325–343 (see also his *Tatian's Diatessaron. Its Creation, Dissemination, Significance and History in Scholarship*, VigChr.S 25 [Leiden 1994], pp. 384–397, 428–432).

[11] Though authors known to have written in both Greek and Syriac are rare, this is not out of the question: for the case of Rabbula of Edessa († 436), see my "Greek and Syriac in Late Antique Syria," in *Literacy and Power in the Ancient World*, edd. A. K. Bowman and G. Woolf (Cambridge 1994), pp. 149–160, esp. 155.

[12] Thus especially Petersen, "New Evidence."

both ἐπισκιάσει at Luke 1:35 and ἐσκήνωσεν at John 1:14[13]; the alteration of John the Baptist's diet from "locusts and honey" to "milk and honey"[14]; and the specification of the room where the wise virgins will meet the Bridegroom as the more intimate "bridal chamber" (*gnona*), rather than the "wedding feast."[15] It is interesting to note that some of these distinctive features are likely to be due to a concern to introduce Old Testament allusions into the harmonized Gospel text, for this would conform with the practice, probably going back to the Syriac Diatessaron, of adapting the text of Old Testament quotations in the Gospels to the text of the Peshitta Old Testament.[16] The existence of these (and other) features of the eastern (and above all, the Syriac) Diatessaron tradition suggests there may be something to be said for Petersen's suggestion that the western Diatessaron tradition goes back to a Harmony based on the one used by Justin, and that the Syriac Diatessaron was the work of Tatian who, while also basing himself on this early Greek harmony, made further adaptations of his own.[17]

---

[13] See my "An early interpretation of Pasah: *aggen* in the Palestinian Targum," in *Interpreting the Hebrew Bible: Essays in Honour of E. I. J. Rosenthal*, edd. J. A. Emerton and S. C. Reif (Cambridge 1982), pp. 27–34, "The lost Old Syriac at Luke 1:35 and the earliest Syriac terms for the incarnation," in *Gospel Traditions in the Second Century*, ed. W. L. Petersen, CJA 3 (Notre Dame [Indiana] 1989), pp. 117–131, and "From Annunciation to Pentecost: The travels of a technical term," in *Eulogema: Studies in Honor of R. Taft SJ*, StAns 110 (1993), pp. 71–91.

[14] See my "The Baptist's diet in Syriac sources," *OrChr* 54 (1970), pp. 113–124. John the Baptist thus already feeds on "the milk and honey" of the Promised Land.

[15] *E.g.* Aphrahat, *Dem.* 6:1, 6:6, 14:16 (ed. Parisot, *PS* I, cols. 241, 248, 269, 612); Ephrem, *Hymni de Fide* 11:18; *Sermones* II.iv.308, 328, 446; *Letter to Publius*, 12; Isaac of Antioch (ed. P. Bedjan, p. 59), etc.; see further, A. Vööbus, *Studies in the History of the Gospel Text in Syriac*, CSCO 128 [Subs. 3] (Louvain 1951), p. 111. The reading had important implications for the Syriac ideal of virginity (male and female); possibly the reading "bridegroom and bride" in Matt 25:1 (also in the Old Syriac and Peshitta), was deliberately intended to counteract this reading in verse 10.

[16] See J. Joosten, "The Old Testament quotations in the Old Syriac and the Peshitta Gospels: a contribution to the study of the Diatessaron," *Textus* 15 (1990), pp. 55–76.

[17] W. L. Petersen, "Textual Evidence of Tatian's Dependence upon Justin's ΑΠΟΜΗΝΜΟΝΕΥΜΑΤΑ," NTS 36 (1990), pp. 512–534, and his *Tatian's Diatessaron*, pp. 346–348, 428–437; similarly, M.-É. Boismard, *Le Diatessaron de Tatien à Justin*, EtB N.S. 15 (Paris 1992). Boimard's further hypothesis, that *CD*

The rationale behind the alteration

These wider questions, however, cannot be pursued further here, since our main concern is with the Syriac Diatessaron reading "bars of Sheol." Before turning to its extensive attestation, we should examine briefly the reasons behind the alteration of "gates" to "bars": why should a phrase that is familiar from the Old Testament[18] be replaced by one that has no exact Old Testament parallel? Robert Murray has made out a strong case[19] for seeing behind the change a desire to link Matt 16:18 with two related passages in the Old Testament, Ps.106 (107):16 and Isaiah 45:2, which were, from at least the second half of the second century onwards,[20] associated with the descent of Christ into Sheol and the liberation of the departed. These two passages read in the Septuagint and Peshitta as follows:

Ps. 106 (107):16:

LXX: ὅτι συνέτριψεν πύλας χαλκᾶς καὶ μοχλοὺς σιδηροὺς συνέκλασεν (lec. var.: συνέθλασεν)

---

combines two harmony sources, Tatian's Diatessaron and a Syriac translation of a harmony going back to Justin, seems much more questionable.

[18] Is. 38:10, Wis. 16:13, III Macc. 5:51; cp. Job 38:17.

[19] R. Murray, *Symbols of Church and Kingdom* (Cambridge 1975), pp. 228–236, 324–327 (based on his earlier "The Rock and the House on the Rock: A chapter in the ecclesiological symbolism of Aphraates and Ephrem," *OrChrP* 30 (1964), pp. 315–362, esp. 341–350, 356–362).

[20] First in a fragment ascribed to Hippolytus; see Murray, *Symbols of Church and Kingdom*, p. 325. Notice the suggestive contexts of both passages: in Ps. 106 (107) the previous verse speaks of the Lord who "brought them out of darkness and the shadow of death," while the following one states that they had "reached the gates of death"; Is. 45:1 commences with the Lord saying to his Messiah (Cyrus, of course, in the original context), "I will begin to open the gates before him, and the gates [so Peshitta, LXX "cities" (see *infra*, n. 21)] shall not be kept closed," and v. 3 continues "I will give to you the treasures that are in the dark." Whether or not the original author of Is. 45 was consciously aware of this, his wording is remarkably similar to that of Ishtar in the Descent of Ishtar into the Underworld: "Open the door,...I will break the door, I will shatter the bolt": see J. B. Pritchard, *Ancient Near Eastern Texts relating to the Old Testament* (Princeton 1969[3]), p. 107.

Syr: ܡܛܠ ܕܬܪܥܐ ܕܢܚܫܐ ܬܒܪ ܘܡܘܟܠܐ ܕܦܪܙܠܐ ܓܕܥ

trans.: because he has shattered the gates of bronze, and the
          bars of iron he has broken

Is. 45:2:

LXX: θύρας χαλκᾶς σύντρίψω
      καὶ μοχλοὺς σιδηροῦς συγκλάσω (lec. var.: συνθλάσω)

Syr: ܬܪܥܐ ܕܢܚܫܐ ܐܬܒܪ
                                        ܘܡܘܟܠܐ ܕܦܪܙܠܐ ܐܓܕܥ

trans.: the gates of bronze shall I shatter,
          and the bars of iron shall I break

That Is. 45 in particular was associated with the Descent in the
Syrian region is suggested by two of the earliest Syriac texts that we
have, the *Odes of Solomon*[21] and the *Acts of Thomas*. *Ode* 17:8–9 (9–
10) has

          ܘܬܒܠܬ ܬܪܥܐ ܕܐܚܝܕܝܢ ܗܘܘ ܘܦܬܚܬ ܬܒܪܘ ܡܘܟܠܐ ܕܦܪܙܠܐ

and I opened gates that were closed and I broke the bars of iron...

a combination which links up with Isaiah 45:1–2 more closely than
with Ps. 106 (107). Although the passage was associated with the
Baptism of Christ in the *Epistle of Barnabas*,[22] it is likely that Plooij
was correct[23] in seeing a reference in the *Odes* to the Descent,

---

[21] It is of course disputed whether or not the *Odes of Solomon* were originally
written in Syriac; the passage in *Ode* 17 fits best with the Peshitta's "gates shall
not be closed," whereas the LXX has cities (πόλεις): this would seem to be an
argument in favour of Syriac as the original language of the *Odes*; it is possible,
however, that πόλεις is a corruption of πύλαι (= Hebrew; the [lunate] sigma
having been occasioned by the following omicron). The dating of the *Odes* is
likewise a matter of uncertainty, with modern opinion ranging from the late first
century to the late third century.

[22] *Barnabas* 11.

[23] D. Plooij, "Der Descensus ad inferos in Aphrahat und den Oden Salomos,"
ZNW 14 (1913), pp. 222–231, esp. 227–228. For the link between Christian
baptism and the Descent, see P. Lundberg, *La typologie baptismale dans l'ancienne
église* (Leipzig/Uppsala 1942), pp. 178–179, and J. Daniélou, *The Theology of*

especially in view of verse 11(12) of the *Ode*, which speaks of the release of prisoners.

In the *Acts of Thomas* (third century) chapter 10 has a probable allusion to Is. 45:1 (rather than verse 2):

ܐܬ݂ܬܐ ܡܫܝܚܐ ܕܐܢܬܐ ܡܫܝܬܐ ܕܘܟܠܐ....ܠܐܠܐ ܠܝ ܐܬܘ

ܠܗܘܢ ܐܢܬܐ ܠܐ ܐܬܐ ܡܪܝܐܣ ܐܠܐ ܠܢ ܕܐܬ ܠܗܘܢ

> you [*sc.* Christ] descended to Sheol...and opened its gates and brought out its prisoners, and trod for them the way[24] upwards by your very divinity.

Clear allusions to Is. 45:1–2 are to be found in two texts from Nag Hammadi, the *Teachings of Silvanus* (Codex VII, p. 110, lines 18–21) and the *Trimorphic Protennoia* (Codex XIII, p. 41, lines 9–11); the former is of particular interest in that the bars are directly connected with the Underworld (AMENTE):

> This one, being God, became man for your sake. It is this one who broke the iron bars (ΝΝΜΟΧΛΟΣ) of the Underworld and the bronze bolts.

The *Teachings of Silvanus* has been variously dated, but the second half of the third century perhaps seems the most likely.[25]

Another very clear allusion to Is. 45:1–2 in the context of the Descent occurs in the Manichaean *Psalms*, of the mid fourth-century:

Jewish Christianity (London 1964), pp. 244–245; see also K. McDonnell's study *The Baptism of Jesus in the Jordan* (Collegeville [Minnesota] 1996), pp. 156–170.

[24] For this non-biblical phrase, very characteristic of early Syriac literature, see Murray, *Symbols of Church and Kingdom*, pp. 299–301.

[25] M. Peel in *Nag Hammadi Codex VII*, ed. B. Pearson (Leiden 1996), pp. 272–274; Y. Janssens, *Les Leçons de Silvanos (NH VII,4)* (Québec 1983), p. 23, gives a much earlier date (end of the second century); as for the *Trimorphic Protennoia*, J. D. Turner suggests that it "may have reached its final form by the mid-second century CE" (in *Nag Hammadi Codices XI, XII, XIII*, ed. C. W. Hedrick [Leiden 1990], p. 401. For the importance of Ps. 106 (107) as the background of the Descent theme in the *Teachings of Silvanus*, see M. L. Peel, "The 'Descensus ad inferos' in the 'Teachings of Silvanus'," *Numen* 26 (1979), pp. 23–49, esp. 30–31, 40–41.

> By his resurrection he opened the gates that were closed: the gates
> and bars (μοχλός) of the men of Hades he broke.[26]

Reminiscences of either Is. 45:2 or Ps. 106 (107) in the context of
Christ's Descent into Sheol can also be found in several passages in
Aphrahat.[27] Clearly, by the fourth century the association of these
Old Testament verses with the Descent was widely familiar.

On the supposition, then, that these two Old Testament
passages (especially Isaiah 45) were already associated with the
Descent when the Syriac Diatessaron was composed,[28] then the
motivation behind the change of wording would seem to be this: in
the Old Testament "gates of Sheol" means little more than "death,"
and none of the passages where it occurs gives any opportunity to
link the phrase with the salvation effected by Christ at his Descent
into Sheol; since "gates" are frequently paired with "bars,"[29] this
provides a convenient means to indicate a more specific link between Matt 16:18 and the Descent theme than is possible with
"gates of Sheol," whose connotations are too general, since "bars of
Sheol" has the merit of drawing attention to these two particular
passages which were specifically associated with the Descent.

It should be mentioned that Stephen Gero has objected to
Murray's explanation of the Syriac Diatessaron's *mukle*, arguing
instead that *mukle* have the sense of "levers" or "crowbars," but
there seem to be no good reasons for accepting this.[30]

---

[26] *A Manichaean Psalm-Book*, ed. C. R. C. Allberry, Part II (Stuttgart 1938), p. 196.

[27] *Dem.* 12:8 (*PS*, Vol. I, col. 524), 14:31 (col. 652), 21:19 (col. 977), 22:4 (col. 997).

[28] If the Syriac Diatessaron was translated from Greek, and this translation was not made by Tatian himself, then a rather later date for it would of course be possible.

[29] *E.g.* Deut. 3:5; Ps.147:2 (13).

[30] S. Gero, "The gates or the bars of Hades. A note on Matthew 16.18," *NTS* 27 (1980), pp. 411-413, where he also tentatively suggests that μοχλοί was the original reading of the Greek. Though *mukla* can occasionally mean "lever" in Syriac, this is not at all common, whereas the association with doors is very frequent. Moreover, once the (most unlikely) suggestion that μοχλοί was the original reading in the Greek is abandoned, it is very difficult to see how *mukle* in the sense of "levers" could ever have arisen, whereas the frequent association of *mukle* with "gates" in the Old Testament provides a ready link (whether or not one accepts an implied association of Ps. 106 (107) and Is. 45 with the Descent).

Attestation of "The bars of Sheol" in Syriac writers

Earlier scholars have drawn attention to a considerable number
of Syriac quotations of, or allusions to, Matt 16:18 in its Diatessaron form[31]: these are to be found not only in native Syriac
writers, but also in early translations from Greek.[32] What is worth
noting, however, is the longevity of these quotations, for they occur
in numerous texts written centuries after the Diatessaron had
ceased to be in use. Some of these will be discussed below, in the
following section, but here attention might be drawn to two
particular instances. In the late sixth-century *Chronicle* of Ps.-
Zacharias Rhetor,[33] the Syriac translation of a letter of Timothy
Ailouros containing a quotation of Matt 16:18 is cited: "and on this
rock (*kepa*) I will build my church, and the bars of Sheol will not
overpower her" (= the church); the same letter happens also to be
quoted in the great *Chronicle* of Michael the Syrian († 1199),[34]
retaining "bars," but with a different word (*šoʿa*) for "rock." A
different translation, however, of Timothy's letter is quoted in a
sixth-century dogmatic florilegium,[35] and there the "gates," which
must have stood in the Greek original, are retained: this conforms
with normal sixth-century translation practice, and it is the
treatment of the Greek quotation in Ps.-Zacharias and Michael that

---

[31] Thus notably F. C. Burkitt, *S. Ephraim's Quotations from the Gospels*, TaS
VII.2, (Cambridge 1901; reprinted Nendeln 1967), p. 30, and *Evangelion da-
Mepharreshe*, Vol. I (Cambridge 1904), pp. 92–93; Euringer, "Der locus
classicus"; L. Leloir, *L'Évangile d'Éphrem d'après les œuvres éditées. Receuil des textes*,
CSCO 180 [Subs. 12] (Louvain 1958), ad locum; R. Köbert, "Zwei Fassungen
von Mt 16,18 bei den Syrern," *Bib* 40 (1959) pp. 1018–1020; I. Ortiz de Urbina,
Vetus Evangelium Syrorum. Diatessaron Tatiani (Matriti 1967), p. 102. Some further
references, especially from Jacob of Serugh, can be found in my "Some aspects
of Greek words in Syriac," in *Synkretismus im syrisch-persischen Kulturgebiet*, ed. A.
Dietrich, AAWG III.96 (1975), pp. 80–108, esp. 95–98, reprinted in my *Syriac
Perspectives on Late Antiquity* (London 1984), as chapter IV.

[32] Thus in the Syriac translations of Titus of Bostra, *Against the Manichaeans*
(ed. P. de Lagarde, p. 185), and of Eusebius, *Theophania* (ed. W. Cureton, pp. 95,
138–139), both preserved in a manuscript dated November A.D. 411. That the
mukle belong to the translator, and not to the original Greek, is indicated by
Eusebius, *h.e.* VI.25.8, where the Greek is of course extant, yet the Syriac (ed.
W. Wright, p. 417) has *mukle*.

[33] At IV.12 (ed. Brooks, Vol. I [= CSCO 83 (Syri 38) (Louvain 1919)], p. 187).

[34] Ed. Chabot, IV, p. 243, col. 1.

[35] Edited by R. Y. Ebied and L. R. Wickham, in *JThS* N.S. 21 (1970), p. 333.

is surprising since adaptation of Greek quotations to a form familiar from the Syriac biblical text is normally confined to early translations (*i.e.* pre-sixth century).[36]

A possible explanation for the occurrence of "bars of Sheol" in these sixth-century texts may be found in two late works by Philoxenus,[37] where he not only quotes the passage with "bars" instead of "gates," but also with *šo'a* (as in Michael's quotation of Timothy Ailouros) instead of *kepa*: elsewhere in these works Philoxenus usually cites the revision of the Peshitta by Polycarp, which he sponsored. Though the reappearance of "bars" in such a revision (when the Peshitta already corresponded to the Greek) would be surprising, the alteration to *šo'a* simply anticipates (as often happens in the Philoxenian) the reading found in the Harklean.

"Bars of Sheol" continues to feature occasionally in seventh- and eighth-century texts. A notable late seventh-century instance is to be found in the influential *Apocalypse* attributed to Methodius;[38] here it is interesting to note that the early Greek and Latin translations do not represent the Syriac original's quotation of Matt 16:18 at all. Probably from the next century the "bars of Sheol" again feature in the quotation of Matt 16:18 in the Dialogue of Sergius the Stylite with a Jew.[39] The Diatessaron reading has even, remarkably, survived into twentieth-century usage, for it appears in a clear allusion to the passage in a report, written in Syriac, of a synod of the Syrian Orthodox Church that was held in November 1981: "For Christ is within his Church...and *the bars of Sheol* will

---

[36] See my "Towards a history of Syriac translation technique," in *Symposium Syriacum*, ed. R. Lavenant, *OrChrA* 221 (Rome 1983), pp. 1–14, reprinted in my *Studies in Syriac Christianity* (Aldershot 1992), as chapter X.

[37] *Commentary on the Prologue of John* (ed. A. de Halleux, CSCO 380 [Syri 165] [Louvain 1977], p. 128); *Letter to the Monks of Senoun* (ed. de Halleux, CSCO 231 [Syri 98] [Louvain 1963], p. 77).

[38] IX.9 (ed. G. J. Reinink, CSCO 540 [Syri 220] [Louvain 1993]); see his note *ad locum*, and more extended discussion in his "Tyrannen und Muslime. Die Gestaltung einer symbolischen Metapher bei Pseudo-Methodios," in *Scripta Signa Vocis. Studies...Presented to J. H. Hospers*, edd. H. L. J. Vanstiphout, K. Jongeling, F. Leemhuis and G. J. Reinink (Groningen 1986), pp. 163–175, esp. 166–170. The Diatessaron reading here may have been derived from the Julian Romance, an important source for the Apocalypse, for it also occurs there (ed. G. Hoffmann, p. 64).

[39] XI.11 (ed. P. Hayman, CSCO 338 [Syri 152] [Louvain 1973]).

not prevail against her."[40] This "afterlife" of Diatessaron (and other archaic) readings is a feature which deserves attention: obviously, such readings cannot be used as evidence for the survival of copies of the Diatessaron (would that this were the case with the late twentieth-century example!); what has evidently happened is that certain archaic readings became fossilized, as it were, through their use in liturgical texts. Sure enough, if one consults the vast hymnaries of the Syriac Churches, the Syrian Orthodox *Fenqitho* and the *Ḥudra* of the Church of the East, numerous examples of the phrase "bars of Sheol," clearly based ultimately on Matt 16:18, can be found.[41]

The various interpretations of "The bars of Sheol"

Even though "the bars" were (in all likelihood) introduced into Matt 16:18 in order to provide a link with the Descent, not all Syriac writers necessarily interpreted the verse in that context, and notable among them is Ephrem, whose *Commentary on the Diatessaron* is the prime witness to the Diatessaron reading. Ephrem's uppermost association in *CD* 14:1–2 is with Matt 7 (the building founded on rock), and it is striking that in his numerous hymns in the *Carmina Nisibena* dealing with the Descent theme he never introduces phraseology reminiscent of Ps. 106 (107)/Is. 45; furthermore, whereas he uses the phrase "gates of Sheol" a number of times[42] (with no reference, of course, to Matt 16:18), he only once employs the term *mukle*, when he says that "Sheol made strong her gates and bars."[43]

The only *madrasha* plausibly attributed to Ephrem that quotes the Diatessaron form of Matt 16:18 is one entitled *On the Church*, printed by Beck at the end of his edition of the *Hymns on Paradise*:[44] here stanza 2 reads

---

[40] *Qolo Suryoyo* (Monastery of St Ephrem, Holland) 23 (Dec.–Jan. 1982), p. 20.

[41] E.g., *Fenqitho* (Mosul 1886), Vol. II, foll. 1b, 25a, 35a, 39a, 42a; Vol. IV, fol. 54a; *Ḥudra* (Trichur 1960), Vol. I, p. 565; II, 568, 604, 637, 641; III, 244, 569.

[42] Thus *Carmina Nisibena* 36:14 (Death says: "I will close the gates of Sheol in the face of the dead [Jesus]"); 37:9 (only the Creator has the key to the gate of Sheol); 41:16 ("Death opened the gates of Sheol and the radiance of the face of our Lord shone forth"), etc.

[43] *Carmina Nisibena* 43:5, reminiscent of the frequent use of ἀσφαλίζειν in Greek homilies by Eusebius of Alexandria and others on the Descent (*e.g.*, Migne, *PG* 86, coll. 385, 520, 722; likewise in the *Gospel of Nicodemus*, 21).

[44] CSCO 174 [Syri 78] (Louvain 1957).

> Bestow upon yourselves, my brethren, the treasure of comfort
> from the words which our Lord spoke concerning his Church:
> "The bars of Sheol are not able to vanquish her."[45]
> If she, then, is stronger even than Sheol,
> who among mortals is able to frighten her? ...

That it is Christ's own prior Descent to Sheol that renders the "bars of Sheol," of Matt 16:18, ineffective against the Church is clearly indicated by a passage in the *Memre* on Nicomedia, preserved only in Armenian translation:

> When her Lord died, his death became life in Sheol,
> ...the Church of Christ is stronger even than death, totally
>   victorious,
> for "The bars of Sheol are not victorious (*yatt'en*)"
> over his Church, as he said.
> Not by vanquishing is she victorious in Sheol:
> she is living, there, like her Lord.[46]

In both these passages we find the apparent variant "vanquish her" (*nezkonah*) in place of "prevail over/withstand" (*nehsnunah*), but even though attestation for "vanquish" here is quite extensive, it is hardly likely to be more than a gloss in origin, albeit one that proved influential.[47]

The next Syriac writer to make use of the Diatessaron reading of Matt 16:18 in the context of the Descent is Jacob of Serugh († 521). His application, in a number of different passages, of the phraseology of Matt 16:18 to Christ, not the Church, again makes it perfectly clear that the reason why "the bars of Sheol will not prevail over the Church" is because they did not prevail over Christ at his resurrection. Thus, for example, (Christ speaks):

---

[45] The Mosul edition of the *Fenqitho* (II, p.12a) quotes the passage with the variant *nakkunah* "harm her."

[46] XIV.135–44 (ed. C. Renoux, *PO* 37, pp. 2–3 [Paris 1975]).

[47] Its occurrence in the Syriac translation of Eusebius's *Theophania* (IV.11) has long been noticed; it can also be found in paraphrases in Jacob of Serugh (ed. Bedjan, Vol. I, pp. 477 and 478); in Isaac of Antioch (ed. Bedjan, p. 785), and in the Syriac translation of (Ps.-) Amphilochius, *Life of Basil* (*Acta Martyrum et Sanctorum*, ed. Bedjan, Vol. VI, p. 330). Quite possibly the gloss originated under the influence of Peshitta Jer. 1:19 and 15:20, "they shall fight with you, but will not vanquish you (*nezkonak*), for I am with you to rescue you, says the Lord"; at Jer. 20:7 *hsen* and *zka* are used together.

> When I die, the bars of Sheol will not prevail over me,
> and Death will not be able to look upon my face when I come
> forth (*sc.* from Sheol).[48]

It is significant, too, that Jacob several times combines "bars of Sheol" with wording derived from Is. 45 (rather than Ps. 106 [107]). Thus:

> The resurrection shines forth, and at it the bars of Sheol are broken (*metgaddmin*),
> and it brings forth from her (*sc.* Sheol) all the treasures hidden there;[49]

or again:

> The bars of Sheol he shattered (*tabbar*) and came forth from the darkness.[50]

It is this latter verb that especially finds favour with later writers in combination with "the bars of Sheol"; thus, an East Syrian writer of a generation later than Jacob, Cyrus of Edessa[51] speaks of Christ as "about to break the bars of Sheol...and to rescue the mortal condition."[52]

This particular combination of "shatter" (*tabbar*, from Isaiah) with "bars of Sheol" (from Matthew) is especially common in subsequent liturgical poetry,[53] thus helping (as we have seen) to preserve this Diatessaron reading, by now totally independent of the Syriac Diatessaron itself.

As was already clear from the situation in the Commentary on the Diatessaron, the use of the Diatessaron text of Matt 16:18 does not necessarily mean that an author will take up the Syriac Diatessaron's hint and associate the passage with the Descent. This

---

[48] Ed. Bedjan, Vol. I, p. 502.

[49] Ed. Bedjan, Vol. V, p. 571.

[50] Ed. Bedjan, Vol. II, p. 632.

[51] Ed. W. Macomber (CSCO 355 [Syri 155] [Louvain 1974], p. 114).

[52] A variation on this, "at his resurrection he shattered (*tabbar*) the bars of death," occurs in the Acts of the Synod of Catholicos Ezekiel, held in 576 (ed. J. B. Chabot, *Synodicon Orientale* [Paris 1904], p. 114); similarly, Isaac of Antioch (ed. Bedjan), p. 734: "he shattered the bars of perdition."

[53] *Hudra*, II, pp. 568, 604, 637, 651, etc.; *Fenqitho*, Vol. V, ff. 274b, 304b, 344a, etc.

also applies to Philoxenus († 523), who identifies the *mukle* as "the afflictions that come from persecutors,"[54] and to the author of the Pseudo-Methodius *Apocalypse* (c. 691/2), who stipulates that they are "the tyrants of paganism."[55]

While both Greek and Syriac[56] writers may apply Ps. 106 (107)/Is. 45 to the Descent independently of Matt 16:18, it is significant that the linking with this of phraseology from Matt 16:18 (such as we found in Jacob of Serugh) appears to be almost entirely confined to Syriac writers. The only exceptions known to me are the *Teachings of Silvanus* (quoted above), a passage in Romanos, and some later Byzantine hymns. Romanos has:

> Ἐγήγερται ὁ Κύριος, ἔτριψε τὰς χαλκᾶς πύλας τοῦ ἅδου
> καὶ σιδηροῦς μοχλοὺς αὐτοῦ συνέθλασε.[57]

> The Lord is risen, he has shattered the bronze gates of Hades
> And broken the iron bars.

Since, however, "gates of Hades" (unlike "bars of Sheol/Hades") is a biblical phrase not confined to Matt 16:18, one cannot be certain that Romanos is really combining these two passages; on the whole, it is more likely that (like the author of the *Teachings of*

---

[54] *Letter to the monks of Senoun*, p. 77. This makes it all the more puzzling why he (or rather, Polycarp) apparently retained the Diatessaron reading *mukle* in his revision (if that is what he is quoting here).

[55] In the *Ḥudra* one encounters the phrase "the gates of Sheol and its tyrants" a number of times (*e.g.* Vol. III, pp.614, 616, 622).

[56] Thus Aphrahat, cited above (in note 27); the same applies to Narsai in two passages cited from Vatican MS Borg. syr. 83 by Murray, *Symbols*, p. 236, both of which are now more readily available, the former in Memra IV, on the Resurrection (ed. F. G. McLeod, *PO* 40,1 [Paris 1979], line 366); and the latter in the Patriarchal Press's edition of Narsai (San Francisco 1970), Vol. I, p. 362. Narsai does indeed once allude to Matt 16:18, but not in the context of the Descent (ed. A. Mingana, II, p. 164, "the gates of Sheol and the bars of Death...").

[57] *First Hymn on the Resurrection*, stanza 20 (= kontakion XL, ed. J. Grosdidier de Matons, *SC* 128 [Paris 1967]). Similar phraseology also occurs in some later liturgical poetry, including the medieval Lament of the Virgin, cited in my "Some aspects," p. 98.

Silvanus) he is simply specifying the context in which Ps. 106 (107)/Is. 45 is to be understood.[58]

The two different scenarios implied

Both Köbert and Murray have noted[59] that the verb *neḥsnun* can be understood in two rather different ways, "prevail over, overcome" (whence the gloss "vanquish"), where the bars of Sheol are, as it were, on the offensive, or "withstand," where they are on the defensive; this double sense is in fact suggested in a passage in Jacob of Serugh[60] where Christ promises his bride (the Church) that "the bars and gates (*sc.* of Sheol) would not confine (*ḥabšin*) her within their palaces or vanquish (*zaken*) her." No doubt connected with these two different understandings of the verb *ḥsen*,[61] is the fact that, when early Syriac writers speak of the Descent of Christ into Sheol, they may either envisage Christ as bursting out of Sheol (*i.e.* at the Resurrection), or breaking into it (to rescue the imprisoned dead). Ephrem, in the *Carmina Nisibena*, definitely sees the gates of Sheol as trying to hold Christ in,[62] and indeed in 41:16 Death himself "opened the gates of Sheol/ and the radiance of the face of our Lord shone forth"—a scenario that conforms with the earlier iconographical tradition, splendidly illustrated in the "Rabbula Gospels of 586," where rays of light emerge from the tomb.[63]

---

[58] As is the case in Tertullian's allusion to the passage in *De carnis resurrectione*, 44: "...*portas adamantinas mortis et aeneas seras inferorum infregit.*"

[59] Kobert, "Zwei Fassungen" and Murray, *Symbols*, pp. 231–232.

[60] Ed. Bedjan, Vol. I, p. 477.

[61] For the basic sense of "get the better of" for *ḥsen* + object, see especially Matt 17:20, where καὶ οὐδὲν ἀδυνατήσει ὑμῖν is rendered *w-meddem la nehsankon* in both the Old Syriac and Peshitta. It was the sense "prevail over" that gave rise to a later development where Christ "makes strong (*ḥassen*, or *sarrar*) the *mukle* of the Church" against her adversaries: thus *e.g. Fenqitho*, Vol. II, fol. 35a; *Ḥudra*, Vol. III, p. 569. This scenario is internalised by the seventh-century writer Martyrius in his *Book of Perfection* (ed. A. de Halleux, CSCO 252 [Syri 110] [Louvain 1965], p. 138), where demonic "enemies" seek to break the *mukle* of the heart, enter it and take away captives.

[62] In 36:14, where Death says "I will close the gates of Sheol before this dead person (= Christ)," the following lines indicate that Christ is envisaged as already being in Sheol.

[63] Illustrated in J. Leroy, *Les manuscrits syriaques à peintures* (Paris 1964), Album, plate 32, and for the iconographical tradition see A. D. Kartsonis, *Anastasis: the Making of an Image* (Princeton 1986), p. 22.

Several passages in Jacob likewise presuppose the "bars of Sheol" as trying to hold Christ and the dead in.[64] The other scenario, where Christ breaks in to Sheol was above all encouraged by the application of Ps. 106 (107)/Is. 45 to the Descent, with its verbs "shatter" and "break," and the background in ancient Mesopotamian myths of descent into the underworld. This latter picture evidently became the dominant one from the sixth century onwards; in Greek (unlike Syriac) tradition this is usually associated also with Ps. 23 (24):7: "Lift up the gates...and the king of glory shall enter in."[65]

The evidence can be summarized as follows: Ps. 106 (107)/Is. 45 had probably come to be associated with the Descent by the end of the second century, and a deliberate allusion to this would seem to be the most likely reason behind the alteration from "gates" to "bars" of Sheol in the Syriac Diatessaron. Once the phrase "the bars of Sheol" had become enshrined in Syriac through the Syriac Diatessaron's change of wording in Matt 16:18, we can observe five different strands of interpretation in early Syriac writers: (1) Ps. 106 (107)/Is. 45 (especially the latter) continue to be employed with reference to the Descent, but without involving use of the phrase "the bars of Sheol" from Matt 16:18; this is the situation in the *Odes of Solomon*, the *Acts of Thomas* and Aphrahat. (2) Both Ps. 106 (107)/Is. 45 and "the bars of Sheol" are conspicuously absent from descriptions of the Descent; this applies most notably to Ephrem's *Carmina Nisibena*. (3) The Syriac Diatessaron's reading "the bars of Sheol" occurs, but the context given to Matt 16:18 is not that of the Descent; this is the pattern found in

---

[64] Thus ed. Bedjan, Vol. II, p. 612, "The Strong One arose and the bars of Sheol did not withstand [lit.: stand before] Him," and later in the same homily (p. 632), "[Christ] who shattered the bars of Sheol and came forth from darkness." In the latter passage Jacob retains the older conception of Christ breaking out of Sheol, even though he has combined it with *tabbar*, from Ps. 106 (107)/Is. 45. See also the passages cited in my "Aspects of Greek words," pp. 96–97.

[65] See the references *supra*, in note 43; this is the scenario of the *Gospel of Nicodemus*, 21. Ps. 23 (24):7 is, of course, also used of the Ascension (*e.g.* Irenaeus, *Proof of the Apostolic Preaching*, 84, in *PO* 12,5). In general for the theme of breaking the gates of the Hades/Sheol, see J. A. MacCullough, *The Harrowing of Hell* (Edinburgh 1930), chap. 13. The theological aspects of the Descent theme are discussed by A. Grillmeier, "Der Gottessohn im Totenreich," *ZKTh* 71 (1949), pp. 1–53, 184–203.

the *Commentary on the Diatessaron.* (4) "The bars of Sheol" and Matt 16:18 are specifically applied to the Descent, but without any hint of wording from Ps.106 (107)/Is. 45; this is the case with Ephrem's *Memre* on Nicomedia and the single *madrasha* "On the Church." (5) "The bars of Sheol" of Matt 16:18 are combined with phraseology taken from Ps. 106 (107)/Is. 45. Even though this combination of passages was in all likelihood the starting point for the Syriac Diatessaron's reading, in subsequent Syriac literature it appears not to be found until Jacob of Serugh, after whose time it features frequently, especially in liturgical texts. In (1) Christ is envisaged as breaking into Sheol, and *ḥsen* will have the sense of "withstand," whereas in (3), where the Descent is not involved, it has the meaning of "overcome" or "get the better of." In (4) Christ is envisaged as bursting out of Sheol, and *ḥsen* here means "get the better of," "have a hold over." In (5) we have a fusion of (1) and (4); as far as Jacob of Serugh is concerned, Christ is sometimes portrayed as breaking in, and sometimes as bursting out (see Figure I, appended at the end of this article). In Matt 16:18, where the object of *ḥsen* is normally seen by Syriac writers as the Church, the sense will be the same as that in (4) where the verse is understood in the context of the Descent: Sheol's failure to get the better of Christ ensures that this will also apply to the Church.

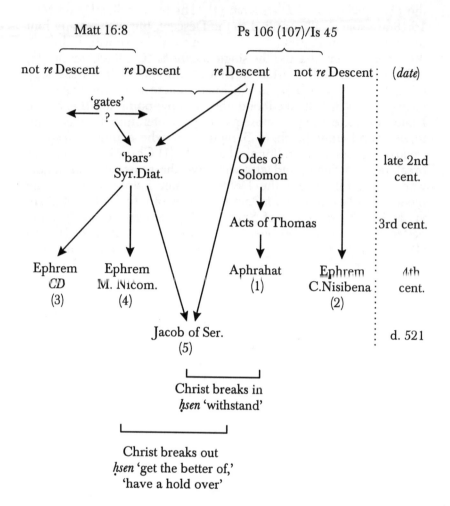

Evolution of terminology

LUKE 23:34a: A PERPETUAL TEXT-CRITICAL CRUX?

Joël Delobel
Katholieke Universiteit Leuven
(Leuven, Belgium)

A glance at Professor Tjitze Baarda's impressive bibliography will prove beyond doubt that extra-canonical traditions, both stories and sayings, have always enjoyed his particular interest. Exhaustive documentation and perspicacity in discussion characterize his numerous contributions in this field. In line with my own interest in the area, I offer this short study on an important saying of Jesus as a small tribute to the highly appreciated scholarship of a distinguished colleague and friend.

Among the various problems concerning the sayings of Jesus,[1] his first words from the cross, according to Luke's passion narrative, continue to puzzle editors and commentators of the third Gospel. In a series of manuscripts, we read: ὁ δὲ Ἰησοῦς ἔλεγεν, Πάτερ, ἄφες αὐτοῖς, οὐ γὰρ οἴδασιν τί ποιοῦσιν. In line with Westcott-Hort, this logion received a very special status in NA^{27}–GNT^{4}, where it is printed within double square brackets, a "treatment" which is given to only a few passages of the New Testament.[2] The

---

[1] Cf. my earlier contributions on this topic: "The Sayings of Jesus in the Textual Tradition. Variant Readings in the Greek Manuscripts of the Gospels," in *Logia. Les paroles de Jésus. The Sayings of Jesus. Mémorial Joseph Coppens*, ed. J. Delobel, BEThL 59 (Leuven 1982), pp. 431–457; "Luke 6:5 in Codex Bezae: The Man Who Worked on Sabbath," in *À cause de l'Évangile. Études sur les Synoptiques et les Actes*, FS J. Dupont, LeDiv 123 (Paris 1985), pp. 453–477; "The Lord's Prayer in the Textual Tradition," in *The New Testament in Early Christianity*, ed. J.-M Sevrin, BEThL 86 (Leuven 1989), pp. 293–309; "Extra-Canonical Sayings of Jesus: Marcion and Some 'Non-received' Logia," in *Gospel Traditions in the Second Century. Origins, Recensions, Text and Transmission*, ed. W. L. Petersen, CJA 3 (Notre Dame [Indiana]/London 1990), pp. 105–116; "Agrapha (Extracanonical Sayings of Jesus)" in *The Oxford Companion to the Bible*, ed. B. M. Metzger & M. D. Coogan (New York/Oxford 1993), pp. 17–18.

[2] Cf. *The Greek New Testament*, ed. K. Aland et al. (Stuttgart 1993^{4}), p. 47*: double square brackets "enclose passages which are regarded as later additions to the text, but which are of evident antiquity and importance."

reason which inspired the GNT-committee to posit this exceptional procedure is formulated by B. M. Metzger as follows:
"...the logion, though probably not a part of the original Gospel
of Luke, bears self-evident tokens of its dominical origin, and was
retained, within double square brackets, in its traditional place
where it had been incorporated by unknown copyists relatively
early in the transmission of the Third Gospel."[3] Such a
motivation is remarkable for several reasons. In the first place,
the indecision concerning the originality of the logion in Luke's
Gospel text: "though probably not a part of the original Gospel of
Luke" is somewhat striking. As is the case with the more numerous examples of words or passages within single square brackets,
the decision is left to the reader. Remarkably enough, however,
at the end of the statement a firm decision is taken, by attributing
the logion to incorporation by "unknown copyists relatively early
in the transmission of the Third Gospel." In addition, the
omission is granted an "A" rating in the fourth edition of GNT.[4]
Nevertheless, the logion is printed in the text, albeit within
double square brackets, because of "self-evident tokens of its
dominical origin."[5] By definition, self-evidence need not to be
argued any further.

No commentator can avoid engaging in a degree of discussion
with respect to this famous saying. Rather than offering an
extensive survey with countless repetitions, I prefer to present the

---

[3] Cf. B. M. Metzger, *A Textual Commentary on the Greek New Testament* (London
1971), p. 180.

[4] In the earlier editions of GNT, the critical apparatus started with the list of
manuscripts in favour of the presence of the text which received a "C" rating.
The editors of the latest critical edition are clearly more confident in rejecting
the originality of the passage.

[5] Metzger's remark is virtually a reformulation of Hort's point of view: cf. *The
New Testament in the Original Greek*, edd. B. F. Westcott & F. J. A. Hort
(Cambridge/London 1881), Vol. 2, "Notes on Select Readings," p. 68: "Few
verses of the Gospels bear in themselves a surer witness to the truth of what they
record than this first of the Words from the Cross: but it need not therefore have
belonged originally to the book in which it is now included. We cannot doubt
that it comes from an extraneous source. Nevertheless, like XXII,43f.; Mt
XVI,2f., it has exceptional claims to be permanently retained, with the necessary
safeguards, in its accustomed place."

main arguments in favour of and against originality.[6] Having weighed up the evidence pro and con, I will then ask whether the negative option taken by several authors as well as the ongoing indecision of many others cannot be overcome by a balanced methodology.

It would appear from the literature that many commentators are impressed by two elements: the *fact* that the logion is absent in several important manuscripts, and the *conviction* that no scribe would omit such a beautiful saying. The respective weight of these two arguments depends on the scholar's emphasis on either external or internal evidence. How strong do these arguments turn out to be on closer inspection, however? An approach which pays equal attention to both external and internal criticism, simultaneously avoiding the separation of the "twins," textual criticism and exegesis,[7] might perhaps lead to a more nuanced conclusion.

The external evidence: A puzzling situation

1. The evidence

According to GNT[4], the verse under question is included (with minor variants) by: ℵ*,[2] A C D[2] L Δ Ψ **0250** *f[1] f[13]* min (18) *Byz* [F G H N] *Lect* it*aur b c e f ff2 l r1* vg syr*c.p.h.pal* cop*bo[pt]* arm eth geo slav Diatessaron Jacobus-Justus*acc to* Hegesipp Irenaeus*lat* Hippolytus Origen*lat* Eusebius Eusebian Canons Ps-Ignatius Apostolic Constitutions Gregory-Nyssa Amphilochius Didymus*dub* Ps-Clementines Ps-Justin Chrysostom Cyril Hesychius Theodoret; Ambrosiaster Hilary Ambrose Jerome Augustine; (with asterisks: E). It is omitted by: 𝔓[75] ℵ[1] B D* W Θ **070** min (3) it*a d* syr*s* cop*sa bo[pt]*.

The evidence is thus striking for all to see. Although it may be correct, as one often hears stated, that the question cannot be decided on the basis of external criticism alone, the text-critical task should not be considered complete therewith.

---

[6] In this article, *originality* means belonging to the original text of the third Gospel, whereas *authenticity* means going back to the historical Jesus. The question of authenticity is not discussed.

[7] Cf. J. Delobel, "Textual Criticism and Exegesis: Siamese Twins?" in *New Testament Textual Criticism, Exegesis and Church History. A Discussion of Methods*, ed. B. Aland & J. Delobel, CBETh 7 (Kampen 1994; 1996[2]), pp. 98–117.

2. In favour of the original absence

The (in)decision of the GNT-committee was strongly inspired by the external evidence, with a well-known, though not exclusive and not entirely ill-founded preference for the combination $\mathfrak{P}^{75}$– B. The committee concluded that the absence of these words from "early and diverse witnesses...is most impressive." It is, indeed, most impressive. Westcott and Hort's choice, which was undoubtedly influenced by the omission in B as well,[8] is confirmed by $\mathfrak{P}^{75}$. In addition, the attestation of these authoritative witnesses combined with D*, not to mention W Q and several manuscripts of the most ancient versions, reinforces the claim for omission. The logion is omitted by ancient witnesses—some of them known for being habitually reliable—which belong to different textual families and various geographical areas.[9] These are highly estimable credentials which can only be challenged by strong arguments to the contrary. One is left wondering, however, whether a certain bias in approach to the evidence does not stand in the way of a full appreciation of the alternative possibility.

3. In favour of the original presence

Evidence in favour of the inclusion of the logion as part of the original text is not insignificant either. The great uncials א and A have an undeniable weight and, here also, various textual families and geographical areas are represented.[10] The fact that there is no early papyrus evidence for the inclusion of the logion constitutes an undeniable weakness. At the same time, however, Ephrem's triple citation of the verse in his *Commentary* on Tatian's Dia-

---

[8] According to Hort, *New Testament*, p. 68: "the documentary distribution suggests that the text was a Western interpolation, of limited range in early times." Apart from the so-called "non-interpolations," the "Western" text stood little chance of being accepted by Westcott and Hort. Given the diversity of its attestation, however, it has been disputed that the logion is to be considered as "Western."

[9] I refer to the short survey by F. G. Untergassmair, *Kreuzweg und Kreuzigung Jesu. Ein Beitrag zur lukanischen Redaktionsgeschichte und zur Frage nach der lukanischen "Kreuzestheologie,"* PaThSt 10 (Paderborn 1980), p. 9. One may contest the "classical" distinction between the families, but the survey does illustrate the variety of textual groups in favour of the omission.

[10] Cf. Untergassmair, *Kreuzweg*. The "addition" of the logion is given by the same textual families as the omission.

tessaron is often too easily overlooked and dismissed.[11] One is often considered to be on less firm ground with indirect evidence compared to Greek manuscripts. The reliability of Diatessaronic variants is particularly debated, given the date and nature of the multiple witnesses and the problem of agreeing upon sound methodological criteria for identifying original Tatianic readings.[12] If there is one point, however, in scholarly research on the Diatessaron on which many scholars do agree, it is the reliability of Ephrem's Commentary for attributing a particular verse or passage to Tatian's original text.[13] This witness brings us back to the second half of the second century, *i.e.* several decades earlier than $\mathfrak{P}^{75}$. Tatian's testimony is confirmed by other second century authors, provided that the logion was part of their original text.[14]

To summarize the matter quite simply: if one is rightly impressed by the third century testimony of $\mathfrak{P}^{75}$, one should not be left unimpressed by the testimony of Tatian, the *terminus ante quem* for the conscious attestation of Luke 23:34a as part of the third Gospel[15] in the middle of the second century. At first sight, the opposition between $\mathfrak{P}^{75}$ and Tatian seems to confirm the correct but somewhat closefisted statement mentioned above that the matter must be left undecided on the basis of external criticism alone. Nevertheless, although Tatian's testimony as such proves neither the originality of the saying nor its authenticity, it is a serious challenge to the attestation of the omission from $\mathfrak{P}^{75}$ on. It would appear, therefore, that from the point of view of external criticism the attestation in favour of the original presence of the logion is stronger than is usually thought. Sound warnings

---

[11] L. Leloir, *Éphrem de Nisibie. Commentaire de l'Évangile concordant ou Diatessaron*, SC 121 (Paris 1966), pp. 192, 376, 384.

[12] Cf. W. L. Petersen, *Tatian's Diatessaron. Its Creation, Dissemination, Significance, & History in Scholarship*, VigChr.S 25 (Leiden 1994), p. 357: "Lacking universally accepted criteria, each scholar decided what readings were 'Diatessaronic'." The thoroughgoing attempt to work out sound criteria is only one of the merits of Petersen's extensive study.

[13] Leloir, *Éphrem*, 25: "Si, d'ailleurs, Éphrem ne cite pas tout l'évangile de Tatien, au moins Tatien a-t-il dit tout ce qu'Éphrem en cite; d'aucun témoin postérieur à Tatien on ne peut dire chose semblable."

[14] W. Radl, *Das Lukas-Evangelium*, EdF 261 (Darmstadt 1988), p. 13, refers to Hegesippus, Marcion, Justin, and Irenaeus.

[15] If one does not attribute the saying to Tatian's own creativity—and I do not know of any author or any argument supporting such a hypothesis—it would seem that he found the verse in his (Gospel-) source(s).

against the "fallacy of the most ancient witness," considered as
the most trustworthy, should not blind us to the importance of
this very early testimony. Should this presumption of originality
—which of course cannot be decisive on its own—be confirmed
by a convincing argument on the level of internal criticism, one
would be inclined to wonder whether the *crux* should remain
undecided after all.

The internal evidence: a decisive argument?

None of the classical causes for accidental addition or omission[16]
can have played a role in this case. The variant under
investigation is of a special nature. Many of the frequently
occurring variants, such as alternative wording, transposition of
words, grammatical changes etc. may be ascribed to the inad-
vertent error of a copyist.[17] The presence or *absence* of a complete
logion of considerable length and striking content, however, can
hardly be attributed to scribal carelessness. Addition or omission
of this kind constitutes a deliberate change to the model. It is
clearly the product of one particular scribe, given that there is
little chance that several scribes in different times and places
would have introduced a change of this nature in exactly the
same Lucan verse independently from one another.[18] The scribe
in question must have had a motive to consciously add or omit
these astonishing words. Any attempt to determine this motive,
however, can only be hypothetical and must presuppose a discussion on the plausibility of the original presence or absence of
the verse in Luke's text. The study of intrinsic probability must,
in this case, precede the discussion of transcriptional probability.

---

[16] No trace of *homeoteleuton, homeoarcton,* etc. Spontaneous harmonisation with
the other Synoptics can hardly be accepted either.

[17] Cf. E. C. Colwell's critical remarks on the carelessness of certain scribes:
"Methods in Evaluating Scribal Habits: A Study of $\mathfrak{P}^{45}$, $\mathfrak{P}^{66}$, $\mathfrak{P}^{75}$," in *Studies in
Methodology in Textual Criticism of the New Testament,* NTTS 9 (Leiden 1969), pp.
106–124; *e.g.* concerning $\mathfrak{P}^{66}$: "The nearly 200 nonsense readings and the 400
itacistic spellings in $\mathfrak{P}^{66}$ are evidence of something less than disciplined attention
to the basic task. To this evidence of carelessnes must be added those singular
readings whose origin baffles speculation, readings that can be given no more
exact a label than carelessnes leading to assorted variant readings" (p. 114).

[18] Metzger, *A Textual Commentary,* p. 180, uses the somewhat misleading plural:
"the logion…had been incorporated by unknown copyists relatively early in the
transmission of the Third Gospel."

1. In defense of the original absence

Three questions have to be answered: (a) Why does the passage not fit in the text (intrinsic probability)? (b) Why did a scribe add it (transcriptional probability)? (c) What is the traditional background of the logion, the copyist's source of inspiration (tradition history)? We now deal with each in turn.

(a) Source critical and redaction critical remarks are employed to prove the absence of the logion in the original text of Luke. The verse is absent in Luke's source, the Marcan passion narrative. In this view, therefore, we are clearly dealing with an addition and a post-Lucan one at that, since, according to the protagonists of the omission theory, the logical flow of Luke's story is interrupted by the insertion, thus making an addition by Luke improbable.

(b) It is argued that had a scribe known of such a wonderful logion, he would certainly have tried to introduce it into the Passion story. The opposite is less probable: once the logion was in the text, no scribe would have dared to leave it out.[19]

(c) It is suggested that the inspiration may come from Acts 7:60, Stephen's prayer before he dies as a martyr. Another or even an additional source of inspiration may have been Isa 53:12: "...yet he bore the sin of many, and made intercession for the transgressors."

2. In defense of the original presence

Again, three questions have to be answered: (a) How does the passage fit in Luke's text (intrinsic probability)? (b) Why would a scribe have omitted the logion (transcriptional probability)? (c) Where did Luke find his inspiration (tradition history)? Once again, we address each in turn.

(a) Exegesis argues that the saying fits well in Luke's terminology,[20] theology, the context. The theological themes of praying for one's enemy,[21] forgiveness[22] and ignorance[23] are

---

[19] See Hort, *New Testament*, p. 69: "Its omission, on the hypothesis of its genuineness, cannot be explained in any reasonable manner."

[20] Cf. the detailed analysis by Untergassmair, *Kreuzweg*, pp. 44–46. Redactional terminology does not necessarily mean redactional creation. It proves that the sentence fits perfectly in Luke's way of writing, without directly affecting the question of authenticity.

[21] Cf. Luke 6:27f. parMatt. Notice the parallel formulation in the Lord's Prayer according to Luke 11:2b–4.

perfectly in line with Luke's own theology. It is also important to note that verse 34a is only one of the numerous Lucan additions and transpositions in comparison to Mark's passion narrative.[24] According to the defenders of originality, v. 34a, like the other "insertions" (diff Mark) in the passage, has a logical function in the context.[25]

(b) Several possible motives for an early omission are put forward, the first of which might have been the polemic between Christians and Jews. Whatever the original meaning of the somewhat vague αὐτοῖς in v. 34a may have been,[26] the logion was

---

[22] See a.o. my article "L'Onction de Jésus par la Pécheresse," in *EThL* 42 (1966), pp. 415–475; esp. 473.

[23] Cf. Acts 3:17; 13:27; comp. Luke 12:47f.

[24] If the hypothesis of a special continuous source for Luke's passion narrative is rejected, the differences between Luke and Mark become all the more striking, especially with respect to our verse: the omission of the offering of wine mingled with myrrh (Mark 15:23); the anticipation of the crucifixion of the two murderers (Mark 15:27); the addition of the logion Luke v. 34a; the rewriting of the scriptural allusion to Ps 22:19 concerning the division of the garments and casting of lots for them in v. 34b (diff Mark 15:24b).

[25] According to Feldkämper, *Der betende Jesus*, p. 259, the two references to the "evildoers" (v. 33c the κακοῦργοι, v. 34a those who crucify Jesus) are perfectly located in between the two traditional (par Mark) references to what is done to Jesus (v. 33b the crucifixion, v. 34b the division of the garments). In addition, there is a logical link between 34a and b, provided that δέ is understood in an explicative rather than in an adversative sense: the evildoers who divide Jesus' garments could not have known (οὐκ οἴδασιν) that they were fulfilling God's will as it was expressed in v. 34b, a quotation of Ps 22:19.

[26] The interpretation of αὐτοῖς as referring to the Jews is strongly rejected by D. Flusser, "'Sie wissen nicht, was sie tun'. Geschichte eines Herrenwortes," in *Kontinuität und Einheit*, FS F. Mussner, ed. P. G. Müller & W. Stenger (Freiburg/Basel/Wien 1981), pp. 393–420. The precise meaning of αὐτοῖς in this context is difficult to determine. There are several possibilities: the immediate context speaks about the two murderers who are crucified together with Jesus (v. 33); about the Roman soldiers (without mentioning them explicitly) who crucify Jesus and divide his garments (v. 33 and 34b); about the Jews in vv. 23–31, a *Sondergut*-text in which Jesus utters severe words with respect to the Jews, and throughout the passion narrative where the responsibility of the Jewish leaders cannot be overlooked. J. H. Petzer, "Anti-judaism and the Textual Problem of Luke 23:34," *FilNeo* 5 (1992), pp. 199–203, proposes an unusual interpretation of the anti-Judaic tendency of the prayer. In his view, Jesus' prayer refers exclusively to the Romans and thus reinforces the guilt of the Jews! The addition

related at an early stage to the fate of the Jews and later anti-Jewish tendencies could not agree with such a prayer for the remission of their sin. This was confirmed by the fact that the prayer seemed to have been contradicted by the actual punishment of the Jews in the destruction of Jerusalem. The scribe who was responsible for the omission may also have sensed a contradiction with the immediate context, the rather negative prophecy in vv. 28–31.[27] Finally, a possible and very simple motive should not be excluded: conscious adaptation to Mark's text.[28]

(c) A *Sondergut*-passage is always particularly difficult to grasp from the point of view of tradition history. The suggestion made above concerning the possible inspiration of Isa 53 may be a valuable one, though the meaning of the Lucan saying does not perfectly coincide with the original meaning of the Isaian text. The preachers of the passion used the Scriptures to interpret the scandal of Jesus' death on the cross. Biblical texts influenced both narrative passages and sayings, but there were different forms of "intertextuality." The relationship with the original meaning and context of the Old Testament quotation or allusion was sometimes rather loose. This may also have been the case here, especially since the Isaian text in question has been the subject of a variety of interpretations within the Jewish tradition itself.[29]

---

in several "Western" witnesses (except for D, *a, d*) corresponds with the omission of the ignorance motif in the "Western" text of Acts. The weakness of this ingenious theory is the debatable interpretation of αὐτοῖς and the divided testimony of the "Western" witnesses for Luke 23:34a. For our discussion, the scribe's interpretation of αὐτοῖς, which inspired a possible omission, is more important than its original meaning.

[27] Cf., for example, W. Radl, *Das Lukas-Evangelium,* p. 13: "...gerade wegen dieser Prophezeiung und ihrer Erfüllung in der Zerstörung Jerusalems ist eine spätere Einfügung schwer vorzustellen."

[28] An unconscious omission of the saying is less likely, given that its "addition" is not the only difference in this verse vis-à-vis Mark. Feldkämper, *Der betende Jesus,* p. 257, reminds us: "Allerdings kommt die gegenseitige Angleichung der synoptischen Texte normalerweise eher duch Hinzufügung als durch Auslassung zustande."

[29] Isa 53:12c: "because he poured out his soul to death and was numbered with the transgressors; yet he bore the sin of many, and made intercession for the transgressors." The sequence of "numbered with the transgressors" and "made intercession for the transgressors" corresponds with the sequence in Luke vv. 33–34a: crucifixion with the two murderers and intercession. Yet, Luke would

3. Jesus and Stephen: the key to the solution?

The relationship between Luke 23:34a and Acts 7:60 in their respective contexts is of particular importance. The most logical line of influence seems to be that Luke's story of Jesus' passion has influenced his way of recounting Stephen's martyrdom.[30] Throughout Acts, a variety of motives, themes and genres from Luke's gospel have clearly influenced the redaction of his second volume. Several details make it evident that the narrative of Jesus' passion had become the model for the story of Stephen's martyrdom in Acts.[31] One can distinguish the following parallel elements:

---

have used the inspiration in a free way: cf. W. Grundmann, *Lukasevangelium*, pp. 432f., according to the Isaiah-texts in Qumran, the passage does not mean "Fürbitte," but "Sühnetod." Feldkämper, *Der betende Jesus*, p. 266, finds the "Lucan" interpretation in the Targum, the Talmud and the Vulgate.

[30] The opposite direction, *i.e.* from Stephen to Jesus, as proposed by the defenders of the original absence of v. 34a, is much more difficult to imagine. Note that a completely different formulation of the saying would then be quite surprising, as is clearly illustrated in the story of James' martyrdom according to Hegesippus, where the logion is repeated literally. Cf. Eusebius, *h.e.*, II.23.16. It seems improbable that the Lucan logion has been copied from James' story, as has been put forward by D. Daube, "'For they know not what they do': Luke 23,34," in *StPatr* 4, TU 79 (Berlin 1961), pp. 58–70; 58: "It would not be the only case of the last words of a lesser figure coming to be attached to a greater one; and the textual position would become fully intelligible." I think that in both James' and in Stephen's case, the opposite move is much more probable, the disciple being presented as following the example of the master.

[31] Cp. R. Pesch, "Der Christ als Nachahmer Christi. Der Tod des Stephanus (Apg 7) im Vergleich mit dem Tod Christi," *BiKi* 24 (1969), pp. 10–11; "Überdies hat Lukas den Prozeß und den Tod des Stefanus dem Prozeß und dem Tod Jesu in wesentlichen Zügen angeglichen, die freilich auch charakteristisch variiert werden und den Christen Stefanus als Nachahmer Christi zeigen" (p. 11).

Stephen (Acts 7) *Jesus (Luke 23)*

the trial before the Sanhedrin	vv. 55, 56, 58b	vv. 66–71
conducted "outside the city"	v. 58	[cp. Luke 20:15 & John 19:17]
the violent treatment	v. 59b	v. 33a
the confident prayer: "receive my spirit"	v. 59b	v. 46b [diff Mark]
the cry "φωνῇ μεγάλῃ"	v. 60a	v. 46
the intercession for the murderers and forgiveness of sins	v. 60b	v. 34a
followed by the death	v. 60c	v. 46c [diff Mark[32]]

The prayer of intercession is surrounded by parallel elements from the Lucan passion narrative. Its presence in the story of Stephen's martyrdom is best explained, therefore, as Lucan redaction in line with *his* way of recounting the passion and death of Jesus. In my opinion, this very strong argument in favour of the originality of Jesus' prayer in Luke 23:34a can hardly be overestimated.[33]

In addition, the theme of ignorance is stressed by Luke in Acts, and applied particularly to the Jews in Acts 3:17 and 13:27.[34] This analogous continuation of a related theological theme through Luke-Acts confirms our view concerning Luke's procedure in shaping the narrative of Stephen's martyrdom.

---

[32] Acts 7:60c: καὶ τοῦτο εἰπὼν ἐκοιμήθη; Luke 23:60c: τοῦτο δὲ εἰπὼν ἐξέπνευσεν.

[33] Cp. G. Schneider, *Die Apostelgeschichte*, HThK 5,1 (Freiburg/Basel/Wien), pp. 478: "Man wird es kaum als Resultat sekundärer Bearbeitung ansehen dürfen, dass die drei letzten Worte des Stephanus drei Worten Jesu entsprechen: V 56 (Luke 22,69); V 59 (Luke 23,46); V 60 (Luke 23,34a)." Cf. already F. Dornseiff, "Lukas der Schriftsteller," *ZNW* 35 (1936), pp. 129–155; 136.

[34] The relationship between "know what you do" and responsibility is also underlined in Luke 6:5 according to codex D (albeit in the opposite way), but this peculiar D-passage has little or no chance to belong to the original text of Luke. See my article "Luke 6,5 in Codex Bezae."

Conclusion

It is ultimately incorrect to suggest that the external evidence related to Luke 23:34a leaves the question of its originality completely open or to propose that a certain bias in favour of original absence is unavoidable because of the authority of $\mathfrak{P}^{75}$–B combined with D. The very early attestation of the saying in Tatian, followed by an extensive and diversified range of witnesses, is a strong counterpart to the testimony of $\mathfrak{P}^{75}$ *cum suis*, and an important, though not decisive element in any dossier in favour of the originality of the logion. Among the numerous arguments on the level of internal criticism in favour of originality, I would particularly stress the parallel between the stories of Jesus' passion and Stephen's martyrdom. This redaction-critical argument is, in my opinion, of major importance if not even decisive in considering v. 34a as an integral part of Luke's original text. I conclude with B. H. Streeter: "Whatever may be the final verdict, it will be worth while to have stated the case, if only to illustrate the fact that the absence from certain Mss. is not necessarily evidence of interpolation."[35]

---

[35] Cf. B. H. Streeter, *The Four Gospels* (London 1924), p. 139.

MARK AND THE TEACHING OF JESUS:
AN EXAMINATION OF
ΛΟΓΟΣ AND ΕΥΑΓΓΕΛΙΟΝ

J. K. Elliott
The University of Leeds
(Leeds, England)

There are innumerable sayings attributed to Jesus in the NT, in the apocrypha and in other sources, patristic and non-Christian. But how does the NT refer to the body of Jesus' sayings? In this essay we shall examine two nouns from the standpoint of Mark's gospel that seem to describe Jesus' proclamation. The nouns are λόγος and εὐαγγέλιον. It is commonly thought they are capable of bearing the same meaning, namely "Christian teaching." We shall look at both of them in turn and we shall see that there has been a change in the meaning, introduced by the church—a revolution in vocabulary visible even within one gospel.

First λόγος.

ΛΟΓΟΣ

Among the many dictionary definitions of the word λόγος in the NT are "declaration," "speech," "the subject-matter," "revelation." Which if any of these fits Mark's usage and which if any is a description of Jesus sayings?

It seems to me as if λόγος is used in Mark in basically two senses: (1) "saying" or "utterance," and (2) "the Christian message." The word occurs 24 times in Mark. We can eliminate the occurrence in 16:20 as part of the longer ending and therefore not written by the same author as the rest of the gospel.

In two places in our printed texts λόγος is not firm in the MS. tradition: at 8:38 $\mathfrak{P}^{45}$ has no space for the word λόγους and it is missing in W *k* Sah. There is a possibility that the noun is secondary. (The saying would then be concerned with Jesus and his followers. λόγους may have been introduced into the MS. tradition from the Lukan parallel.) At 14:39 the phrase τὸν αὐτὸν λόγον εἰπών is not found in D and certain Old Latin MSS. Again, the shorter text is likely to be original, and the longer text due to assimilation to the Matthaean parallel (Matt 26:44). If one does decide to read the phrase in 14:39, λόγος would have a meaning compatible with Mark's usage elsewhere (*i.e.* Jesus' utterance), as we shall see below. The usage in 8:38 (if the longer text is read) would refer to Jesus' teachings in general, but that is not a meaning characteristic of Mark, unless 13:31 can be brought in as support— see further on that verse below.

Several of the firm occurrences are in the interpretation of the parable of the sower (4:14, 15*bis*, 16, 17, 18, 19, 20). That interpretation is commonly understood to be a Christian addition to the original words of Jesus, which arose from the church of Mark's day. λόγος here may be seen as equivalent to εὐαγγέλιον. The interpretation follows the introduction (4:11), in which what it is that is to be revealed is the "mystery" of the kingdom of God. The *timing* of the kingdom's arrival is unlikely to be that mystery. The mystery of the kingdom is more likely to be the *manner* of its inauguration in the person of the messiah. To have that aspect of the messiah's work so described is compatible with our under-standing of the messianic secrecy in Mark's retelling of the story of the ministry in Galilee. The message is messianic in the sense that it tells of the reception of Jesus, who is the inaugurator of the kingdom as its messiah. The early church knew from its experience that that message was often rejected and choked or brought persecution—hence the interpretation of the parable in those terms.

Seven instances elsewhere in Mark refer to an utterance in the immediate context. Unlike the references in the parable of the sower, these seem to reflect the earliest stratum of Marcan usage. They are:

> 5:36 λόγος = the statement that the ruler's daughter is dead (v. 35)
> 7:13 "word of God" = the citation from the Law in v. 10
> 7:29 λόγος = the woman's reply in the preceding verse
> 9:10 λόγος = Jesus' command to silence in v. 9
> 10:22 the saying of Jesus in v. 21 is what dismayed the man
> 10:24 λόγοι = the words of v. 23
> 11:29 λόγος points forward to the question in the next verse

To these we may add an eighth example (13:31 λόγοι) which, on the basis of the usage we have just identified, is unlikely to refer to Jesus' teaching and authority as a whole but to the immediate context, namely particular eschatological prophesies in the chapter. It may also be correct to add 8:32 as a ninth occurrence of λόγος in the sense of "utterance," the reference here being to the prediction of suffering in v. 31. In that verse παρρησίᾳ seems obtrusive if its meaning is "publicly," because Jesus is dealing with his disciples. (Matthew and Luke omit the sentence, possibly because they were both aware of the difficulty.) According to Bauer, παρρησίᾳ can mean "boldly," "confidently" in which case λόγος can clearly refer to the preceding prediction and should not be understood as a reference to Jesus' public teachings. In this context it would be strange if Peter were rebuking Jesus for his overall "message."

On the basis of the preceding examples, the implication of λόγος at 12:13 is that the Pharisees and the Herodians wish to entrap Jesus not in general conversation but with one of his own specific statements (not given in the context).

"The Christian message" is the meaning in the interpretation of the parable of the sower, "utterance" is the sense of most of the other passages we have looked at. We need now to turn to 1:45; 2:2; 4:33. The section 2:1–3:6 stands as a literary unit with its sequence of controversy stories; also in it are to be found explicit messianic statements (2:10, 28) so we may expect a different usage for λόγος in 2:2. λόγος here could perhaps refer to a specific utterance of a particular body of teaching but it is more likely to mean "the good news of the kingdom," "the messianic saving event" and thus serve as a résumé of Jesus' teaching. It may even bear the meaning "the Christian message" or even "the gospel" as it does in, say, Acts 4:29, 31; 8:25; 11:19; 13:46.

At 4:33 the identical form is found as in 2:2 (ἐλάλει αὐτοῖς τὸν λόγον) but there is a textual problem in the phrase.[1] If original, λόγος again seems to be the message about the coming kingdom, or even "the Christian gospel."

In 1:45 λόγος occurs in conjunction with διαφημίζειν, a verb that is not used elsewhere by Mark. (It occurs twice elsewhere in the gospels, both times in Matthew.) The meaning of λόγος is often considered to mean the "event" or "story," which the leper told.

---

[1] At 4:33 our oldest witness 𝔓⁴⁵ is fragmentary, but it looks as if the space available is too small for all the words of v. 33 to fit. πολλαῖς may not have been present: that word is absent from several other witnesses including C W f¹. αὐτοῖς is absent from D 565. τὸν λόγον is not present in Old Latin MSS b c e. It may be worth bearing in mind that 𝔓⁴⁵ could be added to that latter testimony in which case the originality of λόγος in the verse is less strong. On that argument 𝔓⁴⁵ could have read παραβολαῖς ἐλάλει αὐτοῖς although the reading παραβολαῖς πολλαῖς ἐλάλει would have the same result.

But as I have tried to argue in more than one place,[2] Mark 1:45 should not be interpreted as belonging to vv. 40–44. The story of the healing of the leper ends with the command to silence, a command that is obeyed like all such commands, cf. the two stories set in the Decapolis (Mark 5:20; 7:36). There are too many problems in linking v. 45 to the preceding story. αὐτόν in v. 45 is not strong enough to imply a change to "Jesus" as the subject of δύνασθαι. ὁ δέ at the beginning (if it is not ὁ ἐξελθών with the particle interposed) always implies a change of subject in Mark, but the contrast is not with Jesus, the subject of λέγει in v. 44, but with the leper in v. 40. It would be against Marcan practice to have a stranger preach outside the Decapolis: κηρύσσειν is what the Baptist does (1:4, 7) or Jesus (1:14, 38–39) or the apostles (3:14; 6:12; 13:10; 14:9 [16:15, 20]). If κηρύσσειν were to be part of the leper's activity, then the meaning would not be the preaching of the gospel message—the meaning required would be "relate." And, as it parallels διαφημίζειν τὸν λόγον, λόγος would have to bear a meaning ("story") that it does not have elsewhere in Mark (although Matt 28:15; Luke 5:15; 7:7 have that meaning). So, on various counts, the story of the leper must run from v. 40 to v. 44 only. That is how Matthew understood the climax and conclusion of the pericope (Matt 8:1–4 has no parallel to v. 45). Verse 45 on that argument would be related to vv. 38–39. Jesus intends to preach in vv. 38–39; the consequence of his activity is described in v.45. These verses would thus 'sandwich" 40–44 in the way that other Marcan stories are interrupted by an intervening episode (like 6:6b–13 and 30f., or 11:12–14 and 20ff., or 14:1–2 and 10–11). This is perhaps one further dramatic juxtaposition. Thus we may conclude that λόγος once again is likely to have a meaning similar to 2:2 and perhaps 4:33, namely a particular body of Jesus' teaching about the coming of the kingdom.

The meaning suggested for 1:45, 2:2, and 4:33 seems to belong to a later stage in the development of Mark's gospel compared to the meaning in chapters 5–16 "utterance." λόγος in its meaning of Jesus' teaching about the kingdom is a creation of Christian theology, and may be compared to the coining of the noun "baptist." A similar shift in the New Testament is seen in the change in the use of "Lord" meaning God to "Lord" referring to Jesus. The changing

---

[2] "The Conclusion of the Pericope of the Healing of the Leper and Mark i 45," *JThS* 22 (1971), pp. 153–157; "Is ὁ ἐξελθών a Title for Jesus in Mark i 45?" *JThS* 27 (1976), pp. 402–405; "The Healing of the Leper in the Synoptic Parallels," *TZ* 34 (1978), pp. 175–176.

meaning of λόγος within Mark is yet another example of the Christianizing of traditional vocabulary.

Even though λόγος in Mark 2–4 represents a later stratum, εὐαγγέλιον throughout Mark seems to maintain its original pre-Christian meaning except in 1:1.

ΕΥΑΓΓΕΛΙΟΝ

There are 76 occurrences of εὐαγγέλιον in the New Testament, most of which are to be found in the Pauline Epistles. Only 12 are in the gospels: 4 in Matthew, the rest in Mark. εὐαγγέλιον occurs in Mark 1:1, 14, 15; 8:35; 10:29; 13:10; 14:9, and there is one occurrence in the longer ending at 16:15. We shall return to 1:1 later, but the meaning there is different and seems to belong to Mark's redaction. This suggests that 1:14 (on Jesus' lips) is the first non-editorial reference to εὐαγγέλιον in Mark. The meaning is "the divine plan" and it is significant that on this first occurrence εὐαγγέλιον is qualified. The noun is followed by the dependent genitive [τῆς βασιλείας] τοῦ θεοῦ. Elsewhere εὐαγγέλιον is used absolutely although some MSS (A C 𝔐) add τοῦτο after τὸ εὐαγγέλιον in 14:9.

At 1:15 we have πιστεύειν ἐν τῷ εὐαγγελίῳ; at 10:29 ἕνεκεν τοῦ εὐαγγελίου; but it is the occurrences at 1:14; 13:10; 14:9 that demand attention because the verb governing εὐαγγέλιον in these three is κηρύσσειν, and this verb helps us locate the meaning and significance. The verb εὐαγγελίζομαι does not occur in Mark—κηρύσσειν does this work. But it is worth noting that in Luke 4:17–19 where Jesus, quoting from Isa 61 states that the "good news proclaimed" (using the verb εὐαγγελίζομαι) and foretold by the prophets is *God's* deliverance and restoration of Israel at the last—it is a divine action, not a messianic one that is preached.

In the Septuagint εὐαγγελίζομαι is used of divine action by God not the messiah (*e.g.* Psalm 39:9; 67:11; 95:2; Joel 2:32; Nahum 2:1; Isa 40:9; 60:6; 61:1–2). Luke's usage is similar. If these passages speak of salvation it is God's salvation. Similarly in Mark εὐαγγέλιον is not a messianic term (with the possible exception of 1:1 to which we return below). In the epistles εὐαγγέλιον τοῦ Χριστοῦ occurs (1 Cor 9:12; 2 Cor 2:12; 9:13; 10:14; Gal 1:7, etc.) but such a phrase is not Marcan. Mark's meaning is different. For Paul εὐαγγέλιον has become Christian. The noun has developed in meaning. But Mark, either because of his fidelity to his sources or through a conscious archaizing, uses the noun in its older,

Jewish, OT sense even though he, of course, wrote his gospel later than Paul's writing of the epistles.[3]

How is κηρύσσειν used?[4] We may learn from the concordance that, with the exception of 1:7, Mark has κηρύσσειν followed by a direct object (e.g. at 1:4, 14; 5:20; 13:10; 14:9) or by a ἵνα clause (at 6:12), or used absolutely (1:38, 39, 45, where πολλά is likely to be adverbial; 3:14; 7:36). (There is no example in Mark of κηρύσσειν followed by the dative as there is in the rest of the NT.)

Apart from *preaching* the εὐαγγέλιον how else is κηρύσσειν used in Mark? In 1:4 it is used of John's call to repentance (cf. 6:12). In 5:20 it is used of the demoniac's proclamation that Jesus had healed him. (Likewise I suspect this meaning occurs in 7:36 as well: the people "preach" that Jesus had healed the deaf-mute.) If 1:45 has the leper as subject of ἤρξατο then this example of preaching would be connected with healing too—but, as we have

---

[3] Mark deliberately avoids calling Jesus "Lord" in its divine sense and calls Jesus by the simplest title, because he is conscious that to do otherwise would be to use post-Resurrection language of the ministry. (If we think Mark too unsophisticated a writer to distance himself from the subject matter in order to preserve or create the verisimilitude, then I suppose one must consider Mark's archaic usages an indication of his fidelity to his primitive—even pre-Resurrection?—sources.) I prefer to think Mark *was* capable of telling his account of the ministry in as restrained a way as possible. Only the occasional anachronistic elements obtrude, such as the meaning of λόγος as the Christian message. In this context we may consider the textually uncertain words "Son of God" in 1:1. If the longer text is original to Mark, his intention may well have been to show that Jesus Christ, the Son of God was confessed by the Jewish title "Christ" mid-way through the gospel with Peter's confession at Caesarea Philippi, a title that was in all sorts of ways inadequate as a description for Jesus in this gospel as is clear even within the story at Caesarea Philippi where the sequel has Peter compared with Satan for misinterpreting Jesus' distinctive mission. Mark later has Jesus confessed by the second of the two titles found in the longer version of the opening verse. Towards the end of the second half of the gospel the centurion at the foot of the cross recognises Jesus as the Son of God, a title favoured among gentiles. (Compare the different words on the centurion's lips in the Lukan parallel. This shows the uniqueness of those words for Mark.) Despite this argument, I think the words "Son of God" are secondary in Mark 1:1 and are more likely to be a later, scribal addition, motivated by pious considerations and perhaps influenced by the liturgy, rather than that the longer words were accidentally omitted by careless copyists.

[4] The noun "kerygma" is not found in Mark, although it occurs in the gospels twice (in Q).

seen, the subject of ἤρξατο is more likely to be Jesus, in which case the *preaching* is equivalent to his spreading the εὐαγγέλιον.

In 1·7 the verb κηρύσσειν introduces the Baptist's warning. Here recitative λέγων depends on κηρύσσειν and direct speech follows. That makes the usage here somewhat different. But there is textual uncertainty over the originality of κηρύσσειν. D and some Old Latin witnesses read ἔλεγεν αὐτοῖς, and that reading has a good claim to originality.

So, the verb κηρύσσειν is, in general, used in contexts of healing, repentance, and εὐαγγέλιον. How is εὐαγγέλιον used in Mark?

The first thing to note is that it is not followed by a possessive— Jesus does not promote himself as the agent of the εὐαγγέλιον. At 10:29 he distinguishes himself from the gospel. A similar difference occurs in some MSS at 8:35. The noun does not occur on another's lips nor in summaries of the remarks of others.

Matthew agrees with Mark: εὐαγγέλιον and κηρύσσειν occur in Matt 4:23; 9:35; 24:14 where the phrase "gospel of the kingdom" occurs; and 26:13 "this gospel." Matt 4:23 and 9:35 depend on Mark 1:13, 39; Matt 24:14 depends on Mark 13:10; Matt 26:13 parallels Mark 14:9. (There are no Matthaean parallels to Mark 1:1; 8:35; 10:29.)

So far, εὐαγγέλιον in Mark seems to refer to *divine* action. 1:1 is an exception.

MARK 1:1

The late meaning of εὐαγγέλιον as "a gospel book," the sense in which we commonly use it, may well have originated in this verse,[5] but such a meaning would not have been Mark's intention. It was only when a Christian had knowledge of and access to two or more gospels that names or titles would have to be used to differentiate them. It may well have been that Mark's writing was referred to by its opening words, as was the Hebrew practice. Thus it would be "The beginning of the εὐαγγέλιον" book. By extension all comparable literature became known as εὐαγγέλιον books.

But leaving that speculation aside, we note that ἀρχή in Mark is always a temporal expression. This implies that the chronological start of the εὐαγγέλιον of Jesus Christ (equally valid here as a subjective or as an objective genitive) had begun.

---

[5] Cf. M. Hengel, *Die Evangelienübersetzungen* (Heidelberg 1984).

This meaning may make us take εὐαγγέλιον in 1:1 in a different sense from that in the rest of the gospel. In addition there are several peculiar features in this verse.

(a) Only here in Mark do we find the title "Jesus Christ". This phrase occurs for certain in other gospels only at Matt 1:1; John 1:17; 17:3.

(b) Elsewhere in Mark, as we have seen, εὐαγγέλιον occurs only with reference to Jesus' sayings (or as a résumé of Jesus' teaching).

(c) Also it is a rare use of a sentence without a verb (if we punctuate with a full stop at the end of the verse).

Because of its differences is the verse likely to be a title? Many would be attracted to such a suggestion, especially as ἀρχή is anarthrous, but there are snags. First Mark does have some verbless sentences (1:3 (LXX); 1:11 [v.l.: om. ἐγένετο]; 13:8), so 1:1 is not unique. Secondly, as I tried to indicate in an article in *Filología Neotestamentaria*,[6] building on the initial research by G. D. Kilpatrick, καθώς in Mark introducing a quotation *follows* a main clause (as is the case in Mark 4:33; 9:13; 11:6; 14:16,21; 15:8; 16:7 and also in the rest of the NT *e.g.* Luke 2:23; John 6:31; 12:14; Acts 7:42; Rom 1:17; 1 Cor 1:31). That rule obliges us to dispense with the full stop at the end of verse 1, and thus prevents our reading 1:1 as a title.

Where then do we end the sentence that begins in 1:1? If a full stop is to be placed at the end of v. 3 then vv. 1–3 are a unit, and v. 4 is a fresh start. The arrival of the Baptist in the section beginning at v. 4 is shown to be the fulfilment of the prophecy in the introduction. We may paraphrase vv. 1–3 "The beginning of the good news in the life of Jesus Christ *is* what is written in Isaiah...," where ἀρχή is the first of a series; this temporal meaning is consistent with Mark 10:6; 13:8,19. The events run from John to the empty tomb. But the link with the verses preceding is that the *beginning* of the εὐαγγέλιον was the coming of John. Verses 1–3 lead up to v. 4 but are not part of it. The first three verses are Mark the editor speaking: it is an introduction. He is using the language of 65 A.D. Before he starts the narrative in v. 4 where he consciously aims to use language befitting the pre-Easter setting of the events, Mark as editor uses the language of devotion (including the title Jesus Christ) and the later, Christian, use of εὐαγγέλιον. In 1:1 we thus find the most developed meaning of εὐαγγέλιον in the New Testa-

---

[6] "καθώς and ὥσπερ in the New Testament," *FilNeo* 4 (1991), pp. 55–58.

ment, a development that eventually lead to its use to describe a literary genre.

C. H. Turner preferred to put the full stop at the end of v. 4.[7] He took vv. 2–3 as one of Mark's parentheses (like 2:15, 22; 12:12; 13:14; 14:36). On this line of reasoning Turner, following Origen, understood the verb following ἀρχή to be ἐγένετο in v. 4, *i.e.* the beginning of the εὐαγγέλιον about Jesus was John's preaching in the wilderness. But it is abnormal to find Mark's parentheses separating subject and verb. Turner's proposal also ignores the rule about καθώς, a feature of Marcan usage that did not enter his "Notes." So we may reject that proposed punctuation.

Our examination of just two words in only one gospel convinces us that Christianity, while drawing on the language, ideas and background of the Old Testament, succeeded in revolutionising not only theology but also basic vocabulary. This short survey on how these two nouns had their meanings changed to become distinctively Christian is offered in honour of Tjitze Baarda, whose friendship and company I have valued over many years in locations as varied as Abilene, Texas, and Lunel, France, when I have been privileged to share a platform with him. I wish him and his work well.

---

[7] In "Notes on Marcan Usage IV," reprinted in *The Language and Style of the Gospel of Mark*, ed. J. K.Elliott, NovT.S 71 (Leiden 1993), pp. 23–24.

THE NEW TESTAMENT PAPYRI AT OXYRHYNCHUS IN THEIR SOCIAL AND INTELLECTUAL CONTEXT

Eldon Jay Epp
Case Western Reserve University
(Cleveland, Ohio, USA)

*I. At the outset: Sayings of Jesus
and New Testament papyri at Oxyrhynchus*

Collections of sayings of Jesus might well serve as a hallmark of NT discoveries in Egypt in the five decades or so from the last years of the nineteenth century until the middle of the twentieth, and, were it not for Nag Hammadi, the focal point might well have been Oxyrhynchus, where fragments of at least three such lists were discovered in 1897 and 1903 (Oxyrhynchus papyri 1, 654, and 655), all dating in the third century and together preserving portions of seventeen sayings. Of course, nearly a half century later these fragments were identified as portions, in Greek, of the Coptic *Gospel of Thomas*—when the latter was discovered about 1945.[1] In addition, Oxyrhynchus yielded P.Oxy X.1224 (early 4th C.E.), which is a highly fragmentary, poorly preserved papyrus with three sayings. The genre of the document cannot, however, be determined, nor can it be identified with any known gospel.[2] The latter is the case also with P.Oxy V.840 (4th/5th C.E.), a dialogue of Jesus with a chief priest in the Temple, and with P.Oxy XI.1384 (5th C.E.), containing a saying of Jesus on healing. Sayings of Jesus occur also, of course, in eleven other papyri from Oxyrhynchus (NT 𝔓⁵, 𝔓¹⁹, 𝔓²¹, 𝔓²²,

---

[1] P.Oxy IV.654 = Coptic introduction and sayings 1–5; P.Oxy I.1 = sayings 27–31 plus the end portions of 77, 32, 33, 34; and P.Oxy IV.655 = sayings 37–40.

[2] See *New Testament Apocrypha*, edd. W. Schneemelcher and R. McL. Wilson (rev. ed; 2 vols.; Louisville [Kentucky] 1991–92), Vol. 1, p. 100. P.Egerton 2 possibly came from Oxyrhynchus: it was purchased along with other papyri among which nearly all whose provenance could be identified were from Oxyrhynchus. This, however, falls far short of proof (H. I. Bell and T. C. Skeat, *Fragments of an Unknown Gospel and Other Early Christian Papyri* [London 1935] p. 7).

$\mathfrak{P}^{28}$, $\mathfrak{P}^{39}$, $\mathfrak{P}^{69}$, $\mathfrak{P}^{70}$, $\mathfrak{P}^{71}$, $\mathfrak{P}^{77}$, and $\mathfrak{P}^{90}$), though these are randomly preserved portions of the four gospels.

The story of the discovery of P.Oxy I.1, the first of these collections of sayings of Jesus to turn up, and of P.Oxy I.2, the first NT papyrus to appear at Oxyrhynchus, is well enough known, but neither the drama of those moments nor their significance for NT scholarship can be appreciated apart from a thumbnail sketch of the papyrus discoveries that preceded them.

Travellers to Egypt had brought papyrus documents back to Europe since the sixteenth century, but the 1752 discovery of 800 carbonized scrolls at Herculaneum attracted the attention even of King George IV of England—though the scrolls could not be unrolled. Other papyri were studied by Napoleon's scholars and then by numerous other Europeans during the first half of the nineteenth century, but when Ulrich Wilcken brought together and reedited the Greek and Latin papyri of the Ptolemaic period that had been published up to 1891, there were only about 200. In the 1870s, however, a new phase began for the discovery of papyri as Egyptian farmers, seeking fertilizer, began to haul away nitrate-rich soil from ancient villages, thereby uncovering large quantities of papyri that had been deposited in rubbish heaps in the Byzantine period and earlier. Notable sites were Arsinoe (the Fayyûm capital), as well as Hermopolis, Heracleopolis, and elsewhere.[3]

The 1890s saw increased activity, particularly in the purchase of papyrus documents, but also in a more systematic and rational approach to finding additional Greco-Roman papyri, and another fresh phase of discovery was opened when the Egypt Exploration Fund commissioned B. P. Grenfell, A. S. Hunt, and D. G. Hogarth, in 1895, to explore and excavate promising sites, first in the Fayyûm, then Karanis, and, in 1896–97, Oxyrhynchus. They had quite deliberately chosen Oxyrhynchus, where Grenfell and Hunt took over following a brief preliminary survey by Flinders Petrie; notice the opening paragraph of Grenfell's full account of the dramatic first season:

> I had for some time felt that one of the most promising sites in Egypt for finding Greek manuscripts was the city of Oxyrhynchus, the modern Behneseh, situated on the edge of the western desert 120 miles south of Cairo. Being the capital of the Nome,

---

[3] On this early period, see E. G. Turner, *Greek Papyri: An Introduction* (Oxford 1968) pp. 20–27.

it must have been the abode of many rich persons who could afford to possess a library of literary texts. Though the ruins of the old town were known to be fairly extensive, and it was probable that most of them were of the Graeco-Roman period, neither town nor cemetery appeared to have been plundered for antiquities in recent times. Above all, Oxyrhynchus seemed to be a site where fragments of Christian literature might be expected of an earlier date than the fourth century, to which our oldest manuscripts of the New Testament belong; for the place was renowned in the fourth and fifth centuries on account of the number of its churches and monasteries, and the rapid spread of Christianity about Oxyrhynchus, as soon as the new religion was officially recognized, implied that it had already taken a strong hold during the preceding centuries of persecution.[4]

When Grenfell and Hunt began to dig a low mound on January 11, 1897, papyrus fragments became abundant, with most of them retrievable from near the surface. Grenfell increased the number of workmen from 70 to 110 as "the flow of papyri soon became a torrent" so that the two men assigned to making tin boxes for storing the papyri could barely keep up during the next ten weeks. When the discoveries of the second day were being assessed, Hunt's eye caught the uncial letters, ΚΑΡΦΟϹ ("speck"), reminding him of the "mote" and "beam" passage in Matt 7:3–5 par. Luke 6:41–42, though it soon became apparent that four others among the fragment's eight sayings differed radically from the canonical gospels and that the remaining three had only partial parallels. This portion of a collection of "Sayings of Jesus," dated *c.* 200, was designated P.Oxy 1 and given the place of honor as their first published papyrus when the volumes of *The Oxyrhynchus Papyri* began to appear in 1898.

The next day Hunt identified another uncial papyrus, part of a sheet from a codex containing most of Matthew 1. Dating in the third century, it was designated P.Oxy 2, but became the frontispiece in volume 1 of the *Oxyrhynchus Papyri*; it later was accorded the distinction of being Papyrus 1 in the official list of NT papyri[5]—which was to grow to nearly 100 items over the

---

[4] Egypt Exploration Fund, *Archaeological Report 1896–1897*, ed. F. Ll. Griffith (London 1897), p. 1.

[5] In C. R. Gregory, *Die griechischen Handschriften des Neuen Testaments* (Leipzig 1908), p. 45. Note that the papyri follow the uncials, both here and in Gregory,

succeeding century. Although the Matthew papyrus was not the first NT papyrus to be discovered or published, its first position was justified because at the time, as Grenfell and Hunt affirmed, "it may...claim to be a fragment of the oldest known manuscript of any part of the New Testament."[6] Already in 1868, about twenty years after discovering Codex Sinaiticus, Constantin Tischendorf published what was to become $\mathfrak{P}^{11}$, followed by those designated $\mathfrak{P}^7$ and $\mathfrak{P}^8$ in the official list.[7] Meanwhile, $\mathfrak{P}^3$ had been published by Carl Wessely in 1882 and $\mathfrak{P}^{14}$ by J. Rendel Harris in 1890. These first five NT papyri to be presented to the public did not attract much attention, however, because two of them dated in the seventh century, two in the fifth, and one in the fourth—and none, therefore, was older than the two famous mid-fourth century uncial manuscripts, Sinaiticus and Vaticanus, that had led the way in the construction of the critical NT texts of Tischendorf in 1869 and of Westcott-Hort in 1881. Not only that, but these five papyri together contained only 120 NT verses. Thus, the lack of excitement over them is not surprising, but the Oxyrhynchus papyri changed all that, primarily because of their early dates and partly because they issued from a known provenance.

The provenance of early NT manuscripts is all too rarely known. This is the case with nearly all of the major fourth- and fifth-century uncial manuscripts like Codices Sinaiticus (א), Vaticanus (B), Alexandrinus (A), Bezae (D), and Washington-ianus (W).[8] As for the papyri, naturally they come from Egypt,

---

Textkritik des Neuen Testamentes (Leipzig 1909), pp. 1084–1092. The catalogued papyri totaled fourteen at this time.

[6] *The Oxyrhynchus Papyri,* edd. B. P. Grenfell and A. S. Hunt (London 1898–), Vol. I, p. 4.

[7] Published in C. R. Gregory's *Prolegomena* to Tischendorf's *Novum Testamentum Graece* (8th major ed.; 3 vols.; Leipzig 1869–72; for the *Prolegomena*, 1894).

[8] א, B, and A could have originated in Constantinople, though B could have originated in Egypt and A in Caesarea; A, however, is usually assumed to be from Alexandria (for references, see Epp, "The Significance of the Papyri for Determining the Nature of the New Testament Text in the Second Century: A Dynamic View of Textual Transmission," in *Gospel Traditions in the Second Century: Origins, Recensions, Text and Transmission,* ed. W. L. Petersen, CJA 3 (Notre Dame [Indiana]1989), pp. 76–77; reprinted in E. J. Epp and G. D. Fee, *Studies in the Theory and Method of New Testament Textual Criticism,* StD 45 [Grand Rapids (Michigan) 1993], p. 278); D. C. Parker, summarizing other views, constructs an elaborate case that D originated in Berytus (Beirut) (*Codex Bezae:*

but where exactly? One major group, the Chester Beatty ($\mathfrak{P}^{45}$, $\mathfrak{P}^{46}$, $\mathfrak{P}^{47}$) carried with it rumors at the time of purchase that these papyri were found in a pitcher in a ruined church or monastery near Atfih (Aphroditopolis) in the Fayyûm,[9] about a third of the way down the Nile River from Oxyrhynchus toward Alexandria, and it has been surmised that both the Chester Beatty and the other major group, the Bodmer papyri ($\mathfrak{P}^{66}$, $\mathfrak{P}^{72}$, $\mathfrak{P}^{75}$) may have come from the same church library, though proof is lacking.[10] A report accompanying the purchase of $\mathfrak{P}^{52}$, the oldest NT fragment, places its origin either in the Fayyûm or in Oxyrhynchus.[11] $\mathfrak{P}^{4}$ of Luke actually was found *in situ* in a jar walled up in a house at Coptos (modern Qift, just below [north of] Thebes in upper Egypt); it was, however, in the binding of a (presumably Christian) codex of Philo and the house had no evident connection to a church.[12] $\mathfrak{P}^{92}$ was found in 1969 at Madînat Mâdî (modern Narmouthis, between Theadelphia and Tebtunis in the Fayyûm) in a rubble-filled structure near a racing-course,[13] but this does not enlighten us about the origin or use of this manuscript.

The situation is much clearer, of course, regarding the papyri excavated at Oxyrhynchus, though it must be recognized that some of the documents might have been transported for use there from other places in Egypt or beyond.[14] Nevertheless, we

---

An Early Christian Manuscript and Its Text [Cambridge 1992]), pp. 261–78; and H. A. Sanders provides evidence that W was found near the ruined Monastery of the Vinedresser, near Gizeh, near Cairo, in Egypt (*The New Testament Manuscripts in the Freer Collection: Part I: The Washington Manuscript of the Four Gospels* [New York 1912]), pp. 1–4.

[9] Colin H. Roberts, *Manuscript, Society and Belief in Early Christian Egypt*, the Schweich Lectures, 1977 (London 1979), p. 7.

[10] C. H. Roberts, "Books in the Graeco-Roman World and in the New Testament," *Cambridge History of the Bible, Volume 1: From the Beginnings to Jerome*, edd. P. R. Ackroyd and C. F. Evans (Cambridge 1970), p. 56.

[11] Colin H. Roberts, *An Unpublished Fragment of the Fourth Gospel in the John Rylands Library* (Manchester 1935), pp. 24–25; H. I. Bell and T. C. Skeat, *Fragments of an Unknown Gospel and Other Early Christian Papyri* (London 1935), p. 7.

[12] Roberts, *Manuscript*, pp. 8, 13.

[13] Claudio Gallazzi, "Frammenti di un codice con le Epistole di Paoli," *ZPE* 46 (1982), p. 117.

[14] On the rapid transfer of letters, documents, and literature, see Epp, "New Testament Papyrus Manuscripts and Letter Carrying in Greco-Roman Times," in *The Future of Early Christianity: Essays in Honor of Helmut Koester*, edd. B. A.

have twenty-eight NT papyri discovered at one locality; that represents thirty percent of the ninety-four different NT papyri currently known. More remarkable is the fact that twenty of these (plus one uncial found there) are among the forty-eight oldest NT manuscripts—those dating prior to or around the turn of the third/fourth centuries, namely, forty-four papyri and the four oldest uncials, all of which are of special significance because (as noted earlier) they predate the great uncial manuscripts that occupy so prominent a position in NT textual criticism: א, B, A, W, and D. That Oxyrhynchus should have provided forty-four percent of the earliest and most valuable group of papyri is particularly noteworthy.

In addition, the number of NT books covered by the Oxyrhynchus papyri is impressive, for, although highly fragmentary, they contain sections of fifteen of our twenty-seven NT books. Portions of Matthew are found in six papyri; John's Gospel in five; Romans in three; Hebrews, James, and the Apocalypse of John each in two; and Luke, Acts, 1 Corinthians, Galatians, Philippians, 1–2 Thessalonians, 1 John, and Jude are each found in one papyrus. The twelve books not represented are Mark, 2 Corinthians, Ephesians, Colossians, the Pastoral Epistles, Philemon, 1–2 Peter, and 2–3 John, though that is of little significance given the random situation that obtains in excavating rubbish heaps. [1 Peter is found in the uncial P.Oxy XI.1353 = 0206 (4th C.E.).] The twenty papyri (plus 0162) among the forty-eight earliest manuscripts cover Matthew, Luke, John, Acts, Romans, Philippians, 1–2 Thessalonians, Hebrews, James, 1 John, Jude, and Revelation. Yet, among them, only four preserve more than about two dozen verses: $\mathfrak{P}^5$, with about thirty-seven verses of John (3rd C.E.); $\mathfrak{P}^{13}$, with about seventy-nine verses of Hebrews (3rd/4th); $\mathfrak{P}^{15}$, with about twenty-seven verses of 1 Corinthians (3rd); and $\mathfrak{P}^{27}$, with about thirty verses of Romans (3rd). Compared, for example, with our longest gospel, Luke (1,149 verses) or even with our shortest gospel, Mark (661 verses), these papyri are still mere fragments.

Pearson, A. T. Kraabel, G. W. E. Nickelsburg, and N. R. Petersen (Minneapolis [Minnesota] 1991), esp. pp. 55–56. Turner, *Greek Manuscripts of the Ancient World* (Oxford 1971), pp. 20–21; *Greek Papyri*, pp. 49–53, 87, 90, 137, discusses principles for identifying copies made in Oxyrhynchus and the place of finding a text in relation to the place of its writing.

Despite this fragmentary nature of the Oxyrhynchus papyri, they do constitute a remarkable cache of valuable material with a known provenance and they should be allowed, therefore, to inform us about the real-life context in which they were used. Hence, the purpose of this investigation is to place not only the papyrus sayings of Jesus but, more than that, all of the NT papyri found at Oxyrhynchus within the historical and socioeconomic, but particularly the literary, intellectual, and religious environment of the location where they were discovered. This will be attempted through a case study of the city of Oxyrhynchus and its surrounding area as revealed through the other papyri found there, of which about 4,000 have been published in the multi-volume *Oxyrhynchus Papyri* (1898– ; a total of fifty-nine volumes to date), and many others elsewhere, especially in the Italian series, *Papiri greci e latini* (= *PSI*, 1912– ; fifteen volumes to date), since Pistelli and Breccia succeeded Grenfell and Hunt in 1910. For documentation and illustrative purposes, papyri dating in the fourth century and earlier will serve as our primary sources for the obvious reason that we wish to understand the nature of the Oxyrhynchite area in the period when our earliest forty-eight NT manuscripts were current.

II. The general sociocultural context provided by Oxyrhynchus

Ancient Oxyrhynchus covered an area about one and a quarter miles long by one-half mile wide, but its ancient buildings have all but disappeared, for they served during a millennium as a quarry for bricks and limestone, with buildings peeled away down to their foundations. Also, both the city's cemeteries, normally expected to yield papyrus mummy-cases or papyrus rolls in their owners' tombs, proved disappointing, for the Roman cemetery had been situated in a low area and almost all tombs had been affected by dampness; moreover, most bodies had not been mummified. And the ancient Egyptian cemetery had been robbed long ago and dampness had affected the mummies that remained so that they turned to dust when touched. This situation drove Grenfell and Hunt to the rubbish heaps in their search for papyri,[15] and requires that Oxyrhynchus, where archaeological data are sparse, must be understood mainly on the

---

[15] Grenfell, *Archaeological Report 1896–97*, pp. 2–6.

basis of "philological archaeology"that is, the papyrus documents.[16]

The picture of Oxyrhynchus arising in this fashion can only
be hinted at in this present, brief presentation. In recent publications, I have asked but not answered what it might mean for
the NT papyri at Oxyrhynchus when it is recognized that they
were found in a city that we know contained at least two
churches around the turn of the third/fourth centuries—ascertained from records of a night watchman's rounds (see below)—
but a city that was known to have been a significant center of
Christian activity in the fourth and fifth centuries, when Rufinus
reported thirty churches there,[17] and in the early sixth century,
when a bishop and some forty churches are evidenced by P.Oxy
XI.1357 (535–536 C.E.), a calendar of church services at Oxyrhynchus.

The extended question concerns what it might mean for the
NT manuscripts used and preserved there when we realize that
from the papyri the names of some 5,700 residents of the Oxyrhynchite nome can be identified already in the period from ca.
30 B.C.E.–96 C.E.[18] and that the city had some twenty temples
and a theater that seated some eight to twelve thousand people,[19]
permitting a presumption that in Roman times the population
was around 30,000.[20]

The importance of Oxyrhynchus in antiquity is attested by
P.Oxy X.1264 (272 C.E.), where the city is termed λαμπρᾶς καὶ
λαμπροτάτης ("illustrious and most illustrious"), the first of many
occurrences of this two-fold description that replaces the earlier
λαμπρά; possibly the new title arose when the world games, the
Iso-Capitolia, were first held in Oxyrhynchus in the following

---

[16] Turner, *Greek Papyri*, p. 80; cf. Roger S. Bagnall, *Egypt in Late Antiquity*
(Princeton [New Jersey] 1993), pp. 6–7.

[17] *Oxyrhynchus Papyri*, XI, p. 26; Turner, *Greek Papyri*, pp. 81, 150, cf. 28.

[18] B. W. Jones and J. E. G. Whitehorne, *Register of Oxyrhynchites 30 B.C.–A.D.
96*, ASP 25 (Chico [California] 1983).

[19] Turner, *Greek Papyri*, p. 81; Petrie, the excavator in 1922, estimated that the
theater would hold 11,200 spectators (Turner, "Roman Oxyrhynchus," *JEA* 38
[1952], p. 81; for a catalogue of temples, see pp. 82–83).

[20] Julian Krüger, *Oxyrhynchos in der Kaiserzeit: Studien zur Topographie und
Literaturrezeption*, European University Studies, Ser. III, Vol. 441 (Frankfurt am
Main/New York 1990), p. 8, citing I. H. Fichman, "Die Bevölkerungszahl von
Oxyrhynchos in byzantinischer Zeit," *APF* 21 (1971), pp. 111–20.

year, 273.[21] Other indications of importance include the following: (1) The presence of a Roman garrison at Oxyrhynchus at the outset of the second century, attested by the Latin P.Oxy VII.1022 (103 C.E.), which provides the names, ages, and distinguishing marks of six new recruits to be added to the third Ituraean cohort. (Curiously, the first recruit, Veturius Gemellus, reappears forty years later in P.Oxy VII.1035 [143 C.E.] as a "veteran" whose son enters into a rental contract for an iron wool comb or shears.) (2) The recognition of Oxyrhynchus in 202 C.E. by the Emperors Septimius Severus and Marcus Aurelius Antoninus as having a status second to Pelusium but above Memphis in access to imperial benefactions, as shown in two petitions to the Emperors by Aurelius Horion, a high official of the "most illustrious city of Alexandria" who had large landholdings in Oxyrhynchus (P.Oxy IV.705 [200–202 C.E.]). (3) An early fourth century levy upon the city and the Oxyrhynchite nome of thirty-eight pounds of gold (P.Oxy XVII.2106); in the same period, an average of only ten pounds was exacted from seven nomes in the Delta region.[22]

The character of the city can be assessed further, for example, from P.Oxy I.43 (*verso*), a 295 C.E. list of watchmen who made the rounds of the main streets and public buildings, including the temples of Sarapis, Isis, Thoëris, and Caesar; two churches, north and south; the theater; the capitol; three baths; the gymnasium; a Nilometer—to measure the annual floods—and four city gates.[23] Already in the late second century, an Oxyrhynchus municipal account of payments specifies 2,000 drachmai "to Dionysius...in command of the fifty night watchmen" (P.Oxy XVII.2128). Also, the city had "quarters" or regions, perhaps as many as twenty, named for various inhabitants, such as Cretens and Jews (P.Oxy II.335: sale of a house in the Jewish quarter *c.* 83 C.E.); trades or occupations (gooseherds, shepherds, equestrian camp); temples (Sarapis, Thoëris); public buildings (theater, gymnasium, warm baths); and streets or location (South Broad Street quarter, north quarter, south quarter).

Along with the two Christian churches mentioned earlier, P.Oxy IX.1205 refers to a Jewish synagogue that, in 291 C.E.,

---

[21] Turner, "Roman Oxyrhynchus," *JEA* 38 (1952), p. 78. Cf. P.Oxy IX.1199 (3rd C.E.).

[22] See Turner, "Roman Oxyrhynchus," *JEA* 38 (1952), p. 79. I owe the last two references to Turner.

[23] *Oxyrhynchus Papyri*, I, p. 89.

paid fourteen talents of silver (a large sum) to free a woman and her two small children, one of whom was named Jacob.[24] Of course, religion in Oxyrhynchus was dominated by Greek and Roman practices and cults, and by the continuance of traditional Egyptian rites, as attested by innumerable references in the papyri to temples, deities, officiants, festivals, and sacrifices, to say nothing of the inevitable prayers and invocations of the gods in private letters—too numerous to document here.[25]

In addition to religion, the papyri open to us the entire gamut of life and livelihood in Oxyrhynchus through documentary and literary papyri, and through private correspondence. The variety and breadth of classical literature available would have been hard to imagine had the papyri remained undiscovered, as would the range of commerce and agriculture, of transportation, of legal transactions and court activity, of military matters, of politics and government, of cultural and social characteristics, and of work and leisure, as well as the everyday involvements in child rearing, education, marriage and divorce, family joys and sorrows, health and sickness, and natural disasters, all of which are abundantly documented for us at this one location in Egypt.[26]

The location within this socio-economic-cultural milieu of so large a proportion of our extant NT papyri raises again intriguing questions as to how this kind of community impacted upon Christianity up to the fourth century period—and what Christianity's impact upon Oxyrhynchus might have been.

III. The intellectual environment at Oxyrhynchus

More directly relevant to the NT papyri than this brief foray into the sociocultural environment of Oxyrhynchus are the remains and other evidences of intellectual life, particularly the literary works found there and evidences of literary activity, of scholarly editing, and of other literary-critical endeavors. General indica-

---

[24] See *Oxyrhynchus Papyri*, IX, pp. 239–42, and *CPJ*, Vol. 1, p. 94.

[25] See, *e.g.*, Turner, "Roman Oxyrhynchus," *JEA* 38 (1952), pp. 82–83.

[26] Space does not permit detailed documentation; perusal of the volumes of *Oxyrhynchus Papyri* will furnish myriad examples; others may be found in Hugh MacLennan, *Oxyrhynchus: An Economic and Social Study* (Chicago 1968) (though many question his interpretations), and in my recent, popular article, "*Humanitas* in the Greco-Roman Papyri," *Biblical and Humane: A Festschrift for John F. Priest*, edd. L. Bennett Elder, D. L. Barr, and E. Struthers Malbon, Homage Series (Atlanta [Georgia] 1996), pp. 189–213.

tions of such activity at Oxyrhynchus are many, including the following: Already in the third century B.C.E., the peripatetic biographer Satyrus wrote in Oxyrhynchus (notice the extensive P.Oxy IX.1176 [2nd C.E.], *Life of Euripides*), as did the writer and epitomizer, Heraclides Lembus (2nd B.C.E.); in our period, P.Oxy XXIV.2400 (3rd C.E.) lists subjects for student declamations that would require the reading of Thucydides or Euripides; some Oxyrhynchus private letters contain fine expression and writing style, such as P.Oxy XVIII.2190 (1st C.E.) and PSI 1248[27]; the list of titles of Hyperides's speeches in P.Oxy XLVII.3360 (= P.Coll.Youtie I.3) (2nd/3rd C.E.), written in Oxyrhynchus (because it is on the back of a money account), "may illustrate the copying of that author's speeches and their study in that town," and it may, moreover, be a list of books available in someone's library, or a list of books sought, or an account for a scribe's copying work;[28] and P.Oxy VIII.1153 (1st C.E.), a private letter, reports, "I have received through Heraclas the boxes with the books" sent (as the address shows) from Alexandria.

More significant, however, are documents found at Oxyrhynchus identifying individuals as members of the Alexandrian Museum—the most famous among such institutions (originally connected with the arts inspired by the Muses) that housed and provided generous stipends to a group of literary scholars engaged in lecturing and research. For example, P.Oxy XXVII.2471 (*c*. 50 C.E.), which confirms a loan repayment to two brothers, Demetrius and Isidorus, describes Demetrius as "one of those exempt from taxes and maintained in the temple of the Muses." Another Oxyrhynchus document, P.Merton I.19 (31 March 173 C.E.) records the sale of a river boat to Valerius Diodorus, "member of the Museum," and the significant "letter about books" (P.Oxy XVIII.2192), sent to Oxyrhynchus in the second century C.E., also mentions a Diodorus in the context of private book acquisition. The names of both sender and receiver are lost; the three different hands of the fragments complicate the interpretation; the main part of the document was written in a large, flowing, semi-literary hand and in a literary style; following that, the writer in his own hand adds:

---

[27] Cf. Turner, *Greek Papyri*, pp. 84–85, 88; *Greek Manuscripts*, p. 126.
[28] *Collectanea Papyrologica: Texts Published in Honor of H. C. Youtie*, ed. A. E. Hanson, 2 vols, PTA 19 (Bonn 1976), here Vol. 1, pp. 53, 57.

> I pray for your health, my lord brother.... Make and send me copies of books 6 and 7 of Hypsicrates' *Characters in Comedy*. For Harpocration says that they are among Polion's books. But it is likely that others, too, have them. He also has prose epitomes of Thersagoras' work on the myths of tragedy.

At this point a third hand inserts:

> According to Harpocration, Demetrius the bookseller has them. I have instructed Apollonides to send me certain of my own books which you will hear of in good time from Seleucus himself. Should you find any, apart from those which I possess, make copies and send them to me. Diodorus and his friends also have some which I do not have....

The third hand, suggest the editors, may be "a note by another member of the family or circle, correcting and adding to the preceding note." It is now accepted that Harpocration of Alexandria, the author of the *Lexicon of the Ten Orators*, is referred to here, showing that "he was in touch with an intellectual circle in Oxyrhynchus."[29] Turner asserts that the Diodorus here and in P.Merton (above) are the same person, who is to be identified with Valerius Diodorus, the son of Valerius Pollio (= Polion of the papyrus)—two known Alexandrian writers on lexicography.[30] The Merton papyrus makes it likely that Diodorus owned land in Oxyrhynchus, and P.Oxy 2192 could be read to mean that Polion and Diodorus were living in Oxyrhynchus or, more likely, spent time at their property there—and that Harpocration may have visited Polion.[31] It has also been suggested that Seleucus is to be identified with the Alexandrian grammarian.[32] In sum,

---

[29] *OCD*[3], in loc.; this is not in *OCD*[2] and may be based on Turner's work: *JEA* 38 (1952), pp. 91–92 and *Greek Papyri*, p. 87.

[30] Turner, *JEA* 38 (1952), p. 92; *Greek Papyri*, pp. 86–87; *Greek Manuscripts*, p. 114.

[31] Turner, *JEA* 38 (1952), p. 92. He notes (p. 85) that some twenty-four Alexandrian citizens owned property in Oxyrhynchus during the first three centuries.

[32] By B. Hemmerdinger, *REG* 72 (1959), pp. 107–109 (*apud* Turner, *Greek Manuscripts*, p. 114).

the interest of the letter lies in the picture it suggests of a circle of friends at Oxyrhynchus all interested in the acquisition of books and getting their friends to have copies made of works not in their possession. Side by side with this system of private borrowing and copying, we have...an allusion to the book trade.[33]

The natural question, again, is what does it mean for the NT papyri at Oxyrhynchus when it is recognized that they were found in a city where vast numbers of literary texts were in use and were subjected to scholarly analysis and editing?

Actually, the quantity and range of literary works preserved at Oxyrhynchus is enormous, for its rubbish heaps yielded 1,435 papyrus remnants of known and previously unknown classical authors (as catalogued by Krüger).[34] These rolls and codices cover the period from around the turn of the second/first centuries B.C.E. to the turn of the sixth/seventh centuries C.E.—more than 700 years. It would not be fair, therefore, to use the entire lot to characterize Oxyrhynchus at any given point during these centuries, so some reasonable representation must be determined. Since books often last longer than people—papyrus, when kept dry, is very resilient and durable—and since our interest lies mainly in the period from the turn of the first/second to that of the third/fourth centuries C.E. (the period coinciding with our earliest forty-eight NT manuscripts), we can select that 200-year period for investigation. This may suggest that we have

---

[33] P.Oxy XVIII, p. 150.

[34] Krüger, *Oxyrhynchos in der Kaiserzeit,* pp. 227–245; 313–350; cf. the list of Christian and Jewish papyri, pp. 351–354. In 1922, F. Kenyon, "The Library of a Greek of Oxyrhynchus," *JEA* 8 (1922), pp. 130–134, could reckon only 390 literary manuscripts of the Greco-Roman period at Oxyrhynchus (though not counting Homer): 38 from the 1st century, 113 from the 2nd, 121 from the 3rd, 51 from the 4th, etc. *OCD*[3], p. 1088, asserts that "over 70 per cent of surviving literary papyri come from Oxyrhynchus."

Though it is difficult to offer a modern comparison with Oxyrhynchus, a city of some 30,000, residents of the United States might think of a city the size of Fairbanks (30,800) or Juneau, Alaska (26,750), New Castle, Pennsylvania (28,330), Paducah, Kentucky (27,250), Del Rio (30,700) or Texarkana, Texas (31,650), or Walla Walla, Washington (26,500)–recognizable small cities but certainly not major urban centers–and ask about the range and quantity of literary works that might be available there (subtracting the benefits of the printing press and modern distribution methods–and of a system of public education).

in mind the literature available during the lifetime of a 200-year-old Oxyrhynchite and that it would be better to choose a single century, but that difficulty is mitigated if we list the material period by period, so that either the time-frame from about 80–200 or that from 200 to about 325 may be observed separately.

A very quick summary shows that in the period of about 80–200 Oxyrhynchus possessed the following number of copies of works by well-known authors—selected from a much longer list:

Aeschylus	24	Menander	14
Apollonius of Rhodes	10	Pindar	13
Aristophanes	3	Plato	28
Aristotle	2	Plutarch	1
Callimachus	28	Sappho	8
Demosthenes	18	Sophocles	10
Euripides	18	Theocritus	9
Herodotus	11	Theophrastus	1
Hesiod	34	Thucydides	11
Homer	55	Xenophon	6
Isocrates	8		

In addition, the Oxyrhynchus papyri include many other known authors, some 100 anonymous literary works, and three dozen miscellaneous works.

If one moves to the period from about 200 to 325, most of the authors are represented by additional copies (as examples among many others):

Demosthenes	16	Pindar	8
Euripides	16	Plato	21
Herodotus	12	Sappho	7
Hesiod	30	Sophocles	5
Homer	121	Thucydides	13
Menander	17	Xenophon	6

In addition, there are Latin authors like Livy, Sallust, and Virgil, plus many other known authors and nearly 100 each of anonymous literary works and of historical and scientific works.

Literature at Oxyrhynchus, of course, was not limited to classical authors, but the papyri preserve some Jewish writings and numerous copies of Christian writings in addition to NT texts, that is, beyond the 28 NT papyri and six uncials (**071** [P.Oxy III.401], **0162** [VI.847], **0163** [VI.848], **0169** [VIII.1080],

0170 [IX.1169], and **0206** [XI.1353]), of which twenty papyri and the parchment codex **0162** fall into the period up to the turn of the third/fourth centuries. The apocryphal sayings of Jesus have been discussed above (P.Oxy I.1; IV.654, 655; and X.1224), and they date from the same early period. Also within our selected time-frame are portions of Greek (and Latin) Jewish Scripture made for Christian use, though it is difficult to know for certain which were of Christian origin),[35] and various Christian theological texts and treatises, as well as devotional materials. A quick survey, again only through the turn of the third/fourth centuries, shows that some twenty-four items of non-NT Christian literature survive at Oxyrhynchus, including nine apocryphal gospels or sayings of Jesus (*Gospel of Thomas* [I.1; IV.654, 655]; *Sophia Jesu Christi* [VIII.1081]; *Gospel of Mary* [L.3525; P.Ryl III.463]; X.1224; XLI.2949; P.Lond.Christ.1); four copies of the *Shepherd of Hermas* (I.5; III.404; XV.1828; L.3528); and one each of the *Apocalypse of Peter* (P.Vindob.G), the *Acts of Peter* (VI.849),

---

[35] Here is a list compiled from Krüger, *Oxyrhynchos in der Kaiserzeit*, pp. 351–354:

> P.Oxy VII.1010 (4th): 6 Ezra (vellum codex).
> P.Oxy VIII.1073 (4th): Old Latin Genesis (vellum codex).
> P.Oxy VIII.1074 (3rd): Exodus (papyrus codex).
> P.Oxy VIII.1075 (3rd): Exodus (papyrus roll).
> P.Oxy IX.1167 (4th): Genesis (papyrus codex).
> P.Oxy IX.1168 (4th): Joshua (vellum codex).
> P.Oxy X.1226 (3rd/4th): Psalms (papyrus codex).
> P.Oxy XI.1351 (4th): Leviticus (vellum codex).
> P.Oxy XI.1352 (early 4th): Psalms (vellum codex).
> P.Oxy XIII.1594 (late 3rd): Tobit (vellum codex).
> P.Oxy XV.1779 (4th): Psalm 1 (papyrus codex).
> PSI 1163 (4th): Job.
> P.Harr.31 (4th): Psalm 43.
> P.Mil.R.Univ 1.22 (4th): Exodus
> P.Oxy XXXVI.2745 (3rd/4th): Onomasticon of Hebrew Names
>   (verso of land register).
> P.Oxy IX.1173+XI.1356+XVII.2158 (3rd) Philo (papyrus codex–
>   very extensive).

In addition, according to Roberts (*Manuscript*, pp. 74–78), P.Oxy IV.656 (3rd C.E.), Genesis (papyrus codex), is Jewish, while P.Oxy VII.1007 (3rd C.E.), Genesis (parchment codex); P.Oxy IX.1166 (3rd C.E.), Genesis (papyrus roll); and P.Oxy X.1225 (1st half 4th C.E.), Leviticus (papyrus roll) could be either Jewish or Christian.

Irenaeus's *Against Heresies* (P.Oxy III.405, but see IV, pp. 264–65); an apologetic work (XVII.2072); an anti-Jewish dialogue (XVII.2070); a prayer (III.407); and a hymn with musical notation (XV.1786), as well as some gnostic (I.4; XII.1478; P.Harr.107) and other miscellaneous material (II.210). Incidentally, nearly twenty additional items are added if the full 4th century is taken into account, including three more copies of *Hermas* (IX.1172+3526; XIII.1599; L.3527); copies of the *Didache* (XV.1782), the *Acts of John* (VI.850), Aristides' *Apology* (XV.1778), the *Passion of St. Dioskorus* (L.3529), and the *Apocalypse of Baruch* (III.403); an apocalyptic fragment (XVII.2069); a liturgical fragment (XVII.2068); a prayer (VII.1058); three sermons (XIII.1601; 1602; XVII.2073); three amulets (PSI.719; P.Amst 26; SB 10762); and a gnostic charm (VI.924) and a prayer (XII.1566).[36] The anti-Jewish dialogue (P.Oxy XVII.2070 [late 3rd C.E.]) may support Oxyrhynchus as "a Christian intellectual center"[37] at the time, not—to be sure—because of its subject-matter (!), but because the papyrus appears to be an autograph by a local writer, as evidenced by frequent corrections, but especially by alterations to the text by the original hand, which "are difficult to explain except on the hypothesis that we here have a fragment of the author's own manuscript."[38]

Though hardly comparable to the huge classical corpus that had been built up over several centuries, this range—if not the quantity—of Christian literature from within a restricted time-frame is impressive nonetheless, and it suggests an active inter-action of the churches there with the young faith's written traditions.[39] Even the limited quantity, however, seems sufficient

---

[36] Though inferences are risky when assessing randomly preserved data, it is tempting to ask whether apocalyptic interests ran high in Christian Oxyrhynchus because of the large proportion of such literature: ten items out of this list of forty-three. Notice also that two out of the six NT uncial fragments contain the Apocalypse of John (one 4th century, though the other is 5th). It is known, of course, that *Hermas* was used in instructing catechumens—see Tertullian, *de Pud.* 10.39 (Roberts, *Manuscript*, p. 22).

[37] Roberts, *Manuscript*, p. 24, n. 5.

[38] P.Oxy XVII, p. 9. P.Oxy VII.1015 (later 3rd C.E.) may be another autograph (though not Christian), probably of a prize poem (Turner, *Greek Manuscripts*, pp. 90–91).

[39] Recently Harry Y. Gamble, *Books and Readers in the Early Church: A History of Early Christian Texts* (New Haven 1995), estimates a ten- to twenty-percent literacy rate at this time for the Greco-Roman world in general, and for

for C. H. Roberts to suspect that a Christian scriptorium at Oxyrhynchus by or in the third century is "not unlikely."[40]

IV. Literary-critical activity at Oxyrhynchus and the New Testament papyri

In view of the extensive documentation of literary-critical activity at Oxyrhynchus, the next appropriate question is whether the NT papyri and early uncials at that locality were subject to any scholarly analysis or critical editing.

First, however, it is essential to clarify the evidence sought. We are not concerned with *scribal activity* per se, that is, normal or routine manuscript corrections[41] or lection marks, including punctuation, paragraph marks (the *paragraphus*), accent and breathing marks, the *trema* or *diairesis*, the *apostrophe*, etc. $\mathfrak{P}^5$ (P.Oxy II.208+XV.1781 [3rd C.E.]) may serve as a random but typical example, for it shows a few corrections written above the line and an omission due to homeoteleuton placed at the foot of the page, the usual *nomina sacra*, blank spaces as punctuation, and a few rough breathings.

Rather, our search is for editing marks—beyond the copying process—that reveal primarily a *reader's* use and critical reaction to or interaction with the text. Specifically, we are interested in

---

Christians "ordinarily not more than about ten percent in any given setting, and perhaps fewer in many small and provincial congregations that were characteristic of early Christianity" (p. 4, see n. 8; 5–7). The surveys of classical and Christian literature presented above raise the question as to the appropriateness of these figures for Oxyrhynchus (an issue treated by the present writer in a forthcoming article in *Critical Review of Books in Religion*).

[40] Roberts, *Manuscript*, p. 24. Note also that a number of scribes can be identified as producing more than one manuscript (Turner, *JEA* 38 [1952], p. 91; *Greek Papyri*, p. 92; *Greek Manuscripts*, p. 20), though it is not certain whether such items were copied in Oxyrhynchus or, *e.g.*, at Alexandria.

[41] To be sure, it is not always easy to distinguish "normal" or "routine" copying corrections from an activity that might be described as "critical corrections" or "critical editing." For example, the kind of editorial correction applied to $\mathfrak{P}^{66}$ by its scribe–which moves the text of his exemplar toward a Byzantine type of reading (see Fee, *Papyrus Bodmer II ($\mathfrak{P}^{66}$): Its Textual Relationships and Scribal Characteristics*, StD 34 [Salt Lake City 1968], pp. 76–83)– appears to be right on the line between the two, though perhaps leaning toward a critical editing activity. See below, *e.g.*, on signs for "this is what stood in the exemplar."

editor's or scholar's notations or critical marks, such as *glosses* or
scholia (marginal notes, respectively, for explanation and illus-
tration or for elucidating the meaning of difficult passages); *ono-
mastica* (glosses explaining the meaning of names and places);
notes of *commentary*, pointers to a commentary, or indications of a
need for a commentary to a portion of text; and very specific
critical marks or signs, most commonly the χ sign and the > or
diple (διπλῆ), but also the obelus and antisigma, and others.[42]
These notes and signs are employed in literary manuscripts, both
poetry and prose, though not in documentary texts or private
letters (with some rare exceptions).

Both of the common signs, χ and >, as well as others, were
prefixed to a line and apparently were used to indicate a point in
the text that required a clarifying commentary, but each served a
number of other purposes, as observed in the papyri.[43] The χ sign
was employed to indicate something noteworthy in a line, such
as dissent from a reading, an inconsistency, a quotation or a
parallel, an unusual word or form of a word, and other general
uses or specialized uses in certain authors, *e.g.*, Homer, Pindar, or
Plato. The > was used to expose wrong glosses, to mark disputed
words or passages, among other queries. The presence of these
two signs in a text, says Turner, "suggests either that the papyrus
was being marked by a reader who had access to a commentary
(or was making one for himself); or else that it was a copy of a

---

[42] For a convenient discussion, see Turner, *Greek Papyri*, pp. 112–18; cf. 92–95;
on commentaries and scholia, pp. 118–24; idem, *Greek Manuscripts*, pp. 17–18.
Cf. B. M. Metzger, *Manuscripts of the Greek Bible: An Introduction to Greek
Palaeography* (Oxford 1981), pp. 46–48. On the invention of the first critical sign,
the obelus (probably to mark passages whose authenticity was suspect), by
Zenodotus of Ephesus (born *c.* 325 B.C.E.), see Rudolf Pfeiffer, *History of
Classical Scholarship from the Beginnings to the End of the Hellenistic Age* (Oxford
1968; repr. 1978), p. 115; on the additional signs of Aristophanes of Byzantium
(*fl.* 200 B.C.E.), see p. 178; cf. 173–175; on the system of critical signs perfected
by Aristarchus (*c.* 216–144 B.C.E.) for his editions of Homer and on
Alexandrian editing practices, see L. D. Reynolds and N. G. Wilson, *Scribes and
Scholars: A Guide to the Transmission of Greek and Latin Literature* (Oxford 1991[3]),
pp. 10–16, 317; cf. Pfeiffer, *History*, p. 218.

P.Oxy VIII.1086 (1st B.C.E.) is the oldest extant commentary, and it contains
Aristarchean critical signs (*e.g.*, the diple in *ll.* 27, 54, 97). For examples of
extended scholia, see P.Oxy V.841 (1st C.E.); P.Oxy XX.2258 (*c.* 6th C.E.)–
Turner, *Greek Manuscripts*, pp. 67–69.

[43] The following is summarized from Turner, *Greek Papyri*, pp. 116–118.

text so marked," and he points to an instance in P.Oxy 2427 (2nd/3rd C.E.), *fr.* 53, as evidence that a commentary on Epicharmus existed, for the marginal note there reads "the χ was not in Theon's [copies]."[44] Sometimes scholia are introduced by ὅτι...following a lemma, meaning "the sign is placed because...."[45] Closely related are marks, notations, or abbreviations of notations that indicate whether a word or portion of text stood in the exemplar, most commonly ὅ = οὕτως or ὅη̈ = οὕ(τως) ἦν, the equivalent of *sic,* meaning "this is what stood in the exemplar."[46] The clear implication is that the annotator has checked a manuscript exemplar or a commentary.

In short, these critical marks and notations in a literary text indicate literary criticism and other scholarly activity, such as *critical* corrections (as opposed to routine), and there are many instances of such marks in the literary papyri at Oxyrhynchus. Turner provides lists that include twenty-seven manuscripts,[47] and my perusal of the texts and plates of Oxyrhynchus papyri disclosed many more.[48] "Critical marks of this kind, used scru-

---

[44] Turner, *Greek Papyri,* pp. 117 and 184, n. 37; cf. 93–94 and 182 n. 55. See P.Oxy XXIV.2387 (1st B.C.E./1st C.E.) and Turner, *Greek Manuscripts,* pp. 42–43.

[45] See Turner, *Greek Papyri,* pp. 114–115 and his Oxyrhynchus examples: P.Oxy II.221 (1st C.E.), esp. x.24 and pl. VI; and P.Oxy VIII.1086 (1st B.C.E.), ii.55: διπλῆ ὅτι....

[46] Turner, *Greek Manuscripts,* p. 17; *Greek Papyri,* pp. 93 and 182 n. 55, referring to P.Oxy XXIV.2387 (1st B.C.E./1st C.E.) *fr.* 1. See also P.Oxy IX.1174 (late 2nd C.E.), cols. iv, v, vi, viii, ix, xi, xiii, xv; P.Oxy IX.1175, *fr.* 5, i.20 and pl. III; and Turner, *Greek Manuscripts,* p. 66. For its rare occurrence in a documentary papyrus, see P.Oxy III.478 (132 C.E.), *l.* 28.

[47] Turner, *Greek Papyri,* pp. 116–17. Oxyrhynchus examples constitute twenty-seven of the thirty-four in his lists.

[48] Some random examples into the fourth century C.E.:

> P.Oxy IV.687 (two diples where other scholia exist)
> P.Oxy VIII.1082 (marginalia and variants added by different person)
> P.Oxy VIII.1086 (κρηστόν, diple, etc.)
> P.Oxy XI.1371 (sign and marginal notes—see pl. VII)
> P.Oxy XIII.1620 (several signs and marginal notes—see pl. VI)
> P.Oxy XIII.1624 (many corrections, alternative readings by another hand—see pl. VI)
> P.Oxy XV.1808 (signs and marginalia by different hand—see pl. IV)
> P.Oxy XV.1809 (several signs and marginalia by different hand)
> P.Oxy XVIII.2174, *fr.* 16 (diple and antisigma—see pl. X)
> P.Oxy XXIV.2394, *fr.* 1 (signs—see pl. XI)

pulously, are one of the strongest and best indications that the texts in question were scholars' copies."[49]

From the outset of my investigation, I wondered whether such marks were to be found in our early NT papyri—which, if they were, would indicate early critical assessment and scholarly work in the Christian community in those early generations. I have located virtually no discussions of this matter and examination of the published texts and of available plates of the Oxyrhynchus NT papyri so far has turned up few if any certifiable specialized critical marks of this kind, even though a significant number of lines with left margins preserved—where these marks usually occur—are found in the twenty-eight Oxyrhynchus papyri and the six uncials containing the NT.

The most obvious testing ground would be any NT papyri that possess a clear literary character. Among the fourteen earliest Christian papyri (from the second and second/third centuries), C. H. Roberts identified three that are "incontrovertibly literary in style,"[50] two of which are from Oxyrhynchus, though only one contains NT text. The first is P.Oxy III.405 [but see P.Oxy IV, p. 264] (late 2nd C.E.), a portion of a Greek papyrus roll containing fragments of Irenaeus's *Adversus Haereses*, which has a series of diple signs marking the quotation of Matt 3:16–17; if these were made by a user of the text rather than a copyist—apparently unclear (see plate I in the edition)—they would border on critical notations (yet would be of no great significance). The second example is the NT $\mathfrak{P}^{77}$ (P.Oxy XXXIV.2683 [later 2nd or 2nd/3rd C.E.], a leaf with Matt 23:30–39 in an elegant hand, with chapter divisions, punctuation, and breathing marks—all short of the critical signs we are seeking. The third, not from Oxyrhynchus, makes up $\mathfrak{P}^{64}$+$\mathfrak{P}^{67}$+$\mathfrak{P}^{4}$ [Aland does not include $\mathfrak{P}^{4}$] (*c.* 200 C.E.), with portions of Matthew (and Luke), which also has section divisions, as well as punctuation and omission and quotation signs,[51] though judging from the transcriptions and plates, nothing here moves beyond the copyist realm. Examining transcriptions and available plates of other Christian literature from Oxyrhynchus within our time-frame led to the same result, as did a perusal of numerous folios of non-

---

P.Oxy XXV.2430 (marginal notes/corrections by different hand—see pl. V)

[49] Turner, *Greek Papyri*, p. 118.

[50] Roberts, *Manuscript*, p. 23.

[51] Ibid.

Oxyrhynchus papyri, such as $\mathfrak{P}^{45}$, $\mathfrak{P}^{46}$, $\mathfrak{P}^{47}$, $\mathfrak{P}^{66}$, $\mathfrak{P}^{75}$, and others.[52] Naturally, it is always risky to assert that no instances of a given phenomenon exist across a sizable body of literature, so any conclusions remain preliminary at this time and subject to further analysis. At very least, however, it seems safe to say that critical signs indicating scholarly editing—those moving beyond the copying process—rarely if ever occur in the NT papyri at Oxyrhynchus or in other Christian literature there from the early period.

At first this lack of evidence was disconcerting, for would it not have been enlightening to have found in our earliest NT manuscripts some technical marks of literary-critical scholarship and text-critical editing? Would not such marks of scholarly attention, including notice of text-critical judgments, have clarified the origin or development of some textual variants? And would we not have been the richer for such information? Perhaps, but the essentially negative result with respect to critical marks provides clarity about our earliest NT manuscripts in another way—the nature of the codex form as employed in Christianity.

That early Christians very quickly adopted the codex form for their writings—when the roll was normal for literary works—is well established, though the possible reasons for the practice cannot be rehearsed here. What is relevant, however, is that early Christian books were essentially *practical* and produced for use in the life of the Christian community. Included would be NT texts and—even earlier—portions of the Jewish Bible prepared for Christian use. Evidences of this practicality and utilitarianism of our earliest Christian manuscripts are several practices carried over from documentary papyri—and distinct from normal literary conventions—among them the consistent use of the codex form (see below), the virtual absence of a calligraphic

---

[52] A quick reading of Roberts, *Manuscript*, pp. 9–10, 14, 21–25, may give the impression that early Christians frequently placed marks, including "critical signs," in their manuscripts. For the most part, however, he is speaking of lectional or reading aids–punctuation, accents, breathings, diaereses, etc.–as well as customary spacing and paragraph marks. The exceptions include P.Ryl I.1, a copy of Deuteronomy from *c.* 300 and presumably made for Christian use, that has two χ-marks before *ll.* 48–49 (though their purpose is not clear) (see A. S. Hunt, et al., edd., *Catalogue of the Greek Papyri in the John Rylands Library*, 3 vols. [Manchester 1911–1938], Vol. I, pp. 1–3); and P.Grenfell I.5, a copy of Ezekiel that uses Origin's hexaplaric signs (Roberts, *Manuscript*, p. 25).

hand, a lack of strict *scriptio continua*, an enlarged initial letter or one extruded into the margin, the use of symbols rather than words for cardinal numbers, and the use of contractions (notably the *nomina sacra*).[53]

The lack of literary editing in early Christian texts can be explored (and explained) further by considering the very format employed so consistently: the codex. Harry Gamble places the earliest Christian books in the "intermediate phase in the evolving status of the codex—in the late first and early second centuries" and affirms that "the Christians who made them and made use of them did not regard them either as notebooks [the earliest phase] or as fine literature" [the final phase]—"they were practical books for everyday use."[54] Thus, the Oxyrhynchus literary papyri exhibit the critical marks of scholarly editing and literary criticism, as they should, while the NT codices found there do not, which is also as it should be, for they have not yet evolved to the final, literary stage of the codex form, but stand midway in the evolutionary process by virtue of their utilitarian character as writings designed for use in the church.

---

[53] Roberts, *Manuscript*, pp. 12–22, 29.
[54] Gamble, *Books and Readers*, p. 66; cf. pp. 77–78.

DIE HERRENWORTE ÜBER DAS BRAUTGEMACH IM *THOMASEVANGELIUM* UND IM *DIALOG DES ERLÖSERS*

Jan Helderman
Vrije Universiteit Amsterdam
(Amsterdam, the Netherlands)

Das *Thomasevangelium* hat im *Dialog des Erlösers* seinen ersten nunmehr klar gnostisch ausgerichteten Kommentar: "As a commentary on Gos.Thom. 2, the dialogue explains the disciples' place in the eschatological timetable." Dieses Votum wurde abgegeben von Helmut Koester und Elaine Pagels, die sich beide mit dem *Dialog (Dial)* befaßt haben und die Textausgabe der *Coptic Gnostic Library* (in den *Nag Hammadi Studies*) zusammengestellt haben.[1]

Wenn man den Text näher betrachtet, stellt sich in der Tat heraus, daß es im *Dial* sehr viele Parallelen zum Thomasevangelium gibt.[2] Es ist nicht von ungefähr, wenn Koester und Pagels die programmatische Formel von Logion 2 des *Thomasevangeliums* (*TE*), nämlich *suchen, finden, verwirrt sein, sich wundern, herrschen* (bzw. *ruhen*) als roten Faden durch den ganzen *Dial* hindurch bezeichnen.[3] Diesen roten Faden nennen sie treffend die *ordo salutis* des *TE*.[4]

Die Korrelation von *TE* und *Dial* läßt sich auch daran demonstrieren, daß das inhaltsschwere Wort *monachos* (Einsame[r]) sich sowohl im hier zu behandelnden Logion 75 des *TE* findet als auch

---

[1] Vgl. E. Pagels & H. Koester, "Report on the Dialogue of the Savior" (CG III,5), in: R. McL. Wilson, *Nag Hammadi and Gnosis*, NHS 14 (Leiden 1978), pp. 66–74, und S. Emmel (mit E. Pagels & H. Koester), *Nag Hammadi Codex III,5, The Dialogue of the Savior*, NHS 26 (Leiden 1984). Obiges Zitat findet man S. 7.

[2] Man beachte die Liste in Emmel, *Dialogue*, 2–8.

[3] Vgl. Pagels, *Report*, 68, 69 (penultima) und 71 und Emmel, *Dialogue*, 7.

[4] Vgl. Emmel, *Dialogue*, 7. Siehe für die verschiedenen Versionen des Logion 2 *TE*: A. F. J. Klijn, *Jewish-Christian Gospel Tradition* (Leiden 1992), 48–51. Es gilt zu beachten, daß der Kettenspruch des Logion 2 im Grunde basiert auf einem Topos der antiken Philosophie, vgl. die Stellenangabe bei H.-Ch. Puech, B. Blatz, "Andere gnostische Evangelien und verwandte Literatur," in: W. Schneemelcher (Hg.), *Neutestamentliche Apokryphen in deutscher Übersetzung*, Bd. I (Tübingen 1987⁵), 307.

in *Dial* p. 120,26 und 121,18 (beidemal *monochos* geschrieben). Die Einsamen (oder Einsgewordenen) werden in den aufgeführten Stellen im *Dial* auch Auserwählte genannt, wie auch im *TE* in den Logien 23 und 49. Der Topos vom Einsam-Sein bzw. Auserwählt-Sein ist außerordentlich wichtig als Zeichen der Verbundenheit von *TE* und *Dial*.[5] Außer *TE* Logion 75 werden in diesem Beitrag Logion 104 und *Dial* p. 138,14–20 zur Sprache kommen, weil einem an diesen drei Stellen das Brautgemach in einem belangvollen Kontext begegnet, vor allem als Logion/Wort des Herrn. Wie wir sehen werden, kommt das Brautgemach in der Nag Hammadi-Bibliothek öfters vor, aber dann in einer Auseinandersetzung oder Beobachtung des Verfassers.

Die *Dial*-Stelle findet sich im letzten (fünften) Abschnitt des Traktates.[6] In diesem Teil findet ein Gespräch, ein Dialog im wahren Sinn statt zwischen dem Herrn und den Jüngern Matthäus, Judas (anderswo Thomas) und Maria (Mariham).

Dial (datiert um 210[7]), *TE* (datiert um 100[8]), das *Buch des (Athleten) Thomas* (datiert um 220[9]) und die *Thomasakten* (datiert um 225[10]) werden zur Thomastradition oder Thomasschule gerechnet. Eine Tradition, die in Ostsyrien, in der Osrhoene beheimatet war.[11] Ein Merkmal dieses ostsyrischen Christentums war die

---

[5] Vgl. M. Krause, "Der Dialog des Soter in Codex III von Nag Hammadi," in: M. Krause, *Gnosis and Gnosticism*, NHS 8 (Leiden 1977), 28–29, und Ph. Perkins, *The Gnostic Dialogue. The Early Church and the Crisis of Gnosticism* (New York 1980), 107 (ebd. müßte die Anm. 26 Krause, 29 statt 24 sein).

[6] Vgl. die Gliederung des Traktates in fünf Teilen bei Pagels, *Report*, 73, und Emmel, *Dialogue*, 2.

[7] Vgl. Emmel, *Dialogue*, 16.

[8] Vgl. H. Koester, "The Gospel according to Thomas," in: B. Layton, *Nag Hammadi Codex II,2–7*, Vol.I (Leiden 1989), 39.

[9] Vgl. J. D. Turner, "The Book of Thomas the Contender writing to the Perfect," in: Layton, *Nag Hammadi Codex II, 2–7*, 177.

[10] Vgl. J. M. Robinson, *The Nag Hammadi Library in English* (Leiden 1988), 199.

[11] Vgl. Perkins, *Dialogue*, 99–112, B. Layton, *The Gnostic Scriptures* (New York 1987), 359–364 und F. Vouga, *Geschichte des frühen Christentums*, UTB 1773 (Tübingen 1994), 91–92.

Sonderstellung der "Einsamen" (gr. *monachoi*; syr. *ihidaja*), die ein streng asketisches Leben führten.[12]
Wenden wir uns nunmehr den drei Stellen zu.[13]

> *TE* Logion 75:
> *pedzje Iesous wen hah aheratou hirem p^{e}ro alla ^{e}mmonachos netnabōk ehoun epma^{e}nscheleet*
> Jesus sagte: Es stehen viele bei der Tür, doch die Einsamen werden hineingehen ins Brautgemach.

> *TE* Logion 104:
> *pedzjau ^{e}n(Ie)sous dzje amou^{e}nt^{e}nschlèl ^{e}mpow awō ^{e}nt^{e}n^{e}rnèsteue pedzje Iesous dzje ou gar pe pnobe ^{e}ntaiaaf è ^{e}ntaudzjro eroi h^{e}n ou alla hotan erschan pnymphios ei ebol h^{e}m pnymphōn tote marounesteue awō marouschlèl*
> Sie sagten [zu] Jesus: Komm, laß uns heute beten und fasten. Jesus sagte: Was ist denn die Sünde, die ich getan habe, oder worin besiegten sie mich? Wenn aber der Bräutigam aus dem Brautgemach geht, dann mögen sie fasten und beten.

> *Dial* p. 138, 14–20:
> *Pedzjaf ^{e}ngi pdzjois dzje ^{e}ntōt^{e}n pe etna ^{e}rdzjois edzjōou alla hotan ete t^{e}nschanfi ^{e}mp(e)phthonos ebol h^{e}ntèout^{e}n tote tetnati hiōt tèout^{e}n ^{e}mpwoein ^{e}ntet^{e}nbōk ehoun epma ^{e}nscheleet*
> Der Herr sagte: Ihr seid es, die herrschen werdet über sie, aber wenn ihr wegtut den Neid, dann werdet ihr euch in Licht kleiden und hineingehen ins Brautgemach.

In den drei Stellen begegnen wir im Herrenwort der Metapher des Brautgemachs. An sich war die metaphorische Anwendung in der alten Welt weit verbreitet.[14] Folgendes ließe sich hervorheben. Das Brautgemach im metaphorischen Sinne findet sich im Alten Testament in Ps 19:6 und dem genauen Wortsinn nach in Joel 2:16, beidemal mit חֻפָּה. Die Septuaginta hat hier παστός. Im Neuen

---

[12] Vgl. G. Quispel, *Makarius, das Thomasevangelium und das Lied von der Perle*, NovT.S 15 (Leiden 1967), 26, 28 und 108; A. J. van der Aalst, *Aantekeningen bij de Hellenisering van het Christendom* (Den Haag 1974), 44–45 und 48–51. Siehe für Herkunft und Etymologie von *monachos* W. Vycichl, *Dictionnaire étymologique de la langue copte* (Leuven 1983), 173–174.

[13] Wir geben Zitate in Koptisch und Syrisch in einer phonetischen Transkription, inklusive der Vokale "g" wie im französischen *garçon*.

[14] Vgl. J. Schmid, "Brautgemach," *RAC*, Vol. II, 524–528.

Testament findet man in diesem Zusammenhang die Stelle Mk 2:19/Lk 5:34/Mt 9:15 mit οἱ υἱοὶ τοῦ νυμφῶνος (die Hochzeitsgesellen) in genau demselben Kontext wie in Logion 104, nämlich der Fastenfrage.[15] Es sei noch zu bemerken, daß im Minuskel 472 statt ἀπαρθῇ, παρελθῃ steht, also in der Nähe des koptischen "aus...geht," eine Tatsache, auf die der Jubilar am Anfang seiner wissenschaftlichen Laufbahn schon hingewiesen hat.[16]

Wie oben angegeben, ist das koptische Äquivalent für νυμφών *ma^enscheleet* = Ort der Braut. Wir finden dieses Wort sowohl für die neutestamentlichen Stellen,[17] wie in einem vor kurzem aufgefundenen mittelägyptischen (koptischen) Psalmbuch zu Ps 18:6 (LXX-Zählung).[18]

Für ein richtiges Verständnis der Aussagen in den drei Herrenworten scheint es angebracht, nicht nur die Zusammenhänge der Metapher in *TE* und *Dial* anhand des Leitmotives in Logion 2 des *TE* (die *ordo salutis*) zu untersuchen, sondern auch Umschau zu halten, damit wir sachgerechtes Material in Sachen "Brautgemach" im (christlich-)gnostischen und altkirchlichen Schrifttum auf die Spur kommen.

I. Das Brautgemach

Zuerst aber ziehen wir die Brautgemachstellen in der Nag Hammadi Bibliothek in Betracht.

Die überaus große Mehrheit der Stellen findet sich im Philippusevangelium (NCH II). Für das Wort Brautgemach finden wir dort drei Begriffe. Erstens *nymphōn* (νυμφών in koptischer Schrift):

> p. 65,14: Über das irdische "abbildliche Brautgemach" vor dem Tode der Pneumatiker (= die "Bilder"), in dem die pleromatische

---

[15] Vgl. H. Koester, *Ancient Christian Gospels. Their history and development* (London/Philadelphia 1990), 109–110.

[16] Vgl. R. Schippers, *Het evangelie van Thomas* (Kampen 1960). Kapitel VI wurde von T. Baarda geschrieben. Siehe S.153. Die Lesart in 472 wurde im Brief von Fr. Prof. Dr. B. Aland d.d. 18-12-1995 bestätigt. Übrigens stammt 472 aus dem 13. Jhdt.

[17] Vgl. für das sahidische NT: M. Wilmet, *Concordance du Nouveau Testament sahidique, II.3, Les mots autochtones* (Leuven 1959), 1197.

[18] Vgl. G. Gabra, *Der Psalter im Oxyrhynchitischen (Mesokemischen/Mittelägyptischen) Dialekt* (Heidelberg 1995), 98; zu vergleichen W. H. Worrell, *The Coptic Manuscripts in the Freer Collection* (New York 1923), 26.

Hochzeit von jedem "Bild" mit dessen Engel vorweggenommen wird.

p. 67,16: Durch das "abbildliche Brautgemach", ein sakramentaler Ritus bei der Gemeinde hinter dem Philippusevangelium, tritt man in die Wahrheit, d.h. die Wiederherstellung hinein.[19]

p. 67,29–30: "Der Herr tat alles (auf dem Wege der) Mysterien: eine Taufe, eine Salbung, eine Eucharistie, eine Erlösung und ein Brautgemach." Die Gemeinde kannte also fünf Sakramente. Segelberg vermutete, daß die fünf Bäume im Paradies (*TE* Logion 19) auf dieses Brauchtum Bezug nehmen.[20]

p. 69,24–25: In der metaphorischen Deutung des Tempels in Jerusalem ist die Taufe das "Heilige", die Erlösung das "Heilige vom Heiligen"(!) und das Brautgemach das "Heilige der Heiligen." Sehr wichtig ist die Aussage:

p. 69,25–27: "Die Taufe schließt die Auferstehung und die Erlösung ein, während die Erlösung im Brautgemach (sich vollzieht)."

p. 74,21: Der Vater gibt die verschiedenen Heilsgüter durch die Salbung: Auferstehung, Licht, das Kreuz, und den Heiligen Geist im Brautgemach.

p. 82,17: Die Braut darf sich nur ihrem Vater, ihrer Mutter, dem Freund des Bräutigams und den Söhnen des Bräutigams (Begleitern) zeigen. Diesen ist es erlaubt, jeden Tag in das Brautgemach hineinzugehen.

p. 86,5: Hier metaphorisch: "Wenn einer ein Sohn des Brautgemachs wird, wird er das Licht erhalten."

Zweitens *pastos* (παστός in koptischer Schrift):

p. 64,2: Das Brautgemach im herkömmlichen Sinne.

p. 69,36: Im schlecht erhalten gebliebenen Schlußteil der Seite begegnet einem das Wort Brautgemach, siehe oben.

p. 70,20–22: Es handelt sich in dieser Passage um die verhängnisvolle Trennung von Mann und Frau, Adam und Eva: "die Frau wird mit ihrem Mann im Brautgemach vereinigt. Tatsäch-

---

[19] J.-M. Sevrin, "Les Noces Spirituelles dans l'Evangile selon Philippe", *Muséon* 87 (1974), 177–178 Anm. 94, schlägt eine Korrektur vor.

[20] Vgl. E. Segelberg, "The Coptic-Gnostic Gospel according to Philip and its sacramental system," *Numen* 7 (1960), 191 und J. Helderman, *Die Anapausis im Evangelium Veritatis. Eine vergleichende Untersuchung des valentinianisch-gnostischen Heilsgutes der Ruhe im Evangelium Veritatis und in anderen Schriften der Nag Hammadi-Bibliothek* (Leiden 1984), 151.

lich, jene, die im Brautgemach vereinigt sind, werden nicht länger getrennt sein. Darum doch wurde Eva von Adam getrennt, weil sie sich nicht mit ihm im Brautgemach vereinigt hatte."

p. 70,32: Unsicher durch Lakune.

p. 71,9–10: Es wird im Kontext ausgesagt (p. 71,5–16), daß der Vater des Alls sich mit der Jungfrau (= dem Heiligen Geist) als der Frau vereinigte: "Er (wohl der Vater) erschien im *großen Brautgemach.* Sein Leib (= des Sohnes) entstand an dem Tage und er ging aus dem Brautgemach."

p. 71,16: "Es ziemt jedem der Jünger in seine Ruhe (*anapausis*) hineinzugehen." Wir haben es hier mit einem wichtigen Zusammenhang zu tun. Mit dem großen Brautgemach wird wohl das (valentinianisch-gnostische) Pleroma gemeint sein. Da entstand der Christus—Frucht der Zusammenarbeit aller Äonen—als Erlöser.[21]

Drittens *koitōn* (κοιτών in koptischer Schrift):

p. 82,14 (siehe oben): "die Braut, die als eine Buhldirne sich zeigt, wenn sie ihr Schlafzimmer (Brautgemach) verläßt." Es ist nicht unwichtig, daß in dieser Aussage nicht *nymphōn* (siehe oben), sondern ein anderes Wort gewählt wurde, eben *koitōn.*

p. 84,21: Hier wird das Brautgemach das "Heilige im Heiligen" genannt, das verborgen bleibt, während das Innere des Tempels durch das Reißen des Vorhanges offenbart (sichtbar) wurde. Das himmlische Brautgemach bleibt dem Demiurgen verborgen.

p. 85,20–21: Demgegenüber heißt es in bezug auf die Pneumatiker: "das Heiligste des Heiligen (das Allerheiligste) wurde offenbart und das Brautgemach lud uns ein." Für die Gnostiker/Pneumatiker ist jetzt schon in einer sakramentalen Vorwegnahme das Brautgemach im Pleroma zugänglich. Das Pleroma ruft die Gnostiker hinein. Am Ende der Schrift wird über das Zunichtemachen der Trennung gesprochen. Ein Beispiel wird sodann herbeigeführt. Wenn eine Heirat in der Nacht stattfindet, so muß jeder der in das Brautgemach hineingeht, das Licht anzünden."

p. 85,32: Die Mysterien der Gemeinde jedoch finden am hellen Tag statt und demnach wird der Gnostiker als Sohn des Brautgemachs (p. 86,5 siehe oben) das Licht erhalten.

---

[21] Vgl. E. Pagels, "Adam and Eve, Christ and the Church. A Survey of Second Century Controversies Concerning Marriage," in: A. H. B. Logan & A. J. M. Wedderburn, *The New Testament and Gnosis,* Festschrift R. McL. Wilson (Edinburgh 1983), 164.

Auffallend ist, daß die drei griechischen Lehnwörter gewisser-
massen über Anfang, Mitte und Ende der Schrift verteilt sind.
Doch hat *nymphōn* den mehr geweihten Klang. Wie dem auch sei,
es kann festgestellt werden, daß in den fünf Sakramenten oder aber
sakramentalen Riten das eschatologische Heil der Wiedervereini-
gung im Pleroma (dem wahren Brautgemach) antizipiert wird.[22]
Auch ist bemerkenswert, daß Taufe, Salbung und Brautgemach
miteinander verbunden sind, in dem Sinne, daß man der Aussage
Sevrins beipflichten könnte: "le baptême apparaît au moins
comme une réalisation de la 'chambre nuptiale en image'."[23]
Wenn wir nach dieser Auflistung subsumieren, kann festgestellt
werden, daß das Brautgemachsdeuten im *Philippusevangelium* völlig
in Einklang steht mit den bekannten valentinianisch-gnostischen
Aussagen (Prä-Nag Hammadi) über das Brautgemach, laut Irenäus,
Adversus haereses I,7,1 und *Excerpta ex Theodoto*, Kapitel 63–65.[24]
Ebenfalls in der valentinianisch-gnostischen Tradition steht der
Tractatus Tripartitus (NHC, I). Dort wird p. 122,15–16 über das
Brautgemach (*ma ᵉnscheleet*) ausgesagt, es sei für die Auserwählten
(= Pneumatiker), um ihre Einheit mit dem Erlöser zu erleben. Die
Psychiker freuen sich über das Brautgemach, p. 122,21–22, und
das gute Geschick der Pneumatiker. Diese Passage stimmt mit
Excerpta ex Theodoto, 65 vollends überein. Sehr wichtig für unsere
Untersuchung ist p. 128,19–129,16, wo die Taufe acht Namen
bekommt. Der vierte Name ist eben "Brautgemach" (*ma ᵉnscheleet*).
In der Einführung zum zweiten Teil des *Tractatus Tripartitus* haben
die Herausgeber (in diesem Fall war J. Zandee federführend)
richtig bemerkt: "Ici, le fait que le baptême s'appelle 'chambre
nuptiale' doit s'entendre ainsi: c'est déjà au baptême que l'on reçoit
la connaissance et que l'on s'unit au Christ."[25] Auch hier findet sich
der Gedanke des Antizipierens. In p. 135,31—die Stelle ist sehr
schlecht erhalten geblieben—ist vom Brautgemach (nur *eleet* ist zu
lesen) der Pneumatiker (der Auserwählten) die Rede. In den
letzten Zeilen des Traktates wird die Erlösung im Eschaton beschrieben. Nur von den Auserwählten wird gesprochen. In p.
140,9–10 wird das Brautgemach des Vaters im "schönen Osten"

---

[22] Vgl. Sevrin, *Noces*, 188–189.

[23] Vgl. Sevrin, *Noces*, 191.

[24] Vgl. F. M. M. Sagnard, *La gnose valentinienne et le témoignage de Saint Irénée*
(Paris 1947), 46, 414, 417, 419; id., *Extraits de Théodote*, SC 23 (Paris 1970), 184–
189; dazu Sagnard, *Gnose*, 535–536. Vgl. übrigens Helderman, *Anapausis*, 294–
295 (Anm. 99 auf S.328 ist zu streichen).

[25] Vgl. R. Kasser u.a., *Tractatus Tripartitus*. Pars II und III (Bern 1975), 24.

(p. 140,8–9) lokalisiert. Der Traktat wird abgeschlossen mit einer liturgischen Lobpreisung (p. 140,17–25).

Weitere Stellen folgen nun. In der *Exegese über die Seele* (NHC,II) wird die Bekehrung und Erlösung der Seele (als eine Frau, eine Braut vorgestellt) beschrieben.[26] Sie reinigt sich im Brautgemach (*ma ᵉnscheleet*), das sich mit schönen Düften füllt, p. 132,14. Folglich kommt der Bräutigam (der gnostische Erlöser) herab zu ihr im Brautgemach (*ma ᵉnscheleet*), das er schmückt, p. 132, 26.

Auf ähnliche Weise wie in der *Exegese über die Seele* wird das Los der auferweckten, geretteten Seele in der *Authentischen Lehre* (NHC,VI) geschildert. Die Schrift endet folgendermaßen (p. 35,8–11 und 16–18): Sie (die Seele) fand ihren Aufstieg (*anatolè*), sie ruhte in Ihm, der ruht. Sie lehnte sich im Brautgemach (*ma ᵉnscheleet*, p. 35,11)... "Sie erhielt Ruhe von ihren Mühen, während das Licht, das auf sie strahlt, nicht untergeht." Auch wieder ein liturgisches Ende mit der Lobpreisung hier des Lichtes.

Im *Zweiten Logos des großen Seth* (NHC,VII), bekannt durch das Auslachen des Demiurgen durch Christus, der neben dem Kreuz steht, während Simon von Kyrene gekreuzigt wird, begegnet einem das Brautgemach ebenfalls und zwar p. 57,17 (hier mit *pastos*). Da wird das neue und vollkommene Brautgemach des Himmels in einer neuen Heirat dem Christ auf Erden zuteil, der sich mit seiner himmlischen "Hälfte", seinem Zwilling im Brautgemach vereinigt.[27] Das *Heiratskleid*, p. 57,14–15, erinnert an das Lied von der Perle in den *Thomasakten*. Selbstverständlich fällt den Gnostikern dasselbe Heil der Vereinigung zu. Der Traktat endet eindrucksvoll mit den Worten: "Ruhet dann mit Mir, meine Freunde des Geistes und meine Brüder für immerda" (p. 70, 8–10). In den *Lehren des Silvanus* (NHC,VII) schließlich haben wir es mit einer nicht-gnostischen Schrift zu tun. Sie ist eine hellenistische christliche Weisheitsschrift und atmet den Geist der gebildeten Christen in Alexandria. Das Brautgemach (*nymphōn*) begegnet einem hier (p. 94,28) in einem Zusammenhang, wo die Seele als der noetischen Welt entstammend charakterisiert wird: das ist lupenreiner Mittelplatonismus.[28] Demnach heißt es p. 94,25–29: "Als du in eine leibliche Geburt hineinkamst, wurdest du erzeugt. Du entstandst innerhalb des Brautgemachs und du bist erleuchtet

---

[26] Vgl. über das Arteigene der Exegese der Seele, Robinson, *Library*, 190.

[27] Vgl. B. A. Pearson, *Nag Hammadi Codex VII*, NHS 30 (Leiden 1996), 168–169. Anm. zu p. 57,17.

[28] Vgl. Robinson, *Library*, 379–381.

im *Nus* (Verstand)." Die Seele entstammt dem himmlischen Brautgemach.[29]

Wichtig ist hier die Verbindung mit der Erleuchtung. Der φωτισμός wurde schon früh terminus technicus für die Taufe, so bei Justinus Martyr und bei Clemens.[30] In den *Lehren des Silvanus* könnte gleichfalls die Taufe gemeint sein. Bei diesem Rundgang durch die Nag Hammadi Bibliothek lassen wir es bewenden.[31]

Fazit dieser Musterung ist, daß in den gnostischen Texten das Brautgemach (Ort der Vereinigung mit der pleromatischen Welt) in Zusammenhang gebracht wird mit der Taufe, dem Heilsgut der Ruhe, dem Licht und den schönen Düften.

Aus Raumgründen können wir die Manichaeica nicht an und für sich behandeln, nur seien in exemplarischem Sinne einige treffliche Stellen aufgeführt. In den *Psalmen zu Jesus*, Ps 253,1–2, heißt es: "Christus, mein Bräutigam hat mich zu seinem Brautgemach (*ma ᵉnscheleet*) genommen. Ich habe mit Ihm im Lande der Unsterblichen geruht."[32] So spricht der gläubige Manichäer. In Ps 263,1–3 erfährt man: "Laß mich Deinen Brautgemächern, die (voller) Licht sind, wert sein. Jesus Christus empfange mich in deinen Brautgemächern" (beidemal *ma ᵉnscheleet*).[33] In den *Psalmen von Herakleides* wird Ps 281,31–32 so abgeschlossen: "Glorie sei Dir, mein wahrer Bräutigam, Christus der Brautgemächer (*ma ᵉnscheleet*) des Lichtes, und allen seinen heiligen Auserwählten."[34] In einem (unnumerierten) Herakleidespsalm wird am Ende ausgerufen (lasset uns nicht schlafen bis der Herr uns hinüber bringt...) "während er das Kleid seiner Glorie trägt und wir hineingehen in das Brautgemach (*ma ᵉnscheleet*) und wir alle mit Ihm herrschen."[35] Anderenorts in den Herakleidespsalmen ruft der Gläubige aus:

---

[29] Der verdiente Zandee hat sich für lange Zeit mit dieser Schrift befaßt. Vgl. zur obigen Stelle J. Zandee, *"The Teachings of Silvanus" and Clement of Alexandria. A New Document of Alexandrian Theology* (Leiden 1977,) 52–53 (Parallelstellen aus Clemens) und id., *The Teachings of Sylvanus* (sic!) *(Nag Hammadi Codex VII,4)* (Leiden 1991), 204–208 (Parallelstellen aus Origenes und Justinus Martyr).

[30] Vgl. H. Conzelmann s.v. φῶς, *ThWbNT* IX, 349, und Zandee, *Teachings and Clement*, 53.

[31] V. Arnold-Döben, *Die Bildersprache der Gnosis* (Köln 1986) bietet 118–124 nichts Neues.

[32] Siehe C. R. C. Allberry, *A Manichaean Psalm-Book* Part II (Stuttgart 1938), 63, Z.3.

[33] Allberry, *Psalm-Book*, 79, Z.15.

[34] Allberry, *Psalm-Book*, 102, Z.32.

[35] Allberry, *Psalm-Book*, 193, Z.11.

"Ich werde wohnen in Deinen Äonen, Deinen Brautgemächern des Lichtes" (mit *ma ᵉnscheleet*).[36]

II. Kommentar zu den drei Stellen

1. TE Logion 75

Vor dem Hintergrund der oben aufgeführten Stellen aus gnostischen Schriften ist die Aussage über die Einsamen, die ins Brautgemach hineingehen werden, vollends verständlich. Dies ist nämlich ein regelrechtes gnostisches Logion. Es geht hier um die Einheit, die Vereinigung mit dem Erlöser, mit dem himmlischen Selbst.[37] Die Einsamen haben erst einmal die sexuelle Verschiedenheit (Mann und Frau) als eine abscheuliche Hemmung oder aber eine *Entzweiung* überstiegen. Sie sind nur an ihrer Vereinigung mit ihrer ursprünglichen "Heimat," dem Lichtreich interessiert. Sie werden dort hineingehen. Sie gehören nicht zu den bei der Tür Zögernden, die zwar am geistigen Leben interessiert sind, aber noch voll an der hiesigen Welt haften. Die Einsamen sind Asketiker, ihr syrischer Name *ihidaja* kennzeichnet sie. Crossan hat Recht, wenn er sagt: "In all of this, Thomas is profoundly basic to the traditions of sexual ascetism in eastern Syria just as later it would fit well within the Pachomian monastic movement in Upper Egypt."[38]

2. TE Logion 104

Wie anfangs schon darauf hingewiesen wurde, daß Logion 104 auf eine Fastenfrage der Jünger Jesu in den Evangelien Bezug nimmt, diese Frage jedoch erweitert wird mit einer Aussage Jesu über seine Sündlosigkeit, erhebt sich nunmehr die Frage, wie dieses Logion qua talis zu verstehen sei. Vor allem ist deutlich, daß der Verfasser das Fasten abweist. Das tat er zuvor bereits in Log 6 und 14. Für Gnostiker, die schon im Brautgemach sind, ist das Fasten und

---

[36] Allberry, *Psalm-Book*, 197, Z. 5. Vgl. für weiteres A. F. J. Klijn, *The Acts of Thomas*, NovT.S 5 (Leiden 1962), 173, und Arnold-Döben, *Die Bildersprache des Manichäismus* (Köln 1978), 78–85. Auch im neuen Manichaeica-Fund in der Dakhle-Oase (Kellis) begegnet uns der Ausdruck "Brautgemach," vgl. I. Gardner, "A Manichaean Liturgical Codex Found at Kellis," *Orientalia* 62 (1993), 40 und 49.

[37] Vgl. Quispel, *Makarius*, 26–27; K. Koschorke, *Die Polemik der Gnostiker gegen das kirchliche Christentum*, NHS 12 (Leiden 1978), 62–63 und M. Fieger, *Das Thomasevangelium. Einleitung, Kommentar und Systematik* (Münster 1991), 208–209.

[38] Vgl. J. D. Crossan, *Four Other Gospels* (Minneapolis [Minnesota] 1985), 34.

Beten völlig nutzlos und irrelevant. Die Erweiterung über die Sündlosigkeit entstammt dem *Nazoräerevangelium*.[39] Das Logion dürfte sich damit gegen die Gegner der Thomasgemeinde[40] gewandt haben, die das Abweisen des Fastens/Betens kritisierten und die Sündlosigkeit Jesu angezweifelt hatten. Die Kritik scheint somit aus jüdisch-christlichen Kreisen hervorgekommen zu sein. Mag der Kern des Logions die Kritik am Fasten/ Beten gewesen sein, schwieriger ist die kurze Aussage über das aus dem Brautgemach Weggehen zu verstehen. In den synoptischen Evangelien ist erst einmal vom Wegnehmen des Bräutigams die Rede. Damit dürfte das Leiden Christi angedeutet gewesen sein. Bis dahin sollten die Jünger froh sein, weil ihr Herr noch bei ihnen ist. Im Logion jedoch fällt einem das fast majestätisch anmutende Weggehen aus dem Brautgemach auf. *Verläßt* der Erlöser das Brautgemach, d.h. das Pleroma? Aber wohin und warum? Im Gleichnis der zehn Jungfrauen (Mt 25:10) gehen die klugen Jungfrauen mit dem Bräutigam hinein in das Brautgemach und die Tür bleibt für die fünf törichten Jungfrauen verschlossen. Hier verläßt der Bräutigam das Brautgemach. Die Lösung könnte sein, daß es sich hier um einen gnostischen Urteilsspruch handelt. Am Ende der irdischen Geschichte werden die Törichten, die nicht zur Erkenntnis Aufgewachten im Urteil nicht bestehen können. Wie Christus als Sohn des Menschen die himmlische Herrlichkeit verlassen wird um zu urteilen, so wird der "gnostische Jesus" auch seine pleromatische Herrlichkeit (das Brautgemach) verlassen um zu urteilen. Dabei bliebe das *wachet* (γρηγορεῖτε), Mt 25:13, vollends gelten. Denn der Gnostiker ist durch die Erkenntnis aufgewacht und er bleibt weiterhin wach. Die Psychiker jedoch, die nach langem Zögern für das falsche irdische Leben gewählt haben, und die Hyliker werden im Eschaton zunichte gemacht werden. Die Psychiker dahingegen, die das Gesetz befolgt und sich als treue Menschen bewährt haben, werden an jenem Tage am besten fasten und beten.[41] Im *Tractatus Tripartitus* (NHC I) wird das Eschaton deutlich auf der letzten Seite dargestellt: "…Engel …bei einem Lauten der Trompete" (p. 140,4–6). Übrigens ist den Gnostikern nicht das Futurum an sich wichtig, sondern das

---

[39] Vgl. Klijn, *Gospel Tradition*, 102–104.

[40] So Fieger, *Thomasevangelium*, 261.

[41] Vgl. J. Zandee, "Gnostic Ideas on the Fall and Salvation," *Numen* 11 (1964), 49 und 51–52. Im *Tractatus Tripartitus* heißt es von den Hylikern: "sie bleiben bis zum Ende (übrig) für (ihre) Zerstörung," p.139, Z. 7–8, vgl. Kasser, *Tractatus*, 30.

Präsens. Durch ihre Erkenntnis genießen sie jetzt schon antizipierenderweise das Heil (im Brautgemach sich befindend). Burkitt hat in diesem Zusammenhang eine wichtige Beobachtung gemacht:

> the view...is that the prime factor in the rise of the Gnostic systems is connected with what is commonly now called Eschatology, that is to say, the problem raised for the Christian Church by the non-arrival of the Last Day and of the confidently expected Second Coming of Christ.[42]

Es ist in der Tat durchaus möglich, daß die sog. Parusieverzögerung ein bestimmendes Element war für die Entstehung des Gnostizismus (vielleicht schon am Ende des ersten Jahrhunderts[?]).

3. Dial *p. 138,14–20*.

Dieses Herrenwort ist die Antwort Jesu auf die Aussage des Judas gleich zuvor (D. 138,11–14), es seien die Herrscher (*archōn*), die über sie, die Jünger (Gnostiker), herrschen würden. Darauf respondiert der Herr, gerade das Umgekehrte sei der Fall. Es sind *sie* (die Jünger, Maria, Matthäus, Judas an erster Stelle), die über die Archonten herrschen werden. Das ist eine hundertprozentige gnostische Aussage. Unumgänglich aber ist, daß sie sich als vollendete Gnostiker (Pneumatiker) bewähren. Das bedeutet dem Wort des Herrn nach, daß sie den Neid (*phtonos*) überwinden müssen.

Diese Aufforderung findet sich ebenfalls in p. 146,22 in einem schlecht erhalten gebliebenen Herrenwort. Nun war die Neidlosigkeit (ἀφθονία, *m^entaphthonos*) den Gnostikern sehr wichtig. Sie war eine Grundeigenschaft des Vaters. Er erteilt seine Heilsgaben zur Erkenntnis freigebig.[43] Vor allem weiland van Unnik ist diesem Thema in seinen Untersuchungen tiefgründig nachgegangen.[44] So ergibt sich, daß in den *Oden Salomos* die Neidlosigkeit Gottes siebenmal ausführlich zur Sprache kommt. Dasselbe gilt dem

---

[42] Vgl. F. C. Burkitt, *Church & Gnosis. A Study of Christian Thought and Speculation in the Second Century* (Cambridge 1932), 10.

[43] Vgl. Helderman, *Anapausis*, 182 und 223.

[44] Vgl. W. C. van Unnik, "ΑΦΘΟΝΩΣ ΜΕΤΑΔΙΔΩΜΙ" (Brüssel 1971); id., *De ἀφθονία van God in de oudchristelijke literatuur* (Amsterdam 1973), und Th. Nikolaou, *Der Neid bei Johannes Chrysostomus unter Berücksichtigung der griechischen Philosophie* (Bonn 1969).

Philo. Nun werden bekanntlich die Oden wohl Lieder der Ruhe genannt, weil die Ruhe (syr. n^{e}jacha', gr. ἀνάπαυσις) hier öfters begegnet.[45] So z.B. Ode 3,5–6: "und wo seine Ruhe ist, bin auch ich...weil es kein Neid gibt bei dem Herrn, dem höchsten und barmherzigen." Es fällt auf, daß die Neidlosigkeit in dem bisherigen von van Unnik untersuchten Material nur mit Gott in Verbinding gebracht wird und daß demnach "dit motief niet in een paraenetisch verband functioneert."[46] Das ist durch *Dial* nicht länger der Fall. Eigentlich ist das vom gnostischen Blickpunkt her selbstredend: wie der Vater so seine Kinder. Wo nun der Vater neidlos ist, so müssen seine Kinder es eben auch sein. Daß die Jünger im *Dial* erfahren, es gebe keine Mächte, keine Archonten, die sie beherrschen würden, ist eine deutliche Aussage angesichts der Tatsache, daß die Gnostiker "ein Geschlecht sind, über die es kein Königtum gibt (*t^e genea ete m^{e}n m^{e}nt^{e}rro hidzjos*).[47] Die Gnostiker sind die Königlosen, die ἀβασιλευτοί.[48] Der Ausdruck "königlos" war eine der vielen Selbstbezeichnungen der Gnostiker.[49] Es sind gerade die "Königlosen" (= Pneumatiker), die keinem König oder Herrscher dieser Welt oder den Archonten unterstehen; welche als Könige in dieser archontischen Welt urteilen und weiterhin herrschen werden. Das wird klarstens beschrieben im *Ursprung der Welt* (NHC II) p. 125,6–14, wo die Erkennenden, die Pneumatiker die höchste Menschenart bilden als "Königlose" (*at ^{e}rro*) und "Vollendete." Sie werden in den heiligen Ort ihrer Väter hineingehen und sie werden ruhen (*^{e}mton*) in einer Ruhe (*anapausis*)...(sie sind unsterbliche Könige); "sie werden die Götter des Chaos und ihre Kräfte aburteilen."[50] Man sieht hier, wie Ruhen und Herrschen eng miteinander verbunden sind oder miteinander alternieren können. Man braucht nur nochmals auf *TE* Logion 2

---

[45] Vgl. T. Baarda, "Het uitbreiden van mijn handen is zijn teken! Enkele notities bij de gebedshouding in de Oden van Salomo," in: *Loven en Geloven*, Festschrift N. H. Ridderbos (Amsterdam 1975), 249 (nach Holstijn).

[46] Vgl. Van Unnik, *De ἀφθονία*, 49.

[47] So lautet *Sophia Jesu Christi* (NHC III) p. 99,18–19 (nach *Facsimile Edition of the Nag Hammadi Codices. Codex III* (Leiden 1976).

[48] Vgl. M. A. Williams, *The Immovable Race. A Gnostic Designation and the Theme of Stability in Late Antiquity*, NHS 29 (Leiden 1985) 154 (zu SJC p. 99,17–19). Vgl. schon Helderman, *Anapausis*, 211 Anm. 759. Vgl. noch Williams, 174 (zu Hippolytus, *Refutatio omnium haeresium* 5.8,1–2).

[49] Vgl. F. Siegert, "Selbstbezeichnungen der Gnostiker in den Nag Hammadi-Texten", *ZNW* 71 (1980), 129–132.

[50] Vgl. Layton, *Nag Hammadi Codex II*, 86.

hinzuweisen, wo Herrschen und Ruhen die letzte Stufe in der *ordo salutis* sind. Weil wir uns anderenorts ausführlich mit diesen beiden Themen befaßt haben,[51] lassen wir es hierbei bewenden.

Die letzte Stufe des gnostischen Heils wird in *Dial* schließlich folgendermaßen formuliert: "ihr werdet euch in Licht kleiden und hineingehen ins Brautgemach."

Oben erkannten wir den engen Zusammenhang von *Brautgemach* und *Licht* in den Manichäica. Es darf deswegen keinen wundern, daß in den *Acta Thomae* (so beliebt bei den Manichäern) diese Verbindung gleichfalls gelegt wird. Und zwar im Hochzeitslied des Thomas, Kapitel 7, in dem er das Brautgemach so beschreibt: "Ihr Brautgemach ist Licht, duftend nach Balsam und verschiedenem Räucherwerk"(ἧς ἡ παστὸς φωτεινός, ἀποφορὰν ἀπὸ βαλσάμου καὶ παντὸς ἀρώματος διαπνέων).[52] Der syrische Text lautet: " *bēt genunah nahir wᵉ richa dᵉpurqana melē*" (Ihr Brautgemach ist erleuchtet und erfüllt mit dem Duft der Rettung).[53] Auch hier das duftende Brautgemach wie oben bei der *Exegese der Seele*. Weit wichtiger als auf die Parallelstellen ist es, acht zu geben auf den Unterschied zwischen dem griechischen und dem syrischen Text. Dazu bemerkt Klijn: "The difference is that in syr. the baptistery is described and in gr. the heavenly world."[54] Nicht richtig ist Klijns Verweis auf Irenäus *Adversus haereses* I,13,3 für die Gleichsetzung Brautgemach-Taufe. Es handelt sich ebenda überhaupt nicht um die Taufe, sondern um eine freie Invokationsformel der valen-

---

[51] Vgl. J. Helderman, "Anapausis in the Epistula Jacobi Apocrypha", in: R. McL. Wilson, *Nag Hammadi and Gnosis*, 91–92, und id., *Anapausis*, 283. 313–317. H. W. Attridge, *Nag Hammadi Codex I (The Jung Codex) Notes*, NHS 23 (Leiden 1985), 12, weist zu *EpJac* 3,27 hin auf *Acta Thomae* 136, wo es im Wort des Thomas zu Tertia (in der elften Tat) heißt: "καὶ οἱ ἀξίως μεταλαμβάνοντες τῶν ἐκεῖ ἀγαθῶν ἀναπαύονται καὶ ἀναπαυόμενοι βασιλεύουσιν" (M. Bonnet, *Acta Apostolorum Apocrypha*, Vol.II [Leipzig 1903; Neudruck 1959], 243).

[52] Vgl. Bonnet, *Acta*, Vol.II, 109. M. Marcovich, *Studies in Graeco-Roman Religions and Gnosticism* (Leiden 1988), 158, hat seltsamerweise ὁποβαλσάμου statt ἀπὸ βαλσάμου. Vgl. zu *Acta Thomae* 12 noch Marcovich, 165.

[53] Den syrischen Text findet man bei W. Wright, *Apocryphal Acts of the Apostles* (London 1871 [Neudruck 1968]), syr. pag. *qoph- ayin-wau* (= 176), Z. 21–22.

[54] Vgl. Klijn, *Acts* 24, 172. Interessanterweise wird in *Acta Thomae*, 26, vom Siegel (für Taufe und Salbung) gesprochen, vgl. Klijn, 56–57.

tinianisch-gnostischen Markosier in Bezug auf die Vereinigung des Gnostikers mit seinem Engel im Pleroma.[55]

Immerhin sind, wie wir oben vor allem im Hinblick auf das *Philippusevangelium*[56] feststellen konnten, in gnostischen Texten die Taufe und das Brautgemach aufeinander bezogen.

III. Das Brautgemach, die Taufe und die Furt zum ewigen Leben

Die Brautgemachstelle im *Dial* wurde oben untersucht. Wichtig ist zu sehen, daß auch die Taufe im *Dial* vorkommt. Und zwar p. 134,5–8: "Wenn einer nicht erst das Wasser versteht, weiß er nichts. Denn was ist der Nutzen, daß er darin (= im Wasser, H.) getauft wird (*etrefdzjibaptisma*)?"

Diese Aussage ist völlig in Einklang mit dem valentinianisch-gnostischen Denken, vgl. *Excerpta ex Theodoto* 78, den locus classicus der Gnosis schlechthin. *Vor* der überaus bekannten Formel ("Wer waren wir? Was sind wir geworden? Wo waren wir? Wohinein sind wir geworfen? Wohin eilen wir? Wovon sind wir befreit? Was ist Geburt? Was ist Wiedergeburt?"), heißt es dort: "Nicht allein das Bad (λουτρόν) macht uns frei, sondern auch die Erkenntnis (γνῶσις); dann folgt die Formel.[57]

Nun kommt auch anderenorts die Taufe im *Dial* zur Sprache und zwar gleich am Anfang p. 120–124. Diese Seiten des MS stammen vom Verfasser, der im Dialog in der jetzt vorliegenden Form verschiedenes altes Traditionsgut verwendet.[58]

Der Anfang des *Dial* ist eine Initiation (die Taufe) und das Heilsgut der Ruhe (*anapausis*) wird vom Erlöser versprochen. Vielsagend ist, daß in diesem Abschnitt sich die Erwählten und die Einsamen[59] begegnen. Die Einsamen (*monachoi*), die in Logion 75

---

[55] Vgl. Klijn, *Acts*, 173. Ebd. muß im griechischen Text das fehlerhafte καθέδρουν geändert werden in καθίδρυσον. Vgl. dazu Marcovich, *Studies*, 167, und Sagnard, *Gnose*, 417.

[56] Vgl. *Philippusevangelium*, in Layton, *Nag Hammadi Codex II,2-7* (Leiden 1989), p. 69, Z. 25–27.

[57] Vgl. Sagnard, *Extraits*, 202. Vgl. zur Taufformel Emmel, *Dialogue*, 12–13.

[58] *Dial* hat eine komplizierte Entstehungsgeschichte und einen durchdachten Aufbau. Vgl. zum letztgenannten Emmel, *Dialogue*, 2–16. Zum erstgenannten vgl. Robinson, *Library*, 244–246. Zum Schluß heißt es 246: "The Dialogue of the Savior cannot be understood as the simple product of gnostic theology. Rather, it resembles the Gospel of John in its attempt to reinterpret the sayings of Jesus in the horizon of gnostic thought."

[59] Vgl. dazu Zandee, "Gnostic Ideas," 45–47.

TE im Brautgemach sind, hören im *Dial*, p. 120,23–p. 121,1, folgende Heilszusage: "Als Ich (= der Erlöser) aber kam, öffnete Ich den Weg und lehrte sie über den Durchgang, die Furt (*diabasis*), die die Erwählten und die Einsamen (*monachoi*) durchschreiten werden, (sie) die den Vater erkannt haben."[60] Auch p. 123,23–p. 124,1 findet sich die Furt, "the crossing place" (*pma* *ᵉndzjioor*).[61]

Das Wasser der Taufe wird augenscheinlich mit dem Tod, dem Hinübergehen in die himmlische Welt, verbunden, wie man das auch bei Paulus findet (Rom 6:3–11).[62] Den Tod findet man p. 122,3 in einem Zusammenhang, der von den Mächten der Finsternis handelt, die die Initianten, die Täuflinge, bedrohen, im Ausdruck: zur Zeit "der Auflösung" (*ᵉmpbōl ebol*). Das Heil für die Täuflinge ist, daß sie hinübergehen werden zur Welt des Vaters, wo sie herstammen, vgl. *TE* Logien 18 und 49. Vielleicht wird das Durchschreiten, das Hinübergehen noch in *TE* Logion 42 (im kürzesten Logion) angesprochen: "Werdet Vorübergehende" (*schōpᵉ etetᵉn ᵉr parage*)[63]

Eine glänzende Parallele zur διάβασις, zur Furt/"crossing place," wurde bei Aphrem (Ephrem) Syrus (306–373) gefunden in dessen *Prosa-Refutationen des Mani*.[64] In einem Abschnitt, in dem Aphrem die Lehre Bardaisans bekämpft, heißt es, daß durch den Tod Adams die Seelen bei der Furt/"crossing-place" (*maᶜbarta*) behindert wurden. Der Herr hat jedoch das Leben gebracht und die Seelen in das Königreich hinübergeführt. Unser Herr (so sagt Bardaisan) hat gelehrt (folgt Joh 8:51: "So jemand mein Wort wird

---

[60] Vgl. Emmel, *Dialogue*, 10.

[61] Vgl. Emmel, *Dialogue*, 48–49. Vgl. für das koptische *dzjioor* (= διάβασις) W. E. Crum, *A Coptic Dictionary* (Oxford 1939), 82b. Vgl. auch die Übersetzung und Anmerkungen von B. Blatz, in: W. Schneemelcher, *Neutestamentliche Apokryphen*, Vol. I (Tübingen 1987⁵), 248 (mit: Durchgang und Durchquerung).

[62] Vgl. Emmel, *Dialogue*, 13 und Robinson, *Library*, 245.

[63] R. Kasser möchte das *parage* als παρέρχεσθαι verstehen, vgl. alle Angaben bei T. Baarda, "Jesus said: Be Passers-by. On the Meaning and Origin of Logion 42 of the Gospel of Thomas," in: ders., *Early Transmission of Words of Jesus*, edd. J. Helderman/S. J. Noorda (Amsterdam 1983), 179–205, dort 192–193. Im *Zweiten Logos des großen Seth* (NHC VII) bedeutet *parage* p. 56,28 und 58,10 in einem ähnlichen Kontext unmißverständlich "vorübergehen" ("pass by").

[64] C. W. Mitchell, *S. Ephraem's Prose Refutations of Mani, Marcion and Bardaisan*, Vol. I (London 1912), Vol. II, postum herausgegeben von A. A. Bevan und F. C. Burkitt (London 1921). Die englische Übersetzung "cross, crossing-place" wird beigefügt, weil sie in der Diskussion eine wichtige Rolle spielte.

halten, der wird den Tod nicht sehen ewiglich"), daß "dessen Seele nicht gehindert wird, wenn sie durchschreitet die Furt" (when it crosses at the crossing-place): *maʼda baraʼ ʼal maʼbartaʼ*.[65] Auf derselben Folioseite der *Refutatio* Aphrems wird deutlich, daß die Furt (crossing-place) und das Brautgemach des Lichtes (*gᵉnōn nawhᵉraʼ*)[66] eng miteinander verbunden sind. Abgesehen davon, ob Aphrem die Lehren Bardaisans gut wiedergegeben hat,[67] gilt es zu bedenken, daß wir mit Bardaisan in der frühen Zeit (Bardaisan lebte 154–214) des syrischen Christentums angelangt sind. Dieselbe Zeit wie *Dial*, der seinerseits auf *TE* aufbaut! Die Datierung von *TE* und *Dial* führt uns ins zweite Jahrhundert. Ebenfalls wird die Urschrift des *Kindheitsevangeliums des Pseudo-Thomas* im zweiten Jahrhundert angesetzt.[68] In der syrischen Version (Göttinger MS) des *Kindheitsevangeliums* erfahren wir, daß der kleine Jesus an einer Furt (*maʼbarta*) eines Baches spielt.[69] Es bestehen gute Gründe dafür, das Quellgebiet der im Pseudo-Thomas vorgefundenen Traditionen in Syrien zu suchen.

---

[65] Siehe Mitchell, *S. Ephraim's Refutations*, Vol. II, 164 (syr. Text, Fol.86ᵇ Kap. LXXXII–LXXXIII und LXXVII (Übersetzung), vgl. H. J. W. Drijvers, *Bardaisan of Edessa* (Assen 1966), 155, wiederholt von Marcovich, *Studies*, 164. Für *maʼbarta* vgl. K. Brockelmann, *Lexicon Syriacum* (Halle 1928; Neudruck 1982), 508 s.v. Auch in *mandäischen* Texten findet man die Furt bzw. "the crossing place." So bei E. S. Drower, *Alf Trisar Suialia* (Buch der 1012 Fragen), I (Berlin 1960), Nr. 337: (Text S. 99; Übersetzung S. 272) *parwaqa mambarta de nisjmata*, "Erlöser und Furt (crossing place) der Seelen." Es handelt sich um eine Totenzeremonie, bei der ein erlösender Brief eine Rolle spielte. In II, Nr. 378 heißt es (Text S. 101–102; Übersetzung S. 279) *mambarta de bhiria zidqa*, "Die Furt (crossing-place) der auserwählten Gerechten."

[66] Siehe Mitchell, 164 (Kap. LXXXI) und 165 (Kap. LXXXV); LXXVII (Übersetzung), vgl. Drijvers aaO. Vgl. zu *gᵉnon* Brockelmann, *Lexicon*, 122ᵇ und zu *nawhᵉra*, 417ᵇ. Zu beachten ist, daß in der Liturgie der ostsyrischen Kirche das Brautgemach "geistig, nicht mit Händen gemacht, unvergänglich, Gemach des Lichtes, das Allerheiligste" genannt wird. Angabe bei Schmid, *RAC*, Vol. II, 527.

[67] Vgl. mit Recht Drijvers, *Bardaisan*, 154. Derzeit hat T. Jansma scharfe Kritik geübt an Drijvers Methode (T. Jansma, *Natuur, lot en vrijheid* [Wageningen 1969], 19–20, 68, 98 und 144).

[68] Vgl. O. Cullmann, "Kindheitsevangelien," in: Schneemelcher, *Apokryphen*, I, 349–353.

[69] Vgl. W. Baars und J. Helderman, "Neue Materialien zum Text und zur Interpretation des Kindheitsevangeliums des Pseudo-Thomas," *OrChr* 77 (1993), 205 (zum Göttinger syr. MS p.11, Z.2).

Nun hat derzeit Per Lundberg darauf hingewiesen, daß der Ursprungsort des Ruhegedankens wie sie im Gnostizismus sich voll entwickelte, in der Taufliturgie der Kirche zu suchen ist. Auch der Hafen als Metapher für die Geborgenheit durch die Taufe bei Gott ist wie die Ruhe (ἀνάπαυσις) mit der Taufpraxis zu verbinden. Er führt *Ode* 38,3–4 an, wo Hafen der Rettung und Ruhe Heilsgaben der Wahrheit sind. Genau diese beide Themen (Ankunft im Hafen, Ruhe) findet man im Festritual der syrischen Jakobiten wie auch der syrischen Nestorianer.[70] "En partant de cette interprétation cultuelle baptismale de la notion d'ἀνάπαυσις on peut aussi expliquer pourquoi l'eau baptismale a été appelée ὕδωρ ἀναπαύσεως dans certaines liturgies orientales. Comp. la liturgie grecque de l'Epiphanie, ἀνάδειξον τὸ ὕδωρ τοῦτο, ὕδωρ ἀναπαύσεως...ou aqua quietis dans une prière syrienne de consécration de l'eau...."[71] Lundberg liegt daran, die Ruhe in engster Beziehung zur Taufe zu bringen. Die Gnosis habe ihre Terminologie der Ruhe auf die der Kirche aufgebaut: "Il est manifeste que justement les termes cultuels ont été recueillis avec predilection par les gnostiques, qui les ont adaptés aux traits les plus caractéristiques de leur propre religion."[72] Auch Charlesworth pflichtet Bernard bei, als er feststellen möchte: "The clue to this is found in the fact that the baptismal waters were regarded as 'waters of rest' with allusion to Ps xxii (xxiii):2."[73] Auch die Metapher des Schiffes, das die Gläubigen sicher über das Meer des Todes in den Hafen bringt, gehört der Terminologie der Taufpraxis an.[74] Bei dem Meer des Todes ist man der διάβασις im *Dial* eingedenk. Bei all diesem sind die Oden dem Lundberg wichtig (vor allem *Ode* 38).[75] Für Aune sind die Oden Lobpreisungen und "of central

---

[70] Siehe P. Lundberg, *La typologie baptismale dans l'ancienne église* (Uppsala 1942), 78. Das Buch ist jetzt auch vermerkt worden in den Literaturnachträgen des *ThWbNT*, X, 2 S. 999. Durch die Kriegswirren fand Lundbergs Studie nicht die Beachtung, die sie verdiente.

[71] Vgl. Lundberg, *Typologie baptismale*, 83 Anm. 3.

[72] Vgl. Lundberg, *Typologie baptismale*, 83 (vgl. 98) und weiterhin 79–80, 81 Anm. 3 (Hebräerevangelium, vgl. Logion 2 *TE*).

[73] Vgl. J. H. Charlesworth, *The Odes of Solomon. The Syriac Texts* (Missoula [Montana] 1977), 20 Anm. 7 (zu Ode 3,5 vgl. Lundberg, *Typologie baptismale*, 84).

[74] Vgl. Lundberg, *Typologie baptismale*, 85. Wichtig ist 85–86 Anm. 3 mit Hinweis auf Isaak von Ninive (6. Jhdt), der spricht über das Schiff der Reue: (wenn das Ruder der Furcht nicht reguliert,) "in which we cross the ocean of this world unto God, we shall be drowned in the stinking ocean."

importance in the worship services of early Christian communities in Syria."[76]

IV. Kirchliche Christen und (christliche) Gnostiker

Die Gegebenheit, daß Lundberg mit Schwung an die Herkunft der "typologie baptismale" herangegangen ist, hat jedenfalls unseren Verstehenshorizont in bezug auf den Quellgrund der hier behandelten Metaphern erweitert, wenn er auch andererseits einer gewissen Einseitigkeit anheimgefallen ist.[77] So viel ist jedoch sicher, daß (christliche) Gnostiker und kirchliche Christen nicht in zwei voneinander getrennten Welten lebten, quasi durch wasserdichte Schotten voneinander getrennt. Vielmehr wirkten beide Bewegungen in derselben Umwelt der Antike und waren desselben Gedankenklimas teilhaftig. Damals hat van Unnik im Hinblick auf die Gotteslehre bei Aristides und in gnostischen Schriften eine artifizielle Trennung von "Kirche" und "Gnosis" abgewiesen und ihre Teilhaberschaft an derselben geistigen Kultursprache folgendermaßen betont: "Die Vertreter des Gnostizismus stehen mit ihrer Beschreibung des höchsten Gottes also nicht allein, sondern teilen ihre Anschauungen mit einem Mann, dessen Orthodoxie nicht angezweifelt wird."[78]

V. Zusammenfassend ließe sich feststellen, daß unsere "tour d'horizon" dazu geführt hat, daß die *ordo salutis* in Logion 2 *TE* eine nähere Ausfüllung und eine klarere Färbung bekommen hat. Die drei hier untersuchten gnostisch ausgerichteten Herrenworte[79] lehren uns, daß die Klimax der gnostischen Erlösungslehre im Sinne von *ordo salutis, Ruhe* und *Herrschen,* den folgenden zuteil werden wird: den Einsamen (*monachos*) und den Auserwählten. Die Pneumatiker also werden die Ruhe erfahren als eine Vereinigung mit dem Vater im Brautgemach. Dabei gilt es nicht zu zögern. Das

---

[75] Vgl. Lundberg, *Typologie baptismale*, 84 Anm. 2 (zu Ode 38), vgl. ebenfalls Charlesworth, *Odes*, 134 Anm. 16 und 17.

[76] Vgl. D. E. Aune, *The Cultic Setting of Realized Eschatology in Early Christianity* (Leiden, 1972), 193; vgl. 182.

[77] Das gilt der Hafenmetapher (vgl. L. Schlimme, "Hafen" *RAC*, Vol. XIII, 297–305), aber auch der Anapausis und dem Brautgemach.

[78] Vgl. W. C. van Unnik, "Die Gotteslehre bei Aristides und in gnostischen Schriften," *ThZ* 17 (1961), 171. Vgl. Helderman, *Anapausis*, 47–71 (Ruhe in der Umwelt des Gnostizismus).

[79] Vgl. Koester, *Gospels*, 124.

Heilsgut des Herrschens ist den neidlosen Königlosen, die keine
Herrschaft über sich anerkennen, bereitet. Den Hylikern und
Psychikern wird ein ganz anderes Los zugemessen. Den Zutritt zur
Seligkeit im Pleroma werden die Einsamen, Auserwählten, Königlosen mittels des Durchgangs, der Furt (diabasis, *ma'barta*) durch
das "Meer des Todes" erhalten. Dabei ist die Provenienz der
Metapher des Brautgemachs in diesem Zusammenhang der Furt
aus dem kirchlichen liturgischen Brauchtum der Taufe vor allem
im syrischen Raum deutlich erkennbar. Diesbezüglich erwiesen
die *Öden Salomos* sich als äußerst wichtig.[80]

---

[80] Vgl. Baarda, *Loven*, 255, wo er sagt: "Het zou op zichzelf de moeite waard
zijn om dit gegeven uitvoeriger te onderzoeken (nämlich die Verbindung von
Oden und Taufe, H.) dan Plooij in zijn studies heeft gedaan."

"THE FINGER OF GOD"
MISCELLANEOUS NOTES ON LUKE 11:20
AND ITS *UMWELT*

Pieter W. van der Horst
Utrecht University
(Utrecht, the Netherlands)

In the Q version of the Beelzebul controversy we find the following logion:

Lk. 11:20: εἰ δὲ ἐν δακτύλῳ θεοῦ [ἐγὼ] ἐκβάλλω τὰ δαιμόνια,
ἄρα ἔφθασεν ἐφ᾽ ὑμᾶς ἡ βασιλεία τοῦ θεοῦ.

Mt. 12:28: εἰ δὲ ἐν πνεύματι θεοῦ ἐγὼ ἐκβάλλω τὰ δαιμόνια,
ἄρα ἔφθασεν ἐφ᾽ ὑμᾶς ἡ βασιλεία τοῦ θεοῦ.

Apart from the disputed ἐγώ in Luke, the only difference between
these two versions of the logion is Luke's "finger" against Matthew's "spirit." There has been much debate about what may
have been the original reading in Q, each possibility having quite
a number of advocates, as a glance in the standard commentaries
will show.[1] It is not the purpose of this article to go into that
debate (although I am convinced that Luke's "finger" has a much
greater chance of being original than Matthew's "spirit"[2]). As a

---

[1] For two recent and balanced surveys of the various arguments see W. D.
Davies & D. C. Allison, *The Gospel According to Saint Matthew*, ICC, Vol. 2
(Edinburgh 1991), pp. 339–340, and J. Nolland, *Luke 9:21–18:34*, WBC 35b
(Dallas 1993), pp. 639–640. By far the best discussion of the two verses together
is now J. P. Meier, *A Marginal Jew. Rethinking the Historical Jesus,* Vol. II (New
York 1994), pp. 404–423 (with the notes at pp. 457–475, where all the relevant
literature can be found). I have not seen A. George, "Notes sur quelques traits
lucaniens de l'expression 'Par le doigt de Dieu' (Luc XI, 20)," in his *Études sur
l'oeuvre de Luc* (Paris 1978), pp. 128–132, neither could I consult S. V.
McCasland, *By the Finger of God* (New York 1951).

[2] For arguments see Meier, *Marginal Jew*, Vol. II, pp. 410–411; for a different
position (without arguments) see recently G. H. Twelftree, *Jesus the Exorcist. A
Contribution to the Study of the Historical Jesus* (Tübingen 1993), p. 108. Twelftree,
however, rightly concludes: "Jesus believed that while he was operating out of

matter of fact, for the meaning of the logion it does not make much difference whether "finger" or "spirit" is read since both mean God's power here (as does the much more common "hand of God").[3] What I wish to investigate here is what kind of associations the metaphor of the finger(s) of (the) god(s) evoked in the ancient world, among pagan Greeks and Romans as well as among Jews and Christians. As will be seen, this imagery was not a widespread one (in the NT this anthropomorphism never recurs), the idea of a god's hand(s) being much more current, but the "finger of God" did have some particular associations.

Let us begin with the material from the Jewish tradition, since this is likely to form the primary background of the Jesus logion. In the Hebrew Bible, the anthropomorphic expression "finger of God" occurs only in Ex. 8:15 (19), 31:18, Deut. 9:10, and in Ps. 8:4 (but here implicitly and in the plural). In Ex. 8:12–15 (16–19)[4] we find a description of the third plague that the Lord sends upon Egypt, the one of the gnats produced by Aaron's stretching out his hand with his staff and striking the dust of the earth. When the Pharaoh's magicians tried to ape the miracle—which they had successfully done in the two previous cases—and produce gnats as well, they failed and said: "This is the finger of God!" (or: the finger of a god, אֶצְבַּע אֱלֹהִים הִוא — LXX δάκτυλος θεοῦ ἐστιν τοῦτο[5]). This is probably no more than a case of *synecdoche* (or *pars*

---

his own resources, at the same time he believed that it was God who was to be seen as operative in his activity" (p. 165).

[3] As Davies & Allison, *Matthew*, p. 340, n. 35, point out, in 2 Kings 3:15 Targum Jonathan renders *yad YHWH* by the words "a spirit of prophecy from before the Lord" (see D. J. Harrington & A. J. Saldarini, *Targum Jonathan of the Former Prophets*, The Aramaic Bible 10, [Edinburgh 1987], p. 269 with n. 25); and Clement of Alexandria, *Stromateis* VI 16,133,1 (ed. Stählin-Früchtel, p. 499), says that God's finger is to be understood as his power (*dynamis*). In Ps. 8:4 the heavens are the work of God's fingers, whereas in Ps. 33:6 they are the work of his *ruah*. I. H. Marshall, *The Gospel of Luke* (Exeter 1978), p. 475 rightly remarks: "The meaning is the same in both versions." Meier, *Marginal Jew*, Vol. II, p. 463, n. 48: "Both 'finger of God' and 'spirit of God' designate the power of God in action." For alternation of "hand" and "fingers" (plur.) see *e.g.* Psalm 144:1 and Is. 17:8.

[4] The verse numbering in MT and LXX (8:15) is different from that in the Vulgate and many modern versions (8:19).

[5] On this LXX rendering see J. W. Wevers, *Notes on the Greek Text of Exodus* (Atlanta [Georgia] 1990), p. 115.

pro toto) indicating the power of God's hands or God himself.[6] There would seem to be a different nuance in the second and third instances, Ex. 31:18 and Deut. 9:10, where the reference is to the fact that God gave Moses the two tablets of the covenant which were "written with the finger of God" (כְּתֻבִים בְּאֶצְבַּע אֱלֹהִים — LXX γεγραμμένας [ἐν] τῷ δακτύλῳ τοῦ θεοῦ). Here, the expression serves to emphasize the divine origin and character of the commandments. Finally, in Ps. 8:4 it is said that the heavens are "the work of your fingers" (מַעֲשֵׂי אֶצְבְּעֹתֶיךָ — LXX ἔργα τῶν δακτύλων σου), referring to the creation and evidently implying that the heavens testify to God's power and greatness.[7] But this fourth passage differs from the previous ones in that only here the plural (fingers) is used, which can more easily be explained as an alternative for "hand." So in the first (and fourth) instance of the expression, it refers to God's ruling and creative power, in the second and third to his authority.

There can be little doubt that it is the first passage, Ex. 8:15(19), that largely determines the function of the expression in Luke 11:20, for there as well as here it is God's sovereignty over the powers of evil and his intervention on behalf of his people through a human agent that is at the foreground.[8] Forty years ago the French scholar Couroyer tried to demonstrate that Ex. 8:15(19) had an Egyptian background.[9] It is Egyptian magicians who speak these words in Exodus, and indeed the expression *ddb' ndtr* (finger of [a] god) occurs more often in Egyptian than in any other sources. Interestingly enough, as Couroyer observes, the expression "finger of [*name of a god*]" may designate a staff (or another wooden object) so that the word "this" (הוא — τοῦτο) in Ex. 8:15 probably does not refer to the miracle itself but to Aaron's staff. The Egyptian contexts in which this expression occurs, however, are only remotely parallel to the passage in Exodus, and it is for that reason that Couroyer's hypothesis has

---

[6] B. S. Childs, *Exodus* (London 1974), p. 129.

[7] H.-J. Krauss, *Die Psalmen*, BK XV/1 (Neukirchen 1961, reprinted 1972), p. 69: "D.h.: alles trägt die 'persönliche Note' des majestätischen Schaffens und Wirkens Gottes."

[8] R. W. Hall's theory that Luke 11:20 has to be read against the background of Deuteronomy 9:10 ("'The Finger of God': Deuteronomy 9:10 and Luke 11:20," *NTS* 33 [1987], pp. 144–150) has not convinced many exegetes, and rightly so.

[9] B. Couroyer, "Quelques égyptianismes dans l'Exode," *RB* 63 (1956), pp. 209–219; idem, "Le 'doigt de Dieu' (Exode VIII,15)," *RB* 63 (1956), pp. 481–495.

not attracted much support. Moreover, what we are interested in
here is not the background of the expression in Exodus, but in
Luke. Let us therefore first have a brief look at the 'Wirkungs-
geschichte' of these biblical passages in early Jewish sources.

One of the earliest Jewish writers to reflect upon the meaning
of God's finger is Philo of Alexandria.[10] In his *De Vita Mosis* I.112,
when speaking about the plague of the gnats, he deals with the
question of why God took such tiny creatures into his service
instead of more destructive ones: "For what is slighter than a
gnat? Yet so great was its power that all Egypt lost heart and was
forced to cry aloud, "This is the finger of God!"; for as for His
hand, all the inhabitable world from end to end could not stand
against it, or rather not even the whole universe" (transl. F. H.
Colson in *LCL*, slightly adapted). We see that God's finger is
connected, or rather correlated, by Philo with the tiny shape of
the gnats: just as the whole universe would have been destroyed
by God's hand, so Egypt is by his finger, namely the gnats. In this
intervention God uses only a small part of his power. In Philo's
De migratione Abrahami 85, however, we find a different interpretation. After having demonstrated that mastery of language is
needed by the sage in order to defeat the sophists, he illustrates
this from the case of Moses. Use of language in the service of
truth is shown by the story of Moses with Aaron's rod outdoing
the Egyptian magicians. Aaron's rod swallowing those of the
magicians means that all the arguments of the sophists were
devoured, "and the acknowledgement is made that these events
are the finger of God; and the word 'finger' is equivalent to a
divine rescript, declaring that sophistry is ever defeated by
wisdom; for holy writ, speaking of the tables on which the oracles
were engraved, says that they were written by the finger of God.
Therefore the sorcerers can no longer stand before Moses, but fall
as in a wrestling-bout vanquished by the sturdy strength of the
opponent" (transl. F. H. Colson & G. H. Whitaker in *LCL*). Here

---

[10] To be sure, as early as the second century B.C.E. the Jewish exegete and
philosopher Aristobulus (fr. 2, *ap.* Eusebius, *PE* VIII 10,7–9) devotes an
elaborate discussion to biblical anthropomorphisms and tries to demonstrate
that in biblical usage "hands" stands for "power." See the commentary by Carl
Holladay (*Fragments from Hellenistic Jewish Authors. Aristobulus*, Vol. III, TT 39
[TT.PS 13] [Atlanta (Georgia) 1995]). The expression "finger of God" does not
occur in the Dead Sea Scrolls, as I was kindly informed by Dr. F. García
Martínez. It is striking that in all the early forms of "rewritten Bible" this
expression is avoided (*Jubilees*, Pseudo-Philo's *LAB*, Josephus' *Ant.*).

we find an original combination of the two passages in Exodus where the expression "finger of God" occurs, or rather: Philo applies Ex. 31:18 to 8:15(19) in such a way that the following equation is constructed: written by the finger of God = Holy Writ = divine wisdom = ability to do away with the arguments of the sophists (= magicians). Here the finger of God in Ex. 8 is no longer correlated to the tiny gnats but to the two tablets of the Law, and, consequently, the whole story of the third plague is turned into an allegory about anti-sophistic argumentation on the basis of God's Word.

In the long version of *Joseph and Aseneth* we find the expression "finger of God" twice. In 15:12B, after having tried to get to know the name of the heavenly man who appeared to her, Aseneth receives the following answer: "Why do you seek this name of mine, Aseneth? My name is in the heavens in the book of the Most High, written by the finger of God in the beginning of the book, before all the others, because I am the chief of the house of the Most High." In view of the fact that in 15:4 the same heavenly man had already told Aseneth that her name "was written in the book of the living in heaven: in the beginning of the book, as the very first of all, your name was written by my finger," we may infer that it is the heavenly Book of the Living (or the Book of Life) that is here presented as having been written by the finger of God or his viceregent. (The second instance of the expression in *Jos. et As.* is dubious and is referred to in a note).[11]

It is interesting to see how the targumim treat the biblical texts under discussion. Targum Neofiti renders Ex. 8:15 as follows: "This is the finger of might from before the Lord" (a reading in the margin of the ms. has: "this is the might," dropping the finger

---

[11] In *Jos. et As.* 22:13 it is said of Joseph's brother Levi that as a prophet he used "to see letters written in heaven by the finger of God," but the final words are textcritically uncertain. For the long version reconstructed by Chr. Burchard see most conveniently A.-M. Denis, *Concordance grecque des pseudépigraphes d'Ancien Testament* (Louvain 1987), pp. 851–859. Recently there has been an enormous upsurge of interest in *Jos. et As.* See, *e.g.*, G. Bohak, *Joseph and Aseneth and the Jewish Temple in Heliopolis*, EJL 10 (Atlanta [Georgia] 1996 [originally: diss. Princeton 1994]); R. D. Chesnutt, *From Death to Life. Conversion in Joseph and Aseneth*, JSPS 16 (Sheffield 1995); E. McEwan Humphrey, *The Ladies and the Cities. Transformation and Apocalyptic in Joseph and Aseneth, 4 Ezra, the Apocalypse and the Shepherd of Hermas*, JSPE.S 17 (Sheffield 1995); A. Standhartinger, *Das Frauenbild im Judentum der hellenistischen Zeit. Ein Beitrag anhand von "Joseph und Aseneth,"* AGJU 26 (Leiden 1995).

altogether). Pseudo-Jonathan on Ex. 8:15 reads: "This is not from the power of the strength of Moses and Aaron, but it is a plague sent from before the Lord." Here, too, the finger of God has been replaced, as in Neofiti's margin.[12] Targum Onkelos *ad locum* has: "It is a plague from before the Lord."[13] Here "finger" is interpreted as "plague" (for which we will see some parallels later on) not as power or might. So we see that, apart from the half-hearted compromise of Neofiti, here the targumim avoid the anthropomorphic finger of God. When we look at their renderings of the other Exodus passage, however, we get a different picture. At 31:18 we find the following. Neofiti renders: "He gave to Moses...the two tables of the testimony, tables of stone, written by the finger of the Might from before the Lord." Pseudo-Jonathan has: "He gave Moses the two tables of the testimony, tables of sapphire stone from the throne of Glory, which weighed fourty seahs, written with the finger of the Lord."[14] And Onkelos has: "He gave Moses the two tablets of the testimony, stone tablets inscribed with the finger of the Lord."[15] Here *none* of the targumim has dropped the finger. Etan Levine has plausibly suggested that the targumim may have retained the biblical anthropomorphism here "in order to eliminate antinomian allegorization or suggestions that the Torah did not proceed directly from God himself, but through some medium."[16] This is confirmed by the fact that all three targumim retain the finger of God at Deut. 9:10 as well.[17]

When we now turn to the (other) rabbinic sources, we find the following. In Talmud Bavli, *Sanhedrin* 67b, the rabbis reason that the fact that the Egyptian magicians speak of God's finger has to do with the nature of the plague which happens to be one of very small creatures (lice, gnats, maggots, mosquitoes [the precise

---

[12] See M. McNamara, R. Hayward & M. Maher, *Targum Neofiti I: Exodus; Targum Pseudo-Jonathan: Exodus*, The Aramaic Bible 2 (Edinburgh 1994), pp. 35 and 181.

[13] B. Grossfeld, *The Targum Onkelos to Exodus*, The Aramaic Bible 7 (Edinburgh 1988), pp. 20–21.

[14] McNamara, Hayward & Maher, *Targum*, pp. 128 and 250.

[15] Grossfeld, *Targum*, p. 88.

[16] E. Levine, *The Aramaic Version of the Bible* (Berlin/New York 1988), p. 51.

[17] I. Drazin, *Targum Onkelos to Deuteronomy* (New York 1982), p. 127, n. 15 remarks: "Here TO wants to emphasize the sanctity and value of the Ten Commandments and therefore relates them directly to the Lord, and to the Lord alone."

designation is uncertain]). Since the magicians cannot imitate this, Eleazar says: "This proves that a magician cannot produce a creature less than a barley corn in size." We see here the connection between 'finger' and the smallness of the creatures that we already found in Philo. It is impossible to say whether Philo and the rabbis drew upon a common source or whether the rabbis had some knowledge of Philonic exegesis.[18]

In *Mekhilta*, Beshallah VII (*ad* 14:31 [ed. Lauterbach, I, p. 251]), the biblical verse "and Israel saw the great hand" (Ex. 14:31) is commented upon as follows:

> R. Jose the Galilean says: Whence can you prove that the Egyptians were smitten in Egypt with ten plagues and at the sea with fifty plagues? What does it say about them when in Egypt? "Then the magicians said unto Pharaoh: This is the finger of God" (Ex. 8:15). And what does it say about them when at sea? "And Israel saw the great hand" (14:31). Now with how many plagues were they smitten by the finger? With ten plagues. Hence you must conclude that in Egypt they were smitten with ten plagues and at the sea with fifty plagues.

Since a hand has five fingers, the smiting with the hand must have inflicted five times as many plagues, say the rabbis. Again, as in Philo, we see that "hand" and "finger" are not equated, but that punishment by the finger is regarded as less severe and devastating than that by the hand.[19]

A different aspect of the text is emphasized in the haggadic midrash *Exodus Rabba* X 7: "As soon as the magicians realised that they were not able to produce gnats, they recognised that the deeds were those of a God and not of demons (הַמַּעֲשִׂים מַעֲשֵׂה אֱלֹהִים וְלֹא מַעֲשֵׂה שֵׁדִים)." Here the implication seems to be that the demons which supplied the magicians with the power to imitate the first two plagues were not able to reproduce the third one so that "even the magicians are constrained to admit that this third

---

[18] In the same treatise, *Sanhedrin* 95b, we find a discussion of the annihilation of Sennacherib's Assyrian army (Is. 37), and the question is raised, with what they were smitten. Rabbi Eliezer said: With God's hand (quoting Ex. 14:31); but rabbi Joshua said: With God's finger (quoting Ex. 8:15).

[19] Cf. also *Midrash Aggada* on Exodus p. 137: "Wait for Him, He has so far smitten you only with a finger; when He will smite you with the hand, you will be afraid, as it says: 'The great hand etc.' [Ex. 14:31]" (quoted according to Grossfeld, *Onkelos to Exodus* 21).

plague could be wrought only by the superior power of God."[20] Jesus seems to be using a similar line of argumentation in Luke 11:20, for "if the demons are ruled out as the source of Jesus' supernatural power, the only other possible source is God."[21] It must be conceded, however, that it is impossible on the basis of this early medieval midrash to ascertain whether this interpretation was known as early as the first century C.E.

Mekhilta, Pisha II (*ad* 12:2 [ed. Lauterbach, I, p. 15–16]), is the first passage where we read about God's finger without explicit biblical support, although the rabbis point to implicit references in biblical texts. Taking his starting-point in Ex. 12:2 (הַחֹדֶשׁ הַזֶּה — *this* new moon), rabbi Aqiva says:

> This is one of the three things which were difficult for Moses to understand and all of which God pointed out to him with his finger. So also you interpret: "And *these* are they which are unclean to you" (Lev. 11:29). So also you interpret: "And *this* is the work of the candlestick" (Num. 8:4). And some say, Moses found it also hard to understand the ritual slaughtering, for it is said: "Now *this* is what thou shalt do upon the altar" (Ex. 29:38).

It is clear that the repeated use of a demonstrative pronoun (זֶה) in God's speech to Moses induced some rabbis to assume that God repeatedly used his forefinger to point out things to Moses.[22] We find the same motif repeated in Bavli, *Menahot* 29a:

> A Tanna of the school of R. Ishmael stated: Three things presented difficulties to Moses, until the Holy One, blessed be He, showed Moses with his finger, and these they are: the candlestick, the new moon, and the creeping things. The candlestick, as it is written: [Num. 8:4]. The new moon, as it is written: [Ex.

---

[20] Meier, *Marginal Jew*, Vol. II, pp. 411–412.

[21] Meier, *Marginal Jew*, Vol. II, p. 412. Cf. S. R. Garrett, *The Demise of the Devil. Magic and the Demonic in Luke's Writings* (Minneapolis 1989), p. 45: "Jesus was saying that his power was not like the diabolical power of magicians, Egyptian or otherwise, but was rather a triumph of God."

[22] I. Löw, "Die Finger in Litteratur und Folklore der Juden," *Gedenkbuch zur Erinnerung an David Kaufmann*, edd. M. Brann & F. Rosenthal (Breslau 1900), pp. 61–85, here 65, and W. Bacher, *Die Agada der Tannaiten*, Vol. I (Straßburg 1903), p. 315.

12:2]. The creeping things, as it is written: [Lev. 11:29]. Others add also the rules for slaughtering, as it is written: [Ex. 29:38].[23]

Compare also *Pesikta Rabbati* XV 21:

> Rabbi Simeon ben Yohai taught: By three things was Moses baffled: he could not grasp the complicated instructions concerning the making of the candlestick for the Tabernacle; he did not know how to identify the reptiles forbidden as food; he did not understand the mysteries of the moon's changes. God indicated each of the three with his finger, so to speak, to Moses, saying of the candlestick, "This..." (Num. 8:4); of the reptiles, "This..." (Lev. 11:29); and of the moon's changes, "This..." (Ex. 12:2)."[24]

In these passages God's finger has no function other than that of pointing out to Moses difficult matters.

All these haggadic motifs are brought together and both amplified and summed up in an early medieval midrashic work, *Pirqe de Rabbi Eliezer* 48, which deserves to be quoted in full:[25]

> The five fingers of the right hand of the Holy One, blessed be He, all of them appertain to the mystery of the redemption. He showed the little finger of the hand to Noah, (pointing out) how to make the ark, as it is said: "And *this* is how thou shalt make it" (Gen. 6:15). With the second finger, which is next to the little one, He smote the firstborn of the Egyptians, as it is said: "The magicians said unto Pharaoh, This is the finger of God" (Ex. 8:15). With how many plagues were they smitten with the finger? With ten plagues. With the third finger, which is the third starting from the little finger, He wrote the tables (of the

---

[23] Eli Cashdan remarks *ad locum* in the Soncino translation: "The term 'this' implies that something was held up as a pattern or model to illustrate the instructions given."

[24] The tradition is also found in *Sifre Numbers* 61 (*ad* 8:4). Num. 8:4 speaks about the making of the lampstand from *miqshah* (hammered work), which—read as *ma[h] qasheh* (how difficult!)—led to the idea of Moses' finding things difficult (*hiqshah*). See further P. Billerbeck's collection of material *ad* Hebr 8:5 in his *Kommentar zum Neuen Testament aus Talmud und Midrasch*, Vol. III (München 1926), pp. 702–703; and W. Bacher, *Aggada der Tannaiten*, Vol. I, p. 315.

[25] The translation is by G. Friedlander, *Pirke de Rabbi Eliezer* (London 1916; reprinted New York 1965), pp. 382–383.

Law), as it is said: "And he gave unto Moses, when he had made an end of communing with him,...tables of stone, written with the finger of God" (Ex. 31:18). With the fourth finger, which is next to the thumb, the Holy One, blessed be He, showed to Moses what the children of Israel should give for the redemption of their souls, as it is said: "*This* they shall give..." (Ex. 30:13). With the thumb and all the hand the Holy One, blessed be He, will smite in the future all the children of Esau, for they are his foes, and likewise the children of Ishmael, for they are his enemies, as it is said: "Let thine hand be lifted up above thine adversaries, and let all thine enemies be cut off" (Mic. 5:9).[26]

The Jewish evidence for God's finger is not yet exhausted, although with the remaining material we move into quite a different religious atmosphere, namely that of the Merkavah mysticism of Hekhalot literature. In what is usually called *3 Enoch* we find a paragraph (§16)[27] in which the angel Metatron says that God wrote with his finger upon the crown on his (Metatron's) head the letters by means of which the whole universe was created. From his little finger, as §58 states, a consuming fire goes forth to burn the angels when they do not sing the Trishagion (cf. §67); but the same finger(s) can weep and pour forth rivers of tears when the Holy One is sad. In Hekhalot literature we can also find various traditions that go by the name of *Shi'ur Qomah* (literally, "the measurement of the body," *scil.* God's body).[28] It is in these traditions, in which God's bodily parts, as they are seen in mystical ecstasy, are described, named and measured, that we find God's finger again. We will briefly paraphrase here a selected number of passages from various 'treatises'[29] in which *Shi'ur*

---

[26] An elaborate parallel is found in *Midrash Tehillim* 78:15.

[27] Here and in the following passage all paragraph references are to P. Schäfer, *Synopse zur Hekhalot-Literatur* (Tübingen 1982).

[28] For an introduction see G. Scholem, "*Shi'ur Komah*: The Mystical Shape of the Godhead," in his *On the Mystical Shape of the Godhead* (New York 1991), pp. 15–55 (the German original was published in 1962); M. S. Cohen, *The Shi'ur Qomah: Texts and Recensions* (Tübingen 1985), pp. 1–26; P. Schäfer, *Hekhalot-Studien* (Tübingen 1988), pp. 75–83.

[29] On the problematic use of the term 'treatises' in reference to Hekhalot literature see Schäfer, *Hekhalot-Studien*, passim.

Qomah material is to be found.[30] In the *Shi'ur Qomah* fragments in §§482–483, 702, and 950, God's fingers are each said to have the astronomic length of 30,000,000 parasangs (but the indications of length vary between the manuscripts). The names of the fingers are:[31] Tatsmats, Tatmanah, Gagmanats, Ratsmanat, Ratsmastatsnas, Agagmats, Ashashnats, Vashoshni, Gagnashash, Ashashnu, etc.[32] What is striking in these mystical descriptions is the distance from the rabbinic material in various respects.[33] The only aspect I want to emphasize in this connection is that here, in contradistinction to all the Jewish material that we have seen so far, not even one of the four biblical passages about God's finger(s) is quoted or referred to. All that is said about this aspect of God is non-biblical, perhaps apart from the reference to God writing with his own fingers the letters on Metatron's crown, which is reminiscent of God's writing the stone tablets of the Law.

There is a reference to the finger of God in a text of which the religious affiliation is doubtful, that is to say, it is probably heavily syncretistic but there is some debate as to whether or not it may have been influenced by Luke 11:20. It is an ostracon from Eshmunein (Hermoupolis Magna) in Egypt, probably from the third to fourth century (although the dating is uncertain), containing a Greek binding spell in which the god Kronos is invoked to keep Hori from speaking to (or against) Hatros. The spell then continues: "I adjure you by the finger of God [κατὰ τοῦ δακτύλου τοῦ θεοῦ] that he should not open his mouth to (or against) him."[34] Gager surmises that this is a reference to the angel

---

[30] The material can easily be found by means of Schäfer's *Konkordanz zur Hekhalot-Literatur*, 2 vols. (Tübingen 1986–88).

[31] Here too there is a great fluctuation in the manuscript tradition.

[32] More than ten names have been transmitted for God's ten fingers, partly because of the variation in the mss. tradition, partly also because sometimes ten names are given for five fingers. Of course the correct vocalization of these names must remain uncertain. See for similar traditions about the measures and names of God's fingers also the Genizah fragments in P. Schäfer, *Genizah-Fragmente zur Hekhalot-Literatur* (Tübingen 1984), nos. 9 and 19.

[33] See on this aspect also D. J. Halperin, *The Faces of the Chariot. Early Jewish Responses to Ezekiel's Vision* (Tübingen 1988).

[34] For the text see K. Preisendanz, *PGM* II (Leipzig/Berlin 1931; reprinted, Stuttgart 1974), p. 233 = Ostr. 1. Text with German translation in A. Deissmann, *Licht vom Osten* (Tübingen 1923⁴), p. 260; English translation in *Curse Tablets and Binding Spells from the Ancient World*, ed. J. G. Gager (Oxford/New York 1992), no. 111.

Orphamiel, whom we meet in Coptic magical papyri as "the great finger of the Father's right hand."[35] This may be correct. It cannot be ruled out completely, however, that Deissmann and Preisendanz are right in assuming that we have here the same Jewish influence at work that is apparent in Luke 11:20.[36]

When we now turn to the pagan Graeco-Roman material, we find that the expression is much rarer than it already was in the Jewish sources. Actually, it is practically non-existent. Let us quickly review the scanty evidence there is. We will pass over the famous Homeric formula ῥοδοδάκτυλος Ἡώς ("rose-fingered Dawn") since it is only a metaphor for the sunbeams as "a pattern of rays like a spread hand," as is rightly observed by Martin West.[37] A 4th century B.C.E. inscription from the Asclepieion in Epidaurus reports that a blind man called Alketas practiced incubation in the *adyton* and dreamt that the god Asclepius came to him and opened Alketas' eyes with his fingers (τοῖς δακτύλοις διάγειν τὰ ὄμματα) whereupon he could see the trees. When he awoke, he had been healed.[38] A comparable report in Artemidorus' *Oneirocritica* V 89 has it that someone with a stomach ailment went to a temple of Asclepius for incubation and dreamt that the deity offered the fingers of his right hand to the sick man so that he could eat them (τὸν θεὸν ἐκτείναντα τῆς δεξιᾶς ἑαυτοῦ

---

[35] See, *e.g.* A. M. Kropp, *Ausgewählte Koptische Zaubertexte*, 3 vols. (Brussels 1930–31), Vol. II, nos. 15:30; 15:42; 47:14 (4–5). For an English translation see *Ancient Christian Magic. Coptic Texts of Ritual Power*, edd. M. Meyer & R. Smith (San Francisco 1994), p. 291. It should be noted, however, that in Kropp, Vol. II, 15, no. 5.16–23, it is an angel called Nathanael whom we meet as "the great finger" of God. See also Kropp, Vol. III, pp. 43–44. Cf. also the Coptic ritual papyrus from Heidelberg translated in Meyer and Smith, *Ancient Christian Magic*, p. 331 (with note 105).

[36] See the references in note 34.

[37] M. West, *Hesiod. Works and Days* (Oxford 1978), p. 311, who also offers an alternative explanation: "It might also describe a single sliver of red light at the horizon," which is less probable. See also S. West in A. Heubeck, S. West & J. B. Hainsworth, *A Commentary on Homer's Odyssey*, vol. I (Oxford 1988), p. 129. For sunbeams as Aton's fingers in the Echnaton period see K. Groß, *Menschenhand und Gotteshand* (Stuttgart 1985), p. 321, who also refers to the parallel with ῥοδοδάκτυλος Ἡώς.

[38] The text is in R. Herzog, *Die Wunderheilungen von Epidauros* (Leipzig 1931), no. 18, and in L. R. LiDonnici, *The Epidaurian Miracle Inscriptions* (Atlanta 1995), no. A18 (p. 99). Note the parallel with Mk 8:22–26.

χειρὸς τοὺς δακτύλους παρέχειν αὐτῷ ἐσθίειν).[39] It is clear that eating part of the god's body here implies healing because the healing power of the god's hand is appropriated; and that it is the fingers that are offered in this particular case has to do with the fact that Artemidorus draws here on "Traumbüchern, in denen συνταγαί und θεραπεῖαι der Incubationsgötter, also namentlich des Asklepios und Serapis aufgezeichnet waren."[40] The element of *contactus* plays such an important part in ancient healing stories that it is no wonder that the bodily parts that make *contactus* κατ' ἐξοχήν, the fingers (plur., as *pars pro toto* for the hand), have a prominent place in them, as Otto Weinreich has amply illustrated in his classic work on ancient healing miracles. (In this connection mention may be made of the benign demonic powers called Δάκτυλοι or Δάκτυλοι Ἰδαῖοι. The *Daktyloi* originally were a kind of gnomes that came into being when Zeus' mother Rhea, because of the pain at his birth, stuck her fingers into the earth, and who were then entrusted by her with the care of the new-born Zeus at Mt. Ida in Crete; later on they developed into healing demons who also assisted at births, among other things.[41]) Healing and blessing power was probably also attributed to the well-known *tres digiti porrecti* of the so-called Sabazios votive hands,[42] but there are no ancient interpretative texts to this effect and again we find here a plural (three fingers) which is more easily interchangeable with "hand" than one finger. Another curious tale is that of Attis' finger in one of the versions of the Attis myth (this one told by Arnobius on the basis of Alexander Polyhistor) to the effect that Zeus, when asked by Agdistis (who caused Attis' death) to bring Attis back to life, refused, but consented that his body should remain incorruptible, his hair

---

[39] On this passage see O. Weinreich, *Antike Heilungswunder* (Gießen 1909; reprinted, Berlin 1969), pp. 33–34.

[40] Weinreich, *ibid.*, p. 33, n. 6.

[41] See O. Kern in *PW* 4 (1901), pp. 2018–2020, and H. von Geisau in *KP* I (1975), p. 1363.

[42] See *e.g.* R. Fellmann, "Der Sabazioskult," in *Die orientalischen Religionen im Römerreich*, ed. M. J. Vermaseren, EPRO 93 (Leiden 1981), pp. 316–334 with plates at 335–340; S. E. Johnson, "The Present State of Sabazios Research," *ANRW* II 17,3 (Berlin/New York 1984), pp. 1583–1613; for a good recent survey also R. Turcan, *Les cultes orientaux dans le monde romain* (Paris 1989), pp. 313–322. K. Groß, *Menschenhand und Gotteshand*, p. 401, discusses the various proposals to regard the Sabazios hands as testimonies to Jewish influence in Phrygia, which remains speculative even though it cannot be ruled out.

always grow, and his little finger remain in perpetual movement (*Adv. Nat.* V 5–7).[43] It is hard to guess, however, what the origin and meaning of this story are. And, finally, in a magical papyrus (PGM 2.76) we find a reference to a plant with the name "finger of Hermes" (Hermes here being the god of the thieves).[44] That is the end of the pagan material.[45]

It should be clear by now that there is very little affinity between these few and scattered passages from pagan literature and pagan monuments on the one hand and the passage from Luke the background of which we are dealing with on the other. Quite differently from the Jewish material, we nowhere find the element of a god's finger intervening in a salvatory way on behalf of an individual or a people in a hopeless situation (except possibly for the Sabazius hands, but that is perhaps due to Jewish influence; moreover, there we are dealing with three fingers not one). Moreover, apart from the obscure tradition about Attis, none of the texts speak about a finger of the deity in the singular.

We may thus safely conclude that pagan traditions about the finger of a god can hardly have played a role in the mind of Luke (or Jesus), but that it was—not surprisingly—the scriptural and Jewish traditions which form the background of this expression which is unique in the NT. It is the Jewish interpretation of God's finger in Ex. 8:15 as an invincible power in the struggle against (demonic) evil—not its writing or indicating activity—that is in Luke's mind here. This is further confirmed by the consideration that the Egyptian magicians who opposed Moses in Ex. 7–8, called Jannes and Jambres in Jewish tradition, were often regarded in haggadic sources as persons who had made a pact with the devil and his demons.[46] That in such a context a power superior to them, namely God's finger, came to be viewed as the best

---

[43] See A. B. Cook, *Zeus. A Study in Ancient Religion* II 2 (Cambridge 1925), p. 970.

[44] On this passage see K. Groß, *Menschenhand und Gotteshand in Antike und Christentum* (Stuttgart 1985), p. 285. Gross is also the author of the useful article "Finger" in *RAC*, Vol. VII (1969), pp. 909–946.

[45] There is some (Egyptian, Greek, Jewish, Christian) material on mortals being nursed not by divine breasts but by divine fingers, but that is another story: see H. Bechtold-Stäubli, *s.v.* "Finger," *Handwörterbuch des deutschen Aberglaubens* II (1987[=1930]), pp. 1489–1490.

[46] See A. Pietersma, *The Apocryphon of Jannes and Jambres the Magicians* (Leiden 1994), pp. 193–194, 210 *et al.*

'weapon' in the struggle against these evil powers was well-nigh inevitable.

Space forbids dealing with the Patristic exegesis of both the texts from the Torah and from Luke. Many interesting exegetical patterns (comparable to those in rabbinic literature) can be found in their writings as far as the 'finger of God' is concerned. As could be expected, the identification of God's finger with the Holy Spirit looms large in the Patristic material. But the study of that material must be left for another occasion.[47]

---

[47] I mention here just a random selection of passages in alphabetical order of authors: Ambrose, *Expos. in Ev. Luc.*, PL 15, coll. 1722, 1811. Athanasius, *Epist. 4 ad Serapionem* 22, PG 26, col. 673; *De incarn.* 20, PG 26, col. 1020; *Disp. c. Arium* 42, PG 28, col. 496. Augustine, *Civ. Dei* 16,43; *Quaest. in Hept.* II 25, PL 34, col. 604; *De consensu evang.* II 38, PL 34, col. 1118; *De spiritu et littera* I 16, PL 44, col. 218; *Quaest. Ex.* 25; *Serm.* 156,14. Barnabas 4.7; 14.2. Basil, *Epist.* 8,11; *Adv. Eunom.* V, PG 29, coll. 716, 733; *Hom. de ieiunio* I 5, PG 31, col. 169; *Sermo* X 4, PG 32, col. 1252. Clement of Alexandria, *Strom.* 6, [16] 133,1; *Protr.* 4,63,2. Cyril of Alexandria, *Thesaurus: assertio* 34, PG 75, coll. 577–578. Didymus Alex., *De spiritu sancto* 20, PG 39, col. 1051; Epiphanius, *Panar.* 48,4. Eucherius, *Liber formularum spiritalis intelligentiae* 1–2, PL 50, coll. 732, 737. Eusebius, *Dem. Ev.* III 2,22 (93c–d); *Comm. in Pss.* 8.37.143, PG 23, coll. 129, 340; 24, col. 52. Gregory of Nazianze, *Or.* XIX 15 (*Ad Jul.*), PG 35, col. 1061; *Or.* XL 44 (*In sanct. bapt.*), PG 36, col. 421; Gregory of Nyssa, *C. Eunom.* III 6,32–33; *In Basil. fratrem* 21. John Chrysostom, *Hom. in Matt.* 41,2, PG 57, col. 447; *Hom in Act.* 18,3, PG 60, col. 145; *Fragm. in Jer.* 31, PG 64, col. 981; Origen, *Comm. in Joh.* 1,38,281; 10,40,280; *Selecta in Gen.*, PG 12, col. 93; *Sel. in Pss.* 8, PG 12, col. 1184. Tertullian, *Adv. Marc.* 4,26–27. Many more passages can be found in G. W. H. Lampe's *Patristic Greek Lexicon* (Oxford 1968), p. 333, and in the five volumes of the *Biblia Patristica*.

THE SAYINGS ON CONFESSING AND DENYING JESUS IN Q 12:8-9 AND MARK 8:38

Henk Jan de Jonge
University of Leiden
(Leiden, the Netherlands)

Luke 12:8-9 (par. Matt 10:32-33) and Mark 8:38 form an un-deniable cornerstone of any reconstruction of the early history of Christology. In these related passages Jesus speaks about the coming Son of Man in the third person singular without explicitly identifying himself with him. The discussion of these verses often entails the issue whether the words in question can be traced back, in one form or another, to the historical Jesus. The question was answered affirmatively by such exegetes as R. Bultmann and H. Tödt,[1] but negatively by E. Käsemann[2] and P. Vielhauer.[3] According-ing to Käsemann the saying on confessing and denying is an ex-ample of the prophetic genre of the "rules of sacred law"; this genre is the creation of early Christian prophets and a product therefore of the early church's prophetic activity.

Q 12:8-9 and Mark 8:38 can only be construed to be separate witnesses to an earlier, traditional saying in which Jesus refers to the Son of Man as a distinct person if, firstly, Mark 8:38 can be

---

[1] R. Bultmann, *Die Geschichte der synoptischen Tradition* (Göttingen 1958⁴), p. 163: Mark 8:38 and Luke 12:8-9 represent "primäre Überlieferung. Aus ihnen spricht das prophetische Selbstbewusstsein Jesu; irgend welchen spezifisch christlichen Klang haben sie nicht. Auch ist hier zu betonen, dass einige Menschensohnworte offenbar keine christlichen Bildungen, sondern primäre Überlieferungen sind, so das eben genannte Wort Mk 8,38 bzw. Lk 12,8f." H. E. Tödt, *Der Menschensohn in der synoptischen Überlieferung* (Gütersloh 1963²), p. 206: Luke 12:8-9 (par. Matt 10:32-33) and Mark 8:38 par. belong to those sayings "die bei vorsichtiger Kritik als authentische Sprüche Jesu gelten dürfen."

[2] E. Käsemann, "Sätze heiligen Rechtes im Neuen Testament," *NTS* 1 (1954/55), pp. 248-260; reprinted in idem, *Exegetische Versuche und Besinnungen*, 2 vols. (Göttingen 1964³), Vol. 2, pp. 69-82.

[3] P. Vielhauer, "Jesus und der Menschensohn: Zur Diskussion mit Heinz Eduard Tödt und Eduard Schweizer," *ZThK* 60 (1963), pp. 133-177, reprinted in idem, *Aufsätze zum Neuen Testament* (Munich 1965), pp. 92-140. See H. T. Fleddermann, *Mark and Q. A Study of the Overlap Texts*, BEThL 122 (Louvain 1995), p. 149.

shown to be independent of Q 12:8–9 and, secondly, Luke 12:9 can be shown to be independent of Mark 8:38. But the independence of Mark 8:38 over against Q 12:8–9 as well as that of Luke 12:9 over against Mark 8:38 can be called into question. If, for instance, there are good reasons to assume that the phrase ὁ υἱὸς τοῦ ἀνθρώπου in Luke 12:8 is due to the influence of Mark 8:38 on Luke's redaction of Q 12:8–9, the phrase can no longer be ascribed to Q. In that case Q 12:8–9 is not a witness to a saying of Jesus about the Son of Man at all, let alone about the Son of Man as a distinct person. But if Q 12:8 (and 12:9, see below) did contain the phrase ὁ υἱὸς τοῦ ἀνθρώπου, and Mark 8:38 is dependent on Q 12:8–9, then the saying on denying Jesus no longer retains the double attestation.

In the following pages it is our intention, therefore, to address two questions: (1) Is Luke's rewriting of Q 12:8–9 dependent on Mark? and (2) Is Mark 8:38 dependent on Q 12:8–9?

In order to assess the literary relationship between Mark 8:38 and Q 12:8–9 it will first be necessary to try to recover the common source (Q) of Luke 12:8–9 and Matt 10:32–33. Any attempt at reconstructing Q remains, of course, a hazardous enterprise. This applies also to Q 12:8–9. Yet the difficulties are perhaps somewhat less here than in many other cases. First, let us compare Matt 10:32–33 and Luke 12:8–9.[4] (See the table on the facing page.)

---

[4] The Greek text is that of *Synopsis quattuor evangeliorum*, ed. K. Aland (Stuttgart 1988[13]), which is identical with that of N-A[26.27]. There is a considerable amount of textual variation, both in Matthew and in Luke. But the text of N-A[26.27] seems to be acceptable, except for the bracketed article in Matthew, both in v. 32 and v. 33. It should probably be omitted in both cases. See the note appended to this article.

Matt 10:32–33		Luke 12:8–9

<table>
<tr><td></td><td></td><td>8a</td><td>λέγω δὲ ὑμῖν,</td></tr>
<tr><td>32a</td><td>πᾶς οὖν ὅστις
ὁμολογήσει ἐν ἐμοὶ
ἔμπροσθεν τῶν ἀνθρώπων,</td><td></td><td>πᾶς ὃς ἂν
ὁμολογήσει ἐν ἐμοὶ
ἔμπροσθεν τῶν ἀνθρώπων,</td></tr>
<tr><td>b</td><td>ὁμολογήσω
κἀγώ
ἐν αὐτῷ
ἔμπροσθεν
τοῦ πατρός μου
τοῦ ἐν [τοῖς] οὐρανοῖς.</td><td>b</td><td>καὶ ὁ υἱὸς τοῦ ἀνθρώπου
ὁμολογήσει
ἐν αὐτῷ
ἔμπροσθεν
τῶν ἀγγέλων τοῦ θεοῦ.</td></tr>
<tr><td>33a</td><td>ὅστις δ᾽ ἂν
ἀρνήσηταί με
ἔμπροσθεν
τῶν ἀνθρώπων,</td><td>9a</td><td>ὁ δὲ
ἀρνησάμενός με
ἐνώπιον
τῶν ἀνθρώπων,</td></tr>
<tr><td>b</td><td>ἀρνήσομαι κἀγὼ αὐτὸν
ἔμπροσθεν
τοῦ πατρός μου
τοῦ ἐν [τοῖς] οὐρανοῖς.</td><td>b</td><td>ἀπαρνηθήσεται
ἐνώπιον
τῶν ἀγγέλων τοῦ θεοῦ.</td></tr>
</table>

A few brief remarks on Matthew's and Luke's contributions to their redactional shape of these passages and on the underlying text of Q must suffice.

In Luke 12:8a, λέγω δὲ ὑμῖν is probably Luke's addition to the text of Q. Within Luke 12:2–10 a new section begins at v. 8a. Luke marks the transition and the new beginning by inserting the prepositive formula λέγω δὲ ὑμῖν, just as he did in 12:4a and in 11:9.[5] Matthew's οὖν (v. 32a), however, is no less redactional.

ὅστις with the future indicative in Matt 10:32a is typical of Matthew's diction.[6] On the other hand, of twenty instances of ὃς ἂν

---

[5] F. Neirynck, "Recent Developments in the Study of Q," in idem, *Evangelica*, 2 vols., BEThL 60 & 99 (Louvain 1982–1991), Vol. 2 (BEThL 99), pp. 409–464; see especially Neirynck's "Excursus: The λέγω ὑμῖν Formula," pp. 436–449. On Luke 12:9, see p. 442. Contra R. Pesch, "Über die Autorität Jesu. Eine Rückfrage anhand des Bekenner- und Verleugnerspruchs Lk 12,8f par," in *Die Kirche des Anfangs. Für Heinz Schürmann*, edd. R. Schnackenburg, J. Ernst, and J. Wanke (Freiburg/Basel/Vienna 1978), pp. 25–55, see pp. 30–33. On λέγω ὑμῖν in Luke 12:8, see also below.

[6] Pesch, "Autorität," p. 28; R. H. Gundry, *Matthew. A Commentary on his Literary and Theological Art* (Grand Rapids 1982), p. 198.

occurring in Luke, at least ten were taken over from his written sources Mark (7 times) and Q (3 times). Only 3 times is ὃς ἄν in Luke due to Lucan redaction of Marcan material. Obviously, Luke entertained no objections to taking over ὃς ἄν from his sources. He probably did so also in 12:8 and 9.

ὁ υἱὸς τοῦ ἀνθρώπου in Luke 12:8b is almost certainly the reading of Q. If Luke had found κἀγώ in Q, he can hardly have been tempted to change this to ὁ υἱὸς τοῦ ἀνθρώπου. Moreover, Matthew sometimes changes a "Son of Man" reference to a first (or third) person pronoun referring to Jesus since in his (Matthew's) view Jesus and the Son of Man were one and the same person: Matt 5:11 par. Q 6:22; Matt 16:21 par. Mark 8:31.[7]

Luke 12:8 says that if people acknowledge Jesus before others, the Son of Man will acknowledge them "before the angels of God," whereas Matthew 10:32 says that Jesus will acknowledge them "before my Father in heaven." Now it is certain that Matthew's "my Father in heaven" is redactional.[8] But what was the underlying reading of Q? Did Q read what we have in Luke, "before the angels of God," or did it contain only a reference to the person of God, as does Matthew?

The most plausible answer to this question is that Q had what we read in Luke, i.e., ἔμπροσθεν τῶν ἀγγέλων τοῦ θεοῦ (vv. 8 and 9). Matthew looks upon the reward given by the Son of Man as something taking place in heaven (ἐν [τοῖς] οὐρανοῖς, vv. 32 and 33), after Jesus' resurrection and exaltation, when he will plead in favour of the faithful "before the face of God." A similar idea occurs in Rom 8:34 and Heb 7:25. According to Luke, however, the Son of Man will judge the faithful and the unfaithful on the day of the Last Judgement. At that time he will appear with the angels of God, the angels will form a kind of court, and the Son of Man will sit in judgement upon all people.[9]

It is more probable that the futurist eschatological perspective as presented by Luke was changed to the Matthean perspective of an approval or disapproval in heaven than the other way around. If

---

[7] C. M. Tuckett, *Q and the History of Early Christianity. Studies in Q* (Edinburgh 1996), p. 180, n. 50.

[8] See the Appendix to this contribution. To the eleven instances of redactional "the Father in heaven" mentioned there, seven instances of redactional "your (or my) heavenly Father" can be added (5:48; 6:14, 26, 32; 15:13; 18:35; 23:9).

[9] For the Son of Man manifesting himself as the eschatological Judge (not as an advocate in heaven, as in Matt 10:32–33; Rom 8:34, and Heb 7:25), see also Mark 10:37; 13:26–27; 14:62; probably also Mark 8:38. Furthermore Q 17:24, 26, 30.

this is correct, Luke's eschatological view of the Last Judgement in the future, with angels forming a court, must be that of Q. But in the framework of that eschatological view angels had a more or less fixed place, determined by tradition. See, for instance, 1 Enoch 62:9–11: when the Son of Man appears on the Day of Judgement, he will be accompanied by "the angels of punishment" who will punish the sinners and lawless; 4 Ezra 13:52: the Son of Man will come together with "those *qui cum eo sunt*," that is, with the angels;[10] 1 Thess 3:13: Jesus will come "with all his saints", that is, with the angels or the righteous ones turned into heavenly beings; Mark 13:26 "the Son of Man will come with power…and he will send out the angels."[11] Thus, there is a strong traditio-historical justification for taking Luke's reading "before the angels of God" as the text of Q. This conclusion is valid both for Q 12:8 and for 12:9. In 15:10 Luke used the phrase "before the angels of God" once again, probably under the influence of the wording of Luke/Q 12:8–9, but on his own initiative and without a written source.[12] For the parable of the Lost Coin (Luke 15:8–10) shows all signs of being Luke's own creation.[13] It is a Lucan duplicate of the preceding parable of the Lost Sheep which Luke took over from Q.

---

[10] In 4 Ezra (= 2 Esdr) 13 the Son of Man is designated as "Man," in Latin *homo* (vv. 3, 5, and 12) and *vir* (vv. 25 and 32). It is not impossible to understand this *homo* and *vir* as correct renderings of the Hebrew or Aramaic phrase "Son of Man."

[11] See also Rev 3:5: "I will confess your name before my Father and before his angels." But the possibility that this passage is influenced by the synoptic tradition cannot be ruled out. Moreover, the scene of Rev 3:5 is in heaven, not on earth at the end of time.

[12] In 15:10, however, "before the angels of God" means "in heaven," not "at the Last Judgement"; see Luke 15:7. The difference in meaning shows that 15:10 represents another, and probably a more recent, stage of the genesis of Luke's gospel than 12:8–9.

[13] The main person in the parable of the lost coin, which occurs only in Luke, is a woman, whereas the main person in the preceding parable (the lost sheep) is a man. Luke likes to present pairs of a man and a woman: Zechariah and Elisabeth (1:5–80); Simeon and Anna (2:22–38); the possessed man in the synagogue of Capernaum and Simon's mother-in-law (4:31–39); the centurion of Capernaum and the widow of Nain (7:1–17); the crippled woman and the man with dropsy (13:10–17; 14:1–6); the pompous pharisees and the poor widow (20:45–21:4); the man with the withered hand and the crippled woman, both healed by Jesus in a synagogue on the sabbath (6:6–11 and 13:10–17); Ananias and Sapphira (Acts 5:1–11); Aeneas and Dorcas (Acts 9:32–43); Dionysius and Damaris (Acts 17:34); etc.

Q 12:8b and 9b probably had "the angels of God" (τῶν ἀγγέλων τοῦ θεοῦ), not just "God" (τοῦ θεοῦ).[14] There is no compelling reason to assume that "the angels" is a Lucan insertion before "God." Firstly, the mention of a court of "*the angels* of God," in the midst of which the Son of Man will sit in judgement upon all people at the Last Judgement, makes perfect sense, not only in the context of Luke 12:8–9, but also in that of Q 12:8–9.

Secondly, if Q contained "God," not "the angels of God," the wording of Q would have been quite acceptable to Luke. He probably would not have felt the need to change it. See, for example, Luke 1:15: "he will be great in the sight of the Lord (ἐνώπιον κυρίου)"; 12:6 (in the immediate context of our passage 12:8–9): "not one of them is forgotten in God's sight (ἐνώπιον τοῦ θεοῦ)"; and 16:15: "what is prized by human beings is an abomination in the sight of God (ἐνώπιον τοῦ θεοῦ)." Compare also Acts:

4:19: εἰ δίκαιόν ἐστιν ἐνώπιον τοῦ θεοῦ

7:46· εὗρεν χάριν ἐνώπιον τοῦ θεοῦ

10:4: ἀνέβησαν εἰς μνημόσυνον ἔμπροσθεν τοῦ θεοῦ

10:31: αἱ ἐλεημοσύναι σου ἐμνήσθησαν ἐνώπιον τοῦ θεοῦ

Thirdly, in 12:6 Luke left Q's τοῦ θεοῦ unchanged, although the evangelist himself replaced the preposition ἄνευ (cf. Matt 10:29 ἄνευ τοῦ πατρὸς ὑμῶν) with his favourite ἐνώπιον. If he left τοῦ θεοῦ unchanged in 12:6, why would he have changed it in 12:8?

Fourthly, in 12:8a and 8b Luke took over the preposition ἔμπροσθεν from Q, in defiance of his strong preference for ἐνώπιον. This may be an indication that he refrained from interfering in the concluding words of v. 8b at all and that he took over τῶν ἀγγέλων τοῦ θεοῦ from Q, both in 12:8b and 12:9b.

Some reconstructions of Q do not read ἔμπροσθεν τῶν ἀγγέλων τοῦ θεοῦ, but just ἔμπροσθεν τῶν ἀγγέλων (without τοῦ θεοῦ), both in 12:8 and 12:9.[15] But a reference to God occurs both in Matt 10:32b/33b (τοῦ πατρός μου) and in Luke 12:8b/9b (τοῦ θεοῦ). Moreover, as D. Catchpole rightly observed, it would be surprising

---

[14] Here I agree with, *inter alios*, S. Schulz, *Q. Die Spruchquelle der Evangelisten* (Zürich 1972), p. 68, *contra* W. Schenk, *Synopse zur Redenquelle der Evangelien* (Düsseldorf 1981), p. 86.

[15] *E.g.*, Fleddermann, *Mark and Q*, pp. 147, 150. His arguments (p. 147, n. 56) are unconvincing.

if Luke had replaced God with the angels.[16] Luke's τοῦ θεοῦ can therefore best be ascribed to Q, both in 12:8b and in 12:9b.

In all probability, then, the whole phrase ἔμπροσθεν τῶν ἀγγέλων τοῦ θεοῦ in Luke 12:8b and 9b can be ascribed to Q.

In 12:9b Luke uses the passive ἀπαρνηθήσεται with the person denying Jesus as subject, not (as one would expect on the analogy of ὁ υἱὸς τοῦ ἀνθρώπου ὁμολογήσει κτλ. in 8b) the third person singular of the middle voice (ἀρνήσεται) with the Son of Man as subject. The change of voice can be attributed to Luke, who often avoids repetition and likes stylistic variation.[17] Moreover, Luke's preference for the future passive is well-known from other passages.[18] In the present case he did not just change the middle voice to the passive voice, he also switched from the simple ἀρνη- to the compound ἀπαρνη-. All this is characteristic of Luke. He likes to lengthen the forms of the future passive by prefixes.[19] He also likes to change simple verbs in his sources to compound verbs.[20]

Finally, it can be observed that ἐνώπιον, which Luke uses twice in v. 9 where Matthew has ἔμπροσθεν, is very characteristic of Luke's style.[21] In both cases it is Matthew who preserves the wording of Q.

In sum, the Q text of the saying on confessing and denying Jesus may have read as follows:

12:8a Πᾶς ὃς ἂν ὁμολογήσῃ ἐν ἐμοὶ
       ἔμπροσθεν τῶν ἀνθρώπων,
12:8b καὶ ὁ υἱὸς τοῦ ἀνθρώπου ὁμολογήσει ἐν αὐτῷ
       ἔμπροσθεν τῶν ἀγγέλων τοῦ θεοῦ,
12:9a ὃς δ᾽ ἂν ἀρνήσηταί με
       ἔμπροσθεν τῶν ἀνθρώπων,
12:9b καὶ ὁ υἱὸς τοῦ ἀνθρώπου ἀρνήσεται αὐτὸν
       ἔμπροσθεν τῶν ἀγγέλων τοῦ θεοῦ.

---

[16] D. R. Catchpole, "The Angelic Son of Man in Luke 12:8," *NovT* 24 (1982), pp. 255–265; see p. 256.

[17] H. J. Cadbury, *The Style and Literary Method of Luke* (Cambridge [Massachusetts] 1920), p. 83.

[18] Cadbury, *Style*, p. 164.

[19] Cadbury, *Style*, p. 166.

[20] Cadbury, *Style*, p. 166.

[21] J. C. Hawkins, *Horae synopticae* (Oxford 1909²), p. 18 (asterisked; the word does not occur at all in Matt or Mark, 22 times in Luke, and 13 times in Acts).

This reconstruction agrees entirely with that of R. Pesch,[22] except that, according to Pesch, the saying of 12:8a in Q was preceded by the formula ἀμὴν λέγω ὑμῖν.

Is Luke's rewriting of Q 12:8–9 dependent upon Mark?

Here we are not broaching an entirely new question. To a considerable extent the question has already been settled when we established the textual form of Q 12:8–9. As soon as one decides that ὁ υἱὸς τοῦ ἀνθρώπου in Luke 12:8 derives from Q, one can no longer ascribe the phrase in Luke 12:8 to Marcan influence. As soon as one decides that ὃς ἄν in Luke 12:8 derives from Q 12:8, one can no longer attribute the phrase to the influence of Mark 8:38. In a way, then, the question of whether Luke 12:8–9 is dependent on Mark has been treated in the previous section.

Yet a further discussion of the question is not wholly superfluous. Firstly, it is almost generally agreed, for instance, that βλασ-φημήσαντι in the next verse, Luke 12:10, is due to the influence of Mark 3:29 on Luke's reworking of Q 12:10. Consequently, the suspicion that something similar is the case in Luke 12:8–9 is not unjustified. Luke 12:8–9 may contain traces of Marcan influence from other passages than Mark 8:38. Secondly, the question of Marcan influence on Luke 12:8–9 deserves to be looked at somewhat more systematically. "The possibility that Luke adapted 12:8a to Mark 8:38a" is also taken into consideration by R. Pesch, and rightly so.[23]

Let us begin by listing the distinctive readings of Luke 12:8–9 as compared with Q.

	Q	]	Luke's redaction in 12:8–9
12:8a		]	praemittit λέγω δὲ ὑμῖν
9a	ὃς δ᾽ ἄν ἀρνήσηται	]	ὁ δὲ ἀρνησάμενος
	ἔμπροσθεν	]	ἐνώπιον
9b	καὶ ὁ υἱὸς τοῦ ἀνθρώπου]		omittit
	ἀρνήσεται αὐτόν	]	ἀπαρνηθήσεται
	ἔμπροσθεν	]	ἐνώπιον

Of these six instances of Lucan redaction in 12:8–9, none shows the influence of Mark 8:38. Some authors have rightly observed,

---

[22] Pesch, "Autorität," p. 30.
[23] Pesch, "Autorität," p. 28.

however, that λέγω δὲ ὑμῖν in 12:8a may be derived from Mark 3:28.[24] While redacting 12:2–10, Luke certainly had the Marcan saying on sinning against the Holy Spirit (Mark 3:28–30) in mind. This is clear from the fact that, as mentioned above, Luke's βλασφημήσαντι in 12:10 is an echo of Mark 3:28–29 (v. 28 βλασφημήσωσιν, v. 29 βλασφημήσῃ). Mark 3:28 opens with ᾽Αμὴν λέγω ὑμῖν. It is true that Luke did not take over this formula in his corresponding verse 12:10, but he had a reason for this. Luke wanted to create a close connection between his version of the Q saying on sinning against the Holy Spirit (12:10) and the sayings on confessing and denying (12:8–9). He made a new unit out of the combination of vv. 8–9 and v. 10 by linking v. 10 to vv. 8–9 with a redactional καί. The result is a parallelism between v. 8 and v. 10: (8) πᾶς … (10) καὶ πᾶς …. In order to set off the new unit 12:8–10 against its context, Luke used the introductory formula ἀμὴν λέγω ὑμῖν. Possibly, Luke took it over from Mark's saying on sinning against the Holy Spirit (3:28), a passage omitted by Luke in favour of Q 12:10. In conformity with his own style he dropped ἀμήν[25] and inserted δέ. Here, then, we have a possible instance of Marcan influence on Luke's redaction of 12:8.

Yet reasonableness compels us to admit that Marcan influence in the case of λέγω ὑμῖν is just a good possibility. It should be remembered that the formula λέγω ὑμῖν could be prefixed to sayings of Jesus by anybody transmitting the Lord's teaching. At least some cases of λέγω ὑμῖν in Luke are likely to have been added to the Q material by Luke himself.[26] Since Luke inserted λέγω ὑμῖν in 12:4 (the parallel passage Matt 10:27 uses λέγω ὑμῖν quite differently), ὑποδείξω δὲ ὑμῖν in 12:5a, and ναὶ λέγω ὑμῖν in 12:5b, one cannot rule out the possibility that λέγω δὲ ὑμῖν in 12:8a is also due to Luke's own initiative, without any influence from Mark 3:28. Luke seems to use the λέγω ὑμῖν formula to impose structure upon 12:2–10. Consequently, the influence of Mark 3:28 on λέγω ὑμῖν in Luke 12:8 is not certain.

---

[24] H. Schürmann, "Sprachliche Reminiszenzen an abgeänderte oder ausgelassene Bestandteile der Spruchsammlung im Lukas- und Matthäusevangelium," NTS 6 (1959/60), pp. 193–210, esp. 195–199; K. Berger, Die Amen-Worte Jesu, BZNW 39 (Berlin 1970), p. 36: "Der Amen-Einleitung [in Mark 3:28] entspricht aber in Lc 12:8 das λέγω δὲ ὑμῖν;" Neirynck, "The Study of Q," Evangelica, Vol. 2, p. 442.

[25] Cadbury, Style, p. 157.

[26] Neirynck, "The Study of Q," Evangelica, Vol. 2, p. 444.

The other redactional changes Luke made in 12:8–9, however, do not seem to reflect Mark's influence at all. Once again, all depends here on one's reconstruction of Q. In his recent study of Marcan influences on the redaction of Luke 9:51–18:14 (Luke's "great intercalation"), F. Noël has duly recorded H. J. Holtzmann's assessment of the phrase ὁ υἱὸς τοῦ ἀνθρώπου in Luke 12:8.[27] According to Holtzmann,[28] it cannot be ascertained whether ὁ υἱὸς τοῦ ἀνθρώπου in Luke 12:8 derives from Q or from Mark 8:38. The possibility that it is a reminiscence of Mark 8:38 cannot be ruled out. But, as we argued above, it is more plausible that ὁ υἱὸς τοῦ ἀνθρώπου was changed to κἀγώ than that κἀγώ was changed to ὁ υἱὸς τοῦ ἀνθρώπου. Consequently, the latter phrase is best ascribed to Q, not to Marcan influence on Luke's redaction.

Noël himself,[29] in contradistinction to Holtzmann,[30] reckoned with the possibility that τῶν ἀγγέλων in Luke 12:8 and 9 betrays the influence of Mark 8:38. These angels, however, belong to the traditional scenario of the appearance of the Son of Man (see above). As a result the reference to the angels does not need to be denied to Q 12:8–9. In the case of τῶν ἀγγέλων, too, the supposition of Marcan influence is superfluous.

---

[27] Filip Noël, *Van Marcus tot Lucas. De "grote weglating" (Mc 6,45–8,26) en de "grote inlassing" (Lc 9,51–18,14) in de compositie van het Lucasevangelie* (unpublished Ph.D. dissertation, Louvain [supervisor A. Denaux]; Louvain 1996), pp. 129, 176.

[28] H. J. Holtzmann, *Die synoptischen Evangelien* (Leipzig 1863), p. 229.

[29] Noël, *Van Marcus tot Lucas*, p. 176, *ad* Luke 12:8–9, second line.

[30] In his *Die Synoptiker*, Hand-Commentar zum Neuen Testament I.1 (Tübingen/ Leipzig 1901[3]), p. 235, Holtzmann rather seems to rule out the possibility that "the angels" of Luke 12:8–9 are due to Marcan influence on Luke's redaction, for here he calls Matthew's repeated "before my Father in heaven" (12:32–33) "specifisch matthäisch." In *Die synoptischen Evangelien*, p. 183, too, Holtzmann says: "den Engeln Gottes [of the Sayings Source] ist [in Matt 10:] 32. 33 das Angesicht Gottes substituiert." If Holtzmann understood "before my Father in heaven" in Matt 10:32 and 33 as being Matthew's substitute of "before the angels of God" in Q, then he must have regarded "before the angels of God" in Luke 12:8 and 9 as deriving from Q. In that case, however, he cannot have supposed that "the angels of God" in Luke 12:8 and 9 goes back to Mark. True, in *Synoptiker*, p. 370, Holtzmann notices: "anstatt der Beziehung auf Gottes Angesicht Mt [10:] 32 33 erscheinen Lc [12:] 8 und 9 die Engel Gottes." But this observation intends only to record the discrepancy between Matthew and Luke. It does not intend to say that Matthew retained the Q reading and that Luke changed it, whether or not under the influence of Mark.

All in all, then, Mark's influence on Luke 12:8–9 seems to be limited to the insertion of the introductory phrase λέγω δὲ ὑμῖν in v. 8 (δέ is Lucan redaction; see above) and even in that case Mark's influence remains uncertain.

Is Mark 8:38 dependent on Q 12:8–9?

Recently, this question has been answered affirmatively by J. Lambrecht[31] and H. T. Fleddermann.[32] We shall first put Q 12:9 and Mark 8:38 side by side and underline what they have in common. Mark has no parallel to Q 12:8.

Q 12:9		*Mark 8:38*	
9a	ὃς δ᾽ ἂν ἀρνήσηταί με	38a	ὃς γὰρ ἐὰν ἐπαισχυνθῇ με καὶ τοὺς ἐμοὺς λόγους ἐν
	ἔμπροσθεν τῶν ἀνθρώπων,		τῇ γενεᾷ ταύτῃ τῇ μοιχαλίδι καὶ ἁμαρτωλῷ
9b	καὶ ὁ υἱὸς τοῦ ἀνθρώπου ἀρνήσεται αὐτὸν	38b	καὶ ὁ υἱὸς τοῦ ἀνθρώπου ἐπαισχυνθήσεται αὐτὸν ὅταν ἔλθῃ ἐν τῇ δόξῃ τοῦ πατρὸς αὐτοῦ μετὰ
	ἔμπροσθεν τῶν ἀγγέλων τοῦ θεοῦ.		τῶν ἀγγέλων τῶν ἁγίων.

The thematic and syntactic parallelism between Q 12:9 and Mark 8:38 is striking, and although the verbal agreements are not very impressive, they are not lacking. The two passages must be related in some manner. But in order to demonstrate that Mark used Q, it does not suffice to refer to the agreements between the two. Mark can only be proven to be dependent on Q if his text can be shown to be dependent *on Q's redaction*. Q, then, has the following words and phrases in common with Mark 8:38:

---

[31] J. Lambrecht, "Q-Influence on Mark 8,34–9,1," *Logia. Les paroles de Jésus—The Sayings of Jesus. Mémorial Joseph Coppens*, ed. J. Delobel, BEThL 59 (Louvain 1982), pp. 277–304, esp. 285–288.

[32] Fleddermann, *Mark and Q*, pp. 145–151.

Q 12:9

9a ὃς ἄν (ἄν and ἐάν can be taken as interchangeable)
  μὲ
9b καὶ
  ὁ υἱὸς τοῦ ἀνθρώπου
  a future indicative verb in the 3rd pers. sing. + αὐτόν
  τῶν ἀγγέλων

None of these words and phrases of Q can be regarded as redactional or as characteristic of Q's style.

Lambrecht points to several elements in Mark 8:38 that, in his opinion, show that Mark is "clearly dependent on Q."[33] At most, however, he has succeeded in showing that, in many respects, the saying on denying Jesus as transmitted in Mark 8:38 represents a later stage of the tradition than does the saying as preserved in Q. Unfortunately, Lambrecht does not try to demonstrate that Mark 8:38 is dependent on the redaction of Q 12:9. Consequently, his conclusion that "there is no need to postulate a source other than Q"[34] seems to be premature.

Fleddermann argues that the Q saying on denying Jesus fits seamlessly in the overall Q portrayal of the Son of Man. Since it fits so smoothly in Q's Christology, the saying could well come from the Q redactor. If so, the saying shows that Mark knew redactional Q.[35]

This line of reasoning, however, cuts no ice. Firstly, it does not follow from the fact that the image of the Son of Man given in Q 12:9 fits smoothly in Q's Christology, that Q 12:9 belongs to the Q redaction. Secondly, the Q saying on sinning against the Holy Spirit (12:10) has to be regarded as a redactional commentary appended to the saying on denying Jesus, as I shall argue presently. The inconsistency between 12:9 and 12:10 rules out the possibility that Q 12:10 and 12:9 come from the same redactor. Q 12:9 must be regarded, therefore, as pre-redactional.[36]

---

[33] J. Lambrecht, "Q-Influence on Mark," p. 287.

[34] Lambrecht, "Q-Influence on Mark," p. 287.

[35] Fleddermann, *Mark and Q,* p. 151.

[36] H. T. Wrege, "Zur Rolle des Geisteswortes in frühchristlichen Traditionen," *Logia,* ed. J. Delobel, BEThL 59 (Louvain 1982), pp. 373–377, esp. 374; C. M. Tuckett, "The Son of Man in Q," *From Jesus to John* (Festschrift M. de Jonge), ed. M. C. de Boer, JSNT.S 84 (Sheffield 1993), pp. 196–215, esp. 211; idem, *Q and the*

Verse 12:9 asserts that denying Jesus will entail one's perdition at the Last Judgement. Verse 12:10, however, promises that everyone who speaks a word against the Son of Man will be forgiven; only blasphemy against the Holy Spirit will be unforgivable. Obviously, 12:10 intends to add an escape clause to the strict rule of 12:9. Moreover, 12:10 pretends that the phrase "the Son of Man" in 12:9 refers only to the pre-Easter Jesus: those who failed to acknowledge him before Easter may still convert after Easter and be saved. But those who continue to oppose the Holy Spirit after Easter by refusing to convert and confess Jesus, will not be able to be forgiven anymore and cannot be saved.

There can be little doubt that Q 12:10 is a correction of, and a commentary on, the contents of 12:9. If so, 12:9 was written by an earlier hand than 12:10. Q 12:9 does not belong to the final redaction of Q. Consequently, Mark 8:38 has not been proven to be dependent on Q 12:9.

Conclusion

From the above it can be inferred that Q 12:9 and Mark 8:38 go back independently to a common earlier tradition. It is clear that Q 12:9 preserves this tradition more faithfully than Mark 8:38. Mark's version of the saying betrays many unmistakable signs of Mark's redactional hand:

(a) In the post-Easter situation the phrase καὶ τοὺς ἐμοὺς λόγους is synonymous with μέ; together, the two elements form a good example of the principal hallmark of Mark's style, duality.[37]

(b) Duality also results from the juxtaposition of μοιχαλίδι and ἁμαρτωλῷ.

(c) The same applies to the juxtaposition of ἐν τῇ δόξῃ τοῦ πατρὸς αὐτοῦ and μετὰ τῶν ἀγγέλων τῶν ἁγίων.

(d) The order of the substantive τῇ γενεᾷ ταύτῃ and the apposition τῇ μοιχαλίδι καὶ ἁμαρτωλῷ is characteristic of Marcan style.[38]

(e) Finally, the multiplication of forms of cognate verbs or of the same verb (38b ἔλθῃ, 9:1 ἐληλυθυῖαν) also typifies Mark's style, not to mention the parallelism between ἔλθῃ ἐν ... δόξῃ in 38b and ἐληλυθυῖαν ἐν δυνάμει in 9:1.

History of Early Christianity, pp. 239–282, esp. 249–250; F. Neirynck, "Assessment," in Fleddermann, *Mark and Q*, pp. 284–285.

[37] F. Neirynck, *Duality in Mark*, BEThL 31 (revised edition; Louvain 1988), p. 104.

[38] Neirynck, *Duality*, p. 107.

Words and phrases in Mark 8:38 that raise the suspicion of being due to Mark's redaction thus include: γάρ, καὶ τοὺς ἐμοὺς λόγους,[39] ἐν τῇ γενεᾷ ταύτῃ (cf. 8:12 bis, 9:19, 13:30), τῇ μοιχαλίδι καὶ ἁμαρτωλῷ, ὅταν ἔλθῃ ἐν τῇ δόξῃ τοῦ πατρὸς αὐτοῦ, μετά,[40] and probably τῶν ἁγίων. This is an impressive list. In almost all cases in which Q and Mark differ, Q seems to preserve the earlier form of the tradition. It follows that the common tradition behind Mark and Q must have been of this tenor:

> Whoever disavows me before men,
> the Son of Man will also disavow him before the angels of God.[41]

It is impossible to say whether this tradition in its earliest traceable stage was phrased in Greek or in Aramaic. It is equally impossible to say with any certainty whether the saying is of pre- or post-Easter origin. To the latter question we shall give some further consideration presently. Here the conclusion can be drawn that Q 12.9 and Mark 8.38 allow us to reconstruct the common earlier tradition of a saying in which Jesus states that whoever disavows him before men in this world, will receive no favourable sentence from the Son of Man at the Last Judgement. In other words, everybody's definitive fate will depend on whether or not one has disavowed Jesus and his call to comply with the demands of God's Kingdom.

In the reconstructed saying, the future Son of Man is looked upon as the Judge who, on God's behalf, will soon pass sentence on all people. He will judge everyone in accordance with the way each individual has reacted to Jesus. This image of the Son of Man as the central figure of the Last Judgement is retained in Mark 8:38 and, via Q, in Luke 12:8–9. It was changed by Matthew to the image of Jesus as the heavenly advocate, pleading for the faithful before God, but not for the unfaithful (10:32–33).

---

[39] For τοὺς ἐμοὺς λόγους referring to the utterances of Jesus as a whole, see also Mark 10:24 and 13:31. At 8:38 the omission of λόγους in W k sah is probably due to homoioteleuton.

[40] After "the Son of Man," this reference to "his Father" is unfortunate and awkward, although understandable in an author for whom Jesus and the Son of Man were entirely identical.

[41] That is, at the Last Judgement.

Does the primary tradition reconstructed above
reflect something Jesus himself has said?[42]

It remains true that the distinction between the "me" referring to Jesus and the Son of Man must belong to a very early stage of the tradition. But can we be certain that after Jesus' death none of his followers ever again made a distinction between the persons of the terrestrial Jesus and the coming Son of Man?

We may assume that Jesus convinced a number of sympathizers that his ministry and message marked the turn of the ages. Would such a follower of Jesus, after the Master's death, no longer be able to assert that the Son of Man was to judge each one's fate in accordance with each individual's attitude towards Jesus? And could he not say that Jesus himself had said so? Could no Christian after Easter say that whoever rejected *Jesus* would have to reckon with his or her condemnation by the *Son of Man* at the Last Judgement?

Moreover, is it likely that, as long as Jesus and his disciples looked forward to the definitive breakthrough of God's rule on earth, his followers made efforts to remember his words exactly and to transmit them faithfully? Are the recollection, formulation, and transmission of sayings of Jesus not in essence a post-Easter development? If so, how certain can we be that the formulation of such sayings was not affected by the passage of time, the change of situation, the difference in circumstances before and after Jesus' death, new questions, new needs?

On the other hand, it is not absolutely impossible either that at places which Jesus visited as a wandering prophet, his words were remembered or even memorized after he left. His followers and friends can conceivably have cherished the memory of some striking utterance of Jesus and passed it on. With regard to the saying reconstructed above, it cannot be argued that it cannot be pre-Easter because it focusses on the person of Jesus. It does not focus on Jesus, but on each individual's reaction to Jesus: this reaction will turn out to be decisive for each one's fate at the Last Judgement.

All in all, however, we can *neither* be sure that the common tradition behind Q 12:9 and Mark 8:38 reaches back to Jesus before Easter, *nor* that it does not.[43]

---

[42] For a survey of arguments pro and con, none of them compelling, see R. Pesch, "Autorität," pp. 39–41.

[43] It is true that normally, if a passage admits of a satisfactory explanation on a more recent level, an explanation on an earlier level is superfluous. For methodical

But does this really matter? True, it cannot be ascertained whether the saying underlying Q 12:8 and Mark 8:38 goes back to Jesus. If it does, it can still not be ascertained whether Jesus wanted to suggest that he would turn out to be identical with the Son of Man or that he expected the Son of Man to be someone else. Neither can the possibility be ruled out that he wanted to suggest that he would appear to be the Son of Man. In spite of all our ignorance, however, there can be little doubt that the saying underlying Q 12:8 and Mark 8:38 renders correctly Jesus' view of the importance of his mission, no matter whether or not the saying is his.

Jesus regarded himself as God's final envoy whose task was to announce and inaugurate God's Kingdom and to summon his hearers to repentance, conversion, and radical obedience to God's will. Consequently, he must have been convinced that those who refused to acknowledge him and his message could not be saved when God's reign would manifest itself definitively and the Last Judgement would take place. Jesus also shared the belief that, at the crucial moment, the Son of Man would manifest himself and play a central role in the final Judgement.

The saying underlying Q 12:8 and Mark 8:38 thus reflects faithfully Jesus' assessment of the significance of his own role in the realization of God's plan. Anybody who refused to acknowledge this role by not answering adequately to the demands of God's Kingdom, would perish in the Last Judgement. This belief in the correspondence between one's reaction to Jesus and one's ultimate fate fits just as well in a pre-Easter as in a post-Easter context. No matter whether or not the reconstructed saying is authentic, no matter what its date, its contents and message fit just as well in a situation before Jesus' death as after it.

---

reasons, given with the "razor of Occam," an explanation on the earlier level should then be excluded. In the case of the reconstructed saying at issue, however, an explanation on the earlier, i.e., the pre-Easter, level must not be ruled out. The reason is that the distinction the saying makes between Jesus and the Son of Man gives it an extraordinarily primitive complexion. The question arises, therefore, whether in the light of the striking primitiveness of the saying, an explanation on a post-Easter level is really sufficiently satisfactory. Since this question cannot easily be decided, Occam's razor is inapplicable here and a pre-Easter origin cannot be excluded. N.B.: This does not mean that a pre-Easter origin is more probable than a post-Easter origin. Neither is "pre-Easter" the same as "spoken by Jesus."

APPENDIX

Note on the text of Matt 10:32 and 33

In N-A[26 and 27], TGNT[1, 2, 3, and 4], and Aland's *Synopsis*[13] the article τοῖς in Matt 10:32 and 33 is printed in square brackets. The brackets indicate that the editors involved were not sure whether or not the article belonged to Matthew's text. In all Nestle and N-A editions from the 1st to the 25th, both articles were printed without brackets. In my view the word should probably be omitted from the text and relegated to the apparatus in both cases.

Apart from 10:32–33, Matthew has eleven instances of a redactional πατὴρ ἐν (τοῖς) οὐρανοῖς: five times *without* τοῖς (in one of these cases the longer reading occurs as a variant) and six times *with* τοῖς (in three of these cases the shorter reading occurs as a variant). The distribution of cases *with*, and those *without* τοῖς shows a clear and interesting pattern. In all five instances of the shorter reading, "Father" is in the genitive (5:45; 12:50; 18:10; 18:14; 18:19). In all instances of the longer reading "Father" is in another case than the genitive, either the nominative, or the vocative, dative or accusative (5:16; 6:1; 6:9; 7:11; 16:17), except in 7:21 where "Father" is in the genitive. But here the shorter reading occurs as a variant.

It may be concluded that in Matt 10:32–33, where "Father" is in the genitive, the shorter reading (without τοῖς) is probably to be preferred. The insertion of the article can be explained in terms of improvement of style. The shorter reading is indeed the one adopted by Griesbach (1786[2]), C. F. Matthaei (1788[1]; 1803[2]), Tischendorf in his *Octava maior* (1869), Von Soden (1913), Vogels (1922; 1955[4]), and Bover (1943; 1968[5]). H. Greeven,[44] too, has ἐν οὐρανοῖς in v. 32 as well as v. 33, in contradistinction to Huck,[45] who had ἐν τοῖς οὐρανοῖς. In his apparatus Greeven rightly refers to Matt 5:16 and especially 6:9 (the opening of the Lord's Prayer) as well-known passages that may have contributed to the insertion of the article in 10:32 and 33.

---

[44] A. Huck and H. Greeven, *Synopse der drei ersten Evangelien* (Tübingen 1981[13]), no. 72, p. 59.
[45] A. Huck, *Synopse der drei ersten Evangelien* (Tübingen 1950[10]).

MARK 14:25 AMONG JESUS' WORDS ABOUT THE KINGDOM OF GOD

M. de Jonge
University of Leiden
(Leiden, the Netherlands)

1. Introduction

1.1. Among the words on the kingdom of God attributed to Jesus in Mark and Q, the saying "Truly I tell you, I will never again drink of the fruit of the vine until that day when I drink it new in the kingdom of God" in Mark 14:25 has drawn the attention of many. It is one of the few sayings that speak about Jesus' presence at the future manifestation of God's sovereign rule in his creation, and that, at the same time, hints at his death. The part to be played by Jesus is, however, very modest and the saying does not specify how Jesus, after his death, will be able to participate in the eschatological meal. Because of this lack of specifics Mark 14:25 is thought to be early, perhaps even genuinely Jesuanic. J. P. Meier speaks for many when, applying the criterion of discontinuity, he writes: "Mark 14:25 reflects christological, soteriological and eschatological ideas—or the startling lack thereof—that are at variance with almost any stream of early Christian tradition but are perfectly understandable in the mouth of the historical Jesus."[1]

1.2. The purpose of the present essay is to take a closer look at this saying and to determine its contribution to our knowledge of the earliest Christian eschatology and christology, and, if possible, also of Jesus' own expectations concerning his participation in the joy of the future kingdom of God.[2] I shall concentrate

---

[1] J. P. Meier, *A Marginal Jew. Rethinking the Historical Jesus*, Vol. 2 (New York 1994), p. 305. See also H. Patsch, *Abendmahl und historischer Jesus* (Stuttgart 1972), p. 142: "Die Authentizität des eschatologischen Wortes Jesu wird kaum je bestritten. ...Das Wort muß für die Erforschung der eschatologischen Erwartung Jesu als fundamental angesehen werden."

[2] See also M. de Jonge, "Jesus' Rôle in the Future Breakthrough of God's Kingdom," in *Geschichte—Tradition—Reflexion. Festschrift für Martin Hengel zum*

on Mark 14:25 as such, with the parallels in Matt 26:29 and Luke 22:18. We must allow for the possibility that it circulated independently and that its present position in the context of Jesus' last supper with his disciples, immediately after the words connected with the cup in v. 24 "this is my blood of the covenant, which is poured for many" is secondary. Of course, v. 25 presupposes a meal with bread and wine of Jesus together with his disciples at the end of his mission. It reflects a farewell situation in which Jesus speaks about the future meal in the kingdom of God, probably in the light of his impending death. This verse does not necessarily presuppose a supper as described by the Synoptics (and Paul in 1 Corinthians 11) at which Jesus instituted a solemn celebration with bread and wine by his followers after his death.[3]

2. Text, vocabulary and syntax

2.1 The text as printed in the 27th edition of Nestle Aland's *Novum Testamentum Graece* and the fourth edition of the *Greek New Testament* (both from 1993), which is based on A B Δ f^1 f^{13} and a host of other witnesses, is likely to be nearest to the original.[4] The omission of οὐκέτι in a number of important witnesses (amongst which א C L W Ψ) avoids the awkward οὐκέτι οὐ μή and gives a smoother text (cf. Matt 26:29 οὐ μὴ ... ἀπ' ἄρτι and Luke 22:18 οὐ μὴ ... ἀπὸ τοῦ νῦν). The variant οὐ μὴ προσθῶ πεῖν in D and some Old Latin MSS (cf. 565 οὐκέτι οὐ προσθῶ πιεῖν) has drawn attention as a Hebraism.[5] But also this variant may be an attempt to avoid the difficult negation, this time by using a construction

---

70. *Geburtstag*, edd. H. Cancik, H. Lichtenberger, P. Schäfer (Tübingen 1996), Vol. 3, pp. 265–286.

[3] So I shall pass over many questions (in themselves interesting) raised by scholars in connection with Mark 14:22–25 and par., *e.g.* the nature of the last supper, the original form of the words connected with bread and wine, and the origin and nature of the liturgical meal (or meals) in the communities of Jesus' followers.

[4] For details about variants see the apparatus on our verse in *Greek New Testament*[4].

[5] On this see *e.g.* J. Jeremias, *Die Abendmahlsworte Jesu* (Göttingen 1967[4]), pp. 174–175. He thinks that the readings found in B, D and Θ (see below) represent variants of equal value ("gleichwertige Überlieferungs- und Übersetzungsvarianten"); see also M. Black, *An Aramaic Approach to the Gospels and Acts* (Oxford 1954[2]), p. 214 (and 296).

well-known from the LXX.[6] Jeremias also points to the reading οὐκέτι οὐ μὴ προσθῶμεν πιεῖν in Θ and suspects here the influence of the use of the first person plural with singular meaning in Galilean Aramaic; it is much more likely, however, that the plural refers here to Jesus and his disciples (cf. the μεθ' ὑμῶν in Matt. 26:29).

2.2 Much has been written about the Semitisms in our verse.[7] The ἀμὴν λέγω ὑμῖν (Matthew: λέγω δὲ ὑμῖν; Luke: λέγω γὰρ ὑμῖν) is striking; in the Synoptics it only occurs in the mouth of Jesus (John has a double ἀμήν) and no real parallels can be found in the Old Testament and in later Jewish texts. For the evangelists the use of this introduction in solemn sayings was typical of Jesus; whether it represents Jesus' *ipsissima vox* (Jeremias) remains, however, disputed.[8] The awkward οὐκέτι οὐ μή, signalled above, is found eleven times in the LXX as translation of various Hebrew expressions. The use of πίνειν followed by ἐκ, indicating what is drunk (Luke has πίνειν ἀπό), corresponds to Hebrew and Aramaic usage; it is also found in John 4:13, 14 and Rev 14:10, 18:3, as well as in Gen 9:21 (cf. ἀπό in Jer 28:7 [LXX]; Sir 26:12).[9] For "the fruit of the vine" see Num 6:4; Isa 32:12; Hab 3:17 (cf. Judg 13:14; 2 Kgs 18:31). It is regularly used in Jewish prayers, see m. Ber. 6:1 "for over wine a man says: 'who createst the fruit of the vine'" (transl. H. Danby). In ἕως τῆς ἡμέρας ἐκείνης ὅταν the ἐκεῖνος does not receive emphasis and can be missed.[10] Jeremias notes a similar redundancy in a number of other texts (*e.g.* in Mark 14:21) and ascribes this to the

---

[6] See also BDR § 435[4].

[7] A convenient survey can be found in J. Jeremias, *Die Abendmahlsworte Jesu*, pp. 174–177.

[8] On this see especially J. Jeremias, "Kennzeichen der ipsissima vox Jesu" in *Abba, Studien zur neutestamentlichen Theologie und Zeitgeschichte* (Göttingen 1966), pp. 145–152 (originally in the *Festschrift* for A. Wikenhauser [1954]) and K. Berger, *Die Amen-Worte Jesu. Eine Untersuchung zum Problem der Legitimation in apokalyptischer Rede*, BZNW 39 (Berlin 1970); and "Zur Geschichte der Einleitungsformel 'Amen ich sage euch'," *ZNW* 63 (1972), pp. 45–75. Berger found two parallels in the long recension of the *Testament of Abraham* (8:7; 20:2), but the date and provenance of this recension remain disputed. For a survey of recent opinion see J. P. Meier, *A Marginal Jew*, Vol. 2, n. 62 on pp. 367–369.

[9] Compare J. Schlosser, *Le Règne de Dieu dans les dits de Jésus*, EtB (Paris 1980), Vol. 1, pp. 382–383. Classical Greek uses the accusative or the partitive genitive in this case.

[10] See BDR §382, 2.

influence of the pleonastic use of the demonstrative pronoun in
Hebrew and Aramaic. Finally, everyone agrees that the predi-
cative use of καινόν in our verse is Greek, and will definitely not
go back to a Hebrew or Aramaic expression.[11]

These linguistic peculiarities may point to early tradition, or
they may not; they do not necessarily lead us to assume Jesuanic
provenance. Translating this saying back into Aramaic remains a
hazardous undertaking. Semiticizing, "biblical" expressions do
not automatically point to translation from a Semitic original.

3. The parallels in Matthew and Luke

3.1. Matt 26:29 closely resembles Mark 14:25, but tries to remove
a number of difficulties. It smoothes the negative construction
(see 2.1) and reads "*this* fruit of the vine" (establishing a link with
the preceding verse). Matthew also makes Jesus specify that he
will drink the wine anew "with you" (*i.e.* with his disciples), and
indicate his special position at the banquet as Son of the Father
(replacing "in the kingdom of God" by "my Father's kingdom").
By these two changes Matthew answers two questions naturally
asked by readers of Mark: Who else will be present at the meal?
and: What will Jesus' function be? There is no doubt that
Matthew is dependent on Mark in this case, and therefore
presents a secondary text.

3.2. But what about Luke 22:18? This verse is part of 22:15–18
which, in this gospel, forms the introduction to the words about
the bread and the cup in 22:19–20, parallel to Mark 14:22–24
and Matt 26:19–20. Luke 22:18 does not follow "the words of institution" but precedes them. Moreover it has a direct parallel in
v. 16: "For I tell you, I will not eat it (= this Passover, v. 15) until
it is fulfilled in the kingdom of God."

Much has been written on Luke 22:15–20 and its relationship
to the other Synoptic accounts that need not detain us here.[12] The
most likely theory, in my opinion, is that vv. 15–18 go back to
Lukan redaction, and that v. 16 was deliberately formed as a
parallel to v. 18. Schlosser has argued that v. 18 is not directly

---

[11] See especially M. Black, *An Aramaic Approach*, pp. 171–172 who resorts to
the hypothesis of a mistranslation in this case.

[12] See besides J. Jeremias, *Die Abendmahlsworte Jesu* also H. Schürmann, *Das
Passahmahlbericht Lk 22,(7-14,) 15–18*, NTA 19,5 (Münster 1953) and H. Patsch,
Abendmahl und historischer Jesus.

dependent on Mark 14:25.[13] Because of the different endings of the saying in Mark and in Luke, he concludes that Mark and Luke give two versions, independent of one another, of a more primitive logion. He points out that the ἕως οὗ ἡ βασιλεία τοῦ θεοῦ ἔλθῃ cannot have been prompted by a desire on the part of the evangelist to avoid a too realistic picture of Jesus' drinking at the eschatological meal. In fact, a few verses later, in 22:30, Jesus says: "I confer on you, just as my Father has conferred on me, a kingdom, so that you may eat and drink at my table in my kingdom" (a Lukan addition to Q-material, see below). Next, in 14:16–24, he gives the parable of the Great Supper (par. Matt 22:1–10), introducing it with the word of a listener to earlier words of Jesus: "Blessed is anyone who will eat bread in the kingdom of God" (v.15).

Schlosser emphasizes that the combination of βασιλεία τοῦ θεοῦ and ἔρχομαι is also found in Luke 11:2, par. Matt 6:10; Luke 17:20–21 and Mark 9:1. It is typical of words of Jesus and therefore the ending of Luke may be nearer to the original logion than that of Mark. This is, however, far from certain. Luke who had already given a reference to the kingdom of God in v. 16 may have wanted to use a different expression in v. 18, forming it as an analogy to the beginning of the Lord's Prayer.[14] Schlosser's hypothesis of double attestation of an earlier saying of Jesus remains tenuous.

3.3. One final remark under this heading: In Paul's version of the tradition concerning the last supper of Jesus with his disciples in 1 Cor 11:23–26 we find only the words over the bread and the wine. However, in the apostle's own words in v. 26: "For as often as you eat this bread and drink this cup you proclaim the Lord's death until he comes" (cf. also the μαράνα θά in 1 Cor 16:22), there is a reference to Jesus' *parousia*. The coming of the Lord is parallel to the coming of the kingdom of God in the Lukan version. Paul's words show that the connection between the account of the institution of the Eucharist/Holy Supper and God's definitive intervention in the future was made at an early stage in the tradition.

---

[13] See *Le Règne de Dieu*, Vol. 1, pp. 380–389.

[14] So also J. P. Meier, *A Marginal Jew*, Vol. 2, p. 367, n. 60.

4. What is made clear—and what is left open

4.1. Mark 14:25 has to be taken as a unity. The hypothesis that the saying once ended with ἕως τῆς ἡμέρας ἐκείνης, referring to the day of judgment, and that the rest of the verse is a later addition, emphasizing the duration of the time of salvation, is superfluous;[15] the use of ἐκεῖνος here does not call for such an interpretation (see above, 2.2).

4.2. Jesus' solemn declaration should not be taken as a vow of abstinence[16] but as a prediction. Jesus does not announce what he intends to do but what is going to happen "in the kingdom of God", i.e. when God will establish his reign in his entire creation (cf. Luke 11:2, par. Matt 6: 9–10). He speaks authoritatively on the basis of special insight conferred by revelation.[17] J. P. Meier points to the parallels in form between our verse and Mark 9:1; 13:30 ("amen + negated future action + time-span until further experience of the kingdom of God occurs"[18]). In Mark 14:25 Jesus speaks about his own future, as in the other passion predictions (see the amen-sayings Mark 14:8–9, 18, 30). "Der Prophet weiß nicht nur die Geschichte, sondern auch das eng mit

---

[15] See K. Berger, *Die Amen-Worte Jesu*, pp. 54–55, and compare J. Gnilka, *Das Evangelium nach Markus (Mk 8,29–16,20)*, EKK II.2 (Zürich/Einsiedeln/Köln/Neukirchen/Vluyn 1979), p. 243. Schlosser, *Le Règne de Dieu*, pp. 386–387 is rightly critical. W. G. Kümmel, *Verheißung und Erfüllung. Untersuchungen zur eschatologischen Verkündigung Jesu* (Zürich 1953²), pp. 29–36 (a section on "Die Rede vom eschatologischen 'Tag'") states: "Es ist darüber hinaus eindeutig, daß dieser kommende Gerichtstag mit dem Eintritt der Gottesherrschaft zusammenfällt (Mk 14,25)" (p. 31).

[16] J. Jeremias's theory of a "Verzichterklärung Jesu" (*Die Abendmahlsworte Jesu*, pp. 199–210) has been a hot topic in recent discussion. The hypothesis that Jesus pronounced a Nazarite vow (see P. Lebeau, *Le vin nouveau du Royaume. Etude exégétique et patristique sur la Parole eschatologique de Jésus à la Cène* [Paris/Bruges 1966], pp. 81–85, referring to M. Thurian and M. Barth) has recently been revived by M. Wojciechowski, "Le naziréat et la Passion (Mc 14,25a; 15,23)", *Bib.* 65 (1984), pp. 94–96.

[17] On this see K. Berger, *Die Amen-Worte Jesu* in particular.

[18] *A Marginal Jew*, Vol. 2, p. 307. He also points to Matt 10:23; Matt 5:26, par. Luke 12:59; Matt 23:39, par. Luke 13:35 and John 13:38 (p. 306) and remarks that this type of prediction "is a specific case of a more general biblical pattern in which it is prophesied that a person's death will not take place until some saving event occurs." As examples he mentions Luke 2:26; John 21:23 and also Jub. 16:16 (p. 307).

dem künftigen Fortgang verbundene eigene Lebensende voraus—und der Prophetenschüler (Petrus usw.) wird von seinem
Meister belehrt."[19]

4.3. The eschatological nature of our logion is underscored by
the use of the word καινός (cf. the references to the "new
covenant," e.g. in Luke 22:20; 1 Cor 11:25; 2 Cor 3:6; Heb 8:8;
Paul's use of καινὴ κτίσις in Gal 6:15; 2 Cor 5:17 [with "everything old has passed away; see, everything has become new"]
and especially the saying about the new wine that has to be put
into fresh wineskins, in Mark 2:21–22). The drinking of the wine
will take place at a banquet to be held after God's decisive
intervention in the future. In 3.2 we already mentioned the use of
the same imagery in Luke 22:30 and 14:15, 16–24. The most
interesting parallel is the Q-passage Luke 13:28–29, par. Matt
8:11–12 where (many) people will come from all corners of the
earth to take part in a meal in the kingdom of God together with
Abraham, Isaac and Jacob.[20]

4.4. This last passage is particularly important for a better
understanding of Mark 14:25 because it, too, leaves much unsaid.
In Mark 14:25 Jesus' position at the meal is not specified; in Luke
13:28–29 and par. he is not even mentioned. When Abraham,
Isaac and Jacob are portrayed as taking part in the meal, they are
regarded as having risen from the dead (cf. Mark 12:18–27, par.
Matt 22:23–33; Luke 20:27–40), but this is not said explicitly.
How the many other participants at the meal are able to be
present and to take part is not specified. Also our logion simply
refers to Jesus' participation in the meal—with others,
presumably, but not even his disciples are mentioned; it
presupposes the end of his mission among men, but does not
speak explicitly about his death, or about his exaltation or
resurrection enabling him to take part in the meal. Both texts do
not speak about a "coming" of the kingdom (nor our text about a
coming of Jesus); it will manifest itself at God's intervention.

When the meal will take place is clear, but where it is to be
located is left open. It is assumed that in the new dispensation

---

[19] So K. Berger, *Die Amen-Worte Jesu,* p. 67, in the section "Sätze mit betonter
Naherwartung," pp. 58–69; see also "Die Amen-Worte in der Passionsüber-
lieferung," pp. 49–58.

[20] Cf. Isa 25:6–10; 55:1–2; 65:13–14; *1 Enoch* 62:14; *2 Apoc. Bar.* 29:4; 1QSa
2:11–12. On the O.T. and Jewish background of this saying see especially D.
Zeller, "Das Logion Mt 8,11f / Lk 13,28f und das Motiv der 'Völkerwallfahrt',"
BZ 15 (1971), pp. 222–237 and 16 (1972), pp. 84–93.

everything will be different and the meal is a metaphor for unity with God and all his faithful and for participation in the final salvation. With regard to the time and the location of the future meal in which Jesus will take part (with his disciples, according to Matthew) we find an interesting variety in interpretations in the Early Church, from the second century onwards (duly registered by H. Vogels[21] and F. Lebeau[22]).

4.5. Eschatology and christology are always closely connected. This explains why Mark 14:25 also leaves many things open regarding Jesus' place in God's dealings with mankind, during his activity in Galilea and Judea—and later. If his death is envisaged (which seems likely given the farewell situation), nothing is said about the way he is to die and the reason for his death, nor about a possible causal connection between his departure and the manifestation of God's reign. We hear nothing about his resurrection, exaltation or *parousia.* Jesus participates in the banquet, but does not preside over it or procure access to it for others, for instance those closely connected with him. However, the fact that he expresses as his firm conviction that he will share in the final salvation, is highly significant. Although men may want to terminate his preaching of the kingdom of God as well as his healings and exorcisms signifying its inauguration, by putting him to death, the final breakthrough of God's sovereign rule cannot be halted, and Jesus, as messenger of the kingdom, will be personally vindicated.[23]

5. Mark 14:25 and other words of Jesus about the future

5.1. From what has been said so far it is clear that we should avoid overinterpreting Mark 14:25. We may try, however, to throw some more light on it by looking at it again in combination

---

[21] "Mk 14,25 und Parallelen," in *Vom Wort des Lebens. Festschrift für Max Meinertz,* ed. N. Adler, NTA, Erg. Band 1 (Münster 1951), pp. 93–104.

[22] See note 16. The exegetical part of Lebeau's book is disappointing; his survey of patristic exegesis is highly instructive. See also, on the version of the logion in Tatian's *Diatessaron,* A. Baumstark, "Zur Geschichte des Tatiantextes vor Aphrem," *OrChr* 30 (III.8) (1933), pp. 1–12. For the text from *Gos. Eb.* in Epiphanius, *Panarion* 30.22.4–5 and the passage from *Gos. Heb.* in Jerome, *De viris illustribus* 2 (and parallel texts), see A. F. J. Klijn, *Jewish-Christian Gospel Tradition,* VigChr.S 17 (Leiden 1992), pp. 76–77 and 79–86 respectively.

[23] On this see also J. Schlosser, *Le Règne de Dieu,* pp. 394–395 and J. P. Meier, *A Marginal Jew,* pp. 307–309.

with Jesus' other sayings about the future, both with regard to his personal destiny and with the final breakthrough of the kingdom.[24] The question of the possible "authenticity" of our logion and related sayings will have to be discussed at a later stage.

5.2. In the words in the Synoptics concerning the future of the kingdom all emphasis is on the definitive revelation of God's sovereign rule. They do not pay attention to a rôle for Jesus at the final breakthrough, although in the present Jesus plays an important, indeed central, part—when he announces that the kingdom of God has drawn near (Mark 1:14–15) and even inaugurates it in his healings and exorcisms (see Luke 11:20, par. Matt 12:28). He tells his disciples to pray for the coming of God's kingdom (Luke 11:2, par. Matt 6:10); he urges people to believe his message and radically mend their ways (Mark 9:47). They are told to give up everything (Mark 10:17–31, par. Matt 19:19–30; Luke 18:18–30) and expected to accept the kingdom of God as a child (Mark 10:13–16, par. Luke 18:15–17, cf. Matt 19:13–15; 18:3). In this context the term "to enter the kingdom of God" is used (Mark 9:47; 10:15. 23–25; see also Matt 5:20; 7:21; 23:13; Joh 3:5) besides "to inherit eternal life/the kingdom of God" (Mark 10:17; Matt 19:29; 25:34; Jas 2:5 and the Pauline texts 1 Cor 6:9; 15:50; Gal 5:21).

The sayings concerning the future as well as those dealing with the presence of the kingdom, centre around God's dynamic rule, soon to be fully realized, but already manifest in Jesus' activity. Whatever "christology" there is, is theocentric.[25] It does presuppose, however, that the complete realization of God's rule is to bring the vindication of the message preached by Jesus and thereby of his own person and mission. It seems likely that this is also implied in Mark 14:25—a verse that is also in keeping with the other sayings about the future kingdom in not mentioning any special rôle for Jesus.

The same applies to Luke 13:28–29, par. Matt 8:11–12, as we have just seen in 4.4. The picture is different in Luke 22:28–30 which emphasizes that the Father confers a kingdom on Jesus, so that he is able to invite those who have stood by him in his trials

---

[24] On what follows in this section see also my "Jesus' Rôle in the Future Breakthrough of God's Kingdom" (*supra*, n. 2).

[25] See also M. de Jonge, "Christology and Theology in the Context of Early Eschatology, particularly in the Fourth Gospel," in *The Four Gospels 1992. Festschrift Frans Neirynck*, edd. F. Van Segbroeck *et al.*, BEThL 100 (Leuven 1992), Vol. 3, pp. 1835–1853.

to eat and drink at his table in his kingdom and to "sit on thrones judging the twelve tribes of Israel." Matt 19:28 does not speak about table fellowship and connects the last part of this saying with the time "when the Son of man is seated on the throne of his glory." These sayings may be linked with Mark 10:37 where James and John ask Jesus: "Grant us to sit, one at your right hand and one at your left, in your glory" (cf. also v. 40; Matt 20:21 reads: "in your kingdom"). For the evangelist there is clearly a connection between this verse and 8:38–9:1 where he combines two originally unconnected sayings, about the coming of the Son of man "in the glory of his Father with the holy angels" and the coming of the kingdom of God "with power" respectively. Mark 10:37 as such, however, refers to an exaltation in glory of Jesus, not necessarily to his *parousia*.[26]

The evangelists, as well as Paul before them, expected a coming of Jesus from heaven, as Lord or as Son of man, in the near future. The dead would rise from their graves, the final judgment would take place, all wrongdoers would be punished and all satanic powers would be destroyed, and God's faithful would share in the bliss of the new dispensation. There is a great variety in the pictures of the eschatological drama, and none of them are complete. We cannot speak of a fixed scenario into which all predicted events would find a place one after the other. It may be said however, that nearly all our earliest sources assign a central position to Jesus in the events of the future, just as in the past and the present.

How do we account, then, for Mark 14:25 and other passages about God's future rule which do not speak of Jesus' *parousia* and do not highlight the part to be played by him in the final eschatological drama? And can we say something more about the transition from a life on earth to a life in the kingdom of God presupposed in our logion, but not made explicit?

5.3. For an answer to the second question we may look for a moment to 1 Cor 15:20–28, a passage in which the resurrection of Jesus and the resurrection of the faithful are connected. The latter will take place at Jesus' *parousia*; Jesus will destroy every ruler, every authority and every power (the last enemy to be destroyed is death); the end comes when he hands over the kingdom to God the Father.

---

[26] One may note that in Luke 22:28–30 and Matt 19:28, too, neither the Son of man nor the kingdom are said to come.

This passage has been the subject of a thorough investigation by J. Holleman in his recent book *Resurrection and Parousia.*[27] 1 Corinthians 15 emphasizes Jesus' central rôle in the eschato-logical events and establishes a direct link between the resur-rection of "those who belong to Christ" and that of Jesus Christ himself. J. Holleman has shown, however, that traditio-historically we should distinguish two types of resurrection: a col-lective resurrection at the end of times, and a personal resur-rection of certain believers, immediately after their violent death. Jesus' resurrection is essentially that of a martyr vindicated by God, such as is promised to the seven sons and their mother in 2 Maccabees 7. Vindication of a martyr, who has to die because he remains loyal to God and his commandments, may be to the be-nefit of Israel in distress, but it does not, of course, in itself bring about *final* salvation. But because Jesus was seen by his followers as one who had announced and inaugurated God's decisive and definitive intervention in human history, his vindication came to be regarded as the prelude to and the beginning of the escha-tological resurrection—by Paul and perhaps also by other early Christians (but none of those has left us anything in writing).[28]

For our interpretation of Mark 14:25 this may imply that Jesus' death is seen as followed by his resurrection—a resurrection envisaged as the vindication of the one who announced and inaugurated God's kingdom, and who remained faithful to his mission to the end. In his exalted state he takes part in the eschatological meal, sharing in the bliss of God's kingdom. But how, then, is the relation in time between Jesus' exaltation and the manifestation of the kingdom? 1 Cor 15:20–28 presupposes an interim period between Jesus' resurrection and his *parousia*, although Paul expects it to be short.[29] Also in Mark 14:25 the "never again...until that day" suggests some lapse of

---

[27] *Resurrection and Parousia. A Traditio-Historical Study of Paul's Eschatology in 1 Cor 15*, NovT.S 84 (Leiden 1996).

[28] On this see *Resurrection and Parousia*, pp. 158–161. See also H. J. de Jonge, "De opstanding van Jezus. De joodse traditie achter een christelijke belijdenis," in *Jodendom en vroeg christendom: continuïteit en discontinuïteit*, edd. T. Baarda *et al.* (Kampen 1991), pp. 47–61, together with his *Visionaire ervaring en de historische oorsprong van het Christendom* (Inaugural lecture, University of Leiden, 1992). Compare M. de Jonge, *Jesus, The Servant-Messiah* (New Haven/London 1991), pp. 42–48, 56–62.

[29] In 1 Corinthians see 7:26, 29; 10:11 ("...us, on whom the ends of the ages have come").

time between Jesus' death and the meal in God's kingdom; there is, in any case, no indication that Jesus' exaltation and the appearance of God's kingdom will coincide. It is only in connection with vv. 22–24 that v. 25 suggests an interim period *of some length* during which the disciples should continue their communion with Jesus through bread and wine at a community meal.[30] Taken on its own Mark 14:25 does not say more than that Jesus expected to be resurrected/exalted and to be present at the eschatological meal at the final breakthrough of God's sovereign rule; it does not refer to Jesus' *parousia* and it does not give any further specifications concerning a period of "waiting" in between.

5.4. It remains remarkable, then, that our logion presupposes Jesus' vindication after his death and his participation in the joy of the future kingdom without mentioning his *parousia* or assigning to him a central rôle in the final breakthrough of God's sovereign rule. Given the importance of the notion of Jesus' *parousia* in early Christianity and the fact that it is found in the letters of Paul (from his oldest letter, 1 Thessalonians of about 50 C.E., onwards), as well as in Mark and in Q (followed by Matthew and Luke), those passages that fail to mention it, stand out. We may explain this difference as a sign of discontinuity in the Christian tradition, which tended to stress Christ's power and glory and to develop its "christology." If so, the texts about God's future royal rule that do not highlight Jesus' part in it, will belong to an earlier strand in the tradition than those which speak about his *parousia.*

5.5. We should be cautious, however, to call Mark 14:25 a genuine, "authentic", word of the historical Jesus. The wording of this logion does not necessarily point to a word of Jesus himself; (re-)translation into Aramaic remains difficult (see *e.g.* καινόν as predicate). The use of ἀμὴν λέγω ὑμῖν is typical of Jesus in the Synoptics, and the criterion of "multiple attestation" as well as that of "dissimilarity" may be applied to it. That does not mean, however, that every individual saying of Jesus that is so introduced, is a genuine word of Jesus; this introduction may have been added at a later stage to give it more authority. If we see what Matthew did with the word he found in Mark, and notice Luke's extensive redactional activity, we must allow for the possibility that Mark, too, dealt somewhat freely with the word handed down to him.

---

[30] On this see especially J. Schlosser, *Le Règne de Dieu*, pp. 394–398.

In general, I think, we should not try to be too specific about individual sayings, but rather concentrate on historical developments. We are able to distinguish early elements in the tradition and, in some cases, to establish a link between those and the message of Jesus himself. That Jesus expected that God would vindicate his message and make him participate in the joys of the kingdom after his definitive intervention, seems to me certain. After all, he must have taken his own mission seriously. Whether he expressed this conviction in the words found in Mark 14:25 remains, of necessity, uncertain.[31]

---

[31] I thank the members of the N. T. department of the Faculty of Theology in the University of Leiden for a stimulating discussion of an earlier version of this essay, which led to a number of corrections and clarifications.

THE SAYINGS OF Q AND THEIR IMAGE OF JESUS

Helmut Koester
The Divinity School, Harvard University
(Cambridge, Massachusetts, USA)

I. The present situation in Q research and its problems

The synoptic Sayings Gospel (Q) has been the object of intense efforts of scholarship during the last decades, beginning with James M. Robinson's seminal essay "ΛΟΓΟΙ ΣΟΦΩΝ" in the Bultmann Festschrift of 1964[1] and culminating in the International Q Project that published its last installment of the reconstructed Greek text of Q in the *Journal of Biblical Literature* in the fall of 1995.[2] Contrary to the earlier view that the synoptic Sayings Gospel Q grew out of Jesus' eschatological or apocalyptic proclamation,[3] a different perspective recently evolved primarily

---

[1] James M. Robinson, "ΛΟΓΟΙ ΣΟΦΩΝ. Zur Gattung der Spruchquelle Q," in *Zeit und Geschichte: Dankesgabe an Rudolf Bultmann zum 80. Geburtstag*, ed. Erich Dinkler (Tübingen 1964), pp. 77–96; an expanded English translation was published in idem, ed., *The Future of Our Religious Past: Essays in Honor of Rudolf Bultmann* (New York 1971), pp. 84–130 and republished in idem and Helmut Koester, *Trajectories through Early Christianity* (Philadelphia 1971), pp. 71–113.

[2] Milton C. Moreland and James M. Robinson, "The International Q Project: Work Sessions 23–27 May, 22–26 August, 17–18 November 1994," *JBL* 114 (1995), pp. 475–485. The results of previous work sessions were published in *JBL* 109 (1990), pp. 499–501; 110 (1991), pp. 494–498; 111 (1992), pp. 500–508; 112 (1993), pp. 500–506; 113 (1994), pp. 495–500.

[3] Characteristic for this view is Siegfried Schulz, *Q. Die Spruchquelle der Evangelisten* (Zürich 1972), who assumes an enthusiastic-apocalyptic orientation as the matrix of Q. Other more recent studies, however, also maintain that eschatology is the primary element in the composition and redaction of Q; see Dieter Lührmann, *Die Redaktion der Logienquelle*, WMANT 33 (Neukirchen-Vluyn 1969), pp. 93–104; Paul Hoffmann, *Studien zur Theologie der Logienquelle*, NTA N.F. 8 (Münster 1972); also Helmut Koester, *Ancient Christian Gospels: Their History and Development* (Philadelphia 1990), pp. 129–171. For a comprehensive survey of scholarship on Q until 1982, see Frans Neirynck, "Recent Developments in the Study of Q," in *Logia: Les paroles de Jésus—The Sayings of Jesus: Mémorial Joseph Coppens*, ed. Joël Delobel, BEThL 59 (Leuven 1982), pp. 29–75;

among some American scholars, most of whom had participated
in the International Q Project.[4] These scholars agree with most
earlier works assuming that Q was originally composed in Greek[5]
and that it exhibits in all its stages an orientation that is fundamentally different from that found in the Pauline churches.[6] In
other respects, however, they differ from the previous consensus
in several ways:

> (1) There is a good deal of confidence that it is possible to
> distinguish between an original composition of Q and one or
> several later redactions. In its original composition, the model
> for the genre of Q was the "wisdom book," and its orientation
> was sapiential, while only the redaction(s) of Q incorporated
> apocalyptic sayings and judgment sayings, thus introducing an
> apocalyptic perspective.

> (2) Q was composed in Galilee, both in its original form and in
> its second stage. It reflects the small-town and village social,
> economic, and political situation of Lower Galilee, and those
> who composed Q seem to have belonged to the literate class of
> the scribes of these communities.[7]

---

repr. with additional notes in F. Neirynck, *Evangelica II*, BEThL 99 (Leuven
1991), pp. 409–464.

[4] This consensus is largely based upon John Kloppenborg, *The Formation of Q:
Trajectories in Ancient Wisdom Tradition* (Studies in Antiquity and Christianity;
Philadelphia 1987) and it is typically represented in the essays of the recently
published work *Conflict and Invention: Literary, Rhetorical, and Social Studies on the
Sayings Gospel Q*, ed. John S. Kloppenborg (Valley Forge [Pennsylvania] 1995).

[5] Although Q apparently contains a number of sayings that were originally
formulated and transmitted in Aramaic, even the oldest written version of Q was
composed in Greek. There is, however, a new perspective in so far as attempts
have been made to understand the literary and rhetorical structure of Q on the
basis of parallels and analogies from the Greek world.

[6] Only the sayings of Jesus matter, while the narrative of Jesus' passion and
the stories of his appearance after his death are either unknown or ignored.

[7] John S. Kloppenborg, "Conflict and Invention: Recent Studies on Q," in
idem, ed., *Conflict and Invention*, pp. 3–6.

(3) Some scholars in this group have argued that the original composition of Q lacks any eschatological orientation.[8] Rather, its "wisdom" is directed towards the social questions of its time and location. If one wants to reconstruct the teachings of Jesus on the basis of this original version of Q, the corresponding picture of the historical Jesus is that of a wisdom preacher or even of a social revolutionary.

The combination of these three assumptions, however, leads into a vicious circle. To restrict a Greek document to Galilee and to limit it to a single message does not leave room for the diversity of the tradition of Jesus' sayings and for their wide geographical distribution at an early formative stage. Sayings that were collected in the "Inaugural Sermon" of Q (6:20–46)[9] are also found in the letters of Paul.[10] James Robinson and I have argued that the Corinthians were familiar with sayings that have close parallels in the *Gospel of Thomas*.[11] These same sayings have also found their way into Q 10:21–24,[12] most likely into its earliest stage of composition. At the same time, the *Gospel of Thomas* itself is a witness to early collections of sayings that were also incorporated into the first composition of Q.[13] Evidence for such collections of sayings appears in 1 Peter, James, and *1 Clement*.[14] It is hardly possible to restrict the earliest collection and circulation of sayings to a geographically limited area, in which only one

---

[8] John Kloppenborg, however, ascribes an eschatological orientation also to the original composition of Q; see his "The Sayings Gospel Q and the Quest of the Historical Jesus," *HThR* 89 (1996), pp. 337–339.

[9] All references to chapter and verse of "Q" are identical with those numbers in the Gospel of Luke; instead of Q/Luke or Luke I have just used the short formula "Q + chapter and verse."

[10] See my *Ancient Christian Gospels*, pp. 52–55.

[11] James M. Robinson, "Basic Shifts in German Theology," *Interpretation* 16 (1962), pp. 82–86; idem, "ΛΟΓΟΙ ΣΟΦΩΝ," pp. 87–88, n. 39; this footnote was not incorporated into the English translation of this essay, but see idem, "Kerygma and History in the New Testament," in Robinson and Koester, *Trajectories*, pp. 30–34; see my *Ancient Christian Gospels*, pp. 55–62.

[12] For a parallel to the "hidden wisdom which God has predetermined before the ages" (1 Cor 2:7) see also Matt 13:35: "I will utter what has been hidden since the foundation of the world.".

[13] See the documentation in my *Ancient Christian Gospels*, pp. 133–162.

[14] Ibid., pp. 64–75. See also James M. Robinson, "Early Collections of Jesus' Sayings," in Delobel, *Logia: Les paroles de Jésus*, pp. 389–394.

singular ideological perspective determined their selection and composition. It could be argued, however, that the author of Q, living in Galilee, had access only to a particular strand of the otherwise widely distributed and diverse traditions of sayings and that his composition was more uniform than the sayings tradition in general. Yet, that the original composition of Q was in Greek and was based upon sayings circulating in Greek should caution against such a notion. The use of the Greek language cannot simply be explained by drawing an historically problematic image of a thoroughly Hellenized Galilee;[15] rather, the employment of Greek implied necessarily that those who transmitted these sayings participated in a wider cultural context.

The most problematic issue in the understanding of Q as a wisdom book is the question of its religious or philosophical orientation. John Kloppenborg had presented an impressive analysis of two (or even three) stages of the development of Q, in which he identified the earliest stage as a wisdom book.[16] Kloppenborg himself, however, did not claim that the composition of Q as a wisdom book implies an absence of any eschatological orientation, and most scholars engaged in Q research have usually refrained from drawing conclusions from their work with respect to the historical Jesus.[17] Yet Kloppenborg's hypothesis has been used in some publications (Burton L. Mack,[18] Leif

---

[15] See, *e.g.*, Burton Mack, *Who Wrote the New Testament? The Making of the Christian Myth* (San Francisco 1995), pp. 38–39.

[16] *The Formation of Q.* Kloppenborg's thesis is based upon some suggestions that James M. Robinson and I had made in earlier articles as well as on the work of Dieter Lührmann, *Redaktion der Logienquelle*.

[17] Some critics of recent studies of Q have misunderstood scholars such as Kloppenborg and myself by claiming that they were advocating the image of a completely non-eschatological historical Jesus, who was nothing but a Cynic or semi-Gnostic wisdom teacher. See on such criticism Kloppenborg, "The Sayings Gospel Q and the Historical Jesus," p. 336, n. 120.

[18] "Lord of the Logia: Savior or Sage," in *Gospel Origins & Christian Beginnings: In Honor of James M. Robinson*, edd. James E. Goehring et al. (Sonoma [California] 1990), pp. 49–63; idem, *The Lost Gospel: The Book of Q and Christian Origins* (San Francisco 1993); see also idem, *A Myth of Innocence: Mark and Christian Origins* (Philadelphia 1988). In his recent book, *Who Wrote the New Testament?* Mack repeats the Cynic hypothesis regarding the earliest form of Q: "The lifestyle of the Jesus people bears remarkable resemblance to the Greek tradition of popular philosophy characteristic of the Cynics. Cynics also promoted an outrageous lifestyle as a way of criticizing conventional mores, and the themes

E. Vaage[19]) in order to argue that this first stage of Q presented not just wisdom teaching in general, but reflected popular Cynicism. This resulted in the conclusion that Jesus himself must have understood his own mission as that of a social critic in the style of a Hellenistic Cynic preacher—a thesis that was recently critically questioned by Hans-Dieter Betz[20] and James M. Robinson.[21] At the same time, the redaction of Q appears as a secondary transformation of wisdom teaching into eschatological and apocalyptic prophecy and thus as a radical alteration of the view of Jesus from that of a Cynic sage into that of a prophet and apocalyptic visionary.

The reconstruction of the earlier stage of Q may even be influenced by this hypothesis. There is a temptation to relegate to the second stage of Q not only the obviously apocalyptic predictions of the coming of the Son of Man and the clearly secondary judgment sayings but also other sayings of an eschatological or prophetic character. Kloppenborg has doubtlessly furnished the foundation for this reconstruction of the stages of Q. He provided[22] a formal analysis of Q's wisdom instructions, listing all materials that would fit into this formative concept. The question is, whether Kloppenborg's wisdom book should be understood as an ideal construct that helps to understand its formative literary genre or as the reconstruction of an actual document that stood at the beginning of the redactional history of Q. The latter is extremely unlikely for two reasons: (1) Even the inaugural sermon (Q 6:20–49) shows a tension between eschatological prophecy (as distinct from "radical wisdom") and

---

of the two groups, the Cynics and the Jesus people, are largely overlapping" (p. 50). In this book, however, Mack does not claim that the Cynic lifestyle of this Jesus movement necessarily reflected the lifestyle of the historical Jesus (see pp. 45–46).

[19] *The Ethos and Ethics of an Itinerant Intelligence* (Ph.D. dissertation Claremont Graduate School, 1987). For further bibliography on the Cynic hypothesis, see James M. Robinson, "The History-of-Religions Taxonomy of Q: The Cynic Hypothesis," in Holger Preißler and Hubert Seiwert, *Gnosisforschung und Religionsgeschichte: Festschrift für Kurt Rudolph zum 65. Geburtstag* (Marburg 1994), p. 247.

[20] "Jesus and the Cynics: Survey and Analysis of a Hypothesis," *Journal of Religion* 74 (1994), pp. 453–475.

[21] "The History-of-Religions Taxonomy of Q," pp. 247–265.

[22] *The Formation of Q,* pp. 342–345.

the designs of wisdom instruction.[23] (2) As long as external
controls are lacking, internal analysis alone is problematic
because it is hardly possible to assume that an ancient author—
not to speak of one who is primarily a collector of traditional
materials—would strictly adhere to a definition of a literary
genre, which is, after all, the product of modern scholarship. The
merit of Kloppenborg's work is that he has been successful to
isolate certain sections of Q that show how the original author
has "inscribed" his materials in order to create a writing that
presents the ethics of the community. The strategy of this author
is "hortatory and deliberative," while the redactor's strategy is
"epideictic, intent on defending a view of Jesus (and of John, and
the Q people) and characterizing opponents in a negative way."[24]
The question remains, whether there are some Q materials that
cannot be clearly identified as belonging either to the original
purpose of the author or to the redactor's program. Such materials could perhaps be assigned to the original version of Q,
although it may not be possible to detect their exact place in that
composition.

II. The Gospel of Thomas and the stages of the development of Q

I had been impressed by Dieter Lührmann's argument that the Q
sayings about the judgment over this generation did not belong
to the original Q materials but came from the hand of the
redactor.[25] My own suggestion that there may have been an older
edition of Q grew out of the observation that numerous sayings
were shared by Q and the *Gospel of Thomas* but that the latter did
not reveal any knowledge of the sayings about Jesus as the
coming Son of Man.[26] Most of the sayings of Q with parallels in
the *Gospel of Thomas* should therefore be assigned to Q's earliest

---

[23] That the earlier stage of Q includes quite a few sayings that should be
classified as prophetic rather than sapiential has been demonstrated by Richard
Horsley, "Logoi Prophêtôn? Reflections on the Genre of Q," in *The Future of
Early Christianity: Essays in Honor of Helmut Koester*, ed. Birger A. Pearson
(Minneapolis 1991), pp. 195–209.

[24] Kloppenborg, "The Sayings Gospel Q and the Historical Jesus," p. 336.

[25] *Redaktion der Logienquelle*, passim.

[26] See "One Jesus and Four Primitive Gospels," in Robinson and Koester,
Trajectories, pp. 170–172; see also Helmut Koester, "Q and its Relatives," in
James E. Goehring, eds., *Gospel Origins & Christian Beginnings*, pp. 49–63.

stage of composition.[27] As a result, two fixed points appeared in
the development of Q: (1) at the beginning a collection with
many sayings that have parallels in the *Gospel of Thomas*, (2) a
redaction that added the sayings about the coming of the Son of
Man[28] and the judgment over this generation.[29]

While the beginnings of Q are more difficult to determine
with any precision, it is fairly easy to be certain about some
features of Q's final redaction and its eschatology. It is dominated
by sayings of the future judgment and the apocalyptic announcement of the coming of the Son of Man. The first
characteristic of the redaction of Q is the expectation of the
sudden revelation (ἀποκαλύπτεται, Q 17:30) of the Son of Man
ἐν τῇ ἡμέρᾳ αὐτοῦ (Q 17:24) or ἐν τῇ ἡμέρᾳ ἐκείνῃ (Q 17:31).
Since the coming is unexpected, there will be no time to escape
(Q 17:31). The same apocalyptic expectation is found in some
materials of Q 12:39–59; cf. the conclusion of the parable of the
thief: ὅτι ᾗ ὥρᾳ οὐ δοκεῖτε ὁ υἱὸς τοῦ ἀνθρώπου ἔρχεται (Q
12:40). The following parable of the faithful and unfaithful
servants (Q 12:41–46) also illustrates the suddenness of the
coming (Q 12:46), although the title Son of Man has not been
introduced into the allegorizing conclusion of this parable.

A second element that is typical for the redactor is the
announcement of the judgment over "this generation" (γενεὰ
αὕτη, Q 11:29–32, 50–51). Closely related is Q 10:12–15 with the
announcement of judgment over Chorazin, Bethsaida, and
Kaphernaum. ἡ πόλις ἐκείνη corresponds to γενεὰ αὕτη, and the

---

[27] See my *Ancient Christian Gospels*, pp. 138–139 and passim.

[28] Lührmann (*Redaktion der Logienquelle*, pp. 40–41, n. 6, cf. pp. 74–75),
however, did not include the sayings about the Son of Man in the final redaction
but assigned them to the older layer of the Q materials. On the development of
scholarship, see James M. Robinson, "The Q Trajectory: Between John and
Matthew via Jesus," in *The Future of Early Christianity*, ed. Pearson, pp. 178–189.

[29] Such a division of the two stages of Q is not in full agreement with
Kloppenborg (*The Formation of Q*, pp. 102–170), who had identified three
different complexes of sayings that characterize this second stage of Q: (1) The
announcements of judgment (including the Q materials of the preaching of John
the Baptist in Q/Luke 3 and most of the materials of Q 7:1–35 and 16:16). (2)
The controversies (materials in Q 11:14–52). (3) The "Logia Apocalypse" (most
of Q 17:23–37); closely related to this section are the apocalyptic materials in Q
12:39–59. Kloppenborg, however, although arguing for their connection with
the second stage of Q, does not include them into the "Logia Apocalypse" but
considers this section as a separate entity.

distinctive phrase ἐν τῇ ἡμέρᾳ ἐκείνῃ is also used (Q 10:12). The hand of the same redactor is recognizable furthermore in the parable that compares the people "of this generation" (τῆς γενεᾶς ταύτης) to children playing in the market place (Q 7:31–32).

These apocalyptic sayings that were introduced into Q by the redactor come from the same tradition that also furnished the apocalyptic Son of Man sayings to the Gospel of Mark. The Markan apocalypse culminates in the prediction of the coming of the Son of Man (Mark 13:26) and in the statement that "this generation" (ἡ γενεὰ αὕτη) shall not pass away until all this has happened (Mark 13:30). While "this generation" is here referred to without any negative predicates, it is explicitly called "adulterous and sinful" in the Son of Man saying Mark 8:38. There are good reasons to assume that these sayings shared by Mark and the redaction of Q were coined by Christian prophets in Palestine during the turmoil of the sixties of the first century that resulted in the Judaic War, perhaps even as late as during the war itself. It was the answer of the followers of Jesus to the rise of anti Roman revolutionary messianism in Palestine. The apocalypse of Mark 13 reveals the political position of this group. They are warned not to believe any false prophets who proclaimed, "Behold, the Messiah is here" (Mark 13:21–22). Their relationship to the Temple of Jerusalem is fundamentally positive, since the threat of its destruction is seen as a sacrilege (Mark 13:11). The group, however, had suffered persecution from their fellow Israelites (Mark 13:9); divisions ran deep even into the families (Mark 13:12). The prophets do not explicitly condemn the Romans but advise the followers of Jesus to separate and seek refuge elsewhere (Mark 13:14b–16).

The prophets who shaped the materials of the Markan apocalypse belong to Judea (Mark 13:14b), perhaps to the community of Jerusalem.[30] On the other hand, the Son of Man and judgment sayings of the Q community, located outside of Judea,[31] do not reveal the same degree of tribulation; they reflect a different and less urgent experience of persecution and resistance to their mission (cf. the addition of Q 10:12–15 to Q

---

[30] Egon Brandenburger (*Markus 13 und die Apokalyptik*, FRLANT 134 [Göttingen 1984]) has presented a cogent analysis of the apocalyptic source used by Mark and the position of its author.

[31] I hesitate therefore to locate the Q redaction in Galilee because the messianic fervor at the beginning of the Jewish War was no less intense there than it was in Judea.

10:10–11[32]). Both the Jerusalem group and their Q counterparts share the desire to establish an alternative to the two dominating political options of the time: messianic war against Rome or collaboration with the Roman authorities.

III. Eschatology in the earlier stage of the Sayings Gospel Q

John Kloppenborg[33] assigned to the later stage not only the sayings about the judgment of this generation and about the coming of the Son of Man, but also the entire sections, in which they are embedded, namely Q 3:7–9, 16–17; 4:1–13; the Q materials in Luke 7:1–35 and in Luke 11:14–52; Q 12:39–59; 17:23–37.[34] Three observations, however, argue for a more explicit eschatological orientation of the earliest composition of Q: (1) Sayings which are not characteristic for the theology of the redactor are found in these "secondary" sections. (2) Sayings with parallels in the *Gospel of Thomas* appear not only in the sections assigned by Kloppenborg to the first stage of Q—were they are very frequent—but occasionally also in the sections assigned to the redactor. (3) A number of sayings in Kloppenborg's original wisdom book Q are in fact prophetic sayings.

(1) Eschatological sayings in redactorial passages of Q

I shall discuss here only one example, namely Q 12:8–9 (ὃς ἂν ὁμολογήσῃ ἐν ἐμοὶ ἔμπροσθεν τῶν ἀνθρώπων, καὶ ὁ υἱὸς τοῦ ἀνθρώπου ὁμολογήσει κτλ.). It seems, at first glance, to be a secondary addition to a group of wisdom sayings (Q 12:2–7) and a most likely candidate for assignment to the redactor of Q because of the use of the title Son of Man and because of what may be called an "apocalyptic" notion of reward and punishment.[35] Q, however, does not identify the Son of Man with Jesus; Matthew achieves this identification by replacing "the Son of

---

[32] Lührmann, *Redaktion der Logienquelle,* pp. 62–63; Kloppenborg, *Formation of Q,* pp. 196–197.

[33] Ibid., passim.

[34] Ibid., pp. 102–170; moreover, a number of additional sayings in the remaining sections of Q are also assigned to the redactor. Some materials that lack parallels in Matthew are not considered as possibly deriving from Q, *e.g.,* Luke 12:13–21; 17:20b–21; on the latter see ibid., pp. 154–155.

[35] Kloppenborg, ibid., pp. 207–208.

Man" with the first person singular.[36] In Q 12:8–9 the Son of
Man is an angelic figure in the divine court who functions as the
advocate for the faithful—a concept that is not specifically apocalyptic. If this saying can be assigned to the original version of Q,
it would prove that "Son of Man" as a title for a figure of the
divine court was indeed known at an early time in these circles of
Jesus' followers and would later have served as a convenient
foundation for prophets to announce that this Son of Man, now
identified with Jesus, would return as the divinely appointed
judge.

(2) Sayings of the early stage of Q with parallels in the Gospel of
Thomas
Most sayings about John the Baptist (Q 3:2b–4, 16–17, 21–22)
and the account of the temptation of Jesus (Q 4:1–13), assigned
to the secondary stage of Q, lack parallels in the *Gospel of Thomas.*
Parallels are found, however, in the *Gospel of Thomas* to two
sayings in the section that Kloppenborg entitles "John, Jesus, and
This Generation" and assigns entirely to the redactor (Q 7:1–
35)[37]: Q 7:24–26 ("What did you go out into the desert to see?
etc.") has a parallel in *Gos. Thom.* 78, and Q 7:28 ("Among those
born of a woman no one is greater than John") appears in *Gos.
Thom.* 46. While John the Baptist is not explicitly mentioned in
the first of these two sayings, it is evident from the context in Q
that he is the subject of the saying. Moreover, it is probable that
these two sayings belonged together from the beginning. They
were separated by the redactor of Q, who inserted the reference
to Mal 3:1 and Exod 23:20 (Q 7:27). Both sayings are eschatological insofar as they contrast the present time of the kingdom
of God with the past, relegating John the Baptist to the past. They
must have been formulated in the polemic of the early followers
of Jesus with the disciples of John.
   Most of Q 11:14–52 is excluded in Kloppenborg's
reconstruction of the original composition of Q.[38] He allows as
parts of the first stage only Q 11:2–4 (the Lord's Prayer) and Q
11:9–13 (the sayings about asking and receiving);[39] *Gos. Thom.* 92

---

[36] Matt 10:32–33; also the variant in Mark 8:38 presents that (secondary)
identification of the Son of Man with Jesus and includes a secondary reference
to "this generation"—while this reference is absent in Q 12:8–9.

[37] Ibid., pp. 107–121.

[38] Ibid., pp. 141–147.

[39] Ibid., pp. 203–206.

and 94 provide parallels to the latter sayings. There are, moreover, several parallels in the *Gospel of Thomas* to the remaining materials of Q 11:

Q 11:21–22 (The strong man's house)[40]   = *GThom*. 35.
Luke 11:27–28 (True blessedness)   = *GThom*. 79 (=Q?).[41]
Q 11:33 (Light not under a bushel)   = *GThom* 33b.
Q 11:34–36 (The eye as the light of the body) = *GThom* 24.
Q 11:39b–41 (Wash outside of the cup)   = *GThom*. 89.
Q 11:52 (They took the key of knowledge)   = *GThom*. 39.[42]

Most of these sayings are wisdom sayings. The two sayings from the speech against the Pharisees, however, are classified as prophetic sayings by Bultmann.[43] To assign Q 11:52 to a later stratum of the tradition, because here "the kingdom is viewed as a present reality and as a realm into which one can enter even now"[44] is an odd judgment; on the contrary, one must ask, whether it is not exactly this view of the kingdom that is characteristic of the earliest layer of the Q tradition.

Of Q 12:2–59, Kloppenborg assigns only two small sections to the original composition of Q, namely 12:2–12[45] and 12:22–34.[46] The *Gospel of Thomas* presents parallels to Q 12:2 (*Gos. Thom.* 5 and 6b), 12:3 (*Gos. Thom.* 33), 12:22 (*Gos. Thom.* 36[47]), and 12:33 (*Gos. Thom.* 76b). There are, however, in this section of Q a number of further sayings that have parallels in the *Gospel of Thomas:*

---

[40] On the question of the inclusion in Q of this saying, see Koester, *Ancient Christian Gospels,* pp. 142–143; Kloppenborg, *Formation of Q,* p. 125.

[41] There is no parallel in Matthew but the parallel in the *Gospel of Thomas* suggests that this pericope may have stood in Q; see Koester, *Ancient Christian Gospels,* p. 143.

[42] *Gos. Thom.* 102 has preserved another woe against the Pharisees ("Woe to the Pharisees, for they are like a dog sleeping in the food trough of cows: the dog neither eats nor lets the cows eat"). That smaller collections of such woes circulated very early is also evident in Mark 12:38–40.

[43] Rudolf Bultmann, *The History of the Synoptic Tradition* (New York 1968[2]), p. 147.

[44] Kloppenborg, *Formation of Q,* 143, referring to Schürmann.

[45] From which he excludes 12:8–9 [see above] and 12:10.

[46] *Formation of Q,* pp. 206–222.

[47] Parallels to Q 12:25, 27a appear in the Greek version of the *Gospel of Thomas* (*Pap. Oxy.* 655).

Q 12:10 (The blasphemy not forgiven)   = *GThom.* 44.[48]
Luke 12:13–14 (Dividing the inheritance) = *GThom.* 72[49] (Q?).[50]
Luke 12:16–21 (Parable of the rich farmer) = *GThom.* 72.
Q 12:39 (Parable of the thief)   = *GThom.* 103.[51]
Luke 12:49 (Fire on earth)   = *GThom.* 10 (Q?[52]).
Q 12:51–53 (Not peace, but the sword)   = *GThom.* 16.
Q 12:54–56 (Signs of the time)   = *GThom.* 91.

Also Q 17:21–35, mostly formulated by the redactor of Q, contains three sayings with parallels in the *Gospel of Thomas* that should be considered here:

Luke 17:20–21 (When will the kingdom come?) = *GThom.* 113 (Q?[53]).
Luke 17:22 (Seeking and not finding)   = *GThom.* 38 (Q?[54]).
Q 17:34 (Two in one bed)   = *GThom.* 61a.

A surprising number of sayings in this group are eschatological. They reveal an eschatological perspective that is distinctly different from the one introduced by the redactor of Q because the emphasis here is on the presence of the kingdom in Jesus and in his words. In some instances, the version preserved by the *Gospel of Thomas* does not imply the element of watching for an event in the future. The parable of the thief rather emphasizes the *place* of the entry of the robber; it seems to have been reformulated by the redactor of Q so that it would point to the

---

[48] For a discussion of the relationship of the several versions of this saying, see Koester, *Ancient Christian Gospels*, pp. 92–93.

[49] On the relationship of *Gos. Thom.* 72 to Luke 12:13–14, see Gregory J. Riley, "Influence of Thomas Christianity on Luke 12:14 and 5:39," *HThR* 88 (1995), pp. 229–235.

[50] On the question whether this apophthegma and the following parable should be included in Q, see John S. Kloppenborg, *Q Parallels: Synopsis, Critical Notes, & Concordance* (Sonoma [California] 1988), p. 128.

[51] The same parable is also used in *Gos. Thom.* 21; see Koester, *Ancient Christian Gospels*, p. 146.

[52] On the question of the inclusion of this saying in Q, see Kloppenborg, *Q Parallels*, p. 142; idem, *Formation of Q*, p. 151, n. 213. The following saying, Luke 12:50 ("I must be baptized with a baptism…"), however, is certainly a Lukan addition.

[53] On the question of the inclusion of this saying in Q, see Koester, *Ancient Christian Gospels*, pp. 155–156.

[54] Ibid., p. 149, n. 1.

unknown future *time* and therefore motivate the admonition to watchfulness. The original question of the "where?" of the kingdom, which is also evident in Q 12:54–56 and 17:20–21, has been changed by the redactor into the question of "when?"[55] Another element in these sayings is the emphasis upon the urgency of the kingdom's presence (see especially Q 12:49, 51–53; 17:34). These sayings do not speak of judgment to be administered in the form of punishment and reward, but they call to grasp the present moment.

Can the sayings discussed above be incorporated into the final section of the original version of Q? Kloppenborg[56] has singled out several sayings that he assigns to the final section of the original version: Q 13:24 ("Strive to enter through the narrow door"); Q 13:26–27 (a prophetic threat against those who say, "We ate and drank with you"); Q 13:28–29, 30 (a prophetic oracle about the participation of the Gentiles in the kingdom); Q 13:34–35 (Lament over Jerusalem); Q 14:16–24 (parable of the Great Supper = *Gos. Thom.* 64); Q 14:26–27 and 17:33 (three discipleship sayings). If the other sayings with parallels in the *Gospel of Thomas,* which I have discussed above, were incorporated into the final section of Q, the prophetic and eschatological character of this section would become even more evident. To call it the eschatological conclusion of Q in its original form would be more appropriate, while the "Logia Apocalypse" (Q 17:23–37) was composed as the final section of the redaction of Q—incorporating and reinterpreting some of the materials of the original eschatological conclusion of the Sayings Gospel.

(3) Prophetic sayings in Q's original composition
The thesis that the formative genre of Q was a wisdom book has great merit. Indeed, even individual sections of Q have been composed in close correspondence to this genre. Yet this insight can be deceptive. There is an inherent tension between the intent of the sayings incorporated into this wisdom genre and the objective of a wisdom book or speech. The inaugural sermon of Q (6:20b–49) demonstrates this tension.

The beatitudes of this sermon (Q 6:20b–23b) as well as the following curses (6:24–26) seem to correspond to a proper opening of a wisdom book. Blessings for those who fear the Lord and obey the commands of wisdom and curses upon the fools are a

---

[55] Ibid., pp. 153, 155–156.
[56] Ibid., pp. 223–237.

commonplace in wisdom speech.[57] Kloppenborg[58] quotes as an
example Proverbs 3:33:

> The Lord's curse is on the house of the wicked;
> but he blesses the abode of the righteous.

In the inaugural sermon of Q, however, it is neither righteousness
that is praised nor wickedness that is condemned. Rather, blessings and curses refer to social status and to human conditions:
the poor are blessed and the rich are cursed.[59] One might describe the features of these blessings as typical for "sapiential
beatitudes, in particular, serialization and placement at the
beginning of an instruction"[60]—the placement of beatitudes at the
beginning of a variety of documents corresponds to ancient tradition[61] The closest parallels in content, however, are not found
in wisdom literature but in eschatological materials, for example,
in the eschatological hymn, perhaps inherited from the disciples
of John the Baptist,[62] that is preserved as the "Magnificat" (Luke
1:52–53):

> He has brought down the powerful from their thrones
>   and lifted up the lowly.
> He has filled the hungry with good things
>   and sent the rich away empty.

---

[57] Hans Dieter Betz (*The Sermon on the Mount*, Hermeneia [Minneapolis 1995],
p. 586) notes that "series of beatitudes and 'woes' are found in prophetic,
apocalyptic, and wisdom literature."

[58] Ibid., p. 190.

[59] Note that Kloppenborg does not include the woes into either the original
version of Q or its final stage (*Formation of Q*, p. 144; idem, *Q Synopsis*, p. 26).
Most exegetes judge that the curses against the rich have been added by Luke;
see Peter Klein, "Die lukanischen Weherufe," *ZNW* 71 (1980), pp. 150–159;
François Bovon, *Das Evangelium nach Lukas*, EKK 3 (Neukirchen-Vluyn 1989),
Vol. 1, p. 298.

[60] *Formation of Q*, p. 188.

[61] Betz, *Sermon on the Mount*, pp. 97–105.

[62] Bultmann, *History of the Synoptic Tradition*, pp. 296–297; Bovon (*Evangelium
nach Lukas*, pp. 82–83) points to a possible origin in the Pharisaic movement,
rather than in Jewish-Christian or Baptist circles.

Rudolf Bultmann[63] had identified the beatitudes of the inaugural sermon as prophetic sayings. They announce an eschatological moment that calls for a decision in behalf of the kingdom of God. That the followers of Jesus, who remembered the blessings of the poor, the hungry, and those who weep, made this decision and paid a price for it is formulated in the fourth beatitude that blesses Jesus' followers because of their experience of hatred and rejection (Q 6:22–23b).[64]

All the other materials in this section are admonitions and, with respect to their formal structure, they can be classified as sapiential. Yet, to do what the first three admonitions (Q 6:27–35) mandate would in no way be very wise. To love one's enemies, not to retaliate, and to lend to those who will not pay back is decidedly foolish in terms of conventional wisdom. On the contrary, these admonitions state an eschatological alternative to political, social, and economic choices that differ radically from wise behavior. In accordance with the political expectations of Israel, hatred of the Roman occupation forces would seem a national duty. Those who would neither choose to become messianic fanatics nor collaborate with the Romans, but feared God and were willing to obey his commandments, might at least deserve wise counsel that could insure personal success and financial prosperity in spite of the political turmoil. To love the hated Roman occupiers would spell trouble with one's fellow Israelites. Only with the last admonition of this section, "Be merciful" (Q 6:36), the discourse enters the realm of general rules of wise behavior.

The following verses (Q 6:37–49) belong wholly to the world of conventional wisdom: Not to judge in order not to be judged; a blind person cannot lead the blind; a disciple is not above the teacher; the tree is known by its fruit. The initial beatitudes as well as the admonitions to choose radically new political, social, and economic alternatives seem to have opened the possibility of adopting much of what conventional wisdom has taught. The acceptance of the prophecy of the new eschatological existence of the kingdom does not lead into foolishness but into a behavior that has guided people everywhere for centuries. All sapiential

---

[63] *History of the Synoptic Tradition*, pp. 110–111.

[64] 6:23c ("for so their fathers did to the prophets") is most certainly a later addition to Q because none of the parallels to this fourth beatitude (1 Pt 4:14; *Gos. Thom.* 68, 69a) present this clause; cf. Kloppenborg, *Formation of Q,* 173.

sayings in Q 6:37–49 are "international,"[65] while references to the law of Israel and to the fear of the God of Israel, typical for Jewish sapiential literature, are completely missing.

A statement about a fundamentally new eschatological attitude also stands at the beginning of the second "sapiential" speech of Q, 9:57–62 and 10:2–16, 21–24. The introduction of this speech states the radical homelessness of human beings, that is, their separation from their normal social context (Q 9:57–58). This is underlined with the sayings about the dead burying their dead (Q 9:59–60) and the saying that the one who puts his hand to plow and looks back is not fit for the kingdom of God (Q 9:61–62).[66] The following instruction for the messengers of the arrival of the kingdom of God, however, are conventional wisdom: Large harvest and few workers (10:2), the worker is worthy of his food (10:7), and other instructions are common sapiential sayings. A special feature is the conclusion of this speech, Q 10:21–24, comprised of two sayings that present Jesus as the eschatological revealer and praise the disciples for what they see now. If these "Johannine" sayings belong to the first version of Q[67]—the latter may be a variant of *Gos. Thom.* 17 and 38—the original composition of Q makes a strong statement about the eschatological moment that the disciples have been requested to announce.

IV. The original version of Q and its image of Jesus

The composition of the Sayings Gospel Q and its redaction reflect a process in which the community develops a clearer definition of its purpose and identity. In doing so, the collection and composition of sayings puts forward an image of Jesus that mirrors the community's mission in a time that is highly charged with eschatological expectations. The original version of Q does not justify the view that the community of Q began as a rather

---

[65] See Betz, *Sermon on the Mount,* especially his excursus on "Rules for Teachers and Students" (pp. 621–622).

[66] There is no parallel in Matthew but this saying may have been part of Q. "Of all the Lukan *Sondergut,* this has the strongest possibility of deriving from Q since it is found in a Q context, the saying coheres with the preceding sayings formally and it evinces the same theology of discipleship typical of other Q sayings" (Kloppenborg, *Q Parallels,* p. 64). Kloppenborg (*Formation of Q,* pp. 190–192) assigns this saying to the original composition of Q.

[67] Kloppenborg, ibid., pp. 197–203.

innocuous wisdom association that only later developed an eschatological outlook because its members had experienced rejection and persecution.[68] The search for the earliest tradition will hardly lead us "to a social space for cultivating a sane and circumspect society made possible by the wisdom remembered in Jesus' name."[69] On the contrary, the original version of Q insists that the ways of the kingdom of God are becoming a reality in the conduct and experience of the disciples because they follow the voice of an eschatological prophet who announces the presence of the kingdom in their midst.

The image of Jesus that is accessible through the most original version of Q is that of an eschatological prophet. He announces the kingdom's coming to those who have been excluded from the benefits that the society should provide—which most likely included the majority of the people at that time—and he praises the disciples because they are witnesses of events that generations before them have longed to see. This is not a tame and rational Jesus but a divine messenger who brings conflict and division even into the very family. His preaching and teaching instructs the community to understand her own identity as a people who are realizing the eschatological moment in their existence and work, not as fanatics but as human beings who follow the guidance of wisdom in their common life. Jesus also demands that wisdom must govern the conduct of the missionaries, especially when they are not accepted. I can find no indication that the mission of the community has been a failure; on the contrary, the harvest is great and it requires more workers. It is possible that Jesus was also remembered in the common meals of the community. The petition of the Lord's prayer that God's kingdom come is linked to the petition for the daily bread (Q 11:2–4). There is also the eschatological outlook to the banquet, when people will come from everywhere to sit at table in the kingdom of God (Q 13:28–29). References to a liturgy for the common meal celebrations do not appear in Q; one can assume, however, that eschatologically interpreted Jewish meal prayers were used. *Didache* 10–11 has preserved such prayers—a witness for a eucharist under eschatological auspices, albeit without any reference to the death of Jesus.

---

[68] This is the basic thesis of Mack, *A Myth of Innocence*.

[69] Ron Cameron, "The Gospel of Thomas and Christian Origins," in *The Future of Early Christianity*, ed. B. Pearson, p. 392.

Whether the earlier version of Q was the product of a community in Galilee depends upon the judgment sayings against Chorazin, Bethsaida, and Kaphernaum (Q 10:13–15). They may not have been part of the first stage of Q. It should also be remembered that Q 13:34–35 is a lament over Jerusalem. The question of the mission to the Gentiles may have been controversial within the community. This controversy, however, would have begun in the very first years of its existence, as it apparently did in Jerusalem itself and elsewhere, even before Paul began his ministry as a missionary in "Arabia," that is, no later than the year 35 C.E. and, moreover, in the immediate neighborhood of Galilee. The mention of Tyre and Sidon in Q 10:13–14 could well serve as evidence that the Gentile mission of this community had long since been carried into Greek-speaking cities of southern Syria several decades before the original version of Q was composed. The early decades of this community must have been dominated by an eschatological message that was carried to the Gentiles in areas outside of Galilee, although Palestinian connections are still visible in the later apocalyptic redaction of Q.

From the very beginning, the tradition of sayings preserved in the Sayings Gospel Q is dominated by an eschatological orientation. The earliest stage of Q's eschatology is not necessarily a direct reflection of Jesus' preaching. It is also quite likely that other early materials of Jesus' sayings have survived outside of the trajectory of Q and have been incorporated into canonical and extra-canonical gospels independently of Q.[70] As far as Q is concerned, however, its trajectory belongs, from the very beginning to the interpretation of an eschatological tradition of Jesus' sayings, mirroring an image of Jesus as an eschatological prophet in the tradition of Israel. The Jesus of the earliest formation of the Sayings Gospel Q proclaims the arrival of God's kingdom as a challenge to the disciples, who are asked to realize that their own existence belongs to a new eschatological moment. This may not be a direct and unbroken mirror of the preaching of the historical Jesus; but it certainly excludes any recourse to a Jesus who was but a social reformer or a philosopher in the tradition of the Cynic preacher.

---

[70] Kloppenborg, "The Sayings Gospel Q and the Quest of the Historical Jesus," pp. 329–331.

DIE ENDZEITREDE IN DIDACHE 16 UND
DIE JESUS-APOKALYPSE IN MATTHÄUS 24-25

Andreas Lindemann
Kirchliche Hochschule Bethel
(Bethel bei Bielefeld, Deutschland)

Das Schlußkapitel der Didache, zumindest der Abschnitt V.3-8, wird oft als eine "Apokalypse" bezeichnet; tatsächlich aber liegt eine solche nicht vor.[1] Did 16 enthält apokalyptische Elemente, doch der literarischen Gattung nach handelt es sich um eine eschatologische Mahnrede, um Paränese (V.1-2), die in V. 3-8 durch die Ankündigung der (zweifellos als nahe geglaubten) drohenden Endereignisse begründet wird.[2]

Die Frage der in Did 16 verwendeten Tradition(en) wird in der Forschung kontrovers diskutiert. Oft wird vermutet, der Abschnitt habe ursprünglich noch zur "Zwei-Wege-Lehre" (Did 1-6) gehört, oder der Redaktor der Didache habe an die Stelle eines kurzen apokalyptischen Schlusses der Zwei-Wege-Lehre, der sich in Did 6,1 noch zeige, einen eigenen aus Traditionselementen zusammengefügten Schluß gesetzt; es wird schließlich auch vermutet, dem Text liege ein vom Didachisten hierher ge-

---

[1] Vgl. Hans Reinhard Seeliger, "Erwägungen zu Hintergrund und Zweck des apokalyptischen Schlußkapitels der Didache", *StPatr* 21 (Leuven 1989), 185-192, hier 187: "Der erzählerische Rahmen fehlt, jede Mitteilung über den Offenbarer und den Empfänger einer apokalyptischen Botschaft, jede Angabe über den Offenbarungsempfang. Es wird vielmehr eine apokalyptische Botschaft referiert, die schon ergangen zu sein scheint; es wird hier nichts geoffenbart im Sinne des Genus der Apokalypsen, sondern bereits Bekanntes zur Vertiefung des Wissens repetiert".

[2] Vgl. Hans Lohmann, *Drohung und Verheißung. Exegetische Untersuchungen zur Eschatologie bei den Apostolischen Vätern*, BZNW 55 (Berlin 1989), 50: "Der Stoff ist zwar 'apokalyptisch', wird aber nicht als Offenbarung durch Vision oder Audition von Gott her vermittelt, sondern als schlichte Belehrung über die Zukunft mitgeteilt". Die von Lohmann diskutierte Frage, ob "die Naherwartung bereits nachgelassen" habe, liegt dem Text allerdings fern.

stelltes isoliertes Traditionsstück zugrunde.[3] Denkbar ist aber auch, daß Did 16 vom Verfasser bzw. Redaktor der Didache selbst formuliert wurde, zwar unter Verwendung von älterer Überlieferung, aber doch so, daß er selbst die Weisung konzipierte, die seiner Meinung nach den Adressaten seiner Schrift auf deren Weg mitgegeben werden mußte.[4]

Immer schon seit der Entdeckung der Didache ist das enge Verhältnis zwischen Did 16 und den apokalyptischen Abschnitten der synoptischen Evangelien, insbesondere Mt 24, gesehen worden. Liegt dabei unmittelbare literarische Abhängigkeit vor,[5] oder handelt es sich hier wie dort um die Benutzung gemeinsamen apokalyptischen Traditionsguts?[6] Die sorgfältigen Vergleiche zwischen Did 16 und den in Frage kommenden synoptischen Parallelen haben zu sehr unterschiedlichen Ergebnissen geführt: E. Massaux folgert aus seinen Beobachtungen, daß Did 16 literarisch direkt von Mt 24 abhängig ist: "Le texte de Mt. a servi de base à notre auteur qui paraît en donner une sorte de commentaire", wobei auch Einfluß des Lk möglich sei.[7] H. Köster meint, es bestehe eine Abhängigkeit von Did 16 von der in Mk 13 verarbeiteten apokalyptischen Vorlage; die Basis von Did 16 repräsentiere also ein sehr frühes Stadium apokalyptischer Tradition und Literatur.[8] W.-D. Köhler schließlich kommt

---

[3] Vgl. die knappe Übersicht über die Forschungspositionen bei Bruno Steimer, *Vertex Traditionis. Die Gattung der altchristlichen Kirchenordnungen*, BZNW 63 (Berlin 1992), 208 Anm. 79.

[4] Vgl. dazu Seeliger, "Erwägungen" (s. Anm. 1), 188.

[5] Dies ist nach Kurt Niederwimmer, *Die Didache*, KAV 1 (Göttingen 1989), 250–251, die traditionelle These.

[6] Das ist im wesentlichen Niederwimmers eigene Position.

[7] Édouard Massaux, *Influence de l'Évangile de Saint Matthieu sur la littérature chrétienne avant Saint Irénée*, BEThL 75 (réimpression anastatique: Leuven 1986), 637–638. Vgl. die Übersicht a.a.O. 631–638. Ähnliche Übersichten bieten Wolf-Dietrich Köhler, *Die Rezeption des Matthäusevangeliums in der Zeit vor Irenäus*, WUNT II/24 (Tübingen 1987), 51–53 und Clayton N. Jefford, *The Sayings of Jesus in the Teaching of the Twelve Apostles*, VigChr.S 11 (Leiden usw. 1989), 85–87.

[8] So Helmut Köster, *Synoptische Überlieferung bei den Apostolischen Vätern*, TU 65 (Berlin 1957), 189: "Zwingend erweisen läßt sich eine Abhängigkeit der Did.-Apokalypse von den Synoptikern nirgends. Das dürfte sicher sein. Die mannigfachen Berührungen mit den Synoptikern beruhen 1. auf dem Vorkommen auch sonst verbreiteter apokalyptischer Züge und Sätze (Did. 16,1.6.7), 2. darauf, daß ein Teil des Did. 16 und Mk. 13 vorkommenden Stoffes aus ein und derselben jüdischen Apokalypse stammt (Did. 16,4b.5.8), 3. darauf, daß ein

zu dem Ergebnis, daß eine "Abhängigkeit der Didache von
einem synoptischen Evangelium im Sinne einer Orientierung an
ihm...auszuschließen" sei;[9] der Befund lasse sich "am besten"
erklären, "wenn man annimmt, daß Did 16 aus der gleichen Tradition schöpft wie Mt 24", wobei Köhler allerdings voraussetzt,
daß der Didachist Mt "wahrscheinlich kannte", das Evangelium
aber "nicht als in allen Fragen zu rezipierende Autorität" verstand.[10]

Wenn der Verfasser der Didache Mt kannte, so spricht von
vornherein sehr vieles für die Annahme, daß die engen Parallelen zwischen Did 16 und Mt 24 (und 25) auf eine unmittelbare
Benutzung dieses Textes durch den Didachisten zurückgehen. Im
folgenden soll der Versuch gemacht werden, Did 16,1–8 als
eigenständigen Text des Didachisten zu lesen, der damit tatsächlich eine Art "Kommentierung" der Aussagen in Mt 24 (und
25) versucht hat.[11] Es läßt sich ja weder eine als "Quelle" zu
wertende durchgehende Vorlage erkennen, noch läßt es sich
zeigen, daß der Didachist Einzelaussagen aus verstreuten Überlieferungen miteinander kombiniert hat. Die nächstliegende Erklärung des Textbefundes ist die Annahme, daß der Didachist
mit Mt 24 (und 25) vertraut war und daß er seinen Text unter
Aufnahme der dortigen Aussagen redaktionell frei als eine eschatologische Mahnrede gestaltete. Bei diesem Prozeß wurde aus der
apokalyptischen Rede Jesu nun eine Belehrung der Adressaten
durch den Textautor selber, ohne daß Jesus als Sprecher in
Erscheinung tritt. Mit dieser Annahme wird sich die Vermutung
verbinden, daß der Text Did 16, 1–8 in der in der Handschrift H
überlieferten Form vollständig ist und daß insbesondere kein

---

weiteres apokalyptisches Traditionsstück sowohl von Did. 16 als auch von Mt.
(24,10–12) benutzt wird (Did. 16,3.4a.5)". Diese recht komplizierte These hängt
u.a. mit Kösters Vermutung zusammen, daß Did 16 ursprünglich Teil der Zwei-
Wege-Lehre (Did 1–6) gewesen sei, wofür m.E. wenig spricht.

[9] Köhler, *Rezeption* (s. Anm. 7), 53.

[10] Köhler, *Rezeption*, 54. Köhler nimmt an, daß Mt das von Did verwendete
"Evangelium" (8,2: 15,3–4) gewesen sei; der Didachist verweise "zwar für alle
ihm vorrangig wichtigen Fragen abschließend auf das 'Evangelium', er ist aber
durchaus nicht ängstlich darum bemüht, alles, was er sagt, auch im Evangelium
verifizieren zu können" (55–56). Ähnlich urteilt Jefford, *Sayings* (s. Anm. 7), 91.

[11] Vgl. die oben bei Anm. 7 zitierte Position von Massaux. Zu einem
ähnlichen Ergebnis kommt, wenn auch auf anderen Wegen, B. C. Butler, "The
Literary Relations of Didache, Ch. XVI", *JThS* N.S. 11 (1960), 265–283.

nach V. 8 noch folgender Hinweis auf das (apokalyptische) Gericht ergänzt zu werden braucht.

Did 16,1a beginnt "unvermittelt";[12] aber natürlich schließt die Aussage γρηγορεῖτε gut an 15,4 an, so daß durchaus kein Bruch vorliegt. Der Argumentationsgang von Did 15 zu Did 16 ist derselbe, wie er sich in der allegorischen Parabel Mt 25,1–13 findet: Das Handeln der Menschen soll unter der eschatologischen Perspektive stehen. Es ist denkbar, daß der Didachist den Hinweis in 15,4b auf "das Evangelium unseres Herrn" (ὡς ἔχετε ἐν τῷ εὐαγγελίῳ τοῦ κυρίου ἡμῶν) als Indiz dafür verstanden wissen will, daß das Folgende tatsächlich in einer Evangeliumsschrift gefunden werden kann.[13] Mit der Einleitung γρηγορεῖτε ὑπὲρ τῆς ζωῆς ὑμῶν wird daran erinnert, daß das ganze Leben Wachsamkeit erfordert.[14] Mit zwei Metaphern wird das im folgenden näher expliziert. Die erste dieser metaphorischen Aussagen erinnert deutlich an Mt 25,1–13, wobei die Verwendung des Wortes λύχνος anstelle von λαμπάς angesichts von Mt 5,13 leicht zu erklären ist. Der Didachist mahnt zur Wachsamkeit und zur ständigen Bereitschaft für das Kommen des κύριος. Die zweite metaphorische Aussage ist erstaunlich: Die Rede von den "Lenden" begegnet biblisch zum einen mit Blick auf die Zeugungskraft (Apg 2,30; Hebr 7,5.10; vgl. Gen 35,11), zum andern mit Blick auf die Praxis, das Gewand aufzuschürzen, um auf diese Weise beweglicher zu sein (Lk 12,35; Eph 6,14; vgl. Ex 12,11). In der Aussage der Did geht es offenbar weder um das eine noch um das andere; gedacht ist vielmehr an das Bild des Weges, auf dem man nicht ermatten soll, so daß als nächste sachliche Parallele von daher am ehesten eine Aussage wie Hebr 12,3 in Frage kommt. Gemeinsam setzen die beiden Metaphern voraus, daß das Leben als ein Unterwegssein in der Finsternis zu denken ist; es gilt, ausreichend "Licht" zu haben und auf dem Weg nicht müde zu werden.

---

[12] So Niederwimmer, *Didache* (s. Anm. 5), 256; er meint, daß man eigentlich ein οὖν erwarte.

[13] Man braucht nach 15,4 nur einen Doppelpunkt zu setzen, um so den Zusammenhang zu verdeutlichen; in Did 8,2 leitet eine ganz ähnliche Wendung das Zitat des Vaterunsers ein.

[14] Es geht um das irdische, nicht um das ewige Leben (gegen Lohmann, *Drohung* [s. Anm. 2], 46: "Auf den Lebensweg (Did 1–4) bezieht sich diese Mahnung wohl nicht"). Zuzustimmen ist Lohmann aber darin, daß Did 16 nicht "als ursprünglicher Anhang zur Zwei-Wege-Lehre zu verstehen" ist.

Liegt in den beiden metaphorischen Aussagen in Did 16,1b ein Herrenwort vor, das der Didachist zitiert? K. Niederwimmer meint, daß Autor wie Leser der Did, trotz der fehlenden Kennzeichnung, das Logion als ein Herrenwort verstanden haben werden; der Didachist zitiere es "in der Gestalt mündlicher Tradition (oder als Zitat aus einer besonderen Logiensammlung?), in der sie ihm zugänglich war".[15] Aber die Tatsache, daß in V. 1c vom κύριος in der 3. Person gesprochen ist, spricht eher gegen die Vermutung, daß die beiden bildlichen Aussagen in V. 1b als Herrenworte aufgefaßt werden sollen. Wahrscheinlicher ist, daß der Didachist bei den Adressaten die allgemeine Kenntnis der Parabel Mt 25,1–13 voraussetzt und annimmt, daß die Bilder von den Lampen und vom Weg sofort verstanden wurden. Es ist der Verfasser der Did selbst, der sich unmittelbar an seine Leser wendet (sie sind es, die in der 2. Person Pl. angeredet werden) und sie mahnt; auf die Autorität Jesu wird an dieser Stelle nicht Bezug genommen.

In V. 1c sagt der Verfasser positiv und in nicht-metaphorischer Rede, worum es geht: Die Leser sollen bereit (ἕτοιμοι) sein für die Parusie des κύριος, weil sie nicht wissen (können), wann er kommt. Die Aussage erinnert sachlich und in der Formulierung an Mt 24,42 (οὐκ οἴδατε ποίᾳ ἡμέρᾳ ὁ κύριος ὑμῶν ἔρχεται), wobei aber auch Mt 25,13 (οὐκ οἴδατε τὴν ἡμέραν...) anklingen könnte. Wichtig ist die Wendung ὁ κύριος ἡμῶν; sie schließt die Möglichkeit aus, daß die Aussage als ein Herrenwort verstanden werden soll.[16] Der Didachist selbst mahnt seine Adressaten, und er selbst schließt sich in den Kreis der so Ermahnten mit ein.

V. 2a paßt zu den Mahnungen von V. 1. Die Adressaten sollen πυκνῶς zusammenkommen, um ihre ψυχαί zu stärken. Das Adverb πυκνῶς zeigt an, daß die Leser sich "häufig" treffen sollen,[17] weil nur so das für ihr Leben Nötige[18] gesucht (und das

---

[15] Niederwimmer, *Didache* (s. Anm. 5), 257.

[16] Niederwimmer, *Didache*, 257, Anm. 13 hält es "nicht für ausgeschlossen, daß der Didachist bewußt ein Herrenwort aus der Erinnerung seiner mündlichen Tradition zitiert (wobei er in ὁ κύριος ἡμῶν ändert)". A.a.O. 258, Anm. 15: Die Ersetzung von "Menschensohn" durch κύριος "könnte…auch auf das Konto des Didachisten gehen, für den Kyrios *der* Hoheitstitel Jesu ist".

[17] Die oft genannte Übersetzungsalternative "zahlreich" gibt keinen rechten Sinn — wie sollte eine Gruppe ermahnt werden, "zahlreich" zusammenzukommen? Das Wörterbuch von Bauer-Aland nennt als Bedeutung von πυκνῶς nur "häufig, oft" (*Griechisch-deutsches Wörterbuch zu den Schriften des Neuen*

meint wohl: gefunden) werden kann. Diese Mahnung begegnet ganz ähnlich in Ign Eph 13,1, und sie steht auch dort in einem in gewisser Weise eschatologischen Kontext.[19] Was konkret gemeint ist, läßt sich nicht erkennen: Wie oft in der Woche versammelten sich die Christen? Geht es um Gottesdienste (so ja jedenfalls in 14,1), oder geht es um weitere Zusammenkünfte der Gemeinde? Jedenfalls setzt der Didachist voraus, daß es sich um Treffen handelt, die wesentlich zur seelischen Stärkung beitragen, und die deshalb möglichst oft stattfinden sollen.

Das Ziel dieser Zusammenkünfte ist das Erreichen der Vollkommenheit, die ἐν τῷ ἐσχάτῳ καιρῷ gegeben sein soll. Auffallend ist, daß hier tatsächlich vom "Nutzen" gesprochen wird — beim "letzten καιρός" "nützt" ὁ πᾶς χρόνος τῆς πίστεως gar nichts, wenn am Ende die Vollkommenheit nicht erreicht ist. Auch dies erinnert in Aussage und Tendenz deutlich an Mt (vgl. vor allem 5,48; 19,21).[20] Was der Didachist konkret meint, ergibt sich aus dem folgenden V. 3, weshalb zwischen V. 2 und V. 3 kein Einschnitt gemacht werden sollte.[21] Der Didachist betont, daß die Zeit der πίστις im Lichte des ἔσχατος καιρός gesehen werden muß, wobei πίστις ὑμῶν recht formal aufgefaßt zu sein scheint — es geht offenbar darum, daß die Zugehörigkeit zur christlichen Gemeinde für sich genommen eben keinen Nutzen hat.[22]

"Die letzte Zeit" ist, wie V. 3 zeigt, die Zeit der Irrlehre und der Verkehrung der Werte.[23] Falsche Propheten werden in

---

Testaments und der frühchristlichen Literatur [Berlin 1988⁶], 1458). Hätte der Didachist die Zahl der sich Versammelnden im Auge gehabt, so hätte er vermutlich das Prädikativum verwendet (πυκνοὶ συναχθήσεσθε).

[18] Lohmann, *Drohung* (s. Anm. 2), 46 meint, τὰ ἀνήκοντα bezeichne "wohl das rechte christliche Handeln".

[19] Ignatius warnt in Eph 13,1 vor den Mächten Satans und vor dem von ihm drohenden Verderben.

[20] Die Aussage berührt sich eng mit Barn 4,9, doch hat gerade die Verwendung des Verbs τελειοῦν dort keine Entsprechung.

[21] Den Zusammenhang, den der Didachist hergestellt hat, betont Tashio Aono, *Die Entwicklung des paulinischen Gerichtsgedankens bei den Apostolischen Vätern*, EHS XXIII/137 (Bern usw. 1979), 166.

[22] πίστις begegnet in Did nur noch in dem liturgischen Gebet 10,2; das Verb πιστεύω begegnet in Did gar nicht.

[23] Niederwimmer, *Didache* (s. Anm. 5), 259 mit Anm. 25 betont den Zusammenhang von V. 2 und V. 3 mit Recht. Freilich spricht er dann von V. 3–8 als von einer "Apokalypse".

großer Zahl auftreten,[24] ebenso "die Verderber". Von Pseudopropheten hatte die Anweisung für den Umgang mit fremden Wanderaposteln gesprochen (11,4–12); jetzt geht aus 16,3 hervor, daß solche Falschpropheten in der Endzeit nicht nur vereinzelt auftreten, sondern daß sie zahlreich sein werden.[25] Sie erweisen sich dann auch als φθορεῖς (vgl. 5,2), d.h. als Menschen, die die Gemeinde zerstören. Die beiden dann folgenden Aussagen zielen auf die völlige Verkehrung der anerkannten Normen — "Schafe" werden zu "Wölfen", aus Liebe wird Haß werden.[26] Mit der ersten dieser beiden Aussagen ist Mt 7,15 in gewisser Weise verwandt, doch dort geht es darum, daß die Pseudopropheten selbst als "Wölfe im Schafspelz" auftreten, während sich hier die Schafe "verwandeln". Daher brauchen mit den "Schafen" durchaus nicht Irrlehrer gemeint zu sein, sondern es geht um Schafe (möglicherweise: des Hirten Christus?), die sich plötzlich als Wölfe (und also als Feinde Christi und seiner Herde?) erweisen werden. Dasselbe ist gemeint mit der zweiten, nicht-metaphorischen Aussage: Aus der zwischen den Menschen (in der Gemeinde) herrschenden Liebe wird "Haß"[27] werden. Beide Aussagen sind zu lesen vor dem Hintergrund von V. 1–2: Die in V. 3 beschriebene Zeit ist die Phase, in der sich die Glaubenden als die Vollkommenen werden bewähren müssen.

Der Didachist deutet nicht an, daß die hier beschriebene "letzte Zeit" im Sinne eines *vaticinium ex eventu* schon Gegenwart

---

[24] Zur Wendung πληθυνθήσονται οἱ ψευδοπροφῆται vgl. Mt 24,11–12.

[25] Daß es sich bei den hier erwähnten ψευδοπροφῆται "selbstredend nicht um eine Anspielung auf die Pseudopropheten des c 11" handelt (so Steimer, *Vertex* [s. Anm. 3], 209), ist kaum richtig. Auch wenn das Material aus Tradition stammen und also die Übereinstimmung der Begriffe tatsächlich "zufällig" sein sollte, so ist für Did und deren Leser doch klar, daß eben hier wie dort von Pseudopropheten die Rede ist.

[26] Nach der Textausgabe von Klaus Wengst, *Didache (Apostellehre). Barnabasbrief. Zweiter Klemensbrief. Schrift an Diognet*, SUC 2 (Darmstadt 1984), 88 wäre die Wiederholung des Verbs στραφήσεται in der Wendung ἡ ἀγάπη...εἰς μῖσος nicht zu lesen. Aber der Text in *Const Ap* VII 32, dem Wengst mit dieser Lesart folgt, ist kaum als eigener Textzeuge zu nehmen; gleich im nächsten Satz weicht er erheblich von Did 16,4 ab (ψυγήσεται ἡ ἀγάπη τῶν πολλῶν), so daß er zur Rekonstruktion des Urtexts von Did nur mit größter Vorsicht herangezogen werden sollte.

[27] Zu Haß als einem Zeichen der Endzeit vgl. Mt 24,10.

ist[28] — im Gegenteil: Zur Zeit scheint von den angekündigten Bedrängnissen und Gefahren noch wenig zu sehen zu sein, und gerade deshalb muß so dringend vor einem Nachlassen der Aufmerksamkeit gewarnt werden.[29]

In V. 4a wird die Aussage von V. 3 näher expliziert: Haß, Verfolgung und Verrat (vgl. Mt 24,10: ἀλλήλους παραδώσουσιν καὶ μισήσουσιν ἀλλήλους) werden "in den letzten Tagen" überhand nehmen, weil in dieser Zeit die ἀνομία "wachsen" wird.[30] Nach K. Niederwimmer ist gemeint, "daß ein Bruder den anderen verfolgt und verrät" und "daß abgefallene Christen ihre ehemaligen Brüder bei den Behörden denunzieren";[31] aber der Text redet gar nicht speziell von Christen, sondern das Stichwort ἀλλήλους wird einfach darauf hinweisen, daß in der Zeit der

---

[28] Steimer, Vertex (s. Anm. 3), 209 meint, die Endzeit sei hier "nicht als bedrängend nahes Ereignis in Aussicht gestellt". Aber das ist doch fraglich: Die Tendenz geht dahin, ein Überhandnehmen von prinzipiell schon bekannten Negativerfahrungen zu konstatieren; kosmische Katastrophen werden gerade nicht geschildert. Gerade wenn es sich, wie Steimer a.a.O. 312 meint, um einen "Häresietopos" handelt, ist klar, daß die Aussagen zumindest *auch* einen unmittelbaren Gegenwartsbezug haben. Georg Schöllgen, *Didache. Zwölf-Apostel-Lehre*, FC 1 (Freiburg usw. 1991) trennt zu scharf zwischen V. 1.2 ("Der eschatologische Epilog ist...nicht Ausdruck akuter, das Handeln bestimmender Naherwartung, sondern ein Topos der Moralparänese im Kampf gegen die sich zunehmend breitmachende Trägheit in den Gemeinden", 76–77) und V. 3 ("Da schon im 11. Kapitel vom Auftreten von Pseudopropheten in den Gemeinden die Rede war, könnte man meinen, daß der Verfasser sich bereits in der ersten Phase der endzeitlichen Ereignisse wähnt. Doch in bezeichnendem Gegensatz zur Parallelstelle Mt 24,11 ist nicht das Auftreten, sondern erst das zahlenmäßige Anwachsen der Pseudopropheten ein eschatologisches Indiz; von daher ist die erste Phase höchstwahrscheinlich als noch ausstehend gedacht", 77–78). Auch V. 3 enthält, zumindest indirekt, den Aufruf zur Wachsamkeit.

[29] Auf den fehlenden Gegenwartsbezug verweisen auch Philipp Vielhauer/ Georg Strecker, "Apokalypsen und Verwandtes. Einleitung", in *Neutestamentliche Apokryphen in deutscher Übersetzung*, II. Band: *Apostolisches. Apokalypsen und Verwandtes*, hg. v. Wilhelm Schneemelcher (Tübingen 1989⁵), 536–537. Ihre Schlußfolgerung, Did 16 habe also nicht den Zweck, die "Gemeinde zu mahnen und zu trösten", sondern der Verfasser wolle "einen Gesamtentwurf der letzten Dinge in übersichtlicher Knappheit und klarer Gliederung" geben, so daß man Did 16 als "ein katechismusartiges Stück" anzusehen habe, wird aber der Funktion von VV. 1–2 im Textganzen nicht gerecht.

[30] Zu ἀνομία vgl. wiederum Mt 24,12, aber auch Mt 7,23.

[31] Niederwimmer, *Didache* (s. Anm. 5), 261.

wachsenden ἀνομία ein wechselseitiges Verfolgen und Hassen eintreten wird (vgl. etwa Apk 6,4), das nicht nur das Verhältnis von Christinnen und Christen untereinander betrifft. V. 4b schildert dann die Offenbarung des "Weltverführers". Obwohl das Stichwort "Antichrist" nicht begegnet,[32] entspricht die Beschreibung ganz dem mit diesem Begriff bezeichneten Typ des eschatologischen Widersachers Christi.[33] Die Bezeichnung κοσμοπλανής[34] ist ungewöhnlich, erinnert aber an 2 Joh 7.[35] Die über sein Wirken gemachte Aussage erinnert inhaltlich an Mt 24,24.21: Er erscheint ὡς υἱὸς θεοῦ, also als Pseudochristus; er tut Zeichen und Wunder; er empfängt die Herrschaft über die ganze Erde;[36] er wird Freveltaten von bis dahin nicht bekanntem Ausmaß begehen.[37] Woran beim Begriff ἀθέμιτα konkret zu denken ist, bleibt unklar;[38] daß es speziell um Christenverfolgungen geht, ist jedenfalls nicht ersichtlich.

K. Niederwimmer meint, die Aussagen in V. 4b stünden nicht in literarischer Abhängigkeit von Mt 24; "wenn eine Relation zur synoptischen Überlieferung vorläge, müßte sie in einer Relation zu einer zu postulierenden vormarkinischen Apokalypse beste-

---

[32] Das Stichwort ἀντίχριστος begegnet in den Schriften der Apostolischen Väter nur Pol Phil 7,1 (in enger Anlehnung an 1 Joh 4,2–3); es bezeichnet dort nicht den apokalyptischen Gegenspieler Christi, sondern "Irrlehrer" bzw. vom Glauben Abgefallene, die als solche Christusfeinde sind.

[33] Vgl. dazu L. J. Lietaert Peerbolte, *The Antecedents of Antichrist. A Traditio-Historical Study of the Earliest Christian Views on Eschatological Opponents*, JSJ.S 49 (Leiden 1996), vor allem 96–113.

[34] Das Wort ist hapaxlegomenon; in *Const Ap* VII 32,2 ist es in κοσμοπλάνος korrigiert worden, was einige Textausgaben übernehmen.

[35] Vgl. auch Apk 12,9: Der Teufel verführt die ganze οἰκουμένη.

[36] Vgl. Apk 13,7. In der synoptischen Tradition begegnet eine entsprechende Aussage nicht; vgl. aber Lk 4,6 Q. Auffallend ist, daß das logische Subjekt zu παραδοθήσεται nicht genannt ist; liegt tatsächlich ein "*passivum divinum*" vor (so Lohmann, *Drohung* [s. Anm. 2], 47)?

[37] Zu den ἀθέμιτα vgl. die Aussage über die θλῖψις in Mt 24,21. Dabei ist das Stichwort θλῖψις nicht einfach durch ἀθέμιτα ersetzt worden; vielmehr erscheinen die Frevel so tatsächlich als die Taten des κοσμοπλάνης und nicht als ein Verhängnis.

[38] Vgl. Lietaert Peerbolte, *Antecedents* (s. Anm. 33), 182: "The observation that the deceiver will commit lawless deeds is largely traditional. Although the exact words have no parallels, the activities of the ungodly one in 2 Thess 2,1–12, and those of the Beast in Rev 13,1–10 can perfectly be summarised as 'committing lawless deeds' (ἀθέμιτα ποιεῖν)".

hen".[39] Aber wenn man berücksichtigt, wie nahe die meisten Aussagen von Did 16, teilweise bis ins Detail der Formulierung hinein, bei Mt 24 (und 25) stehen, spricht doch vieles für die Vermutung, daß auch hier wie allgemein in Did 16 eine unmittelbare literarische Beziehung zu Mt 24 besteht, auch wenn diese nicht der Abhängigkeit entspricht, wie sie zwischen Mt und Mk vorliegt.

V. 5a beschreibt im Bild des Feuers die Prüfung, der die Menschen "danach" (τότε) ausgesetzt sein werden. Die Wendung ἡ κτίσις τῶν ἀνθρώπων ist singulär; daß entgegen dem Wortlaut "faktisch nicht das ganze Menschengeschlecht gemeint ist, sondern nur die Christen",[40] wird auch durch V. 5b nicht erwiesen (s. unten). Gesagt wird, daß die ganze Menschheit dem "Prüfungsfeuer" ausgesetzt werden wird,[41] und daß dabei "viele" zugrundegehen werden. Die Wendung σκανδαλισθήσονται πολλοί stimmt zwar mit Mt 24,10 überein; aber dort ist durch den Kontext (V. 9) klargestellt, daß es um Christen geht, die in der Verfolgung "zu Fall kommen". In Did 10,5 macht der Kontext dagegen deutlich, daß es einfach "viele Menschen" sind, die in der eschatologischen Prüfung scheitern und umkommen. Die Sachdifferenz bedeutet also nicht von vornherein, daß eine literarische Beziehung zu Mt 24 nicht vorliegt; offensichtlich hat der Didachist gegenüber Mt 24,10 die "Prüfungssituation" weiter gefaßt.

Die Verheißung für die, die im Glauben ausharren (V. 5b), entspricht weithin Mt 24,13 (ὁ δὲ ὑπομείνας εἰς τέλος, οὗτος σωθήσεται). Der Wechsel vom Singular in den Plural legt sich sprachlich vom Kontext her nahe; und daß der Didachist auf die πίστις der Ausharrenden verweist, ergibt sich gerade dadurch, daß nach seiner Darstellung das Prüfungsfeuer ja gerade alle Menschen erfaßt: Es sind eben die Glaubenden, die gerettet werden,[42] weil ihr Glaube ihnen dazu die Kraft gibt. Der Hinweis

---

[39] Niederwimmer, *Didache* (s. Anm. 5), 263 Anm. 15.

[40] So Niederwimmer, *Didache*, 263. Auch Schöllgen, *Didache* (s. Anm. 28), 78 spricht von der "Feuerprobe der Christen".

[41] Zu dieser Metapher vgl. 1 Kor 3,13; 1 Petr 1,7. Vgl. in der Sache Did 11,11, wo von Gottes κρίσις über die Propheten gesprochen ist.

[42] Daß hier die Wendung εἰς τέλος fehlt, ist vom Kontext her naheliegend — vom "Ende" ist an dieser Stelle noch nicht die Rede.

auf das, was rettet (ὑπ' αὐτοῦ τοῦ καταθέματος[43]), ist schwer zu erklären; am nächsten liegt es wohl doch, κατάθεμα auf Christus zu beziehen — es ist der von seinen Feinden (oder am Kreuz von Gott) Verfluchte, der die Glaubenden zur Rettung führen wird.[44] Der Didachist redet in 16,5 vom eschatologischen Gericht, das für die einen den Untergang, für die anderen aber Rettung bedeutet.[45]

Diese Auslegung wird dadurch bestätigt, daß in V. 6 das Gericht als bereits geschehen vorausgesetzt ist; jetzt nämlich werden "die Zeichen der Wahrheit" offenbar werden, deren Ziel die Auferstehung der Toten ist und an deren Ende die Parusie steht.[46] Die Aussage erinnert an Mt 24,30; dort ist vom "Zeichen des Menschensohnes" die Rede, das offenbar nicht näher beschrieben zu werden braucht, sondern das im Augenblick

---

[43] Jean-Paul Audet, *La Didachè. Instructions des Apôtres*, EtB (Paris 1958), 242 liest (mit der georgischen Übersetzung) ἀπ' αὐτοῦ anstelle von ὑπ' αὐτοῦ. Zur Kritik vgl. Butler (s. Anm. 11), 275.

[44] Vgl. Niederwimmer, *Didache* (s. Anm. 5), 264–265. Eindrucksvoll ist in diesem Zusammenhang die in *MartPol* 9,3 dargestellte Szene. Eine ganz andere Interpretation vertritt Aaron Milavec, "The Saving Efficacy of the Burning Process in Didache 16.5", in *The Didache in Context. Essays on Its Text, History and Transmission*, hg. v. Clayton N. Jefford, NovT.S 77 (Leiden 1995), 131–155. Er meint, eine Soteriologie, die dem Fluchtod Jesu im Sinne von Gal 3,13 rettende Kraft zuspreche, liege dem theologischen Denken der Did ganz fern. Denkbar sei, daß entsprechend apokalyptischem und prophetischem Sprachgebrauch vom eschatologischen Feuer die Rede sei, das die Glaubenden retten werde. Auch Milavec gibt aber keine Erklärung dafür, warum hier der Begriff κατάθεμα verwendet wird. Die christologische Deutung, wonach mit κατάθεμα Christus bezeichnet ist, wird mit guten Gründen unterstützt von Nancy Pardee, "The Curse that Saves (Didache 16.5)" in demselben Sammelband (a.a.O. 156–176). Möglicherweise muß es am Ende bei der Auskunft bleiben, die schon Rudolf Knopf, *Die Lehre der zwölf Apostel. Die zwei Clemensbriefe*, HNT Erg.band. Die Apostolischen Väter I (Tübingen 1920), 39 gab: "Die Ausdrucksweise [ist] nicht eben klar. Aber das mag freilich Absicht sein, es wird dunkel für Wissende gesprochen".

[45] Anders Aono, *Entwicklung* (s. Anm. 21), 170; die Aussage schildere nicht das Gericht Gottes, sondern "nur den schrecklichen Zustand der Endzeit". Aber Paulus meint mit der sehr ähnlichen Aussage in 1 Kor 3,13 (auf die Aono selbst hinweist) zweifellos das Gericht.

[46] Zu beachten ist die Parallelität von V. 4b (καὶ τότε φανήσεται) und v. 5 (τότε ἥξει ἡ κτίσις τῶν ἀνθρώπων...) auf der einen Seite und V. 6 (καὶ τότε φανήσεται τὰ σημεῖα) und V. 8 (τότε ὄψεται ὁ κόσμος τὸν κύριον) auf der anderen Seite.

seiner Erscheinung gleichsam für sich selbst sprechen wird.[47] Der Didachist unterscheidet drei σημεῖα voneinander, die aber alle auf die ἀλήθεια verweisen.[48] Die Erklärung des ersten "Zeichens" bereitet größte Schwierigkeiten:[49] Was ist mit der ἐκπέτασις ἐν οὐρανῷ sachlich gemeint?[50] Zu beachten ist jedenfalls, daß es sich um das erste von insgesamt drei "Zeichen" handelt: Die ἐκπέτασις ἐν οὐρανῷ ist keine unmittelbare Begleiterscheinung der Parusie, von der ja erst in V. 8 die Rede sein wird; vielmehr handelt es sich um das erste Vorzeichen der Parusie des κύριος. Dann aber liegt die traditionelle Auslegung wohl doch am nächsten: "Zuerst" wird der Himmel selbst "ausgespannt" werden, d.h. ein Vorgang, wie er etwa in Apk 6,14 geschildert ist, wird geradezu umgekehrt werden — die Offenbarung der Wahrheit beginnt damit, daß die Weltordnung (wieder)hergestellt wird.[51] Dazu paßt, daß als zweites Zeichen der Trompetenstoß

---

[47] Die Debatte darüber, woran konkret bei dem in Mt 24,30 erwähnten "Zeichen" zu denken sei, ist von daher im Grunde unnötig. Für den Apokalyptiker kommt es auf die Feststellung an, daß das σημεῖον im Moment seines Erscheinens als solches unmißverständlich ist.

[48] "Wahrheit" ist hier offenbar gesehen im Gegenüber zum κοσμοπλάνης. Die Konstruktion σημεῖα τῆς ἀληθείας muß nicht unbedingt als Hebraismus (für σημεῖα ἀληθινά) erklärt werden (so Niederwimmer, *Didache* [s. Anm. 5], 265); es geht um Zeichen, die auf "die Wahrheit" verweisen.

[49] Vgl. die bei Niederwimmer, *Didache*, 265–267 referierten Positionen.

[50] Wengst, *Didache* (s. Anm. 26), 99–100, Anm. 139, und Niederwimmer, *Didache*, 266 halten diejenige Auslegung für die wahrscheinlichste, die in Anlehnung an *Didask* 49,8 an "die Ausbreitung des Kreuzes am Himmel" denkt; vorausgesetzt sei möglicherweise die in *EvPetr* 10,39 belegte Vorstellung, daß das Kreuz mit Christus in den Himmel aufgenommen wurde, und nun kündige es die unmittelbar bevorstehende Parusie an. Aber der Verweis auf die *Didascalia* trägt wenig aus, denn dort handelt es sich um eine allegorische Deutung der Aussage von Mt 5,17–18; gedeutet wird der Satz "*Iota, id est unus apex, non transiet a lege*". Jota "*significatur per decalogum, nomen Iesu. Apex uero signum est extensionis ligni*". Die *Didascalia* verweist zusätzlich auf die Verklärung Jesu: "*Nam et Moyses et Helias erant cum domino in montem, id est lex et profetae*". Eine apokalyptische Vorstellung von der himmlischen Epiphanie des Kreuzes im Zusammenhang der Parusie läßt sich hieraus nicht ableiten. Wenig wahrscheinlich ist auch die These von Alfred Stuiber, "Die drei σημεῖα von Didache XVI", *JAC* 24 (1981), 42–44, daß an die "am Himmel ausgebreitete Standarte" Christi zu denken sei.

[51] Vgl. Audet, *Didachè* (s. Anm. 43), 473, der ebenfalls auf Apk 6,14 verweist. Die Wendung ἐν οὐρανῷ meint dann nicht, daß die ἐκπέτασις "am Himmel"

erfolgt (vgl. 1 Thess 4,16; 1 Kor 15,52); anders als in Mt 24,30–31 geht die Parusie nicht dem Trompetenstoß voraus, sondern sie folgt ihm — und zwar sogar erst nach der Totenauferstehung. Die φωνὴ σάλπιγγος ist also das Zeichen, das die Totenauferstehung einleitet, nicht "Begleitmusik" für die Parusie. Man braucht hier in der Tat nicht unbedingt mit literarischer Abhängigkeit von Paulus oder auch von Mt 24,31 zu rechnen,[52] aber es genügt auch nicht, pauschal darauf zu verweisen, daß "überall das gleiche, verbreitete Motiv jüdisch-christlicher Apokalyptik zugrunde" liege.[53] Denn die spezifischen Elemente der eschatologischen Aussagen in Did 16,6–8, nämlich die Abfolge 1) "Öffnung" am Himmel, 2) Trompetenstoß, 3) Auferstehung der Toten und erst dann (V. 8) die Parusie, sind doch überaus auffällig.[54] Das dritte Zeichen ist die ἀνάστασις νεκρῶν; dieser Ausdruck wird geradezu "technisch" verwendet, d.h. es wird ein als bekannt vorausgesetzter Sachverhalt angekündigt und nicht etwa ein Vorgang beschrieben. Gerade deshalb bedarf die Aussage einer Präzisierung, die der Didachist in V. 7 vornimmt.[55]

Wenn in V. 7 gesagt wird, daß "nicht alle" Toten auferstehen werden, sondern nur οἱ ἅγιοι, so deutet nichts darauf hin, daß damit auf eine zu erwartende Abfolge von zwei Auferstehungen

---

geschieht, sondern daß sie als erstes der Zeichen "am Himmel" sichtbar sein wird.

[52] So m.R. Niederwimmer, *Didache* (s. Anm. 5), 267, Anm. 26.

[53] So Niederwimmer ebenda unter Verweis auf Köster, *Überlieferung* (s. Anm. 8), 189, und vor allem auf John S. Kloppenborg, "Didache 16,6–8 and Special Matthean Tradition", *ZNW* 70 (1979), 54–67, hier 66.

[54] In 1 Thess 4,16–17, einem von Paulus zitierten apokalyptischen Traditionsstück, geschieht die Parusie, während die eschatologische Trompete erschallt, und zugleich (!) geschieht die Auferstehung der Toten ἐν Χριστῷ, so daß dann die Begegnung der Entrückten mit dem Herrn "in der Luft" erfolgt. Über Letzteres ist in Did 16,6–8 im einzelnen nichts gesagt; klar ist aber, daß auch in Did die Auferstehung der Toten nicht *nach* der Parusie geschieht, sondern vorher.

[55] Der "Kommentar" in V. 7 muß nicht bedeuten, daß in V. 6 eine "Vorlage" zitiert ist, die der Didachist korrigieren müßte. Es ist gut denkbar, daß der Verfasser der Did seine eigene Aussage vor dem Mißverständnis schützen will, der von ihm ganz selbstverständlich verwendete Ausdruck ἀνάστασις νεκρῶν bezeichne eine Auferstehung *aller* Toten.

(im Sinne von Apk 20) hingewiesen sein könnte.[56] Es wird einfach festgestellt, daß nur οἱ ἅγιοι, mit denen zweifellos die Christen gemeint sind, auferstehen werden, die anderen Toten dagegen nicht. Als Beleg dafür wird in V. 7b das ausdrücklich mit ὡς ἐρρέθη eingeleitete Zitat von Sach 14,5 LXX angeführt, auf das auch in Mt 25,31a angespielt zu sein scheint.[57] Daß der Didachist anders als LXX nicht κύριος ὁ θεός μου liest,[58] sondern ὁ κύριος, ist nicht verwunderlich, denn er bezieht den κύριος-Titel natürlich auf Christus und nicht auf Gott. Verwendet wird das Zitat in erster Linie, um die Aussage von V. 7a zu belegen, daß eben "nicht alle (Toten)", sondern nur πάντες οἱ ἅγιοι (μετ' αὐτοῦ) an der ἀνάστασις νεκρῶν teilhaben werden. Zugleich hat der Wortlaut des Zitats den Vorteil, mit der Verbform ἥξει auf das bevorstehende "Kommen" des Herrn hinzuweisen, so daß sich nun die abschließende Aussage zur Parusie gut anschließen kann.[59]

---

[56] Niederwimmer, *Didache* (s. Anm. 5), 267 paraphrasiert: Der Didachist gebe den Kommentar, daß "mit ἀνάστασις νεκρῶν...(noch) nicht die allgemeine Totenerweckung gemeint [sei], sondern (erst) die Auferweckung der 'Heiligen'". Diese Deutung hat aber keinen Anhalt am Text. Schöllgen, *Didache* (s. Anm. 28), 80–81, meint, es sei "eine spätere generelle Auferstehung der Toten...nicht notwendig ausgeschlossen"; darauf weise schon der in H verlorene Schluß, der sicherstelle, "daß während der eschatologischen Ereignisse ein Endgericht stattfinden wird, in dessen Verlauf alle Menschen gemäß ihren Werken gerichtet werden". Dagegen jetzt m.R. Seeliger, "Schlußkapitel" (s. Anm. 1), 189: Did 16,7 wendet sich "ausdrücklich gegen die Vorstellung der allgemeinen Totenauferstehung...Der Didache nach werden ausdrücklich nur die Heiligen gerettet", womit sich diese Schrift auch deutlich von Apk 20,11–21,8 unterscheide.

[57] Daß das Zitat nicht aus Mt 25,31, sondern unmittelbar aus LXX übernommen wurde, liegt auf der Hand; der Wortlaut ist erheblich verschieden, so daß man fragen kann, ob bei Mt überhaupt eine Anspielung auf Sach 14,5 vorliegt. Die Tatsache, daß Did in der Textfassung von 16,7 weitgehend dem LXX-Text von Sach 14 folgt und nicht Mt 25,31, muß nicht bedeuten, daß Did hier von Mt "unabhängig" ist (so Kloppenborg; s. Anm. 53); es kommt bei der Benutzung von Vorlagen häufig vor, daß dort zitierte Quellen bei der Übernahme korrigiert werden.

[58] In LXX ist so das hebräische יהוה אֱלֹהַי ganz korrekt wieder gegeben.

[59] Daß das Zitat davon spricht, daß die Heiligen "zusammen mit dem κύριος" kommen, läßt der Didachist unberücksichtigt; ursprünglich sind πάντες οἱ ἅγιοι die Engel als die Begleiter Jahwes bei dessen Ankunft, und dieser Aspekt ist in

Als Höhepunkt und Abschluß des eschatologischen Geschehens erfolgt (V. 8) die Parusie des κύριος. Angesichts der Nähe von V. 6 zu Mt 24,30a.31 fällt es schwer, die Aussage und Formulierung in V. 8 nicht von Mt 24,30b her zu lesen. Die Wendung ὄψεται ὁ κόσμος steht offenbar anstelle von πᾶσαι αἱ φυλαὶ τῆς γῆς...ὄψονται,[60] und statt des Titels "Menschensohn" gebraucht der Didachist natürlich wieder den Titel κύριος. Wichtig ist die fast wörtliche Übereinstimmung in der Wendung ἐρχόμενον ἐπάνω[61] τῶν νεφελῶν τοῦ οὐρανοῦ, die die Vermutung nahelegt, daß der Didachist unmittelbar Mt 24,30 seiner eigenen Formulierung zugrundegelegt hat.[62] Die Auskunft, der Verfasser der Did zitiere "gemeinapokalyptisches Gut (von Dan. her)",[63] wird diesem Befund — und der großen Zahl der bisher schon beobachteten Parallelen zwischen Did 16 und Mt 24 (und 25) — nicht gerecht.[64]

Endet die Didache tatsächlich mit der Rede von der Parusie des κύριος, wie es der hier endende Text der Handschrift H vorauszusetzen scheint? Das wird in der Forschung weithin bezweifelt. Unter Hinweis auf die äußere Gestalt des Textes in der Handschrift wird argumentiert, daß nach Meinung des Kopisten von H "der Schluß der Did. fehlt".[65] Bestätigt werde dies durch die — freilich unterschiedlichen — Fassungen des

---

Mt 25,31 auch noch enthalten. In Did 16,7 entspricht diese Vorstellung nicht dem vom Didachisten angesteuerten Ziel (s. aber unten Anm. 72).

[60] Das vorangehende Verb κόψονται ist natürlich entfallen, weil die Aussage der Sache nach ja schon in V. 4–5 enthalten gewesen war.

[61] Mt hat hier ἐπί.

[62] Die "Grundstelle" (so Niederwimmer, *Didache* [s. Anm. 5], 268) Dan 7,13 ist sowohl in LXX wie bei Theodotion sprachlich anders aufgebaut (vgl. Niederwimmer, ebenda, Anm. 2), während Did und Mt hier übereinstimmen.

[63] Niederwimmer, *Didache*, 268. Er wendet sich m.R. gegen die These, V. 8 stamme aus der in Mk 13 verarbeiteten Vorlage.

[64] Auch Christopher M. Tuckett, "Synoptic Tradition in the Didache", in *The New Testament in Early Christianity. La réception des écrits néotestamentaires dans le christianisme primitif,* hg. v. Jean-Marie Sevrin, BEThL 86 (Leuven 1989), 197–230, kommt zu dem Ergebnis, daß in Did 16 die Kenntnis von Mt 24 vorauszusetzen ist. Ihm ist dabei der Aspekt wichtig, daß Did kein Beleg für eine von Mk unabhängige Mt-Fassung ist. Dagegen Kloppenborg (s. Anm. 53), 67: "Matthew combined Marcan tradition with another free-floating apocalyptic tradition which had been incorporated into the Didache quite independently of Matthew".

[65] Niederwimmer, *Didache* (s. Anm. 5), 268. Vgl. a.a.O. 247, Anm. 2.

Textschlusses in *Const Ap* VII 32 und in der georgischen Übersetzung. Insbesondere aber spreche auch der Aufbau von Did
16,3–8 im Ganzen für eine solche Annahme: "Der Leser erwartet
eine Schilderung des Weltgerichts. Damit muß ursprünglich auch
der Text der Did. geschlossen haben".[66] Aber diese Voraussetzung ist mehr als fraglich. Natürlich verbindet sich in den
traditionellen kirchlichen (vor allem Bekenntnis-) Aussagen mit
der Parusie auch die Gerichtsvorstellung;[67] insofern ist die von K.
Niederwimmer erwähnte Erwartung "des Lesers" durchaus verständlich. Aber eben dies macht es gerade auch verständlich, daß
frühe Rezipienten der Didache die ihnen als fehlend erschei-
nenden Aussagen ergänzt haben[68] und daß der im Jahre 1056

---

[66] Niederwimmer, *Didache*, 268. Ähnlich Wengst, *Didache* (s. Anm. 26), 20: "Es
fehlt offenbar eine Aussage darüber, was dann geschieht, wenn der Herr auf den
Wolken des Himmels gekommen ist. Und in der Tat bieten CA und G
unabhängig voneinander weitergehende Aussagen, aus denen sich mit größer
Wahrscheinlichkeit eine Gerichtsaussage als ursprünglicher Schluß der Didache
rekonstruieren läßt". Wengst bietet (a.a.O. 90) den Text ἀποδοῦναι ἑκάστῳ κατὰ
τὴν πρᾶξιν αὐτοῦ, d.h. den gemeinsamen Textausschnitt aus *Const Ap* VII 32
und der georgischen Übersetzung. Boudewijn Dehandschutter, "The Text of the
Didache: Some Comments on the Edition of Klaus Wengst" (in dem in Anm. 44
genannten Sammelband, 37–46, hier 44, Anm. 44) hält es für "evident that H is
deficient" und meint, Wengst biete "only a cautious solution". Zur Kritik vgl.
Schöllgen, *Didache* (s. Anm. 28), 81. Er meint, die georgische Übersetzung habe
den ursprünglichen Text wohl weitgehend bewahrt, doch blieben so viele
Unsicherheiten, daß auf eine Rekonstruktion verzichtet werden müsse. Die
grundsätzlichen Bedenken gegenüber der (ja nur in einer deutschen
Übersetzung bekannten) georgischen Übersetzung gelten auch und in be-
sonderer Weise für den Schluß der Did. Vgl. zur Sache *La Doctrine des Douze
Apôtres (Didachè)*, hg. v. Willy Rordorf/André Tuilier, SC 248 (Paris 1978), 115–
116, Anm. 2, und Niederwimmer, *Didache* (s. Anm. 5), 44–45.

[67] Hier ist schon allein an den Schluß des zweiten Artikels des "Apostolischen
Glaubensbekenntnisses" zu erinnern.

[68] *Const Ap* VII 32 ist ja durchgängig eine Bearbeitung von Did 16 und
keineswegs ein "Textzeuge"; etliches ist gestrichen, manches ist ergänzt worden.
Daß gerade am Schluß die Notwendigkeit gesehen wurde, den Text zu
ergänzen, ist naheliegend. Vgl. dazu Adolf Harnack, *Die Lehre der zwölf Apostel
nebst Untersuchungen zur ältesten Geschichte der Kirchenverfassung und des Kirchenrechts* (Leipzig 1884), 178, der feststellt, "dass der Bearbeiter bei seinen
Correcturen immerhin noch conservativ verfahren ist, soweit er es irgend
vermochte, dass er aber bis auf sehr Weniges Alles getilgt oder im Geiste des 4.
Jahrhunderts umgearbeitet hat, was für die neue Zeit nicht mehr passte".

schreibende Kopist der Handschrift H den Eindruck haben konnte, es fehle noch etwas.[69] Tatsächlich braucht jedoch für die frühe Zeit der christlichen Eschatologie keineswegs als zwingend angesehen zu werden, daß sich mit der Erwartung der Totenauferstehung und der Parusie des κύριος auch die Vorstellung eines dann folgenden Gerichts verband. Weder in 1 Thess 4,13–18 noch in 1 Kor 15 begegnet der Gerichtsgedanke; umgekehrt ist in 2 Kor 4,16–5,10, wo vom Gericht gesprochen wird (5,10), von der Parusie nicht die Rede. Dasselbe gilt für Mk 13: Der in der Parusie gekommene Menschensohn (13,26) sendet seine Engel aus, um die ἐκλεκτοί zu sammeln (13,27) — von einem Gericht über die anderen Menschen ist nicht die Rede. In der Mt-Parallele ändert sich das erst dadurch, daß in 25,1–30 zwei Gerichtsgleichnisse und in 25,31–46 das große Bild vom Endgericht über πάντα τὰ ἔθνη angefügt werden.[70]

Entscheidend ist freilich die Beobachtung, daß in Did 16,1–8 der Endgerichtsgedanke keineswegs fehlt und deshalb auch nicht "ergänzt" zu werden braucht. In VV. 4–5 ist deutlich davon die Rede, daß alle Menschen in das "Feuer der Bewährung" kommen und daß dabei nur die Glaubenden gerettet werden.[71] Wenn dann in VV. 6–7 gesagt wird, daß nur "die Heiligen" auferstehen werden, dann ist damit das eschatologische Endgericht durchaus umfassend dargestellt: Die in der Endzeit Lebenden müssen durch das Gericht hindurch, und die Toten werden dadurch gerichtet, daß die einen auferstehen werden und

---

Offensichtlich hat er Fehlendes, das im 4. Jahrh. zu sagen unerläßlich schien, ergänzt.

[69] Niederwimmer, *Didache* (s. Anm. 5), 268: "Der Schreiber hat nach οὐρανοῦ einen Punkt gesetzt und den Rest der Zeile leer gelassen, übrigens auch den Rest der Seite. Offenkundig signalisiert der Kopist damit, daß nach seiner Überzeugung der Schluß der Did. fehlt und d.h., daß damit auch der Schluß der Did.-Apokalypse nicht erhalten ist".

[70] Zur Auslegung von Mt 25,31–46 vgl. vor allem Egon Brandenburger, *Das Recht des Weltenrichters. Untersuchung zu Matthäus 25,31–46*, SBS 99 (Stuttgart 1980).

[71] Dies betont nachdrücklich auch Milavec (s. Anm. 44), 151–154; er verweist darauf, daß Did 16,5 in *Const Ap* fehlt, was zeige "that this section of the Didache was no longer adequately understood or adequately appreciated as the final judgement". Der von *Const Ap* geschaffene "Langtext" sei dementsprechend "a testimony to the frailty of culturally and historically conditioned understandings" (154).

die anderen im Tode bleiben.[72] Das Ziel der Endereignisse ist das
für den κόσμος sichtbar werdende Kommen des κύριος — mit
diesem gleichermaßen eschatologischen wie christologischen
Ausblick endet die Didache.[73]

Der Verfasser bzw. Redaktor der Didache hat bei der Abfassung des eschatologischen Schlußabschnitts seines Werkes die
synoptische Apokalypse in der Fassung von Mt 24 (und 25)
literarisch verwendet;[74] er übernahm dabei Einzelaspekte und
bestimmte Formulierungen, ohne dem Mt-Text im Aufbau und
in der Tendenz durchgängig zu folgen.[75] Der Grund für diesen
vergleichsweise "freien" Umgang des Didachisten mit der bei Mt
bewahrten Jesusüberlieferung liegt auf der Hand: Die Apokalypse in Mt 24.25 ist, ebenso wie die Vorlage Mk 13, gestaltet
als eine Rede, in der es gerade darauf ankommt, daß der
Sprecher Jesus ist; der irdische Jesus der geschichtlichen Vergangenheit sagt eine Zukunft an, die zur Zeit der Abfassung des
Mt zumindest teilweise Gegenwart bzw. schon geschichtliche

---

[72] Darauf, daß vom Gericht schon die Rede war, verweisen auch Vielhauer/
Strecker (s. Anm. 29), 536; sie meinen freilich, es fehle gleichwohl in V. 8 etwas,
und zwar "die Sammlung der Erwählten (Mt 24,31) bzw. die Vereinigung der
Gläubigen mit dem Kyrios (1 Thess 4,17)". Aber die Zugehörigkeit der ἅγιοι
zum Herrn war im Zitat in V. 7 deutlich ausgesagt worden.

[73] Vgl. Aono, *Entwicklung* (s. Anm. 21), 171: "Die Parusie des Herrn ist
bemerkenswerterweise als ein frohes Ereignis beschrieben, und nicht mit dem
negativen Gericht verbunden". Aono meint allerdings, daß auch in Did 16,5
nicht an das Gericht gedacht sei, was m.E. fraglich ist.

[74] So auch Tuckett (s. Anm. 64), 208: "The pattern of parallels between the
Didache and Matthew is thus most easily explained if the Didache here
presupposes Matthew's finished gospel".

[75] Aono, *Entwicklung* (s. Anm. 21), 186, meint, es müsse "die Hypothese
gewagt werden, dass der [Verfasser] der Did wahrscheinlich nicht einmal ein
schriftliches Exemplar des MtEv vor sich hatte, dass er aber die zitierten Sätze
aus dem Gedächtnis kannte, weil sie wörtlich oder mit Varianten immer wieder
in der Gemeinde gesprochen wurden". Vgl. die Schlußüberlegung bei Seeliger
(s. Anm. 1), 192: Es sei "denkbar, daß hier die wichtigsten Inhalte prophetischer
Verkündigung für die Gemeinden referiert werden, die keinen Propheten
haben. Angesichts der Gefahr der Pseudopropheten wird die wahre Prophetie,
das aber heißt Apokalyptik, in Grundzügen festgehalten. Das ist, sofern man
einen Propheten hat, unnötig. Sofern man keinen hat, aber dringend geboten.
So wundert es nicht, daß das apokalyptische Schlußkapitel der Didache sich als
Bezugnahme auf ein Genus der Offenbarungsliteratur liest, selbst aber keine
Apokalypse ist, sondern nur ein Aide-mémoire apokalyptischer Theologie".

Vergangenheit ist. Insofern erfüllt die "synoptische Apokalypse" eines der wesentlichen Elemente apokalyptischer Literatur, denn sie bietet Geschichtsdarstellung in Futurform und nennt als fiktiven Sprecher eine Gestalt der Vergangenheit.[76] Did 16 hingegen ist von vornherein als ein Text entworfen, in dem der Didachist selbst zu Wort kommt und in dem die Angeredeten auch die unmittelbaren Adressaten des Textes sind, weshalb Did 16 eben auch nicht als "Apokalypse" bezeichnet werden sollte.

Die Endzeitrede der Didache vermittelt den Lesern des Textes die eschatologische Perspektive der ihnen in den vorangegangenen Kapiteln teilweise sehr detailliert mitgeteilten Weisungen. Die einleitenden Aufforderungen in VV. 1.2a (γρηγορεῖτε / γίνεσθε / πυκνῶς) sind unmittelbare paränetische Anweisungen, die sich an die gegenwärtigen Leser der Schrift richten; es handelt sich nicht, wie in Mt 24,25, um "Vorhersagen", die bezogen auf die Sprechersituation erst in der "Zukunft" Bedeutung haben werden. Die Forderung der Vollkommenheit (V. 2b) signalisiert, in welcher Weise es auf das Verhalten der Leser in der "letzten Zeit" ankommen wird: In der Endzeit, die in VV. 3–5 beschrieben wird, werden Gefahren, Gefährdungen und religiöse Verführungen überhand nehmen; und eben darin wird sich das Gericht vollziehen, das mit dem Untergang derer endet, die nicht im Glauben auszuharren vermögen, während die Glaubenden gerettet werden. Danach bricht dann die Zeit der ἀλήθεια an, in der nach entsprechenden "Zeichen" der Welt die Epiphanie des κύριος in seiner Parusie sichtbar werden wird. Dieser eschatologische Ausblick der Did ist vollständig — es gibt keinen Grund für die Annahme, daß in dieser Zeichnung des Geschehens der "letzten Zeit" irgendetwas fehlt bzw. "weggebrochen" ist.[77]

Von wesentlicher Bedeutung für die Auslegung von Did 16 ist die Tatsache, daß der Verfasser der Didache sich für seine Weisungen auf das "im Evangelium" Überlieferte, d.h. auf die apokalyptische Jesustradition berufen konnte (15,3-4), und daß er die Aussagen über den eschatologischen Ernst, der hinter diesen Weisungen steht, ebenfalls aus "dem Evangelium" zu gewinnen vermochte. Insofern ist Did 16 ein bedeutsamer Beleg

---

[76] Vgl. dazu Vielhauer/Strecker (s. Anm. 29), 493–497 zum literarischen Charakter von Apokalypsen.

[77] Vgl. dazu Niederwimmer, *Didache* (s. Anm. 5) 269: Der Text in *Const Ap* VII 32,4-5 ist, "(wenn überhaupt, dann) eine sehr freie Wiedergabe der Did." (vgl. oben Anm. 68).

für die fortdauernde Wirkung der apokalyptischen Jesustradition
auch in einer paränetischen Schrift, der apokalyptisches Denken
im Grunde ganz fernliegt.

DOUBLE VOCATIVES

Gerard Mussies
Utrecht University
(Utrecht, the Netherlands)

1. Introduction

The use of a double vocative κύριε κύριε, as occurring in Matt 7:21 "Not everyone who says to me 'Lord, Lord/Sir, sir' will enter the kingdom of heaven," has not attracted much attention in the field of NT grammar and stylistics. The well-known works of such scholars as Robertson (1915²), Radermacher (1925²), Abel (1927), Blass-Debrunner(1959¹⁰), Moulton-Howard-Turner, and Zerwick (1963) do not in fact even mention the existence of the phenomenon as such. This silence on the matter may have arisen from the implicit assumption on their part that such reduplications were semantically not different from single vocatives, and a symptom only of the emotional attitude of the speaker(s), just like what happens nowadays in modern languages. As such these double vocatives would then be comparable to repeated exclamations like σταύρωσον σταύρωσον αὐτόν (Luke 23:21 = John 19:6), ἆρον ἆρον (John 19:15), or μεγάλη ἡ Ἄρτεμις Ἐφεσίων, μεγάλη ἡ Ἄρτεμις Ἐφεσίων (Acts 19:34 B), which last was even kept up for two hours at a stretch.[1]

Such an explanation from the speaker's emotion or expressivity is indeed the one that is worded by grammars of more extensive periods of Greek and Latin than that which is covered by the writings of the NT only. Schwyzer speaks very briefly about "expressiv verdoppelte Vokative," adducing *int. al.* the instances Ζεῦ Ζεῦ and παῖ παῖ from Aeschylus *Choeph.* 246 and 653.[2] Hofmann, equally curtly, remarks: "Die Gemination des

---

[1] In the LXX *e.g.* Judith 13:11 ἀνοίξατε ἀνοίξατε δή; Job 19:21 ἐλεήσατέ με, ἐλεήσατέ με.

[2] E. Schwyzer and A. Debrunner, *Griechische Grammatik* II (München 1966³), p. 60.

Vokativs, z.B. Pl(au)t(us) *Mil.* 313 *Sceledre, Sceledre,* ist affektisch."[3]
Elsewhere he is much more elaborate on the matter:

> Sie (*scil.* die Gemination in der Alltagssprache) stellt sich ohne
> weiteres bei gesteigerter Aktion und im Affekt ein, sei es dass es
> gilt sich stimmlich auf weitere Entfernung geltend zu machen
> (*heus heus* zunächst dort, wo einfaches *heus* nicht genügt), sei es
> dass der überströmende Affekt in der Doppelung die
> Möglichkeit findet, sich stärker auszuleben. Das eigentliche
> Gebiet der Gemination ist daher ausser den Interjektionen...der
> Imperativ und der Vokativ.[4]

As almost all of the instances which these authors adduce[5] are
from the stage, figuring either in tragedies or comedies, the

---

[3] J. B. Hofmann and A. Szantyr, *Lateinische Syntax und Stilistik* (München
1965), p. 26.

[4] J. B. Hofmann, *Lateinische Umgangssprache* (Heidelberg 1978[4]), pp. 58–59.

[5] Schwyzer's instances, which can easily be extended (for example, why ignore
the oldest and only example from Homer E 31; 455 "Ares Ares, ruin of man"?
cf. J. Wackernagel, *Sprachliche Untersuchungen zu Homer* [Göttingen 1970[2]], p.
230), require some comment. Aeschylus *Cho.* 653 has properly speaking ὦ παῖ
παῖ, while it is 652 that has παῖ παῖ. Euripides *Hec.* 171 and Aristophanes *Nub.*
1164 have both ὦ τέκνον ὦ παῖ, which are semantical duplications only that do
not belong here; *Nub.* 1167, however, has ὦ φίλος, ὦ φίλος. J. B. Hofmann's
(1978, p. 59) two instances from Petronius are not defendable. "*Carpe, carpe*"
(36,7), a command to a carver named Carpus, is explained in the context itself
as a pun consisting of two homonyms, a vocative and an imperative, hence:
"*Carpus, carve*"; "*Glyco, Glyco*" (45,9) is in reality "*Glyco? Glyco dedit suos*" ("Glyco?
Glyco gave away his own flesh and blood"). The material quoted by these
scholars is then: Aeschylus *Cho.* 246; 652; Aristophanes *Nub.* 1167; Plautus
Bacch. 814; *Curc.* 626; (*Merc.* 683); *Mil.* 313; (415); *Most.* 373; *Rud.* 523; 1235;
Trin. 1094 (triple voc.); Terence *Ad.* 256; *Andr.* 282; *Eun.* 91; (*Hec.* 856); Cicero
Ad Quintum 1,3,1 (triple voc.). Instances in brackets are of the discontinuous type
"*Palaestrio, o Palaestrio*" (Plautus *Mil.* 415) and the like, and are therefore impure
duplications. To these the following can be added, partly from D. Fehling, *Die
Wiederholungsfiguren und ihr Gebrauch bei den Griechen vor Gorgias* (Berlin 1969),
pp. 169–173, partly from elsewhere, but no completeness can be claimed:
Homer E 31; 455; Herodotus 1,86 (triple voc. deducible from: ἐς τρὶς ὀνομάσαι·
Σόλων); Archilochus 118 (L–B); Sappho frg 164 (*Lyra Graeca*, Vol. 1, pp. 296–
298); Aeschylus *Ag.* 1073; 1077; 1080; 1085; 1489; 1537; *Cho.* 382; 855; *Pers.*
675; *Supp.* 890; Sophocles *Ai.* 854; *O.C.* 1627; (*Ph.* 759–760); 797; Euripides
Andr. 319; Aristophanes *Pax* 114; 236 (triple voc.); 246; 255; *Vesp.* 995; Plato

emotional character of such duplications is in most cases evident from the context, or can at least easily be interpreted in this vain. The emotions themselves may be bemoaning, reproaching, rebuking, wondering, admiring, pleading, especially so when gods are invoked, or they may vary from a cry for help (Plautus *Curc.* 626) to a joyful salutation (Terence *Hec.* 856). On the whole it seems that the more serious feelings are preponderant, even in comedies.

This general explanation seems also to be applicable to our particular instance Matt 7:21, but only as long as the following verses 22–23 are also taken into account: "For many will say on that day: 'Lord, Lord, did not we prophesy in your name, did not we throw out demons in your name, and did not we perform many powers in your name?' And then I shall confess to them: I never knew you, get out from me, you doers of lawlessness!" However, according to the opinion of many commentators 7:21 was originally an independent saying,[6] and the verses 22–23, which lend it an eschatological colour, a later addition. The distribution in Luke of the synoptic parallels to these portions may corroborate this assumption. The parallel to Matt 7:21 is Luke 6:46 "Why do you call me 'Lord, Lord' and do not do what I say?" It has there no sequel comparable to Matt 7:22–23, but introduces the parable of the man who built without laying a foundation, while what corresponds to Matt 7:22–23 figures in another context, in Luke 13:22–30, following upon the words "Sir, Sir, open up." If the general explanation of emotionality is applied to Matt 7:21 as a separate logion, one fails to see, however, what specific emotions are now involved, and rather gets the impression that Jesus saw the double vocative as flattery, by means of which people expected to be allowed into the Kingdom.

Tim. 22b; *Axiochus* 364a; *Anacreontea* 1,1,13; Corpus Herm. *Ascl.* 24; PGM 7, 529; 687; 19, 1; 2; 4; 6; 37,335; Cretan sorcery tablet, line 4 (published by R. Wünsch, *RMP* 55 (1900), p. 508; triple voc.); *Carm.Pop.* 25; *Hist. mon. in Aeg.* 8,3; *Hist. Laus.* 67, 1b (triple voc.). In Aeschylus' choral lyrics there are many duplications of all kinds of word-forms, and it is often difficult to say whether it is a nominative or a vocative *e.g. Prom* 694 "oh, oh, fate, fate!" (cf. Fehling, *Wiederholungsfiguren*, pp. 170–171).

[6] *E.g.* E. Klostermann, *Das Matthäusevangelium*, HNT 4 (Tübingen 1971[4]), pp. 70–71; U. Luz, *Das Evangelium nach Matthäus (Matt 1–7)*, EKK I/1, (Zürich etc. 1985), pp. 402; R. Schnackenburg, *Matthäusevangelium 1,1–16,20*, NEB (Würzburg 1985), p. 76.

There is therefore some reason to review the NT material as a whole and see if apart from emotion or expressiveness there may be some additional shade of meaning.

2. NT material

Besides Matt 7:21, our starting-point, this material appears to be as follows:

(a) Matt 7:22 "Many will say to me on that day 'Lord, Lord' (κύριε, κύριε) did we not prophesy in your name?" (Luke 13:26 lacks the vocative[7]).

(b) Matt 23:7 (in MSS D W 𝔐 etc.) "(The Pharisees love) greetings in the market places and to be called 'Rabbi, rabbi' (ῥαββί, ῥαββί) by the people" (ℵ B L Δ Θ etc.: ῥαββί; absent in parr. Mark 12:38 and Luke 20:46).

(c) Matt 23:37 "Jerusalem, Jerusalem, you who kill the prophets" etc. (= Luke 13:24).

(d) Matt 25:11 "Later the other virgins also came, saying 'Sir, sir' (κύριε, κύριε), open up for us" (= Luke 13:25 A D W Θ Ψ 𝔐 etc., but in a different context; 𝔓[75] ℵ B L etc.: κύριε).

(e) Matt 27:46 "My God, my God, (ἠλί, ἠλί / θεέ μου, θεέ μου) why have you forsaken me?" (= Mark 15:34 ἐλωί, ἐλωί / ὁ θεός μου, ὁ θεός μου).

(f) Mark 14:45 (A 016 𝔐 etc.): "When he (Judas) arrived he immediately approached him, kissed him and said 'Rabbi, rabbi'" (ℵ B C* D L Δ Θ Ψ etc.: 'Rabbi'; C[2], W, etc.: 'Greetings, Rabbi' (χαῖρε ῥαββί), as in par. Matt 26:49; different in parr. Luke 22:47 and John 18:4).

(g) Luke 7:14 (D) "Young man, young man (νεανίσκε, νεανίσκε) I say to you, get up" (remaining mss.: νεανίσκε).

(h) Luke 8:24 "Master, master (ἐπιστάτα, ἐπιστάτα), we are drowning!" (ℵ[c] W Γ lat boh goth: ἐπιστάτα; D: κύριε, κύριε; parr. Matt 8:25 κύριε; Mark 4:38 διδάσκαλε).

(i) Luke 10:41: "Martha, Martha, you are worried and upset by many things."

(j) Luke 22:31: "Simon, Simon, Satan has tried to sift you as wheat."

---

[7] The term "vocative" will denote not only vocatives in the proper sense like κύριε, but also nominatives and indeclinables used "as vocative," as in Mark 15:34 ὁ θεός μου and Matt 23:7 ῥαββί.

(k) Acts 9:4 (22:7; 26:14): "Saul, Saul, why do you persecute me?"

It may be clear that not all of these instances can with absolute certainty be ascribed to the personal style of either Jesus or the gospel writers.

Firstly, (e) the word from the Cross in Matt 27:46/Mark 15:34 can be set apart as an OT quotation from Psalm 22:2: אלי אלי. It demonstrates however, that the double address was not a phenomenon peculiar to Koine Greek or to the NT period, and it also shows in its various Greek renderings that the articles and the possessive suffix or pronoun could be included in the gemination: Psalm 21:2 LXX: ὁ θεός, ὁ θεός μου; Matt 27:46: θεέ μου, θεέ μου; Mark 15:34: ὁ θεός μου, ὁ θεός μου.

Furthermore, a number of instances are uncertain in that they are not attested by the entire textual transmission. From this point of view the following are at least doubtful: (b) Matt 23:7; (d) Luke 13:25; (f) Mark 14:45; (g) Luke 7:14; and (h) Luke 8:24.

In this list, (f) Mark 14:45, Judas greeting Jesus in Gethsemane, is interesting for two reasons. The double vocative variant ῥαββί, ῥαββί may have arisen from a single vocative and could owe its very occurrence in the manuscripts to a combination with our opening instance (a) Matt 7:(21–)22. The addition of a second vocative in Mark 14:45 was then felt by the copyist(s) as a fulfillment of the warning formulated in Matt 7:21–22. It was Judas, among other people, who addressed the Lord in this way and ended in Hell. This variant shows at the same time that a double vocative needed not to be followed by any further words. Schwyzer *l.c.* seems to say in his brevity that double vocatives were used only at the beginning of a sentence, except for preceding interjections like ὦ; but what he means to say in fact is that they do not occur in the middle or at the end of a sentence, not that they cannot be a person's only utterance for the time being. And so there is no need to assume that in Matt 7:21 and Luke 6:46 κύριε, κύριε are meant as "Lord, Lord,...," as an opening formula of statements that have now been omitted.

Thirdly, (h) Luke 8:24 ἐπιστάτα, ἐπιστάτα (in D: κύριε, κύριε) may well be an innovation that goes back to Luke himself, although a number of manuscripts and versions have here one vocative, like Matt and Mark. The former might then in their turn reflect a harmonization to the gospels of Matt and Mark, a harmonization which undid the Lucan doubling but retained the specific Lucan word.[8]

The NT instances that remain if we should eliminate these doubtful cases all happen to figure admittedly in the words of Jesus, either his own words or those that he makes other persons say. So Schürmann concluded, therefore and also because of "die mit der Verdoppelung gegebene feierliche Getragenheit," that the double vocative may have been one of the characteristics of the *Ipsissima Vox*.[9] This may have been true, but it cannot mean that it was as such unique to Jesus. In fact Psalm 22:2, which Jesus quotes, proves that in any case the OT contained also instances of double address.

3. OT Material

The OT instances known to me are the following. First those four persons that are so addressed by *God*, cases which the later rabbinical commentators knew quite well and especially wanted to provide with an explanation, namely Abraham (Gen 22:11), Jacob (Gen 46:2; cf. Josephus *Ant* 2,172 δὶς ὀνομαστὶ καλέσας), Moses (Ex 3:4), and Samuel (1 Sa 3:4 and 3:6 MT [v. 10 LXX]).[10] Furthermore Eliyah whom Elisha acclaimed at his ascension by "My father, my father (LXX πάτερ πάτερ), Israel's chariotry and drivers" (2 Kgs 2:12), and Elisha who was later, on his sick bed, spoken to in exactly the same way by a weeping king Joash of Israel (2 Kgs 13:14). Instances of non-persons are also there: "Altar, altar, thus speaks the Lord" (by an anonymous prophet, 1 Kgs 13:2), "Land, land, land, listen..." (by Jeremiah in 22:29 MT; LXX γῆ, γῆ).

King David's wailing complaint in 2 Sa 19:1 "My son Abshalom, my son, my son Abshalom, oh that I had died instead of you, Abshalom my son, my son" (cf. 19:5 My son Abshalom, Abshalom my son, my son") is not simply an address, but comes

---

[8] Cf also E. Hofmann, *Ausdrucksverstärkung. Untersuchungen zur etymologischen Verstärkung und zum Gebrauch der Steigerungsadverbia im Balto-Slavischen und in anderen indogermanischen Sprachen* (Göttingen 1930), p. 24.

[9] H. Schürmann, "Die Sprache des Christus. Beobachtungen zu den synoptischen Herrenworten," in *Traditionsgeschichtliche Untersuchungen zu den synoptischen Evangelien* (Düsseldorf 1968), p. 93.

[10] References can be found in H. L. Strack and P. Billerbeck, *Kommentar zum Neuen Testament aus Talmud und Midrasch, Das Evangelium nach Markus, Lukas und Johannes und die Apostelgeschichte* (München 1924), p. 258 (ad Luke 22:31).

clearly under the heading of emotional repetition, like 2 Kgs 13:14. Compare the similar situation in Aeschylus *Persians* 675–678 where the dead king Darius I is addressed: "Why (did), lord, lord, these doubly formidable, twice lamentable losses (befall) this country as a whole?" These latter two also happen to be the only Greek instances encountered thus far of a sentence-medial occurrence of double address.[11]

Finally it may seem that God twice addresses *Himself* by His unspoken name in Ex 34:6 MT: "and He called out: Yhwh, Yhwh, El, merciful and gracious," etc. (LXX κύριος ὁ θεός). This is not the case if the former "Yhwh" would be taken as the subject of the immediately preceding verb *wayyiqra,* although this verb itself can well be linked with a still earlier occurring "Yhwh" in the sentence. In either case, however, it is doubtful that these words are a self-address because the sequel to them is in the 3rd person: "and He will certainly not leave (the guilty) unpunished." Even if this verse was originally a cultic formula, as it is some-times supposed,[12] it could well have been in the 3rd person, as is proved by *e.g.* Psalms 11, 98, and 100, and cannot therefore be considered to belong to our material.

The MT does not contain any instance of an *'adôn, 'adôn* or the like, that might have been the model of our starting point Matt 7:21/Luke 6:46. As it is Jesus, who is here intended, the example will not have been provided by the seventeen Septuagintal occurrences of κύριε κύριε, since it is there without exception God who is so spoken to, but they may have been the model for Matt 25:11/Luke 13: 25 "Lord, Lord, open up," where God is invoked rather than Jesus. The corresponding MT-pas-sages never contain a doubled vocative of one and the same word, but have nearly always two different words, either יהוה אדני or אדני יהוה, like Ps 8:2, 10 יהוה אדנינו, corresponding to κύριε ὁ κύριος ἡμῶν.[13] The occurrences at Esth 4:17b, 2 Macc 1:24 and 3

---

[11] Also Ez 21:5 μηδαμῶς κύριε κύριε, but the initial adverb corresponds in the MT with an adverb (אהה), and the double vocative with two different words, for which see below. Aeschylus *Cho.* 653–654 might be a further case but the editions waver here in their punctuation. The various instances in *PGM* are difficult to class (see below).

[12] So J. Scharbert, *Exodus,* NEB 24 (Würzburg 1989), p. 128, n. 6f: "eine aus dem Kult stammende Bekenntnisformel."

[13] The LXX instances are Dt 3:24; 9:26; Jdg 6:22A; 16:28A; 3 Kgdms 8:53; 1 Chron 17:24; Esth 4: 17b; 2 Macc 1:24; 3 Macc 2:2; Ps 68(69): 7; 108(109): 21; 139(140):8; 140(141):8; Amos 7:2,5; Jer 28(51):62; Ez 21:5. (We have not

Macc 2:1 may reflect similar phrases if they rest on Hebrew originals, or else may imitate the other LXX instances.[14] The double κύριε κύριε of Matt 7:21/Luke 6:46 must have had, then, another background than the LXX. In the case of Jesus the most likely Semitic word rendered here, we think, is not *adôn* or *adôni*, but rather *rabb[oun]i*. In Mark Jesus is so addressed on four occasions, two of them (9:5; 10:51) being matched in Matt 17:4; 20:33/Luke 18:41 by κύριε, although in the three gospels διδάσκαλε is a more frequent address, itself probably also a reflection of *rabb[oun]i*.[15]

4. Double address in OT/NT apocrypha and the Talmud

The OT apocryphal literature has somewhat more examples of double address, especially of Abraham, either in the context of Genesis 22, so *Jubil* 18:1,10, or otherwise: *Jubil* 23:3; *Apc Abr* 8:2; 9:1 (+ "speaking twice"); 19:1; 20:1; *Test Abr* (A) 11. Other persons, however, can also be called in this way by God or an angel: Adam (*Apc Mos* 41), Asnath (*Jos et As* 14:4, 6), Ezra (*IV Ezra* 14:2), Job (*Test Job* 3:1; but in 24:1 by his wife[16]), and the archangel Michael *Test Abr* A 15).[17] The NT apocrypha also contain examples: *Prot Jac* 4,1 "Αννα, "Αννα and 4,2 Ἰωακείμ, Ἰωακείμ; *Act Petr cum Sim* 5 "*vox humana de caelo dicens mihi "Theon, Theon," bis nomine meo <me> vocavit et dixit mihi....*"[18]

In the Rabbinical literature the phenomenon is not lacking either. The following survey is based mainly on Strack-Billerbeck

---

included Ps 129(130):1–2, 3. The vocatives do follow here upon one another, but belong to different lines or cola.) The discontinuous case κύριέ μου κύριε at 2 Kgdms (2 Sam) 7:18, 19, 19, 20, 22, 25, 28, 29 corresponds in each instance likewise with two different Hebrew words. At 1 Chron 17:24 and Jer 51:62 the MT has only יהוה.

[14] A doubtful instance is κύριε κύριε in *T.Abr.* A 4,5–6, where the archangel Michael speaks to God, and part of the manuscript tradition has δέσποτα κύριε, which may also stem from Gen 15:8 LXX (Abraham speaking to God).

[15] Cf. John 20:16: ῥαββουνί, ὃ λέγεται διδάσκαλε.

[16] Also by his wife in 25,9 P and moreover preceded by another word, which sounds odd; mss S V slav have here one "Job" only.

[17] This list does not claim to be complete and is partly based on B. Schaller, *Das Testament Hiobs,* JSHRZ III.3 (Gütersloh 1979), p. 327 n. III 1 d.

[18] R. A. Lipsius and M. Bonnet, *Acta Apostolorum Apocrypha* (1891; reprinted, Hildesheim 1959), Vol. I, p. 50.

(1922).[19] Except for the various discussions and explanations of the above OT passages where people are addressed by God,[20] it is striking that in the Rabbinical passages as far as collected[21] the speakers are only ordinary persons and once even a fox. They may address other persons, *e.g.* the priest Zachariah (*bGitt* 57b; cf 2 Chr 24:20–22) and R.Chiyyah (*Pesiq* 178b), or non-persons, a country in *pShabb* 15b: "Galilee, Galilee," and such a thing as a vineyard, spoken to by a fox, who complains about its narrow entrance in *Qoh.R.* 5,14/29a. Just as happened in 1 Kgs 13:2, an altar is also spoken to, but now by the words: "Luqos, luqos,/Wolf, wolf, how long will you swallow the money of the Israelites without helping them in the hour of oppression?" In all likelihood the god Apollo(-Lykeios) was here intended (*bSukka* 56b). More words also than just the name may be reduplicated: "Chiyyah my son, Chiyyah my son" (*Pesiq.* 178b), "Mother of Menachem, mother of Menachem" (*pBerach* 2,5a,16).

5. Various Shades of Meaning

(a) The explanation from the speakers' emotion and passion given for the Classical Greek and Latin double vocatives is certainly also valid for many of the OT, Jewish, and Christian instances. With only a few exceptions, all of these are at least introductions to statements of a serious, though not always clearly emotional character.

(b) Sometimes, however, the main reason for their occurrence may be a purely natural one. Just as in the classical scenes of persons knocking on a door (Aeschylus *Cho* 652–653) or trying to awaken someone who is asleep (Plautus *Most* 373 "*Callidamates, Callidamates, vigila*"), the repetition of the name may simply be due to the distance that has to be bridged or to other physical impediments that have to be overcome like sleep or even death.[22]

---

[19] Strack–Billerbeck, *o.c., Das Evangelium nach Matthäus erläutert aus Talmud und Midrasch* (München 1922), p. 943 (ad Matt 23:37); cf. G. Dalman, *Die Worte Jesu* (Leipzig 1930[2]), p. 186, who adds *pShabb* 15b; a further instance is *bMeg* 15a.

[20] See *supra*, note 10.

[21] *pBerach* 2,5a,16; *pShabb* 8,11a,35; 15b; *bSukka* 56b; *bMeg* 15a; *bGitt* 57b; *bMakk* 24a; *Lev.R.* 25,5/123c; *Qoh.R.* 5,14/29a; *Pesiq* 178b.

[22] Such doublings can have come about in different ways. On the one hand they can be thought of as the final stage of a process which may have been as follows: on a preceding occasion a single cry had had no result and had to be followed by a louder cry; on subsequent occasions speakers replaced the earlier

Just distance might account for all instances of God in heaven
being invoked by people on earth, as in the prayers and psalms
quoted above and Matt 27:46/Ps 22:2, and of people on earth
being summoned by God, so Abraham apparently from heaven
(Gen 22:11, Moses at some distance from the burning bush (Ex
3:4), Saul on the road to Damascus (Acts 9:4 parr.), and in a
number of instances from the Apocrypha.[23] Here might also
belong Eliyah who ascends to heaven and is acclamated by
Elisha, who stays on earth (2 Kgs 2:12). Distance in itself might
already be a sufficient explanation of these cases, although
emotion may sometimes also be involved. In several of them the
person who is called reacts by saying "Here I am" before the
actual message is delivered to him.[24] Special obstacles have to be
overcome in the following:

> Gen 46:2 to the sleeping Jacob.
> 1 Sam 3:4–10 to the sleeping Samuel.
> Matt 25.11 and Luke 13:25 "Sir, sir/Lord, Lord, open up for
>   us!"
> Luke 8:24 ἐπιστάτα, ἐπιστάτα, to awaken the sleeping Jesus.
> Luke 7: 14 D: νεανίσκε, νεανίσκε, to raise a dead boy.
> T.Job 3,1 to awaken the sleeping Job.
> Apc Mos 41 God calling the dead and buried Adam.
> bGitt 57b the Babylonian general Nebuzaradan, calling the dead
>   priest Zachariah, who had been killed two centuries
>   earlier.

(c) In virtually all the remaining Jewish-Christian instances of
the double vocative the addressees are no longer called but
simply spoken to, and they never react by saying "Here I am."
The explanation here must therefore be different from that given

---

sequence by two cries in immediate succession. On the other hand one can
imagine the double cry as the relic of a stage, still represented by babies and
animals, in which the cry was repeated on and on.

[23] T.Job 3:1; Jub 18:1,10; Jos As 14:4,6; Apc Abr 8:2; 9:1; 19:1; 20:1; T.Abr. (A)
14:15; 4 Ezr 14:2; Act Petri cum Sim 5. In pBerach 2,5a,16 an Arab passing by calls
to a Jew ploughing his field: "Jew, Jew, unyoke your ox."

[24] Also in T.Job 3:1 and Apc.Mos. 41. Not in Acts 9:4 (9:10 is the only NT
instance, but after a single vocative); T.Abr. A 14:15; Act Petri cum Sim 5; pBerach
2,5a,16. Here the double vocative is immediately followed by the speaker's
statement to the person he has called. 2 Kgs 2:12 is of a different character and
should perhaps be classed with the invocations of God.

for the foregoing cases. The energy originally applied in order to overcome some natural or physical hindrance, is now needed as it were to deal with a situation which is still difficult but in a psychical sense. Otherwise stated, the use of the double vocative, which was first concrete, has now grown more abstract. This implies that the statements following upon it are not so much of an everyday nature, but nearly always important and serious, and often of an admonishing character. This may explain the following:

> Matt 7:22–23 people pleading with Jesus to be allowed to enter the Kingdom.
>
> Luke 10:41 Martha being reproached for caring too much about the household.
>
> Luke 22:31 Jesus telling Simon Peter that the disciples' quarrel about their future status in the Kingdom is actually the work of the Satan.
>
> *pBerach* 2,5a,16 "Mother of Menachem, mother of Menachem, come and buy for your son." She answered: "I had rather strangle him," etc.
>
> *Pesiq* 178b "Chiyyah my son, Chiyyah my son, is it little in your eyes that I sold something that has been created in six days?"
>
> *pShabbath* 8,11a,35 "Old man, old man, you are either a wine drinker, a usurer or a swine breeder."
>
> *Lev.Rabbah* 25,5/123c "Old man, old man, if you rise early you don't have to work late."
>
> Matt 23:37–Luke 13:34 the City of Jerusalem being rebuked for having killed her prophets. Clement of Alexandria comments on this passage which he quotes in *Paed.* 1,9,79: "And the reduplication (ἐπαναδίπλωσις) of the name gives strength to the rebuke." This instance of a town being addressed in a serious way has its parallels in:
>
>> *pShabbath* 15b "Galilee, Galilee, your hatred of the Law will class you in the end among the oppressors of Faith," said by R.Jehochanan ben Zakkay because during his 18 year stay in Galilee people had only twice consulted him concerning questions of the Law.[25]

---

[25] Adduced by G. Dalman, *Die Worte Jesu* (Leipzig 1930^2), Vol. I, p. 186. Countries etc. are still so addressed in some modern national hymns. Cf. also

Cf. Aristophanes *Pax* 246 "Oh Megara, Megara,
how will you be crushed in a moment...,"
and Corpus Herm. *Ascl.* 24 "Oh Egypt, Egypt, of
your cults only fables will remain...."

(d) Yet another shade of meaning seems to be attached to the
use of double, triple etc. vocatives in the magical papyri (*e.g.* *PGM*
36,26–29 Σηθ seven times), and on amulets. In this context they
are clearly part of a larger collection of repeated and partly
repeated elements, such as spell-words (*e.g.* *PGM* 36, 30–34 βρακ
seven times), imperatives (*e.g.* *PGM* 12,333 κρύβε, κρύβε), and
adverbs (especially the ubiquitous ἤδη ἤδη ταχὺ ταχύ).[26] All these
repetitions have the only purpose of compelling the invoked or
rather summoned gods and demons to comply with the wishes
and demands of the exorcist. This practice has no parallel in the
OT/NT, but the following Talmudic anecdote comes close to it:
b*Meg* 15a "Our rabbis taught: Rachab inspired lust by her (very)
name.... R.Isaac said: Whoever says 'Rachab, Rachab' at once
has a pollution. R.Nachman said to him: I say 'Rachab, Rachab'
and nothing happens to me. He replied: I was speaking of one
who knows her and is intimate with her." Here R.Isaac,
mockingly, repeats the name more or less as a serious sorcerer
would repeat a magic word or formula. This is, however, exceptional, for otherwise the rabbinical explanations for the occasions
where God addresses the patriarchs Abraham and Jacob or the
prophets Moses and Samuel by calling them twice, are of quite a
different nature.

(e) "Abraham, Abraham" etc. was explained as an expression
of love and encouragement, comparable to the above emotional
explanation under a), by R.Simeon b.Yochai (*c.* 150 C.E.) and
R.Chiyyah (*c.* 200 C.E.) (*Gen.R.* 56/35d; *Nu.R.* 14/178a; so also
Ex.R. 2/68d in the case of Moses). But R.Eliezer b.Jacob (*c.* 150
C.E.) took it to refer both to Abraham himself and to the generations after him (*Gen.R.* 56/35d; 74/47b), and "Moses, Moses,"
was otherwise taken to express that he was the same person
before and after God had spoken to him (*Nu.R.* 14/178a), or else
that he had taught the Torah in his earthly life and would

---

the film title "New York, New York" (M. Scorsese, 1977), which carries a much
more emotional load than a simple "New York" ever would.

[26] Cf. also the curious disappearance schemata, for instance the one at *PGM*
35,27–29 which should be printed as: Ιαω Σαβαωθ, Αω Σαβαωθ, Ω Σαβαωθ,
Σαβαωθ, Α{α}βαωθ, Βαωθ, Αωθ, Ωθ, Θ.

continue to do so in the next (*Ex.R.* 2/68d). This last explanation, partaking of this life and of the life to come, was even extended by R.Abba b.Kahana (*c.* 310 C.E.) to hold for those cases where there is in the text a succession of two identical names but no double *address*, the first name being the final word of one sentence, the second name being the opening word of the next. This happens to be so in Gen 6:10 "This is the story of *Noah. Noah* was righteous...," and so also Terah, Abraham's suspected half-pagan father, was not excluded from the future life, since his name occurs in a similar configuration in Gen 11:27 (*Gen.R.* 30/18b).

Interestingly, a similarly comprehensive explanation as for these four OT patriarchs and prophets has incidentally been formulated in the Church for some of the double addresses uttered by Jesus. The Persian church father Aphrahat states in his *Demonstration* 8,14 that the three persons whom Jesus raised from the dead, were all raised "with two words," comparable to the explanation given above under (b): the daughter of Jairus, the young man at Nain, and Lazarus. He quotes each time the actual words of Jesus, which contain then in his quotations double vocatives, with the exception, curiously enough, of "Lazarus." In the Ethiopic text entitled *On the Resurrection of the Dead* , which was edited by E. Cerulli and shown by Baarda to be the translation of Aphrahat's treatise, the name of "Lazarus" is doubled as well as "young man," but now it is the vocative "daughter" which has been left to stay single.[27] Together these texts may indicate, however, that there existed some gospel manuscripts which read double vocatives in the respective stories. The extant NT manuscript tradition actually attests to this, albeit only seldom. Indeed, at Mark 5:41 Vetus Latina ms. *e* has *puella, puella,* but apparently par.Luke 8:54 contains nowhere anything comparable, at Luke 7:14 D *a ff*[2] read νεανίσκε, νεανίσκε etc., and at John 11:43 C[3], Diatess.Pers. 3,34, Eth (ed. Walton) have Λάζαρε, Λάζαρε or the like.[28]

The existence of such fanciful exegesis around double vocatives does not, however, mean that these were no longer understood in any ordinary sense. Explanations like "Abraham, Abraham" = "Abraham and your posterity" are rather to be evaluated as instances of the allegorical method of exegesis of the

---

[27] T. Baarda, "Another Treatise of Aphrahat the Persian Sage in Ethiopic Translation," *NTS* 27 (1980/81), pp. 632–640, esp. 633–634.

[28] Cf. Baarda, "Another Treatise," p. 632.

time. Not content with the obvious and self-evident interpretation
of a passage, one endeavoured in addition to delve a deeper
meaning or *sensus plenior* from its wording. But remarkably, it was
not Philo of Alexandria, who led the allegorical way in connection with this particular idiom, although he happens to discuss
Gen 22:11 on two different occasions, the story of God who
prevents Abraham from killing and sacrificing his son. In his
treatise *On Abraham* 176 he draws special attention to the double
address, but evidently sees it only as the expression of the urgent
nature of God's counter-command: "Twice He called the father
by name, turning him round and drawing him back so as to
prevent him from carrying out the slaughter." This would then be
in line with the emotional explanation under (a) above. On the
second occasion, however, in the treatise *On Dreams* 1, 193–195,
Philo interprets the double address rather as a way to draw
people's attention, in line with explanation (b) above. He
involves now Gen 22:1–2, too, the beginning of the story,
because it contains in the LXX version, which he quotes literally,
a further instance of "Abraham, Abraham," against the majority
of the MT manuscripts. He also adduces and quotes now Ex 3:4,
the story of God calling Moses twice by name from the burning
bush, in order to illustrate his explanation, which is that persons
so addressed "may prick up their ears and listen with calmness
and attention."[29]

(f) The attentive reader will have noticed that Matt 7:21 was
not yet included in any of the foregoing explanations. For if all
those commentaries are right which suppose that the Jesus-saying
in this verse was originally complete as it stands, its double
vocative did not introduce any further statement, although this is
precisely what is suggested by the addition of vv. 22–23. It could
then either summarize the introduction to all statements ever
made to the person of Jesus, and would have to be followed by
some dots to indicate that these statements have been left out, or
it could be some polite salutation that one might use as such,
without necessarily saying anything more. The former possibility
is in itself not very probable in the light of the material which has
been discussed thus far. Why should one not have called Jesus by
crying from afar "Sir, sir!"? Or why should an important remark
to him starting with "Sir, sir,..." have been reprehensible in
general? It seems therefore that the latter possibility, that of the
salutation, is the one which we should consider seriously. Matt

---

[29]No such explanation is given in the *Life of Moses* 1, 71ss.

7:21 would then be exactly comparable to two further NT passages which up to now have likewise been left out of the discussion, and which also contain greetings: Matt 23:7 about the Pharisees who like to be saluted by the man in the street by "Rabbi, rabbi," and Mark 14:45 where Judas in Gethsemane greets Jesus by saying "Rabbi, rabbi." The purport of Matt 7:21 could then be paraphrased as: "Those who only greet me reverentially, but neglect my demand to honour and obey God, will never enter the Kingdom." As the social context of this salutation is Jesus' earthly life, the rendering "Sir, sir" seems slightly more appropriate as long as this saying is considered in isolation,[30] whereas "Lord, Lord" is more fitting in Matt 7:22–23, where "on that day" refers to the Last Judgment. In par. Luke 13:23–30, however, the vocatives "Lord, Lord"/"Lord" do not refer any longer to Jesus himself, but to God. The secondary character of Luke's redaction of this Jesus-saying may also appear from the fact that in the synoptic gospels Jesus only rarely refers to God by "[the] Lord" only, as Dalman has pointed out, and that the few actual occurrences are themselves uncertain.[31] Dalman mentions here Mark 5:19 "and tell them how much the Lord has done to you," where D and par. Luke 8:39 have ὁ θεός, as well as to Luke 20:37 "when he [Moses] calls the Lord 'the God of Abraham'...," where parr. Matt 22:31 and Mark 12:26 do not have it. He might have added that in Mark 5:19 Jesus perhaps refers to himself, as in Mark 11:3 "the Lord needs it" = Matt 21:3 = Luke 19:31, and he does not discuss Mark 13:20 "if the Lord had not cut short those days," where par. Matt 24:22 has a *passivum divinum.*

These three NT instances of double vocatives as a reverential way of salutation have a very illuminating Talmudic parallel in *bMakk* 24a which says of king Jehoshaphat of Judah that "whenever he saw a wise scholar he rose from his throne, and embraced and kissed him, calling him: My father, my father, my teacher, my teacher [*rabbî*], my lord, my lord [*mârî*]."

---

[30] "Sir"/κύριε was the normal way to address unknown or unrecognized persons respectfully, Jesus is so spoken to in John 5:7 and 20:15, the disciple Philip in John 12:21, Paul and Silas in Acts 16:30. A son addresses his own father in this way at Matt 21:30. According to Epictetus *Encheiridion* 40 all women after the age of fourteen were called κυρία.

[31] G. Dalman, *Die Worte Jesu* (Leipzig 1930²), Vol. I, p. 146. In expressions such as "Lord of heaven and earth" (Matt 11:25 = Luke 10:21) "lord" is purely an appellative.

ΟΥΔΕ ΕΓΩ ΣΕ [ΚΑΤΑ]ΚΡΙΝΩ.
JOHN 8:11, THE *PROTEVANGELIUM IACOBI*, AND THE HISTORY OF THE *PERICOPE ADULTERAE*

William L. Petersen
The Pennsylvania State University
(University Park, Pennsylvania, USA)

Many *Leitmotive* run through Tjitze Baarda's scholarship: the Diatessaron, the *Gospel of Thomas*, Syriac studies, Paul's epistle to the Galatians, and New Testament textual criticism. There is, however, one theme which embraces his professional career, and that is the Gospel of John. Many years ago he wrote his dissertation on the text of the Gospel of John in the *Demonstrations* of Aphrahat.[1] Now, in the year of his retirement, he and I co-direct a six-person team at the Netherlands Institute for Advanced Studies, investigating the text of the Gospel of John in the Diatessaron. It seems fitting, therefore, to offer him a study of a saying of Jesus drawn from the "Spiritual Gospel."

I. Prologue

Among the most-studied passages in the Gospel of John are the twelve verses which tell of the woman caught in adultery—the so-called *pericope adulterae* (John 7:53–8:11). This story contains one of the best-known sayings in world literature, namely: "Let him who is without sin cast the first stone." It also contains another saying of Jesus, less well-known, perhaps, but certainly more important: οὐδὲ ἐγώ σε [κατα]κρίνω[2] ("Neither do I

---

[1] Tj. Baarda, *The Gospel Quotations of Aphrahat the Persian Sage. I. Aphrahat's Text of the Fourth Gospel*, 2 vols. (Meppel [the Netherlands] 1975).

[2] While most apparatuses (*e.g.*, N-A[27]/UBS[4]) provide no variants to κατακρίνω, C. von Tischendorf, *Novum Testamentum Graece* (Lipsiae 1869[8]), Vol. I, p. 834, provides two: κρίνω (read by many unspecified MSS) and κρινῶ (read by E F G K). Tischendorf also notes a similar division in the Latins, with *iudico* (= κρίνω) read by *e* and *condemnabo* (= κατακρίνω) read by *c ff*[2] *g l*[mg] (cp. A. Jülicher, *Itala. I. Matthäus-evangelium* [Berlin 1963], p. 87, who refines Tischendorf's list slightly, listing *damnabo* as the reading of *ff*[2], *condemnabo* as the reading of *aur c [j] r*[7] *vg*, *condemno* as the reading of *d*, and *iudico* as the reading of *e*). Similarly, H. von

[condemn/] judge you"). The author of the *pericope adulterae* also thought this saying the more important, for he placed it at the end of the story, where it functions as a brilliant *coup de théâtre*.

The theological and literary genius of the story has not escaped notice. F. C. Baur praised "die hohe absolute Wahrheit" of the narrative, whose lesson was "der eigentliche Mittelpunkt des christlichen Bewußtseins."[3] The textual critic H. von Soden was moved as well: he concluded a thirty-seven page excursus on the textual history of these verses with a single word having nothing to do with the text: "Meisterstil."[4]

The problem, as all scholars know, is that the entire twelve verses of the *pericope adulterae* are completely absent from *all* of the oldest manuscripts of the Gospel of John.[5] They first appear in a Greek manuscript of John only in the early fifth century. Thereafter, their spread in the manuscript tradition is very slow; it is not until the thirteenth century or so that a majority of new manuscripts include the verses. H. J. Vogels put the predicament well when he remarked:

> Das Problem beginnt erst bei der Frage, wie es möglich war, daß ein so umfangreiches und inhaltschweres Stück Eingang in die Hss fand und sich so stark und sicher durchsetzte, daß Ambrosius und Augustinus es für echt ansahen und Hieronymus ihm Aufnahme in die Vulgata gewährte.[6]

Scholarship has, almost universally, regarded the episode as "insérée dans l'évangile."[7] The reasons are massive, convincing, and obvious. First, as already noted, its utter absence from all the Greek manuscripts of John before the early fifth century—and

---

Soden, *Die Schriften des Neuen Testaments*, Teil 2 (Göttingen 1911[2]), p. 428, in the apparatus: κρίνω is read by his μ[5] group (which consists of about 130 MSS, among them: 343 529 548 563 785 1379 [all Gregory numbers]). See his discussion in idem, Teil 1.1, pp. 487–488, and esp. Teil 1.2, pp. 739–745. I have not been able to locate any listing of the entire μ[5] group; one can, however, deduce a partial list from the information on pp. 739–741.

[3] F. C. Baur, *Kritische Untersuchungen über die kanonischen Evangelien, ihr Verhältnis zu einander, ihren Charakter und Ursprung* (Tübingen 1847), p. 171.

[4] Von Soden, *Die Schriften*, Teil I.1, p. 523.

[5] See *infra*, n. 12.

[6] H. J. Vogels, *Handbuch der Textkritik des Neuen Testaments* (Bonn 1955[2]), p. 161.

[7] M.-J. Lagrange, *Évangile selon Saint Jean* (Paris 1948[3]), p. 222.

then its only gradual penetration of the tradition—speak against it. Second, when it finally enters the gospel manuscript tradition, it intrudes in no fewer than *five* different places[8]; such "bouncing around" in the manuscript tradition is one of the characteristics of a "floating" logion, as scribes try to fit it in, first here, then there. Third, the literary features of the passage are not Johannine,[9] suggesting that some other writer composed it. Fourth, in its present position (*viz. post* John 7:52), it interrupts the flow of the narrative, which moves quite smoothly from John 7:52 to John 8:12.[10] Fifth, the passage appears unknown to any church father prior to the late fourth century; no earlier father cites it. Sixth, the vast majority of scholars have found—in a report in Eusebius's *Historia ecclesiastica* (III.39.17)—a convenient explanation for the genesis of the story, its absence from the early manuscripts of John, and its gradual encroachment upon the gospel tradition. Writing about 300 C.E., Eusebius passes on a report which he says comes from Papias (*fl. c.* 130): the *Gospel according to the Hebrews* contained a story about "a woman accused of many sins before the Lord."[11] According to this scenario, the origin of the passage lies in a Judaic-Christian gospel, from which it eventually passed into the Gospel of John.

This is a very convincing array of evidence and argumentation. However, new facts (or at least facts unknown to those drawing these conclusions) can alter the balance of the evidence.

II. Known evidence for the pericope adulterae

Before plunging into the matter at hand, it is necessary to review briefly the textual evidence for the *pericope adulterae*. This can be broadly divided into four categories, each of which will be

---

[8] They are: (1) after John 7:52 (the "normal" position); (2) at the end of John (*i.e., post* John 21:25), as an appendix of sorts; (3) after John 7:44 (in some Georgian MSS); (4) after Luke 21:38 (in the MSS of *f*[13]); (5) after John 7:36 (MS 225); see any of the standard handbooks or editions for further specifics.

[9] On the differences in style, vocabulary, etc., between the *pericope adulterae* and either John or Luke, see U. Becker, *Jesus und die Ehebrecherin*, BZNW 28 (Berlin 1963), pp. 43–74, esp. 68–74.

[10] See, *e.g.*, Becker, *Ehebrecherin*, p. 79.

[11] *Eusèbe de Césarée. Histoire ecclésiastique, Livres I–IV*, ed. G. Bardy, SC 31 (Paris 1952), p. 157: ἐκτέθειται [Παπίας] δὲ καὶ ἄλλην ἱστορίαν περὶ γυναικὸς ἐπὶ πολλαῖς ἁμαρτίαις διαβληθείσης ἐπὶ τοῦ κυρίου, ἣν τὸ καθ᾽ Ἑβραίους εὐαγγέλιον περιέχει.

considered in turn: (1) Greek NT manuscripts, (2) the versions, (3) patristic and (4) apocryphal sources.

(1) In the Greek manuscript tradition of the Gospel of John, the *pericope adulterae* makes its first appearance in the early fifth-century Codex Bezae Cantabrigiensis (D).[12] Although absent from all sixth- and seventh-century manuscripts, it reappears in a lone eighth-century manuscript, Codex Basiliensis (E). In the ninth century it is read by ten manuscripts (F G H K M U Π Ω 565 892). In the tenth century, it is read by three manuscripts (Γ 1076 1582). While Codex Bezae belongs to the Western Text type, all of the later manuscripts belong—broadly speaking—to the Byzantine Text type. After the tenth century, the number of manuscripts with the passage expands, for the story is insinuating itself into the Byzantine Text, the most reproduced form of the text in this later period. Among the many manuscripts which read it are: 28 700 1006 1570 (all XI cent.) 225 1071 (both XII) as well as the manuscripts of the Lake Group (f^1 [XII and later][13]) and the Ferrar Group (f^{13} [XIII and later][14]). Von Soden states that, in total, about a thousand manuscripts offer the passage.[15]

(2) Among the *versions*, the passage first appears in the Old *Latin* half of bilingual Codex Bezae (*d*; early fifth cent.), and two other fifth-century codices of the Vetus Latina (*b**[16] and *ff*²). Later

---

[12] The passage is absent from $\mathfrak{P}^{66}$ (which dates from about 200), $\mathfrak{P}^{75}$ (third cent.), and from the fourth-century MSS ℵ B and the fifth-century MSS A C T W. As for Codex Bezae, D. C. Parker, *Codex Bezae. An early Christian manuscript and its text* (Cambridge 1992), dates the MS to "about 400" (p. 281), and places its origin in Berytus (pp. 267–278).

[13] These MSS place the passage *post* John 21:25.

[14] These MSS place the passage *post Luke* (!) 21:38.

[15] Von Soden, *Die Schriften*, Teil I, Abt. 1, p. 487.

[16] For some inexplicable reason, Eb. Nestle, *Introduction to the Textual Criticism of the Greek New Testament*, trans. from the 2ⁿᵈ German edition (London 1901), p. 142 (italics added), when commenting on the Georgian version, states in an aside that "in Old Latin Codex b, the passage from vii.44 onwards *has been erased*" (cp. p. 283, where the assertion is repeated). B. F. Westcott and F. J. A. Hort, *Introduction to the New Testament in the original Greek* [Cambridge 1896²; reprinted Peabody (Mass.) 1988], p. 85, leave a similar impression when they speak of the "obliteration" of the passage in MS *b*. U. Becker, *Ehebrecherin*, p. 31, speaks—ambiguously—of a "Lücke" at this point in MS *b*.

In contrast to these assertions, consider the words of the manuscript's editor, E. S. Buchanan, *The Four Gospels from The Codex Veronensis...*, OLBT 6 (Oxford 1911), pp. viii–ix (italics added): "The two centre leaves of Q.[uire] xiii which

Vetus Latina manuscripts with the passage are: *c e r'* and *[j]*.[17] Despite the divided evidence of the Vetus Latina, Jerome included it in his Vulgate (translated *c.* 383); therefore, the Vulgate must be counted among the oldest Latin witnesses offering indirect evidence for the passage in the Gospel of John.[18] The story is also found in all major Western Diatessaronic witnesses, including Latin Codex Fuldensis, the Middle Dutch Liège Harmony, and the Old High German Codex Sangallensis.

As for the *Syriac* versions, the passage is absent from all Eastern witnesses to the Diatessaron. Baarda has correctly remarked that it "was not transmitted in the early Syriac versions. Not only Sy[s.c] and Sy[p], but even the original text of Sy[h] are witnesses of this state of affairs."[19] Even the evidence of the eleventh- and twelfth-century manuscripts of the Palestinian Syriac Lectionary (Syr[pal]) is divided.[20]

---

contained the pericope de adultera have vanished and left no trace behind. *The passage has not been erased.* The text of *b* must have been closely akin to that of *ff;* for the two lost leaves in *b* would be exactly filled by the text of *ff.*" [It should be noted that—in what may be only a striking coincidence—some MSS of the Georgian version place the *pericope adulterae* after John 7:44, that is, exactly at the point at which MS *b* breaks off (see B. M. Metzger, *A Textual Commentary on the Greek New Testament* [corrected edition; Stuttgart 1975], p. 221, n. 4)].

[17] MS *j* contains only vv. 6–7.

[18] "Indirect" because we have no Vulgate MSS of the gospels before the fifth century, the date of Sankt Gallen MS 1395 (Σ); yet, because of Jerome's comments (see *infra,* n. 32), we can be quite certain it stood in the Vulgate of 383.

[19] Tj. Baarda, *The Gospel Quotations of Aphrahat,* Vol. I, p. 125. Baarda's statement is correct for all the ancient witnesses to these versions; J. Gwynn, *Remnants of the Later Syriac Versions of the Bible,* part I [NT] (London/Oxford 1909), pp. 2, 3, and 46, notes that several very late (fifteenth cent. and later) Peshitta MSS give the passage.

[20] Of the three known MSS, the passage is found in MS "A" (which gives John 8:1,3–11; dated 1030); MSS "B" (dated 1104) and "C" (dated 1118) lack the full passage (all three give John 7:37–8:2, as do fragments of an unknown lectionary, found in the binding of MS "B"). See A. S. Lewis and M. D. Gibson, *The Palestinian Syriac Lectionary of the Gospels* (London 1899), pp. xii (dating), lv (variants in the Syriac MSS against the Greek), 242–243 (text of MS "A"), 58–60 (text of John 7:37–8:2 in all three MSS), 320 (fragments from the binding of MS "B"); cp. esp. the remarks of Lewis on p. xv, where she suggests that the original *pericope adulterae* consisted of only John 8:2–8:11. (Cp. her suggestion with Gwynn, *Remnants,* pp. 46–49, where he presents the "Mara" form of the passage, which commences with John 8:2 [cp. *infra,* n. 40])

In the *Armenian* version, the passage is absent from the three oldest Armenian manuscripts, dating from 887 C.E. (Moscow, Inst. Lazareff), 901/902 (Venice, San Lazaro MS 1144), and 986 (Erevan, Matenadaran MS 7445).[21] The first manuscript with the story is a codex dating from 989 C.E. discovered in 1891 by F. C. Conybeare at Edschmiadzin.[22] Its version of the story is, however, different from the standard form found in John.[23] For example, the woman is accused of "sins" (Arm: *malitiis*), and the concluding dialogue with the woman is abbreviated: Jesus' final words are, "Go in peace, and present the offering for sins, as in their law is written"; it lacks the words οὐδὲ ἐγώ σε [κατα]κρίνω.

The *Georgian* version also lacks the story in all of its oldest manuscripts (the codices of Adysh [dated 897], Opiza [913], and Tbet' [995]).[24]

(3) To the *Patristic* evidence, commencing with the *Greek*. Almost all modern scholarship mentions—with varying enthusiasm—a comment attributed to Papias, which survives only because Eusebius included it in his *h.e.* (III.39.17). Eusebius says that Papias "set forth another narrative about a woman who was accused before the Lord of many sins (ἐπὶ πολλαῖς ἁμαρτίαις),

---

[21] Metzger, *A Textual Commentary*, p. 220, n. 2, quotes a note in J. Zohrab's edition (1805) as reporting that only "five of the thirty manuscripts we used preserve [the *pericope adulterae* in its usual position in John].... The remainder usually placing it as a separate section at the end of the Gospel.... But in six of the older manuscripts the passage is completely omitted in both places." Tracking these six MSS is difficult: F. G. Kenyon, *The Text of the Greek Bible*, revised by A. W. Adams (London 1975), pp. 132–133, gives the dates of four MSS which omit the pericope, three of which can be identified from the list of Armenian MSS in B. M. Metzger, *The Early Versions of the New Testament* (Oxford 1977), pp. 158–161.

[22] Now housed in the Matenadaran in Erevan, catalogue no. MS 2374; formerly it had been catalogued (and was sometimes referenced) as Edschmiadzin MS 229.

[23] These differences led Conybeare, "The Last Twelve Verses of St. Mark's Gospel," *Exp*, fifth series, Vol. 2 (1895), pp. 401–421, to argue that the form of the story found in the Armenian codex was older than any other: "I have nowhere met with it in the more archaic form in which the Edschmiadzin codex gives it" (p. 406); "The shorter text of the Edschmiadzin codex represents the form in which Papias and the Hebrew Gospel gave the episode" (p. 408).

[24] See Metzger, *A Textual Commentary*, p. 220, n. 3 (cp. also *supra*, nn. 8 and 16).

which is contained in the *Gospel according to the Hebrews*."[25] Although a majority of scholars interpret this reference as an allusion to the *pericope adulterae* (or some *Ur*-form of it),[26] there are four rather obvious reasons for not doing so. (1) The Papias/ Eusebius report contains no direct quotation or paraphrase from the story; there is, therefore, no assurance that it is the *pericope adulterae* which is being referenced. (2) Papias's report is much more congruent with the Lucan version of the "Anointing at Bethany" (Luke 7:36–50, which, in v. 47, informs us that αἱ ἁμαρτίαι αὐτῆς were πολλαί [cf. also vv. 37, 39, 48]: note the verbal similarity with the πολλαῖς ἁμαρτίαις of Papias's report) than with the *pericope adulterae*. (3) The Papias/Eusebius account—which speaks of the woman's unspecified "sins" as πολλαῖ ("*many*")—disagrees with the Johannine *pericope adulterae*, in which the woman is charged with only *one* sin, namely, a single instance of adultery.[27] (4) The language used by Eusebius and the context in which he places this report in the *h.e.* do not make it clear whether *Papias* said the story was from the *Gospel according to the Hebrews*, or whether *Eusebius*—as a courtesy to his readers (or, perhaps, as a display of his erudition?)—supplied this information.

If one sets aside this ambiguous Papias/Eusebius reference, then the oldest Greek patristic reference to the *pericope adulterae* occurs in a *Commentary on Ecclesiastes* by Didymus the Blind (∗*c*.

---

[25] See *supra*, n. 11.

[26] So, for example, Becker, *Ehebrecherin*, pp. 105–116, B. D. Ehrman, "Jesus and the Adulteress," *NTS* 34 (1988), pp. 29–30, and D. Lührmann, "Die Geschichte von einer Sünderin und andere apokryphe Jesusüberlieferungen bei Didymos von Alexandrien," *NovT* 32 (1990), pp. 304–307. The report is viewed ambiguously by J. H. Bernard, *A Critical and Exegetical Commentary on the Gospel According to St. John*, ed. A. H. McNeile, ICC (Edinburgh 1928; reprinted 1963), Vol. 2, p. 716. A. F. J. Klijn, *Jewish-Christian Gospel Tradition*, VigChr.S 17 (Leiden 1992), pp. 116–119 (Frag. XXXVII), regards the report as untrustworthy, however, for he categorizes it as "Spurious and Doubtful."

[27] This remains so even if a much-discussed variant in verse 3 in Codex Bezae were accepted as the text (D and 1071 read ἐπὶ ἁμαρτίᾳ instead of ἐπὶ μοιχείᾳ): first, this substitution still leaves the disjunction between the plural and the singular unresolved (Papias/Eusebius = plural ["*many* sins"]; John = singular ["in sin" or "in adultery"]); second, that the issue is "adultery" (and not some unstipulated "sin[s]") is made explicit in all MSS of John—including D and 1071—in v. 4.

313–† 398).[28] But as with the Armenian MS Edschmiadzin *anni* 989 (see above), Didymus's story deviates considerably from what we now have in John: the woman is accused of ἁμαρτία ("a sin"); no attempt is made by the Jews to entrap Jesus who, instead, intervenes of his own volition; the story's most famous line becomes "He who has not sinned, let him take a stone and cast it"; the story ends there, and lacks the writing on the ground; also missing is the concluding dialogue between Jesus and the woman, which contains the saying we are investigating.

After Didymus, the next known Greek patristic reference occurs in the twelfth-century writer Euthymius Zigabenus, who states that τοῖς ἀκριβέσιν ἀντιγράφοις ἢ οὐχ εὕρηται ἢ ὠβέλισται ("in the most accurate manuscripts [the story] either is not to be found or has been obelized").[29]

Among *Latin* writers, no fewer than five reference the passage at about the same date. The oldest of these appears to be Pacien of Barcelona († 379–397), whose brief comments indicate only that he knew a story in which the Lord did not condemn an "adulteress" (= John, but not Papias/Eusebius) and that it stood in a "gospel."[30]

Ambrose of Milan (*c.* 378) knows the passage, quotes snippets of it ("Let him who is without sin..."; the woman is an "adulteress"), but never indicates where he found the story. He provides an important insight into the reception of the episode when he remarks that some were disturbed by it, because Jesus did not condemn the adulteress.[31]

Jerome also knows the passage and includes it in his Vulgate (383). In his *adversus Pelagianos* II.17, he observes that "*in Evangelio secundum Joannem in multis et Graecis et Latinis codicibus*

---

[28] *Didymos der Blinde. Kommentar zum Ecclesiastes (Tura-Papyrus). Teil IV (Komm. zu Eccl. Kap. 7–8,8)*, edd. J. Kramer and B. Krebber, PTA 16 (Bonn 1972), p. 88 (fol. 223, lines 7–13); the editors remark on the parallel with John on p. 89, n. 1.

[29] *Comm. Io.*, Migne, PG 129, col. 1280D.

[30] See his *Contra Tractatvs Novatianorum* XX.2 (cited here after *Pacien de Barcelone. Écrits*, ed. C. Granado, et al., SC 410 [Paris 1995], p. 254 [the text is also available in Migne, PL 13, col. 1077A]): "*Nolite in Euangelio legere quod pepercerit Dominus etiam adulterae confitenti, quam nemo damnarat,...*"

[31] Ambrose, *Apologia David altera* I.1.1–3 (*S. Ambrosii opera*, pars 2, ed. C. Schenkl, CSEL 32 [Pragae/Vindobonae/Lipsiae 1897], pp. 359–360); cp. idem, *Ep.* I.25 (ed. Migne, PL 16, col. 1041A), and *Apologia David* X.51 (*Ambroise de Milan. Apologie de David*, ed. P. Hadot and M. Cordier, SC 239 [Paris 1977], p. 142).

invenitur de adultera muliere, quae accusata est apud Dominum" ("in the Gospel according to John, in many manuscripts, both Greek and Latin, is found [the story] of the adulterous woman, who is accused before the Lord").[32]

Rufinus seems to be the first to link the Papias/Eusebius report with the *pericope adulterae*. In 402 C.E. he translated Eusebius's *h.e.* into Latin, and apparently altered the indefinite Papias/Eusebius phrase "[a woman accused of] *many sins*" to "an *adulterous* woman [who is accused by the Jews before the Lord]."[33] This change is, however, of little value for discerning what *Eusebius* meant; it only suggests how *Rufinus* understood Eusebius.

Often overlooked is the fact that both Jerome and Rufinus were students of Didymus the Blind in Alexandria, the last head of the city's famed catechetical school.[34] This suggests that the evidence of these three men should be considered collectively, rather than in isolation.[35]

Ambrose's famous protégé, Augustine of Hippo (*c.* 415), remarks tellingly that "certain persons of scant faith—or better, I believe, enemies of the true faith—fearing that their wives be given impunity in sinning, removed from their manuscripts the Lord's act of kindness toward the adulteress, as if…[the Lord] had given permission to sin."[36] This testimony, together with the

---

[32] Jerome, *adv. Pelag.* II.17 (ed. Migne, PL 23, col. 579AB).

[33] Rufinus substituted "*muliere adultera*" for Eusebius's γυναικὸς ἐπὶ πολλαῖς ἁμαρτίαις. See Th. Mommsen's edition of the Latin translation (*Die lateinische Übersetzung des Rufinus*), published in *Eusebius Werke II. Die Kirchengeschichte I*, ed. E. Schwartz, GCS 9.1 (Leipzig 1903), p. 293: "…*de muliere adultera, quae accusata est a Judeis apud dominum…*" ("…concerning the *adulterous woman* who is accused by the Jews before the Lord"). One cannot (*pace* Klijn, *Jewish-Christian*, p. 117, n. 149) categorically rule out the possibility that Rufinus was translating from (older? more reliable?) Greek MSS of Eusebius accessible to him at that early date, which read ἐπὶ μοιχείᾳ.

[34] See J. Quasten, *Patrology* (Utrecht 1950; reprinted Westminster [Maryland] 1983), Vol. III, p. 85. Only Lührmann, "Die Geschichte," p. 292, n. 16, remarks on the teacher-student relationship between Didymus and Jerome—but even Lührmann ignores Rufinus's link with Didymus.

[35] Jerome's strong endorsement of the passage as Johannine suggests that Didymus might have known it as part of John as well; Rufinus's apparent alteration of the *h.e.* (which brings it closer to the version of the story now found in the Johannine text) may well point in the same direction.

[36] Augustine, *De adulterinis coniugiis*, VII.6 (*Sancti Avreli Avgvstini*, Sec. V, Pars III, ed. I. Zycha, CSEL 41 [Pragae/Vindobonae/Lipsiae 1900], pp. 387–388). It

remark of Ambrose about the unease caused by the passage, and the omission in many sources of the words οὐδὲ ἐγώ σε [κατα]κρίνω, suggest a motive for the suppression of the story—which Augustine unambiguously says occurred.

In *Syrian* patristic sources, the story is wanting before the late sixth century. It is absent from Aphrahat's writings,[37] and it is not found anywhere in voluminous works of the other great fourth-century Syrian father, Ephrem. It first appears in a late sixth- or early seventh-century Syriac manuscript (British Library, Add. 17202) which is a translation (or expanded version) of an anonymous *Historia ecclesiastica* originally composed in Greek and sometimes attributed to Zacharias Rhetor (of Mitylene; † *c.* 550).[38] The story is prefaced with a remark that it came from "the Gospel of the holy Bishop Mara, in...a chapter which belongs uniquely to John...and in other copies [of John's gospel] this passage is not found." Mara († *c.* 527) was bishop of Amida; he is reported to have fled to Alexandria *c.* 525, amassed a substantial library, had a good command of Greek, and—presumably—translated this passage from a Greek manuscript he came across there.[39] This "Mara" version of the pericope, which consists only

---

is ironic that those (see, *e.g.*, *infra*, n. 98) who would defend the originality of the *pericope adulterae* as part of the Gospel of John *because* of its presence in the Byzantine Text (or Textus Receptus) enthusiastically cite Augustine on this matter; they fail to note the absurdity, however, of arguing that such a theologically motivated excision occurred here, *but nowhere else in the entire NT*. This is indeed cutting the evidence to fit your theories.

[37] See *supra*, n. 19.

[38] Bk. 8.7 (*Historia ecclesiastica. Zachariae Rhetori vulgo adscripta, II*, ed. E. W. Brooks, Syriac text in CSCO 84 [Syri 39] [Parisiis 1921; reprinted Louvain n.d. (probably 1974)], pp. 86 [line 24]–87 [line 20], and Latin translation in CSCO 88 [Syri 42] [Lovanii 1924; reprinted Louvain 1965], pp. 59–60 [Becker's reference (*Ehebrecherin*, p. 16, n. 29) is incorrect]). See also J. Gwynn, *Remnants*, pp. 3 (Gwynn's MS *h*), 46–47 (the "Mara" introduction), 48–49 (Syriac text), 91–92 (Greek reverse translation). On (Ps.-)Zacharias Rhetor, see B. Altaner, *Patrology* (London 1961), p. 276, or the Introduction of E. W. Brook's English translation (*The Syriac Chronicle known as that of Zachariah of Mitylene* [London 1899], pp. 1–10, esp. 1–5). A. Baumstark's brief reference, *Geschichte der syrischen Literatur* (Bonn 1922), pp. 183–184, is so short as to be useless.

[39] On Mara, see (Ps.-)Zacharias Rhetor, *Hist. Eccl.*, 8.5 and 8.7 (CSCO 88, pp. 54 and 57–60, resp.); his command of Greek is also mentioned in a manuscript (Dublin, Trinity College, B.2.9; dated 1197) of Dionysius bar Salibi's *Commentary on the gospels* (cp. Gwynn, *Remnants*, pp. 47 and 3 [Gwynn's MS *f*]).

of John 8:2–11, deviates considerably from the standard Johannine form. There is no attempt to entrap Jesus, who voluntarily interpolates himself into the scene; there follows a revised, less-pointed version of the challenge to the sinless one to cast the first stone; when finally alone with the woman, only Jesus speaks, and while he directs her not to commit this sin again, the words οὐδὲ ἐγώ σε [κατα]κρίνω are once again lacking.[40]

The next Syrian father to mention the story appears to be Agapius (Mahboub) of Hierapolis (Syria). In his *Kitab al-'Unvan* (*Universal History*), composed about 942 in Arabic, he refers to "a sage" (usually understood to be Papias, who was Bishop of Hierapolis in the early second century) who came to Hierapolis and wrote five books (presumably Papias's *Explanation of the Sayings of the Lord*); in his book on the Gospel of John, this "sage" recounted (according to Agapius) that "in the book of John the Evangelist, there is the matter of a woman who was an adulteress," and offers a précis of the story.[41] Despite the fact that this version is obviously abbreviated (there is no writing on the ground, no dialogue between Jesus and the woman), there are nevertheless differences between it and the standard form of the story. These are most obvious in the (apparently) direct quotations from Papias's book: Jesus' challenge to the mob becomes, "The one among you who is certain of his innocence of the sin of which she is accused, let him witness against her with the proof that he is [innocent]."

Finally, commencing with a manuscript of Dionysius bar Salibi's *Commentary* on the gospels dating from 1197 (Dublin, Trinity College, B.2.9), we find the standard Johannine version of the story; it is introduced by a statement asserting that "[it] is not found in all the copies; but the Abbot Mar Paul found it [in one of the Alexandrian copies], and translated it from Greek into

---

[40] *Hist. eccl.* 8.7 (CSCO 88, pp. 59–60 [*supra*, n. 38]); cp. Gwynn, *Remnants*, pp. 43–49.

[41] *Kitab al-'Unvan. Histoire universelle écrite par Agapius (Mahboub) de Menbidj*, ed. A. Vasiliev, PO tome 7, pars 4 (Paris 1909), pp. 504–505 (Arabic text and French translation). See also J. Linder, "Papias und die Perikope von der Ehebrecherin (Jon [*sic*] 7,53–8,11) bei Agapius von Mambig," ZKTh 40 (1916), pp. 191–199. Note that this description of what Papias (presumably) wrote—which explicitly describes the woman as "an adulteress"—is at odds with Eusebius's account of what Papias reported ("a woman accused of many sins"). Might Papias's text have been correctly preserved by Agapius, and erroneously transmitted by Eusebius (whose error Rufinus attempted to correct)?

Syriac...from the Gospel of John."[42] "Abbot Paul" is often presumed to be Paul of Tella or his contemporary, Abbot Paul.[43]

(4) In the *apocrypha*, we are told that the oldest evidence for
the *pericope adulterae* is the *Didascalia apostolorum*. Originally
composed in Greek, it survives today only in translations into
Syriac (complete, very early) and Latin (partially preserved in a
palimpsest in Verona).[44] In *Didascalia 7* we find portions of the
story quoted (including John 8:11), as a cautionary example
directed at bishops: when dealing with sinners, they should be as
indulgent, merciful, instructive, and reticent as Jesus was with the
adulteress. Since the *Didascalia* is usually dated to the first half of

---

[42] Gwynn, *Remnants*, p. 41 (text); the MS is Gwynn's *f* (p. 3: Dionysius bar
Salibi's *Commentary* on the gospels, which *also* contains the older "Mara"
tradition and its version of the story [cp. *supra*, nn. 38–40]).

[43] Both Pauls flourished in the first quarter of the seventh cent.; on Paul of
Tella (who resided in Alexandria from 615 to 617), see Baumstark, *Geschichte*,
pp. 186–188; "Abbot Paul" is reported to have translated the works of Gregory
Nazianzus into Syriac in 624.

[44] The Syriac text was first published by P. de Lagarde, *Didascalia apostolorum
syriace* (Leipzig 1854); only 100 copies were printed; one resides in the Oriental
Reading Room of the Library of the University of Leiden. The passage in
question is found on p. 31. It is perhaps more readily available in *The Didascalia
apostolorum in Syriac*, ed. M. D. Gibson, HSem 1 (London 1903), p. ܣܓ (= p. 63),
with an accompanying English translation in her *The Didascalia apostolorum in
English*, HSem 2 (London 1903), pp. 39–40. A German translation of the Syriac
is found in H. Achelis and J. Flemming, *Die ältesten Quellen des Orientalischen
Kirchenrechts. Zweites Buch. Die Syrische Didaskalia*, TU 25 (N.S. 10.2) (Leipzig
1904), p. 39. The Latin palimpsest was edited by E. Hauler, *Didascaliae
apostolorum fragmenta Veronensia latina* (Leipzig 1900). F. X. Funk, *Didascalia et
Constitutiones apostolorum* (Paderbornae 1905; reprinted, Torino 1962), presents a
Latin text, reconstructed from the Syriac and the Verona palimpsest, on facing
pages with the related but later work, the *Apostolic Constitutions*. Another English
translation is found in R. H. Connolly, *Didascalia Apostolorum. The Syriac version
translated and accompanied by the Verona Latin fragments* (Oxford 1929).

the third century,[45] it is, in absolute terms, the oldest reference—or so we are told—to the story.

We have reached the end of our *tour d'horizon*. The various forms in which the story is found suggest that it changed over time, either evolving (with the addition of v. 11, for example) or, alternatively, "shrinking" (through the suppression of v. 11 [recall the testimony of Augustine]). Citing such differences as *(a)* the transgression of the woman (adultery, or an unstipulated sin), *(b)* the manner in which Jesus is brought into the matter (by the Jews to entrap him, or of his own volition), *(c)* the presence or absence of Jesus writing on the ground, and *(d)* the presence or absence of Jesus' concluding dialogue with the woman (including our text in v. 11), B. D. Ehrman has suggested that there were originally two distinct stories, one known to Papias and Didymus (and found in the *Gospel according to the Hebrews*), and another known to the author of the *Didascalia apostolorum*; the present *pericope adulterae* is the result of the combination of these two originally independent stories.[46] D. Lührmann criticized this reconstruction, arguing that the present Johannine account is simply a more-developed form of the story which stood in the *Gospel according to the Hebrews*, which was known to Papias and Eusebius and Didymus in a primitive form, and which gradually evolved into the story which now stands in John and the *Didascalia apostolorum*.[47]

Tracing the history of the story would be facilitated if the full range of evidence were considered (for example, both of the reconstructions just outlined ignore the evidence of Armenian codex Edschmiadzin *anni* 989 as well as Agapius of Hierapolis). But all of these reconstructions have proceeded on the assumption that the oldest evidence for the story (excluding the ambiguous Papias/Eusebius report) is the third century *Didascalia apostolorum*; in doing so, they have ignored or dismissed the most ancient evidence for the *pericope adulterae*.

---

[45] On the date, see esp. P. Galtier, "La date de la Didascalie des Apôtres," *RHE* 42 (1947), pp. 315–351, who would place it in the first half of the third century (esp. p. 351: "le première moitié du IIIe siècle"). See also Gibson (*The Didascalia apostolorum in Syriac*, p. v ["third century"]), and Achelis and Flemming (*Die ältesten Quellen*, p. 377 [third century, with a weak preference for the latter half]). As for its provenance, Achelis and Flemming, p. 366, opt for Coele-Syria; Connolly, *Didascalia Apostolorum*, p. lxxxix, specifies the Antioch-Edessa region, but would not exclude southern Syria or Palestine.

[46] B. D. Ehrman, "Jesus and the Adulteress," pp. 24–44, esp. 32, 37–38.

[47] D. Lührmann, "Die Geschichte" (*supra*, n. 26), pp. 289–316, esp. 310–312.

III. John 8:11 and the Protevangelium Iacobi

Given what has been described by commentators and textual
critics as the oldest evidence for the *pericope adulterae,* your author
was surprised to find the following words in the *Protevangelium
Iacobi.* They are uttered by a male Jewish religious judge, adjudi-
cating a case of sexual misconduct:

> Εἰ Κύριος ὁ Θεὸς οὐκ ἐφανέρωσεν τὸ ἁμάρτημα ὑμῶν, <u>οὐδὲ ἐγὼ
> κρίνω ὑμᾶς</u>. Καὶ ἀπέλυσεν αὐτούς.[48]

> "If the Lord God has not made your [pl.] sin manifest, *neither do
> I condemn you* [pl.]." And he let them go.
> — *Protev. Iac.* XVI.3

The *Protevangelium Iacobi* is an apocryphal Christian romance,
dating from the second half of the second century.[49] The judge in
this instance is the (High ?) Priest, who is acquitting a pregnant
young woman/girl (Mary), and her "guardian" (Joseph).

The plot of the *Protevangelium* is well-known; it is sufficient to
say that Mary, a young girl pledged to the Temple, must leave
when her first menses occurs. By lot she is placed in the care of
an older widower, Joseph. When Mary is later discovered to be
pregnant, a crowd of Jews brings her and Joseph before the Priest
to be tried for their self-evident sexual sin. Joseph is subjected to
a trial by ordeal: he drinks a poison, and is sent into the
wilderness. When he returns alive—a sign of his innocence—
Mary is put to the same test. When she too returns alive, the
Priest pronounces the words given above—which, allowing for
the plural (ὑμᾶς, that is, Mary and Joseph) in place of the
singular, and the transposition of the last two words, are an *exact*
parallel for the text of John 8:11:

---

[48] É. de Strycker, *La forme la plus ancienne du Protévangile de Jacques,* SH 33
(Bruxelles 1961), p. 140.

[49] De Strycker, *La forme,* p. 417, sets the *terminus post quem* as "le deuxième
quart du IIe siècle" (because of its knowledge of II Peter), and gives his dating
("la seconde moitié du IIe siècle") on p. 418.

Protev. Iac.: οὐδὲ ἐγὼ [κατα]κρίνω[50] ὑμᾶς
John 8:11: οὐδὲ ἐγώ σε [κατα]κρίνω

The question poses itself: Is this parallelism the result of chance, or does the *Protevangelium* betray knowledge of the story which now stands in the Gospel of John?

First, one must ask whether or not the passage belongs to the oldest stratum of the *Protevangelium*. The answer is that although scholarship recognizes the interpolation of certain blocks of material into the *Protevangelium*,[51] the section with this passage is universally regarded as part of the oldest layer of the work.[52] Indeed, the lengthy section telling of Mary's birth, placement in the Temple, "adoption" by Joseph, pregnancy, and trial (chaps. I–XVI) presupposes her acquittal—which finally occurs in XVI.3 with these words which parallel John 8:11. Structurally, then, the passage does not appear to be a later addition.

Next, one must see if there are any textual variants within the *Protevangelium* which might affect the apparent parallel with John 8:11. Since the oldest manuscript of the *Protevangelium*—Bodmer Papyrus 5 (Greek; fourth cent.)[53]—contains these words, no textual difficulties are obvious. Among the many languages and manuscripts in which the *Protevangelium* survives, only two variants appear. (1) The verb is found in both the simple (κρίνω: "judge") and the compound (κατακρίνω; "condemn") form. This is of no moment for our investigation, for the identical phenome-

---

[50] Although de Strycker, *La forme*, p. 140, does not show any MSS in any language reading κατακρίνω (the only variant he offers is between the present [κρίνω] and the future tense [κρινῶ]), C. von Tischendorf, *Evangelia apocrypha* (Leipzig 1876[2]; reprinted Hildesheim 1966), p. 31, in the apparatus, lists one MS (Tischendorf's "E," which is Paris, Bib. Nat., 1468 [XI cent.]) with κατακρίνω. I trust in Tischendorf.

[51] *E.g.*, the death of Zacharias (*Protev. Iac.* XXII–XXIV) is universally considered a later addition.

[52] On the source criticism of the *Protevangelium*, see de Strycker, *La forme*, pp. 6–13 (with bibliography and summary of earlier studies).

[53] *Papyrus Bodmer V. Nativité de Marie*, ed. M. Testuz (Cologny/Genève 1958). It is noteworthy that this papyrus—although containing the full text of the passage under examination—generally has a "short" text, which caused de Strycker, *La forme*, to describe it as "un abrégement arbitraire de l'original" (p. 34). This is further evidence that the portion of the *Protevangelium* which contains the parallel with John 8:11 is part of the work's oldest stratum.

non is found in the Gospel of John as well.[54] (2) One of the two
extant Armenian recensions, Arm[b] (a paper manuscript which
dates from after the fall of Constantinople [*i.e.*, *post* 1453]), omits
the words which parallel John 8:11. However, the other Armenian recension, Arm[a] (paleography and codicology suggest a
late thirteenth- or early fourteenth-century date), includes the
words, in agreement with the entire Greek tradition.[55] This division of the Armenian is of no significance for our investigation,
for the entire Armenian version is described by its editor, H.
Quecke, as "assez gravement corrompu," with the sense of the
original text frequently being lost.[56]

The question still remains, however, whether the parallel is
the result of chance or of dependence—either direct or indirect.
Since one cannot logically prove that a parallel is the result of
"chance," one must shape the investigation as a *negative* inquiry
by hypothesizing that the parallel *is* the result of chance, and then
seek to disprove the hypothesis. One way to do this is to see if
there are specific "fingerprints" associated with this passage in the
Protevangelium which might reveal something about its origin.

It is here that form criticism comes to our aid, revealing a
wealth of parallels between the *Protevangelium* and the Johannine
pericope adulterae. (1) In both, the words are part of a "confrontation story."[57] (2) In both, the accusation is one of sexual
misconduct, and (3) in both the accused is female. (4) In both, the
accusation is made by the same group: the Jews, especially
religiously scrupulous Jews. (5) In both, the accused is presented
to the judge for a ruling; in neither story does the judge
interpolate himself into the situation. (6) In both, the scene is the
same, in that the accused woman is *brought* by a crowd to stand

---

[54] See *supra*, n. 2 (for MSS of John) and n. 50 (for MSS of the *Protevangelium*).

[55] H. Quecke made Latin translations of the Armenian versions; they are
published in de Strycker, who used them when constructing his apparatus. See
Quecke in de Strycker, *La forme*, p. 455 (for the "first" Armenian recension
[Arm[a]], which gives the reading, in agreement with the Greek), and p. 467
(where the "second" Armenian recension [Arm[b]] omits the words). Quecke's
dating of the manuscripts is in de Strycker, pp. 442–443.

[56] Quecke remarks: "il s'écarte fréquemment de la teneur originale de la
version...il est dénué de sens" (Quecke in de Strycker, *La forme*, p. 443).

[57] V. Taylor, *The Formation of the Gospel Tradition* (London 1957 [= second
edition of 1935, reprinted]), pp. 83–84, perversely (in your author's opinion)
classifies the *pericope adulterae* as a "pronouncement story"; Becker, *Ehebrecherin*,
p. 83, correctly classifies it as a "confrontation" story.

before a *male* religious figure. (7) In both, the words are spoken as the dramatic climax to a tension-filled scene. (8) In both, the woman is acquitted, despite overwhelming evidence of her guilt (according to John 8:4, the woman is "caught" in the act of adultery; in the *Protevangelium* it is visually self-evident that Mary is pregnant [XV.1: "Annas (the scribe who alerts the authorities concerning Mary)...*saw* Mary great with child"]).

Because of the form-critical congruity of these features and because of the virtually verbatim literary agreement, we are driven to conclude that some sort of dependence exists between the *Protevangelium* and the *pericope adulterae*. Furthermore, we may stipulate that the form of the *pericope adulterae* from which the *Protevangelium* borrowed these words must have been similar to the form the episode now has in the Gospel of John, in that the transgression was (1) explicitly sexual in nature, (2) the accused was presented by a mob to the authority figure for judgement, and (3) the story contained the words "Neither do I judge you." All of these features—while present in the *Protevangelium* and in the Gospel of John's version of the story—are not only absent from Papias/Eusebius and Didymus the Blind, but specifically contradict their information[58]; therefore, we may reject them as possible sources for the words.

The words "Neither do I judge you" are, then, *textual* evidence that three constitutive elements of the *pericope adulterae*, as it is now know to us from the Gospel of John, were known in the second half of the second century, the date assigned to the *Protevangelium Iacobi*.[59]

The evidence of the *Protevangelium* is important for three reasons. (1) It establishes the presence of these three distinctive elements in the story *as far back as we can find evidence for it.* Working without the evidence of the *Protevangelium*, Ehrman and Lührmann[60] presumed that these elements were later accretions, absent from its earliest form of the story (for, indeed, they are absent from Didymus and Papias/Eusebius). Such a position is no longer tenable. (2) In absolute terms, it moves back the date for the first reference to the story from the third century (the date of

---

[58] Papias/Eusebius, for example, speaks of "many sins," and says nothing of their nature; in Didymus's account, rather than a mob bringing the woman to Jesus for judgement, Jesus interpolates himself into the scene to defend her.

[59] See *supra*, n. 49.

[60] Lührmann was aware of the *Protevangelium*'s evidence, but dismissed it (see *infra*, n. 68).

the *Didascalia apostolorum*) to the second half of the second century—or between fifty and one hundred years earlier. And this earliest evidence for the story shares recognizable, distinctive elements with the Johannine version of the story. (3) As we will see, it provides additional information for determining the provenance of the story.[61]

IV. Previous Scholarship

Despite the apparent relevance of the *Protevangelium*'s words to the matter of the origin of the *pericope adulterae*, none of the major commentaries (over forty were consulted, in English, French, German and Dutch) even mentions the parallel.

Apparently the first scholar to comment on the parallel was F. C. Conybeare. A specialist in the Armenian tradition, it was he who discovered the Armenian manuscript Edschmiadzin *anni* 989 (this is the same Armenian manuscript mentioned above [see §II]; it was introduced in the review of the versional evidence for the *pericope adulterae*). In passing, Conybeare noted that the words οὐδὲ ἐγώ σε [κατα]κρίνω were absent from this Armenian manuscript, but present in both John and in the *Protevangelium Iacobi*.[62] He did not pursue the matter, however, for his principal concern was the presence in this manuscript of the "long" ending of Mark with a gloss attributing it to a certain "Ariston."

The next recognition of the parallel seems to be in A. Meyer's article on the *Protevangelium* in E. Hennecke's *Handbuch zu den Neutestamentlichen Apokryphen* (1904). Meyer's negative appraisal sets the tone for subsequent scholarship. In a curious twist of logic, he remarks "Selbst wenn eine Erinnerung an dies Wort [*viz.* John 8:11] vorläge, was nicht notwendig anzunehmen ist, so wäre damit noch nicht Rückgang aufs Joh.-Ev. erwiesen, da bekanntlich die Geschichte von der Ehebrecherin ursprünglich nicht dazu gehörte."[63] While one may excuse Meyer's failure

---

[61] See *infra*, n. 99.

[62] Conybeare, "On the Last Twelve Verses," pp. 405–408, 416–417. Conybeare is also the only scholar to comment upon the difference between the *Protevangelium*'s κρίνω and the canonical text's κατακρίνω: "In the Greek texts of the *Protevangelium* there is the same variation between κρίνω and κατακρίνω as in the MSS. at John viii.11" (p. 416).

[63] A. Meyer, in E. Hennecke, *Handbuch zu den Neutestamentlichen Apokryphen* (Tübingen 1904), p. 124. I thank Dr. Johan Vos of Amsterdam for calling to my attention this and the sources consulted in the next two notes.

to apply form-critical analysis to the passage (for he was writing before the development of form-critical tools), it is more difficult to excuse his logic. According to it, the literary parallel to John 8:11 in the *Protevangelium* need not be taken as evidence of the presence of the *pericope adulterae* in John, because "ursprünglich" the *pericope adulterae* was not part of John. Meyer's error is that he presumes the point under investigation (*viz.*, that John did not originally contain the *pericope adulterae*); the consequence is that he dismisses the evidence of the *Protevangelium*—as he would (presumably) *any* evidence which might suggest that the *pericope adulterae* were originally part of John.

Similar logic is found in other scholars: there is an obvious reluctance (all too apparent from our vantage point) even to acknowledge that a verbal parallel exists between the *Protevangelium* and John. An example is the Dutch scholar H. Bakels, who grudgingly admits that the *Protevangelium* gives "Ongeveer dezelfde uitdrukking" ("*Approximately* the same expression") as John; he hastens to add, however, "Dit wil niet zeggen dat het Voorevangelie haar aan Johannes heeft ontleend" ("This is not to say that the Protevangelium has borrowed [the expression] from John").[64] The reasons are two-fold: according to Bakels, John was composed ± 125, while the *Protevangelium* (again, according to Bakels) was written "vóór het jaar 100 [before the year 100]"; second, Bakels (using Meyer's *a priori* reasoning) points to the fact that the *pericope adulterae* was not originally part of John, hence the *Protevangelium* could not be dependent upon John. Another example is W. Michaelis, who—even in the age of form criticism—limits his remarks to the following, relegated to a note: "Kaum Zusammenhang mit Joh 8, 11."[65] "Kaum"? One wonders what is required for "Zusammenhang," if not the virtually verbatim literary parallel and form-critical congruity between the two sources!

The most extensive study to date of the *pericope adulterae*, U. Becker's 1963 monograph *Jesus und die Ehebrecherin*, also noted the parallel with the *Protevangelium*, and even applied form criticism to it, finding three points of congruity.[66] But Becker's

---

[64] *Nieuwtestamentische Apocriefen of het nadere over Jezus* (Amsterdam 1922), Deel I, p. 147, n. 1.

[65] *Die apokryphen Schriften zum Neuen Testament* (Bremen 1962³), p. 94.

[66] BZNW 28 (Berlin 1963), p. 118; the three points of congruity are: (1) both are set in scenes of judgement; (2) in both the transgression is sexual; (3) in both the accused is acquitted.

conclusion is consistent with Meyer: even the new form-critical
parallels do not allow one to admit dependence. Becker offers
two arguments. First, he attempts to dilute his own form-critical
findings by observing that the theme of the acquittal of a woman
is also found in the Susanna story and other "volkstümliche[n]
Erzählungen"; hence, a link with John is not necessary. (This
silently ignores, of course, the *facts* that [1] none of these "volkstümliche[n] Erzählungen" has a verbal parallel with the *pericope
adulterae*, and that [2] none has the extensive, explicit form-
critical congruence we have found between the *Protevangelium*
and the *pericope adulterae*.) Second, despite the fact that the
Protevangelium contains other apparent citations from other New
and Old Testament books, introduced "ohne Einführungs- oder
Zitationsformel und für seine Zwecke leicht modifiziert,"..."eine
Benutzung des vierten Evangelisten im Protevgl. Jakobi nicht
nachweisbar ist"[67]; on the other hand, an acquaintance with
"judenchristliche[n] Traditionsstoffe[n]" is demonstrable. Since
Johannine dependence is out of the question for Becker, he concludes that the *pericope adulterae* originated in the *Gospel according
to the Hebrews* (he accepts that the Papias/Eusebius report references the *pericope adulterae*, and not Luke 7:36–50, or some other
[perhaps unknown] story), and that from there it later spread to
both John and the *Protevangelium*. One wonders what it would
take to establish use of John in the *Protevangelium*, for apparently
a virtually verbatim literary parallel and extensive form-critical
congruency are, in Becker's eyes, insufficient.

More recently, D. Lührmann logged the parallel in a note in
an article, but then dismissed it, referring the reader to Becker's
argumentation.[68]

Leaving aside (1) the fallacious logic of Meyer (namely,
"since the *pericope adulterae* was not part of John, the passage in
the *Protevangelium* cannot be dependent upon John")—which
assumes the point under examination, (2) the erroneous dating of
the *Protevangelium* by Bakels, and (3) Becker's purely rhetorical
argument that the *Protevangelium's* words might stem from the
Susanna story or "volkstümliche[n] Erzählungen" (which, however, begs the question at hand, namely, the existence of a virtually verbatim literary parallel), one is left with only one substantive argument against dependence, and that is Becker's assertion that use of John in the *Protevangelium* is "nicht nachweisbar."

---

[67] Ibid., p. 119.

[68] D. Lührmann, "Die Geschichte," p. 311, n. 103; cp. p. 291, n. 12.

IV. The Protevangelium Iacobi *and the Gospel of John*

Becker's statement leaves one with the impression that there are no other parallels between the *Protevangelium Iacobi* and distinctively Johannine material; absent further parallels, dependence might correctly be described as "nicht nachweisbar." But this is not the case, for although Becker does not mention it, at least one[69] other parallel between the *Protevangelium* and the Gospel of John is known to exist.[70]

According to the *Protevangelium*, after Mary and Joseph are freed by the Priest with the words "neither do I judge you," they depart for Bethlehem. En route, Mary goes into labour. Joseph finds a cave[71] where he leaves Mary while he goes to get a midwife. In a manner and in language which evokes the sphere of the birth of the Buddha,[72] Mary gives birth without travail, and Jesus is born in a cloud and light. The midwife exits the cave in amazement, and comes upon Salome.[73] She tells Salome of the

---

[69] De Strycker, *La forme*, p. 436, actually lists a *third* parallel between John and the *Protevangelium*, namely, between John 6:17b (καὶ σκοτία ἤδη ἐγεγόνει) and *Protev. Iac.* XIV.1 (καὶ κατέλαβεν αὐτὸν νύξ; in de Strycker's edition, p. 128, lines 5–6). Your author regards this parallel as dubious for two reasons: (1) the parallelism is far from exact (different words are used [darkness::night, became::overcame]), and (2) the expressions are "generic" and, unlike the other two parallels discussed in the text above, have no distinctive qualities.

[70] The passage about to be discussed has been noted by de Strycker; the *Biblia Patristica*; Meyer in Hennecke, *Handbuch*, p. 127; Michaelis, *Die apokryphen Schriften*, p. 95; H. Bakels, *Nieuwtestamentische Apocriefen*, p. 152; and H. R. Smid, *Protevangelium Iacobi. A Commentary* (Assen 1965), p. 140. Once again, I am indebted to Dr. Vos, who drew my attention to the last four of these sources consulted (Meyer through Smid).

[71] This tradition of Jesus' birth in a cave is also known to Justin Martyr, Ephrem Syrus, and Romanos Melodos, and has, of course, overtones of Mythraic rites and the birth of that god (the references may be found in W. L. Petersen, "A New Testimonium to a Judaic-Christian Gospel Fragment from a Hymn of Romanos the Melodist," *VigChr* 50 [1996], pp. 115–116, n. 48).

[72] The parallels are striking, not only with the account in the *Protevangelium*, but also with the canonical accounts: cp. Asvaghosha's *The Buddha-Karita*, Bk. I, 9–55 (available in *World of the Buddha*, ed. L. Stryk [Garden City (New Jersey) 1968], pp. 12–17).

[73] The name is popular in apocryphal literature (cp. the *Gospel of Thomas*, log. 61, or the *Gospel of the Egyptians* [see *The Apocryphal New Testament*, ed. J. K.

"wonder" she has just seen. Salome, however, scoffs and says that she "will not believe that a virgin has brought forth *unless I can put my finger* (ἐὰν μὴ βάλω τὸν δάκτυλόν μου) and prove her nature (τὴν φύσιν αὐτῆς)" (*Protev. Iac.* XIX.3).[74] De Strycker's notes liken this passage to John 20:25 (uniquely Johannine), where the words are spoken by the apostle Thomas, who will not believe that Jesus has risen "*unless I* can see the holes that the nails made in his hands and *can put my finger* (ἐὰν μὴ...βάλω τὸν δάκτυλόν μου) into the holes they made." Placing the two passages side-by-side, one sees that they are identical:

> *Protev. Iac.*: ἐὰν μὴ βάλω τὸν δάκτυλόν μου
> John 20:25: ἐὰν μὴ...βάλω τὸν δάκτυλόν μου

The literary parallelism is, once again, beyond dispute. However, before pronouncing on the legitimacy of this parallel as evidence for dependence upon the Gospel of John, we must first determine—as we did in the other case—whether this passage is genuinely part of the *Protevangelium* and, if so, if there are any textual variants which might affect its use as a parallel for John 20:25.

As for the passage's position within the *Protevangelium*, it appears to belong to the oldest stratum of the text: the main aim of the work is to establish Mary's virginity *post partum*—for which this examination provides the definitive proof. As for variants, they are present; both Tischendorf and de Strycker, however, adopt the text given above. This is the text found in the oldest manuscript of the *Protevangelium* (Bodmer Papyrus 5; fourth cent.), and most other early manuscripts.[75] Later manuscripts

---

Elliott (Oxford 1993), pp. 143 and 16–19, respectively]), but found in the canonical gospels only in Mark 16:1.

[74] De Strycker, *La forme*, p. 158, lines 6–7 (15–16).

[75] De Strycker lists MSS D (XI cent.) and F[b] (XI) as reading the text with P.Bodmer 5 (IV); substituting "hand" for "finger" are MSS G (XII) and H (XV–XVII); reading "unless I examine her nature" (omitting the Johannine parallel—and the offensive digital examination) are MSS B (XII–XIII cent.), I (XIII–XIV), L (XVI), and R (*c.* 1600). The reading "unless I see [I will not believe]" is found in MSS A (X–XIV), (C) (X), and E (XI). The versions are as follows: the Latin agrees with the Bodmer Papyrus, with one MS substituting "hand" for "finger"; the Georgian follows the Bodmer Papyrus; the Aethiopic and the Syriac read with MSS A (C) E ("unless I see"), with some of the Syriac interpolating "with my eyes" *post* "see"; the Armenian has its own garbled reading; cf. de Strycker,

sometimes substitute "hand" for "finger" (a substitution also found in manuscripts of John: in א*). The tendency of history would certainly be to move *away* from such a direct demand for a digital gynecological examination of the Mother of God; and indeed, this is what later manuscripts offer: "unless I *see* [+ with my eyes] her nature," etc. But the logic of the variants, as well as the dates of the manuscripts, unequivocally posit the explicit Johannine parallel as the oldest text, as do both modern editors.

The question remains whether the *Protevangelium*'s word-choice is a random event (and therefore unrelated to the Gospel of John), or whether there is literary dependence (once again, either directly upon John, or upon a common source). Form-critical analysis once again provides an impressive list of parallels. (1) Both statements are uttered by a doubter. (2) The thing doubted is one of the major "miracles" which bracket Jesus' earthly existence (the virgin birth in the *Protevangelium*; his resurrection in John). (3) The method of examination is identical: in both a digit is used. (4) In both cases the result of the examination is identical: the doubter is converted into a believer (after Jesus reappears and orders Thomas to perform a digital examination of his wounds, Thomas offers his confession [John 20:28]; after performing her digital examination, Salome's hand is immediately afflicted with "fire," which is cured by touching the infant Jesus—which elicits a confession of faith [*Protev. Iac.* XX.4]). This form-critical congruity indicates that some sort of dependence exists between the two texts. It suggests that (unless one wishes to posit a common, pre-Johannine source) the author of the *Protevangelium*—*pace* Becker—both knew and used the Gospel of John.

It is important to note that *both of these parallels display exactly the same literary technique*. In each case, a few words of direct speech have been lifted from passages which are now part of John—*and only known through John*[76]—and are inserted into the

---

p. 158 in the apparatus, and pp. 30–45 for the MSS. De Stryker's reasoning for preferring the reading with the digital examination is made explicit in a remark on p. 159: "Une partie des variantes provient de Jn. 20.25; les autres semblent dues au désir d'atténuer le réalisme du passage."

[76] Here we deliberately ignore (and dismiss) the placement of the *pericope adulterae* in the Gospel of Luke by the Ferrar Group (*f*[13])—MSS which date from the twelfth cent. and later. We must also clarify our claim that the passage is "only known through John": what we mean is that, in the late second century, when the *Protevangelium* was being composed, there is no other known source

mouths of different people—*but in situations which are form-critically identical*—in the *Protevangelium.*[77] Although the *explicit* details of the situations may have changed, the *implicit* details remain unchanged.

V. *The origin of the* pericope adulterae

By now it should be clear that we can trace the existence of certain constitutive elements of the Johannine *pericope adulterae*—including οὐδὲ ἐγώ σε [κατα]κρίνω—to the last half of the second century, if not earlier. The question remains, however, whence did the author of the *Protevangelium Iacobi* acquire these words?[78]

There are three[79] possibilities for the origin of the clause in the *Protevangelium Iacobi.* (1) It is the original creation of the unknown author of the apocryphal work. In that case, it would not be drawn from any source. (2) It is drawn from the Gospel of John, whose text already contained the *pericope adulterae* in the second half of the second century. (3) Both the Gospel of John and the *Protevangelium Iacobi* independently drew on some earlier, now-unknown document (perhaps, *e.g.,* the *Gospel according to the Hebrews*), and independently preserve this clause.

The first option (the complete independence of the *Protevangelium*) is untenable. The verbal parallels are too exact; the con-

---

from which the "digital examination" might be derived. Similarly for the clause "Neither do I judge you": it is uniquely Johannine among the gospels, canonical or non-canonical; after the *Protevangelium* the first source to cite the clause is the Syriac *Didascalia apostolorum*, which cites it and Jesus' actions in the story as a model for bishops to emulate when dealing with sinners.

[77] This technique is used elsewhere in the *Protevangelium*, and with other gospels: *e.g.,* at *Protev. Iac.* V.2 (ed. de Strycker, p. 88, lines 5–6), when Mary's mother *Anna* gives birth to her and is told that the child is a girl, *Anna* says Ἐμεγαλύνθη ἡ ψυχή μου ("My soul is magnified...")—which is part of the "Magnificat" spoken by *Mary* at the Annunciation in the Gospel of Luke (Luke 1:46: Μεγαλύνει ἡ ψυχή μου).

[78] It should be noted that the author of the *Protevangelium*—like other authors of other early apocryphal works—seems wont to lift his material from "authoritative" sources. This suggests that the source in which οὐδὲ ἐγώ σε [κατα]κρίνω stood had some *gravitas* in the eyes of the *Protevangelium*'s author.

[79] We exclude at the outset the possibility that the entire *pericope adulterae* in the Gospel of John grew from this one clause in the *Protevangelium Iacobi*; therefore we limit our investigation to the question of whence the *Protevangelium* derives the text.

text in which the words are uttered is too similar; and, of course, like virtually all apocryphal documents, the *Protevangelium* displays knowledge of the ([proto-]canonical) gospel tradition, including another passage (the digital examination which causes belief) known only from the Gospel of John.

The second option (dependence of the *Protevangelium* upon the Gospel of John) has become much more likely than generally presumed, given the discovery of a *second* parallel between the *Protevangelium* and another uniquely Johannine passage, namely the "digital examination" of Mary's hymen/Jesus' wounds. There is admittedly much evidence against this possibility—it has been enumerated above (cf. §I, *Prologue*). However, *all* of the commentators who have so authoritatively stated that the *pericope adulterae* was not part of the early text of the Gospel of John have been either ignorant of or willfully ignored both this parallel and its significance.

The third option (mutual dependence upon an earlier, unknown source) is also possible. We have no knowledge of the extent or genre of the source, nor can we stipulate the precise context in which the saying occurred. However, given the similar contexts in John and the *Protevangelium*, it seems reasonable to presume that the words were uttered by a male authority figure/judge (presumably Jesus) to a woman accused of a capital crime, whose nature was almost certainly sexual; she was presented to him by a mob demanding a judgement. While we cannot stipulate the name of this source, tradition has—perhaps—given us one in Papias's report (as transmitted by Eusebius): the mysterious *Gospel according to the Hebrews*.[80] What little we know of this Judaic-Christian gospel fits the known parameters of our source: it must antedate 150 C.E. (the *Gospel according to the Hebrews* does[81]); it probably was composed in Greek (apparently it was[82]); it must preserve narratives about Jesus as well as *logia* (it does);

---

[80] The matter of the number and assignation of fragments to the three Judaic-Christian gospels hypothesized by modern scholarship is fraught with problems: cp. Petersen, "A New Testimonium," *VigChr* 50 (1996), p. 105, and idem, *Tatian's Diatessaron*, VigChr.S 25 (Leiden 1994), pp. 29–32. Therefore, it is possible that the name and/or date and/or provenance of one of the other Judaic-Christian gospels should be substituted for those given. Also, recall once again (see *supra*, in the text at nn. 26 and 27) the numerous arguments *against* identifying the Papias/Eusebius report with the *pericope adulterae*.

[81] Cp. the date suggested by Klijn, *Jewish-Christian*, p. 30.

[82] Ibid., p. 33.

and it must have circulated in Egypt[83] at this early date (apparently it did[84]).

One way to gauge the likelihood that this *logion* entered the *Protevangelium* from the *Gospel according to the Hebrews*, is to examine the *Protevangelium* for indications that it preserves elements otherwise known to be part of the Judaic-Christian gospel tradition. There appears to be only one passage which offers an explicit parallel, and that is at *Protev. Iac.* XIX.2: when Jesus is born in the cave, a cloud appears, καὶ ἐφάνη φῶς μέγα ἐν τῷ σπηλαίῳ ("and *a great light* appeared in the cave"). According to the report of the late fourth-century writer Epiphanius (*Pan.* 30.13.7), when Jesus was baptized in the Jordan, the "Hebrew gospel" stated that καὶ εὐθὺς περιέλαμψε τὸν τόπον φῶς μέγα ("and immediately *a great light* shone around the place"). The verbal parallelism (φῶς μέγα ["a great light"]) is exact, and while the circumstances are not identical, there is no denying the similarities—and concomitant confusion among early Christians[85]—between Jesus' birth and baptism. Hence, it is not surprising to find a description associated with Jesus' baptism in a Judaic-Christian gospel transposed to Jesus' birth, as it appears to be in the *Protevangelium*.

While this link with the Judaic-Christian gospel tradition is fairly clear, it is not unambiguous, for the same tradition of a light at Jesus' baptism is found not just in the fragment of a Judaic-Christian gospel quoted by Epiphanius, but much earlier, in Justin Martyr (*Dial.* 88.3), several Diatessaronic witnesses,[86] and in two Vetus Latina manuscripts (*ante* Matt. 3:16: *a* [fourth cent.; our earliest Vetus Latina manuscript]; *g'* [sixth cent.]). Therefore, it is not clear whether this variant circulated only in a Judaic-

---

[83] The *Protevangelium*'s provenance, according to de Strycker, *La forme*, p. 423.

[84] Egyptian provenance is presumed for the *Gospel according to the Hebrews*; see, for example, Klijn, *Jewish-Christian*, p. 30.

[85] Recall the interesting variant in many very early sources (Justin, Clement, Origen, Augustine, the *Gospel of the Ebionites*, D, *d*, etc.) at Luke 3:22: *at Jesus' baptism*, the voice from heaven states "You are my Son; today I have begotten you." This, and the linked variant (found in many of the same sources) which has the "Holy Spirit" in the form of the "dove" either "entering into him," or "rested upon him," or "rest in [him]," suggests that there was, in addition to the virgin birth tradition, another tradition, according to which Jesus' conception was by sexual intercourse (cp. Epiphanius, *Pan.* 30.13.7; 30.14.4; Jerome, *Comm. Is.* at 11:2), and his "divinity" was acquired only at his baptism.

[86] For the evidence, see Petersen, *Tatian's Diatessaron*, pp. 14–20.

Christian gospel, or whether at one time—in very early, second-century Christianity—it circulated in an *Ur*-version of one of the (proto-)canonical gospels. If it were (as the evidence of *a* and *g '* suggests) part of a very early recension of the Gospel of Matthew, then the *Protevangelium* might be dependent upon it for this reading, and not upon a Judaic-Christian gospel.

We have exhausted the evidence available to us, and still no answer to the question of the origin of the *pericope adulterae* is obvious. It might have come from a Judaic-Christian gospel—perhaps the *Gospel according to the Hebrews.* There is much to commend this viewpoint, which has been popular since it was first suggested to modern scholarship by J. Drusius (1595),[87] from which it passed to the Dutch polymath Hugo Grotius (1641),[88] and thence to J. A. Fabricius (1703–1719).[89] Apparently this was also the understanding of Rufinus, as evidenced by the alterations he apparently made when translating Eusebius's *h.e.* into Latin.[90] It would explain why Eusebius preserved Papias's remark (he did so because it was "new" information).[91] It would explain the non-Johannine style of the language in the pericope,[92] and its awkward position in the manuscripts of John (and Luke):[93] bumped about, marked with obeli and asterisks, adorned with cautionary marginal glosses. It would also explain the absence of the pericope from all the oldest manuscripts of John.

---

[87] J. Drusius, *De quaesitis per epistolam* (Franeker 1595), Ep. 25: *"...ut suspicari merito quis possit ex Evangelio illo [ad Hebraeos] in nostra exemplaria eam [narrationem de muliere adultera] dimanasse."* My good friend, Prof. H. J. de Jonge of Leiden, rescued me from an error (I would have credited Grotius with the introduction of the idea) by drawing my attention to this reference in Drusius, for which he deserves the credit.

[88] H. Grotius, *Annotationes in Libros Evangeliorum* (Amsterdami 1641), p. 4b: *"...historia de adultera, quam nos a Ioanne proditam habemus, in illorum [Nazaraeorum] Evangelio legebatur"* (for Grotius and most scholars before 1920, the *Gospel according to the Hebrews* and the *Gospel of the Nazoraeans* were identical).

[89] J. A. Fabricius, *Codex Apocryphus Novi Testamenti* (Hamburgi 1703–1719²), p. 358: *"quod non vere sit Johannis, aut ex Evangelio ad Hebraeos illuc insertum,..."*

[90] See *supra*, n. 33.

[91] This is, after all, the context in which Eusebius places *all* of the "stories from Papias" he transmits: "And he [Papias] also presents other strange/unheard of (ξένος) stories and teachings of the Savior, which came to him from the unwritten tradition, and certain tales/myths" (Eusebius, *h.e.* III.39.11).

[92] See *supra*, n. 9.

[93] See *supra*, n. 8.

On the other hand, we can be certain that *some* form of the *pericope adulterae*—in a form similar to that which it now has in the Gospel of John—was known to the author of the *Protevangelium Iacobi*, which was composed in the second half of the second century. And the *Protevangelium* cites another *uniquely* Johannine passage (the digital examination) in exactly the same "transposed" fashion. When commentators penned their opinion that the *pericope adulterae* was not part of the Gospel of John, they did so under the mistaken impression that there was no evidence for the *pericope adulterae* before the *Didascalia apostolorum* (that is, before the first half of the third century). We now know better.

Similarly, when Becker opted for the *Gospel according to the Hebrews* as the source of the *pericope adulterae*, he did so under the mistaken impression that the *Protevangelium* evinced no dependence upon the Gospel of John. Here too, we now know better.

Finally, since the testimonies of Papias/Eusebius, Didymus the Blind, Agapius of Hierapolis, and the Armenian MS Edschmiadzin *anni* 989 contain neither the words οὐδὲ ἐγώ σε [κατα]κρίνω nor stipulate the nature of the woman's sin[s], it has been suggested that these writers were referencing some story other than (or in an earlier form than) the one now found in the Gospel of John. The inference is that the story which now stands in John is either a later fusion of two earlier stories (so Ehrman),[94] or a later, more developed version of a story which stood in the *Gospel according to the Hebrews* (so Lührmann).[95] Here we do not know better, but our evidence casts doubt upon either scenario, for now we know that (1) the words of Jesus οὐδὲ ἐγώ σε [κατα]κρίνω—conspicuous by their absence from so many of the early accounts (Papias/Eusebius, Didymus, the Syriac "Mara" tradition, Armenian MS Edschmiadzin *anni* 989)—*were* known in the second century, and (2) this saying of Jesus *was* linked to a story about a woman whose transgression was not some vague, unstipulated "sin[s]," but rather a sin which was specifically sexual in nature; furthermore, (3) this story did *not* have Jesus come to the woman's rescue uninvited (as he does in Didymus and the Syriac "Mara" tradition), but rather has the woman presented to him for judgement and sentencing. And these three points are consistent with the *pericope adulterae* as it now stands in the Gospel of John.

---

[94] So Ehrman (*supra*, n. 46), the one circulating in the *Gospel according to the Hebrews*, and the other known from the *Didascalia apostolorum*.

[95] So Lührmann (*supra*, n. 47).

Despite the more complete picture we now have before us, we are still left with the problem of deciding which source—the Gospel of John, the *Gospel according to the Hebrews*, or some other as-yet-undiscovered source (another *Gospel according to Thomas?*[96] Papias's *Explanation of the Sayings of the Lord?*[97])—first contained the *pericope adulterae*. Solving that problem is a very difficult task, fraught with uncertainty. Indeed, it is a problem which, given our present state of knowledge of the sources, cannot be solved.

VI. Postscript

In the course of our investigation, we have indirectly come across several things which are worthy of special mention. First, many commentaries offer an inadequate depiction of the textual evidence. For example, none of the more than forty commentaries consulted mentions the *Protevangelium Iacobi* in connexion with the *pericope adulterae*.

Second, we have found that much can be learned by reading widely in earlier, apparently unrelated scholarship. This was how we stumbled upon the fact that it was Conybeare who apparently first discovered the *Protevangelium*'s parallel with John 8:11.[98]

Third, it is important to double-check the explicit and implicit assertions of authors. If one had accepted Becker's assertion that dependence of the *Protevangelium* upon John was "nicht nachweisbar," then one would not have investigated de Stryker's edition, and discovered that a second, verbatim parallel existed.

---

[96] A marginal gloss stating "This section [the *pericope adulterae*] is from the Gospel of Thomas," is found in Greek MS 1006 (eleventh cent.); cp. Becker, *Ehebrecherin*, p. 145. Of course, the Coptic *Gospel according to Thomas*—at least in the form in which it has come down to us—lacks this story.

[97] Might the story have *originated* (that is, first been written down/composed by Papias, dependent only upon oral traditions) here? If so, then it would be Eusebius, not Papias, who (erroneously?) attributed the story to the *Gospel according to the Hebrews* (cp. *supra*, n. 41).

[98] The irony is heavy when Z. C. Hodges, "The Woman Taken in Adultery: The Text," *BS* 136 (1979), pp. 318–332, takes Metzger to task for ignoring evidence (p. 320: he faults Metzger for ignoring Jerome and for only mentioning [but not quoting] Augustine), for Hodges himself (1) utterly ignores Becker's monograph (whose twenty-nine pages of textual evidence surpass both the length and the coverage of Hodges' entire article), and (2) ignores the evidence of the *Protevangelium*—evidence which, had he know it, he could have used in his defense of the "Majority Text" (which presents the story at John 7.53ff.).

Fourth, while some scholars have debated the genesis of the *pericope adulterae* and sought to reconstruct the various stages in its evolution, this has usually been done with incomplete evidence. Sources such as the Armenian MS Edschmiadzin *anni* 989, Agapius of Hierapolis, and the *Protevangelium Iacobi* have been ignored, even though they have much to contribute to the necessary task of tracing the form(s) in which the story circulated, as well as the date and original provenance of the story (namely, Egypt, probably in or near Alexandria, in the second century[99]).

Fifth and finally, the more one delves into the puzzle of the origins of the *pericope adulterae*, the more one sees how difficult it is to cut the knot cleanly. Deciding for either position leaves messy problems remaining. For example, if one were to conclude that the story originated in the *Gospel according to the Hebrews*, then, *mutatis mutandis*, should we not suspect the same genesis for the *other* story which was *also* adapted by the author of the *Protevangelium Iacobi*, and which is *also* now known only from John, namely, the "Doubting Thomas" episode with the saying "unless I put my finger..."? Is this story also originally from the *Gospel according to the Hebrews*? And why, if the *pericope adulterae* originated in the *Gospel according to the Hebrews*, does Papias/Eusebius report that she is accused of "*many* sins" when, in fact, she is accused of only *one* sin, a single instance of adultery? On the other hand, if one were to conclude that the story originated in the Gospel of John, why, then, are *all* of the most ancient witnesses—in *all* of the languages—lacking these verses?[100] And if the verses were originally part of the Gospel of John, then what can account not only for their insertion at no fewer than *five* different places in the gospels—including Luke!—but also for the *non*-Johannine vocabulary and style found in the passage?[101] Neither solution resolves these issues in a satisfactory manner.

All of these points are, I think, close to the heart of Tjitze Baarda, who is the most circumspect scholar I know. Some of this caution may arise from his character; but there is no doubt that

---

[99] The confluence of the provenances of (1) the *Protevangelium Iacobi* (*viz.*, Egypt [see *supra*, n. 83]), (2) the *Gospel according to the Hebrews* (see *supra*, n. 84), (3) Didymus the Blind, and (4) the Syrian reports that the story was copied from *Alexandrian* MSS by either Bishop Mara (so [Ps.-]Zacharias Rhetor) or "Mar Paul" (see *supra*, nn. 39 and 43), suggests that the *pericope adulterae* originated in Egypt (probably in Alexandria), in the first half of the second century.

[100] Recall that Augustine provides a possible explanation (see *supra*, n. 36).

[101] See *supra*, n. 9.

much of it stems from his encyclopedic knowledge of the texts of ancient Christianity, in nearly all of her many languages. His publications are distinguished by a careful summary of previous scholarship, often giving not just the preferred texts of earlier editions, but even the variant readings found in the apparatuses—stretching back to Erasmus, Beza, Grotius, Mill, and Fabricius.[102] Before theorizing about *Ur*-forms of a pericope, he exhaustively excavates the literature of early Christianity, logging every allusion, paraphrase, and citation; only then does he begin to assemble the evidence and see where *it* leads *him*. His discreet criticism of many commentaries comes from having assembled a vast collection and observed the uncritical transmission of defective information from one to another. To guard against this, he continually forces himself to emulate the Renaissance dictum, *Ad fontes!*

Although it was never my good fortune to have been a student of Tjitze Baarda, it has been my great privilege to sit at his elbow for over fifteen years, and to learn from one of the true masters of our discipline. This small contribution has sought not only to bring to scholars' attention something of great importance which has been inexplicably ignored, but also to illustrate several constitutive elements of our honoree's style of scholarship.

Behind the scholar, however, there always stands the man; and in this case, it is a creature singularly composed: a magnanimous friend, mentor, and colleague who, in his daily life, demonstrates that he has learned what few ever do, namely, the true, profound meaning of the words οὐδὲ ἐγώ σε κρίνω.

---

[102] An example is his address "Textual Criticism on the Threshold of a New Century: A Step Forward?" delivered 22 November, 1993, in Washington, D.C., at the Annual Meeting of the Society of Biblical Literature.

The author gratefully acknowledges a summer stipend from The Pennsylvania State University's Institute for the Arts and Humanistic Studies, which facilitated research for this article. Also gratefully acknowledged is a sabbatical leave granted during the fall semester, 1996, by the university's College of Liberal Arts, without which research on this article and editorial work on this volume would have been impossible.

GALILEAN UPSTARTS: A SOT'S CYNICAL DISCIPLES?[1]

James M. Robinson
The Institute for Antiquity and Christianity
Claremont Graduate School
(Claremont, California, USA)

1. Introduction

During the Spring Semester of 1986 Leif E. Vaage was completing his dissertation at Claremont Graduate School, Ron Cameron was spending a sabbatical at Claremont, and Burton Mack was the senior New Testament colleague in residence at Claremont, while I was on sabbatical working in the Papyrus Collection of the Egyptian Museums in Berlin and teaching in Hans Küng's Ecumenical Institute at the University of Tübingen. It was during this period of my absence that the hypothesis of the Cynic Q must have ripened among them.[2] For it appeared first in Vaage's dissertation,[3] then in Cameron's essay on Q 7:18–35 as a *chreia*

---

[1] This paper was presented at the Annual Meeting of the Society of Biblical Literature in Chicago on 21 November 1994, in a Panel Review of Leif E. Vaage, *Galilean Upstarts: Jesus' First Followers According to Q* (Valley Forge [Pennsylvania] 1994). Page references to this work are included in the text in parentheses. Subsequent related essays by Vaage include a rebuttal of Christopher M. Tuckett, "A Cynic Q?," *Bib.* 70 (1989), pp. 349–376, entitled "Q and Cynicism: On Comparison and Social Identity," *The Gospel Behind the Gospels: Current Studies on Q*, ed. Ronald A. Piper, NovT.S 75 (Leiden 1994), pp. 199–229, and a defense of a non-apocalyptic, Cynic John: "More Than a Prophet, and Demon-Possessed: Q and the 'Historical' John," *Conflict and Invention: Literary, Rhetorical, and Social Studies on the Sayings Gospel Q*, ed. John S. Kloppenborg (Valley Forge [Pennsylvania] 1995), pp. 181–202.

[2] For a critical survey of other and prior advocates of the Cynic Jesus, going back to Friedrich Nietzsche, see Hans Dieter Betz, "Jesus and the Cynics: Survey and Analysis of a Hypothesis," *JR* 74 (1994), pp. 453–475.

[3] Leif E. Vaage, *Q: The Ethos and Ethics of an Itinerant Intelligence* (unpublished Ph.D. dissertation, Claremont Graduate School, 1987). He reports that he lit upon the Cynic hypothesis on his own. He had already presented a paper entitled "To Wear Soft Raiment," concerning the Cynic term occurring in Q

elaboration,[4] and then in Mack's popularizing best-seller.[5] Vaage's first book, *Galilean Upstarts*, brings this development to completion.

My interest in the Cynic hypothesis was first engendered by Vaage, then a Claremont doctoral student and my research associate, who pointed to the striking parallel between the role model of the ravens and wild flowers (Q 12:22–31) and the point scored by Dio Chrysostom, *Or.* 10.15–16 (quoted p. 62), that the good life is living according to nature like the beasts and birds who, by owning no property, are just that much better off than are humans. No matter what else one may think of the Cynic hypothesis, such a striking parallel cannot simply be ruled to be irrelevant, as no more than a striking coincidence, especially in view of the comment by England's leading exponent of a Cynic Q, F. Gerald Downing (quoted by Vaage, p. 169, n. 48): "Apart from references to the short life of grass—Isa. 40.7–8, etc.—there seem to be no close Jewish parallels."[6] Yet to maintain that the

---

7:25, at the Annual Meeting of the Society of Biblical Literature at Anaheim, California, in November 1985.

[4] Ron Cameron, "'What Have You Come Out To See?': Characterizations of John and Jesus in the Gospels," *Semeia* 49 (1990), pp. 35–69. The essay, pp. 41–44, contains a number of references to Vaage's dissertation, and, pp. 46, 48–50, to Burton Mack's Occasional Paper 10 of the Institute for Antiquity and Christianity, *Anecdotes and Arguments: The Chreia in Antiquity and Early Christianity* (Claremont, CA 1987). There Mack emphasizes the correlation of the *chreia* with the Cynics, and refers to Vaage's paper "To Wear Soft Raiment" to document "evidence that Jesus was remembered in contrast to John the Baptist (Jesus' behavior is reminiscent of a 'hedonistic' Cynic; John's is described as that of the 'ascetic' type)." Cameron's addition to this position was to argue that Q 7:19–35 was a *chreia* elaboration, just as Mack, pp. 34–36, argued that Mark 2:18–22 was a *chreia* elaboration also about John and Jesus.

[5] Burton L. Mack, *The Lost Gospel: The Book of Q and Christian Origins* (San Francisco 1993). See my essay, "The History-of-Religions Taxonomy of Q: The Cynic Hypothesis," in *Gnosisforschung und Religionsgeschichte. Festschrift für Kurt Rudolph zum 65. Geburtstag*, edd. Holger Preißler and Hubert Seiwert (Marburg 1994 [1995]), pp. 247–265.

[6] This overlooks some pseudepigraphic, rabbinic and Mandaean evidence: Rudolf Bultmann, *The History of the Synoptic Tradition*, tr. by John Marsh (revised edition: New York 1968), p. 106, n. 3. Martin Hengel, *The Charismatic Leader and his Followers*, tr. by James Greig (New York 1981), p. 49, n. 41, points out that the rabbinic references are from the second century C.E., and are so unusual in

Q people were "like" the Cynics does not say much, since it remains unclear whether they are more or less "like" the Cynics than they are to other alternatives with which they could be—but in fact have not been—carefully compared.

Vaage (p. 180, n. 20) can quote Peter Brown to the effect that "the holy man drew his powers from outside the human race: by going to live in the desert, in close identification with an animal kingdom that stood, in the imagination of contemporaries, for the opposite pole of all human society." Similarly (p. 185, n. 1): "Although I have alluded in this book on more than one occasion to both the Cynics and the persons whom Q represents as 'ascetic,' it remains an open question, how exactly each might fit into a general history of 'asceticism' in the ancient Mediterranean world." To point to Jesus as a "holy man" or "ascetic" would not have drawn the attention (and angry criticism) that the classification as "Cynic" has effected. But it might have provided a more durable point of departure, open to refinement that might or might not lead to a Cynic specificity.

Critics of the Cynic hypothesis for their part should desist from their shocked, indeed reproachful tone about the Cynic comparison until they have shown that Q 12:22–31 has a closer matrix elsewhere. For it, like the Sermon on the Mount in which it occurs, simply cannot be removed from its central position in defining Jesus and the movement he launched. For it stands at the center of the formative stratum of Q: The closest parallel is the Lord's Prayer, where "thy kingdom come" is defined not by Matthew's moralistic addition, "thy will be done on earth as it is in heaven," but instead by the subsistence concern: "give us this day our ration of bread." Both Q texts conform to the striking life style of the Q movement presented in the formative stratum by the Workers' ("Mission") Instructions (Q 10:4–9), to take along neither a backpack for provisions nor a supply of cash, but to knock on unfamiliar doors trusting in God's gift of hospitality: dinner, bed and breakfast.

To be sure, not all of the Q people may have lived this way. The itinerants are referred to (Q 10:2,7b) as "workers"[7] who are

---

rabbinic Judaism as to raise the question "whether pronouncements by Jesus may have not found their way into rabbinic tradition via Jewish Christianity."

[7] Vaage, *Galilean Upstarts,* pp. 111–114, ascribes both references to the late redactional stratum, "especially if Q's redactional polemic against 'this generation' signals not only the announcement of judgment, but also and indeed precisely thereby the establishment of clearer social boundaries and the concomi-

sent out in answer to the prayer of persons not explicitly so designated (Q 10:2), and who are admitted for the night by someone
designated instead a "son of peace" (Q 10:6). Not all of such
hosts promptly dropped out of their home life to take up itinerancy themselves, but no doubt in some (most?) cases stayed at
home, perhaps ultimately to provide a "safe house," a "house
church," as seems to be emerging already in Matthew's redaction
(Matt 10:11): "And whatever town or village you enter, find out
who is worthy in it, and stay with him until you depart." Yet,
however welcome, indeed indispensable, such supporters may
have been, the message of Q and presumably of Jesus was not
primarily directed to them, but rather to those who gave up such
security for the primitive life of nature.

Here then one strikes upon the existential issue that is—or
should be—the nub of the hostile reception that the Cynic
hypothesis has received: We, the academics, and the educated
public who read our popular scholarship, do not live at the
subsistence level, but instead have refrigerators with food to last
longer than a day's ration, a savings account for a rainy day,
annuities for security in old age—and do not wish to be
reproached for so doing. Our consciences will not permit us! We
believe in God, and give thanks to him for the food we eat—but
we do not throw caution to the wind and literally entrust to God
our daily survival. After all, we have family responsibilities, etc.
We have wised up. We are, in short, like the moral, religious
Jews of Jesus' environment, and of main-line Christians down
through the centuries. A life style based on the earliest stratum of
Q is too much to expect of us!

There is of course a tremendous cultural gulf between our
cosmopolitan, technologically advanced society of affluence, and
the relatively "simple," subsistence-level status of First Century
Galilee. Carrying a club would in any case not protect against
gang violence today, nor would emptying our wallets, much less
our bank accounts, to the nearest beggars or street people, cure
our social evils. We reassure ourselves with the rationalization
that "charity" is surely less effective than the elimination of aspects of society that condemn many to poverty—without of
course really favoring the "socialism" this would suggest. But in
fact a hermeneutic of practice is called for, to seek to define what

---

tant consolidation of a more distinctive group–identity by the later tradents of
Q" (p. 114). Perhaps this is an early designation of a function moving toward a
"church office"!

life style today best implements what Jesus and the Q people called for then, at least to whatever extent one still cherishes such ideals of "following in their footsteps," being "disciples," etc. Ultimately, the Cynic hypothesis is offensive because it puts our status as Christians basically in question.

There have been down through the centuries of Christian history more and less "committed" or "radical" Christians. The martyrs, the ascetics, monks and nuns, crusaders, reformers, missionaries (not to speak of other ordained clergy) have in varying cultural climates and interpretations represented a fuller commitment. The *modus vivendi* has been that the "radicals" were tolerated, even supported, by the "main-line" Christians, so long as the life style of the majority was not as such invalidated. Yet, ill-advised as many such "radicals" may have been, they, rather than we, represent a recognizable continuity with the Jesus movement.

In this sense the final assessment of the Cynic hypothesis is not primarily focused on historical questions about the Cynics. To argue that the closest "Cynic" parallel to Q 12:31 is actually from the Stoic Seneca ("kingdom of wisdom," p. 62) does not violate basically the Cynic hypothesis, since the debate about what Q is most like is not really which religion one is to choose as most similar within the history of religions (or, especially in the Hellenistic Age, among moral philosophies offering a way of life). Rather the basic problem is that Jesus and his followers were in their life style more like ascetic Cynics (or Stoics) than like us.

The sophisticated methodological Introduction of *Galilean Upstarts* makes clear that a discussion partner who, in all naïveté, just wants the facts, will not only be disappointed on principle, but will in effect be ruled out of the academic discussion. The critical historical reconstruction of Jesus and his immediate followers is our myth (pp. 4–6), but, if it is a constitutive ingredient of the myth we live by, we nonetheless are to take it seriously and work at it conscientiously. We are not free to replace it with the myth of some other age or culture, *e.g.* a precritical gullibility that may have functioned in the Middle Ages, since we can only be ourselves, in our given time and space.

The clarification the Introduction presents as to what the Q-Cynic discussion is all about (or should be all about) is very helpful. Vaage does not propose to "derive" the Q posture from Cynicism. Hence the question of whether there were Cynics in the time and space of Q loses its cogency. It is not a matter of historical causation, "origins or genealogical derivation" (p. 10).

Jesus and the Q people need never to have seen or heard a
Cynic, or even heard one described. It is rather a matter of
typology. Among the various life styles, understandings of existence, social formations—which are more similar, which less?
Thus the question is more like that in "comparative religion,"
when religions from quite distinct cultures are compared even
though it is extremely unlikely that one religion was in contact
with the other.

Parties on both sides of the debate have at times lapsed into
the kind of argument about historical causation that Vaage is
opposing (p. 10: "the abiding conceptual confusion of comparison with genealogy"), so that the blurring of the distinction as
one studies the discussion is quite understandable. But, since
one's position might be quite different, depending on which
meaning one has in view, it is important to be clear as to what
the Q-Cynic comparison is intended to be. It is for Vaage hardly
a question as to whether the Q people "were" Cynics, but rather
whether they resembled Cynics more than they resembled other
alternatives (including ourselves). One should thus note that
Vaage's Cynic "claim" has become much more "modest" than
that published previously by Q-Cynic scholarship. It would only
mean that within the varieties of religious experience (or of social
formation, or of understandings of existence, or the like), these
two are the most similar.[8]

2. The alcoholic Jesus

Vaage describes his basic method as an archeological approach
comparable to working down through a tell, stratum by stratum,
in the order in which the strata lie from the surface of the tell at
the top downward:[9]

---

[8] Vaage, "Q and Cynicism: On Comparison and Social Identity," builds upon
this insight he derives from Jonathan Z. Smith, *Drudgery Divine: On the Comparison of Early Christianities and the Religions of Late Antiquity* (Chicago 1990).

[9] Leif E. Vaage, "Q[1] and the Historical Jesus: Some Peculiar Sayings (7:33–34;
9:57–58, 59–60; 14:26–27)," *Forum* 5,2 (1989), pp. 159–176. On p. 159 he refers
to his unpublished "Paper presented to the 1988 Spring meeting of the Jesus
Seminar, Sonoma, CA," "An Archeological Approach to the Work of the Jesus
Seminar." The quotations that follow are from the paper distributed for that
meeting, pp. 1, 2, 3.

My assumption is that if any stratum of these documents corresponds to Jesus, it will be the earliest. All later strata as they are progressively discerned can thus be removed and displaced to one side (exactly as is done on any dig). By then collecting the lowest stratum of the various texts, we will have created the primary data base that we are seeking....

In archeological terms, then, as a kind of principle one could say that the later the stratum in which a given saying, etc. occurs, the stronger the black vote against its pertinence to Jesus...

Using thus a stratigraphical analysis of Mark and Q, one would have at the end of an investigative survey of relevant research a set of sayings, etc. constituting the formative stratum of these documents which, precisely for this reason, the Jesus Seminar could claim with confidence as its primary data base for a description of the historical Jesus.

In the case of Q, the strata established by John S. Kloppenborg are followed:[10]

> Key to Kloppenborg's description of this kind of analysis is the use of strictly literary criteria for determining earlier/later strata in a document.

Vaage maintains that only this literary-critical procedure provides real objectivity:[11]

> Precisely because the stratigraphical analysis of a text has per se *absolutely nothing to do with a description of Jesus*, its aid in determining the data base for this project is enormous. For the material such an approach will give us as primary will be free from interest in the question.

This approach in terms of the earliest written stratum means one is less dependent on assessing oral tradition:[12]

---

[10] Vaage, "An Archeological Approach to the Work of the Jesus Seminar," p. 4. See John S. Kloppenborg, *The Formation of Q,* Studies in Antiquity and Christianity (Philadelphia 1987).

[11] Vaage, "An Archeological Approach to the Work of the Jesus Seminar," p. 5. The emphasis comes from Vaage.

[12] "An Archeological Approach to the Work of the Jesus Seminar," pp. 5–6.

The approach here proposed suspends (for the time being) all notions and derivative habits of explanation which would invoke a so-called free-floating oral tradition, whereby sayings, etc. of the historical Jesus could conceivably find their way into stratigraphically later levels of the inscribed texts that we presently possess....

I am not denying the erstwhile existence of an oral tradition nor limiting its life to only a very few years. I am simply observing that we have no clear access to it in the way we do to the set of written texts that today constitute for us the Jesus tradition.... That is why stratigraphical analysis on the basis of literary criteria is the necessary first step toward establishing the Jesus Seminar's primary data base.

This sounds all very objective in principle, until Vaage becomes fascinated with building his presentation of Jesus on a saying that Kloppenborg's "strictly literary criteria" assign to the secondary stratum. The analysis ceases to have *"absolutely nothing to do with a description of Jesus,"* "free from interest in the question," and enters into a series of maneuvers that end in special pleading.

Q 7:18–35, ascribed by Kloppenborg to the redactional level, is separated by Vaage into those sayings not ascribing superiority to Jesus over John (7:24b–26, 28a, 33–34), which Vaage hence ascribes to the formative stratum, and those with such an invidious distinction, ascribed to the redactional stratum, which thus "contrasts sharply with the strikingly different characterizations" in the other sayings (p. 110).

We are thus asked to assume that Appendix One: "The Formative Stratum of Q: Agreement and Disagreement with John S. Kloppenborg, *The Formation of Q*" (pp. 107–120), out of purely literary considerations and with complete disinterest in the historical John and Jesus, just by coincidence puts back into the formative stratum precisely those sayings that then Chapter Five: "Memory: John and Jesus: Earliest Recollections (7:24B–26, 28A, 33–34; 9:57–60; 14:26–27)" (pp. 87–102) uses for the presentation of the Cynic John and Jesus. I must admit to being too cynical to take this claim to disinterested objectivity at face value. The joy ride was just too much of a high to be missed.

Vaage does not require that these sayings were spoken by Jesus, but rather that they accurately characterize him:[13]

---

[13] Vaage, "Q^1 and the Historical Jesus," pp. 173–174.

The question is not exactly whether or not we think Jesus ever said one or more of the sayings in 7:33–34, 9:57–60, 14:26–27, nor even whether these sayings in some way would reflect the structure or whatever of his voice. The immediate issue is rather whether we think, after clarifying their sense and rhetorical import, that the characterizations made here of certain kinds of behavior and relation to local society apply to an historical description of this person. Is the sort of style depicted in these sayings reminiscent of that particular man?

Even though sayings elevating John may be old, indeed in some instances such as 7:28a are usually thought to go back to Jesus, the ascription of them to the written formative stratum of Q (though just where remains unknown), rather than simply to oral tradition, is required by Vaage's method. Yet this calls for some special pleading (p. 108):

> It is finally impossible to imagine how the hand responsible for Q's secondary elaboration would ever have willingly included these sayings in its composition, were it not that they already had a place in Q's initial literary presentation.

It is nonetheless not "impossible" for Vaage to imagine how 7:35, where John and Jesus are also thought of as equal spokespersons for Wisdom, was admitted first in the redactional stratum without being previously in the formative stratum: "the focus of attention has shifted instead to another problem, namely, how adequately to describe 'this generation'" (p. 109), so that 7:35 functions "as patent evidence of this generation's clear culpability…merely to underscore the utterly feckless folly of this generation's irresolute regard" (p. 109–110). Why could the redactor not have also been distracted by these or other such concerns sufficiently to have introduced 7:24b–26, 28a, 33–34 from oral tradition, or to have created them, in spite of the equality between John and Jesus they tolerate?

Vaage seems hardly to sense the implicit challenge posed by Ron Cameron's interpretation of 7:18–35 as a *chreia* elaboration, which, if valid,[14] would do the "impossible" of explaining why

---

[14] Cameron's argumentation in "'What Have You Come Out To See?'" is far from convincing, indeed seems contrived, in spite of the disclaimer (p. 50): "Naturally, we should not expect the elaboration pattern to be employed in a wooden way." The *chreia*'s saying is first said to be 7:23, but is then thought to

the redactor came to incorporate such varying materials (namely, in order to fill out the elaboration), without having to postulate that Q 7:24b–26, 28a, 33–34 were present in the formative stratum (p. 186, n. 7):

> Cameron's effort to describe the logic of the redactional composition of Q 7:18–35 as a chreia elaboration presupposes that the various sayings contained within this section are not all of the same tradition-historical provenance.

Yet what Vaage's method calls for is precisely what is lacking in Cameron's presupposition, namely that the sayings in tension to the redactional stratum were not just from a divergent "tradition-historical provenance," somewhere in "free-floating oral tradition," but were already written down in the formative stratum. Were Cameron not such a strong ally in the Cynic interpretation of Q, his method would no doubt have of necessity (and rightly) been rejected as inadequate.

Vaage concedes (p. 187, n. 13): "Where 7:24b–26 and 7:33–34 originally appeared in Q's formative stratum can no longer be determined." Kloppenborg was much more cautious in ascribing individual sayings that were not part of sapiential discourses to the written formative layer if he did not know where they belonged. But Vaage's stratigraphical method, giving exclusive priority to the earliest written layer, requires him to ascribe what he wants to build upon precisely to that layer, though its location in that layer, and the justification for ascribing it (somewhere) to that layer, remain unknown.

Vaage does not explain why the redactor did not omit sayings that stand in tension to his view, but simply asserts (p. 187, n. 13):

> ...it is easier to explain the evident "containment strategies" exercised upon the sayings in 7:24b–26, 33–34 as part of the secondary stratum's general effort to recast the previous version of Q than it is to imagine the Q-redactor self-consciously incorporating the same material into the document only, then, to rectify it immediately.

---

have been shifted to 7:22 when the elaboration took place. The *chreia* that is supposed to have here its elaboration is about Jesus, but part of the elaboration is only about John.

Vaage argued especially that Q 7:33–34 was derived from the formative stratum:[15]

> The fact that 7:33–34 is otherwise unparalleled in early Christian literature makes it difficult to argue that the saying was ever "independent" in the form-critical sense of "free-floating." The most economical solution would be, in my opinion, to recognize in 7:33–34 a saying from Q's formative stratum; one whose current (secondary) placement at the end of 7:18–35 is both propitious and awkward....
>
> Only with great difficulty can the saying in 7:33–34 be seen as a creation of Q^2 (although it now clearly forms part of the redactional composition, 7:18–35). Neither can it easily be argued that 7:33–34 ever existed independently of Q. Thus, its stratigraphical location as a saying likely was originally Q^1 (though the impossibility of discerning where exactly in the earlier document 7:33–34 was placed makes this a somewhat abstract conclusion). This assessment is largely the result of the lack of any other convincing explanation.

The ascription of the material to the formative stratum is just as largely the result of Vaage's logic that requires it to be there, if it is to be considered constitutive of the historical Jesus.

A substantive problem is however neither mentioned nor resolved: The formative stratum makes no reference to John, just as it is not prophetic/apocalyptic in orientation. Vaage is the first to propose locating John there, which he can do only at the cost of arguing that John is not prophetic/apocalyptic, but rather Cynic.[16]

---

[15] Vaage, "The Son of Man Sayings in Q," p. 113.

[16] Vaage, *Galilean Upstarts,* pp. 96–102, argues that John was a Cynic, since Q 7:25 contrasts John with the "soft" life-style against which Cynic polemics are directed. The same saying occurs in the *Gospel of Thomas,* 78. Yet it is here not even certain that the saying, which does not identify the person intended, had John in view. Cameron, "'What Have You Come Out To See?',", pp. 44–45, raises the question: "But is there any reason to think that John is being referred to here in *Thomas?* It is Jesus who is the speaker; conceivably he or his followers are implicitly being characterized.... Yet there is no mention of John in this passage, nor any reference to the figure of a prophet. Is there any reason to imagine that *Gos. Thomas* might attest to an earlier stage of the tradition, which was further interpreted when it came to be elaborated in its Q context?" In the case of Q, Cameron, p. 56, does conclude: "Indeed, the contrast with life in kings'

Once Q 7:34 is put back into the formative stratum, it is ascribed the status of providing "the picture that emerges from the 'depths' of the synoptic tradition at the level of Q's formative stratum" (p. 88). This picture is that "of a bit of a hellion and wanderer on the wild, even illicit, side of things" (pp. 88–89); further (p. 88):

> Jesus is said in 7:34 to have eaten and drunk frequently enough and in sufficient quantity to become notorious for his generous consumption.

Similarly (p. 110):

> It is the fog of a hangover that envelopes the fearless feaster in 7:34. Any scandal provoked by Jesus from the perspective of this saying alone would not be the result of eschatological surprise and wonder,[17] but the direct consequence of his low-life associations.
>
> In 7:33–34, John stands on a par with the omnivorous sot, though at the opposite end of the behavioral spectrum.

Similarly:[18]

> His behavior is notably unorthodox, having neither the serious ascetic demon-possessed demeanor of a prophet like John nor the least trace of a "civilized"—"natural"—way of being. The

---

courts indicates that John's lifestyle was the opposite of such luxury.... i.e., a recognizable Cynic." But even if the use of μαλακός suggests a Cynic affinity for the formulation of the saying, this would not indicate that the person intended by the saying was a Cynic, but only that the person who composed the saying shared such a Cynic usage. And all this tenuous argumentation is considered strong enough to cancel as redactional the evidence of the apocalyptic sayings ascribed to John in Q 3, which themselves show no overlap in vocabulary with Q's own apocalyptic redactional language!

[17] Vaage, "The Son of Man Sayings in Q," 123, is basically correct with regard to the non-eschatological nature of the idiom son of man as a reference to Jesus in Q 7:34 and 9:57–58. See my essay, "The Son of Man in the Sayings Gospel Q," *Tradition und Translation: Zum Problem der interkulturellen Übersetzbarkeit religiöser Phänomene – Festschrift für Carsten Colpe zum 65. Geburtstag*, edd. Christoph Elsas *et al.* (Berlin/New York 1994), pp. 315–335, especially "2. Son of Man Sayings Referring to Jesus' Public Ministry," pp. 319–325.

[18] Vaage, "The Son of Man Sayings in Q," p. 123.

son of man is in this instance simultaneously an eater and drinker to excess, carousing with socially disreputable types, and wont to spend the night wherever it finds him (or he happens to fall down, if what is said of him in 7:34 was true).

There is a logical flaw imbedded in this interpretation: Q 7:33–34 contains quite parallel descriptions of John and Jesus. First a description of each is presented as factual: "came neither eating nor drinking," "came eating and drinking." This is followed by a description in each case introduced with the same quotation formula disassociating the Q community from the view presented, i.e. it is presented as a slur ("and you[19] say"): "He has a demon," "behold, a glutton and a drunkard, a friend of tax collectors and sinners."

In the case of John, Vaage interprets the slur as such: The accusation that one is a demoniac is merely a common slur of the time, and need not be (and never has been) interpreted factually, or hardly even in terms of a psychiatric equivalent, as valid of John. Contrary to the usual treatment of John as a prophet like Elijah (2 Kings 1:8), or the newer comparison of him with the *Bedouin,*[20] Vaage classifies John as a Cynic, though obviously a quite different kind of Cynic than was Jesus (p. 88):

> Both characterizations of John, namely, as demented and ascetic, are paralleled by similar well-known descriptions of the Cynics. The spare diet of many of these ersatz-mongrels, restricting themselves to water and a few mean vegetables, is common knowledge. And Diogenes, the archetypal Cynic, at one point is supposed to have been called by Plato "Socrates gone mad." At the level of Q's formative stratum, John appears as one more of these same "dog-gone" philosophers.

But the slur on Jesus is taken at face value, as historically accurate. Vaage does in fact invite his readers to consider Jesus as such a sot that in a drunken stupor he staggers to the ground and lies there, passed out, until he has slept it off. Is this really a

---

[19] The International Q Project decided (*JBL* 114 [1995], pp. 479–480) that Q here reads in the second person (with Luke) rather than the third person (with Matthew).

[20] Philip Vielhauer, "Tracht und Speise Johannes des Täufers," *Aufsätze zum Neuen Testament,* TB 31 (Munich 1965), pp. 47–54. This essay is omitted from Vaage's discussion and bibliography.

legitimate deconstruction of Jesus' inclusiveness toward tax-collectors and sinners?

Furthermore the second person plural formulation of Q 7:33–34 is hardly the usual formulation in the formative stratum, where the second person plural is normally addressed to the Q people themselves (e.g. Q 6:27: "love your enemies"), whereas the evil environment is hardly addressed, even rhetorically, as present. Rather it reflects the redactional stratum, where the second person plural addresses rhetorically such negative groups as (Q 3:7) "you brood of vipers," and in the immediately preceding context (Q 7:32), where the couplet about the children piping for a dance or wailing for a dirge involves a criticism of "this generation" (Q 7:31), which is addressed in the second person plural as responding neither to the piping nor the wailing. Q 7:33–34 is literarily secondary to Q 7:31–32, in that it provides its interpretation, as Kloppenborg and his predecessors have maintained. Vaage would have to argue that Q 7:33–34, though created by the formative stratum, was then secondarily edited by the redactional stratum. But such a discussion is absent.

There is of course usually in a slur an element of truth that is distorted: John was surely different, eccentric enough to be thought to be abnormal, or, as an invidious caricature, a demoniac. Jesus did transcend the conventional barrier of ostracism between good society and outcasts, did befriend tax collectors and sinners, according to the Synoptic Gospels.[21] And he is presented as accepting invitations to dine with prosperous hosts capable of throwing a sumptuous banquet. The Workers' ("Mission") Instructions also advocate eating and drinking whatever a host provides,[22] who thereby becomes a "son of peace" (Q 10:6).

This assumption of eating a square meal when available does not stand in tension to the Q people's ascetic (lack of) provisions

---

[21] The quite uncertain conclusion of the International Q Project (*JBL* 114 [1995], p. 479) that Luke 7:29–30 was not in Q may, in fact, be in need of revision, since Q 7:29–30 would have suggested already the intended meaning of Q 7:33–34. In any case, this view is well documented in the Synoptic Gospels themselves.

[22] This would be the case irrespective of whether Q 10:7–8 is in Q. Vaage argues (pp. 128–131) that these verses were not in Q, but the International Q Project decided, though with considerable uncertainty (*JBL* 114 [1995], p. 480), to include them. In any case, when one accepts hospitality as indicated in Q 10:6, it is common wisdom that one eats what is set before one. "Beggars are not choosers." "One does not look a gift horse in the mouth."

for the road (Q 10:4), when understood within the context of the document to which it is ascribed, the formative stratum of Q. For taking adequate provisions in a backpack and coin purse would involve hoarding at the expense of beggars one passed by on the side of the road, rather than giving away what one had (Q 6:29–30). It would, from the viewpoint of the formative stratum, involve assuring oneself of the next meal, rather than asking God each day anew for bread (Q 11:3) and leaving its provision up to God (Q 12:22–29), who knows of one's need (Q 12:30); one is to trust God to provide it (Q 11:9–13), while one focuses one's own attention on God's rule (Q 11:2; 12:31). If, as Vaage maintains, Q 7:34 is a creation of the formative stratum, its meaning must have been consistent with that stratum.

It is indeed highly improbable that the formative stratum of Q would not have remembered Jesus in the context of these sayings it ascribed to him. Yet this is what Vaage proposes (p. 88):

> Far from worrying about where his next meal would come from, as 12:22 admonishes not to, Jesus, according to 7:34, apparently ate and drank well and often enough to be suspected of overindulgence. Perhaps for this reason, he saw no cause for concern about these things.

That is to say, Jesus lived so high on the hog that he did not need to worry about food and drink, and so advised the poor and hungry not to worry about subsistence. This might be ascribed to Marie Antoinette, who, on hearing the populace had no bread, is said to have suggested that they could eat cake. But the Q community that remembered Jesus and recorded Q 7:34 obviously did not interpret this saying that way—unless they were very cynical about ascribing the major texts of their formative stratum to such a phony.

This interpretation, so obviously isolated from the bulk of the formative stratum of Q, is strengthened by appeal to another Q text from that stratum (p. 89):

> Lest we think, however, that such a view is only a polemical caricature, an isolated aberration, a false impression, the same distinctive memory tradition surfaces elsewhere in two other peculiar sayings from Q's formative stratum, namely, in the pair of sayings about "discipleship" or following the "son of man" in 9:57–58, 59–60.

According to Q 9:57–58, "the son of man has no place to lay his head." The saying has to do with warning an all-too-eager volunteer. Yet this meaning which the saying had in that Q context is ignored. Instead (pp. 89–90):

> The situation described in 9:58 is that of every tramp and street-person, though other persons in antiquity were also some-times homeless....
>
> This characterization of Jesus, without a place to lay his head, may sound tamer than the statement in 7:34 referring to him as "a glutton and a drunkard, a friend of tax-collectors and sinners."...
>
> Not only prone to rowdiness, Jesus was also remembered in Q's formative stratum as someone decidedly shiftless.

This presentation, originally made at the Jesus Seminar (Toronto, 20 October 1989), was intentionally provocative:[23]

> The man emerges here as neither apocalyptical seer nor sapiential sage. He was rather a bit of an imp, in Socrates' terms a social gad-fly, an irritant on the skin of conventional mores and values, a marginal figure in the provincial context of Galilee and Judea whose style of life and appeal to others was to go a different way than the "normal" one. The "religious" character of this posture is neither primary nor secondary. It is simply part of the cultural setting in which Jesus will have lived and moved.

This playing down of exclusive trust in God's concrete intervention on one's behalf is for Vaage's view of Jesus indispensable, since the Cynics were anything but religious in that sense, in that they at best made occasional allusions to God as nature, using religion indeed only as "part of the cultural setting," but in fact trusting in their own cunning ($\mu\hat{\eta}\tau\iota\varsigma$). The formative stratum of Q is on the other hand specifically religious in the sense that for survival they are dependent on God (Q 11:9–13; 12:22–30), whose reign happening (Q 10:9; 11:2,22; 12:31) is how they made sense of their counter-cultural conduct. The Q people clearly had a different variety of religious experience from that of the Cynics. Modern scholarship, for which religion is to be treated as a part of the cultural setting, should not "modern-

---

[23] Vaage, "Q[1] and the Historical Jesus," p. 175. This is paraphrased in *Galilean Upstarts*, p. 102.

ize" the text by reading back into it what is here but not there. The Cynic hypothesis at times seems no more than a sophisticated instance of "the peril of modernizing Jesus." We continue to paint Jesus in our own image.

Vaage concluded by affirming the historicity of this material he had moved back from the redactional stratum to the formative stratum of Q:[24]

> The Jesus Seminar has enjoyed a certain notoriety to dat[e]. If in our imagination of the historical Jesus we choose to move in the direction indicated by this set of sayings from Q (7:33–34; 9:57–58, 59–60; 14:26–27) such enjoyment will likely increase. Certain persons may see red. I recommend that we meet their challenge by voting the same color in every instance.

The presentation achieved its objective of notoriety in the local press,[25] though, surprisingly enough, somewhat less interest in the Jesus Seminar itself, which published Q 7:33–34 in gray (probably not authentic), Q 9:58,60 in pink (probably authentic), Q 14:26 in pink and Q 14:27 in black (not authentic).[26] If even the Jesus Seminar is this negative regarding Q 7:34, the historical Jesus as "hellion," "sot," "gad-fly," "imp" has presumably already disappeared from the pages of history.

A basic problem with Vaage's form of presentation is that it intermingles two distinct dimensions: There is on the one hand the offensively abnormal marginality of the Jesus movement, calling upon all "haves" to share fully with the "have-nots" to the extent of self-impoverishment, a call that society rejects, indeed resents and seeks to discredit with lame slurs. And, on the other hand, there is a quite distinct dimension, namely that caricature itself, which Vaage cannot help but accentuate for its PR value, and for the shocked responses which he relishes. That can indeed

---

[24] Vaage, "Q[1] and the Historical Jesus," p. 175.

[25] The write-up by a theology student Barry Henaut in the local paper, the *Globe* of 19 October, 1989, featured Vaage's up-coming presentation. The newspaper article was entitled "Was Jesus a 'party animal'?" It also picked up the idiom "social gadfly" and the sentence "Jesus, beyond being a bit raucous, appears now also shiftless," later published in "The Son of Man Sayings in Q," p. 175.

[26] Robert W. Funk, Roy W. Hoover, and the Jesus Seminar, *The Five Gospels: The Search for the Authentic Words of Jesus* (New York 1993).

be lots of fun (p. 106: like the Cynics, the Galilean upstarts thus achieved "a higher form of happiness,...the uncommon pleasures of unsettling thought and action"). This is all the more so, the stuffier and more suffocating the pious atmosphere has become. A grim reaction in fact discredits itself! But the more serious task of identifying Jesus, and communicating the kind of person he really was to an intelligent and involved lay public (the original goal of the Jesus Seminar), is actually impeded by Vaage's not only distractingly offensive[27] but also unhistorical portrayal of Jesus as an alcoholic. For the initial hermeneutical objective (Vaage's own point of departure was Paul Ricoeur) has been replaced by a deconstructionist agenda whose (anti)theological bias is the only way to explain the muddling of an otherwise sophisticated methodology. J. Edgar Hoover carried out extensive research to seek to pin something on Martin Luther King, so as to be able to discredit the civil rights movement that King symbolized. He only succeeded in discrediting the FBI.

Yet all this alcoholism is hardly the meaning of the formative stratum of Q, which Vaage maintains his book is elucidating. That layer contained such things as the Sermon (Q 6:20–49), the Workers' ("Mission") Instructions (Q 10:3–11, 16), the Prayer (Q 11:2–4, 9–13), The Ravens and Wild Flowers (Q12:22–31). Did readers of this formative stratum think the speaker was "prone to rowdiness,...someone decidedly shiftless?" Did they not rather think that, by hearing and doing what the person Vaage characterizes as a "sot" etc. said, they would be building upon a solid foundation (Q 6:47–49)? It may well be that to the establishment of that day Jesus came across with Cynic-like, or, more generally, ascetic-like marginality and offensiveness. But the Q community itself saw all this more from the inside, indeed shared it and emulated it. Of course, Vaage concedes this point (p. 102): "For the persons whom Q represents, no one could have embodied better their own social practice." This may well be true of

---

[27] Rudolf Bultmann's proposal to demythologize the kerygma was largely motivated by the recognition that post-Enlightenment people were often not able to work their way through its jungle of mythological conceptualizations to the existential "offense of the cross," but took offense at the assumption they should believe literally this mythology and thus were turned off even before they got to the substance of the matter, where an existential decision was called for. Vaage's attention-grabbing rhetoric, with its excessive formulations (does he himself take them literally?), functions in a similar way to the kerygma's mythological rhetoric.

their austerity and marginality, but not of the caricature they present as a slur and Vaage as historical fact. What Vaage is in fact doing, in spite of his archeological method, is presenting Jesus in isolation from the formative stratum of Q to which he appeals.

Vaage presents himself as using a rigorously empirical, positivistic, inductive, objective, focused approach to the language of Q 7:34 and the saying cited in Q 9:58:[28]

> When I speak about the linguistical peculiarity of a saying, I have in mind the extant Greek text of Q. It is the wording of a given unit of this document that is perceived to be striking and strange. After noting such a fact, the question then will be: What is the historiographical significance or worth of odd talk? Is it a clue to anything or simply the combination of coincidence and modern distance from an ancient tongue?

For Vaage, it has immense historiographical significance, for it turns out to be, in fact if not in theory, his basic criterion for authenticity:[29]

> In examining the origins of a movement like early Christianity where we are wont to imagine the figure of Jesus, what place do we give to peculiar phenomena, whether linguistical or otherwise? Are they always wiggles, aberrations, slight deviations of basic patterns? Or are they the manifestation of a certain particularity within historical experience, appearances of the other side to every set of norms?...
>
> In what follows, I would argue that we favour what is peculiar over what is common, insofar as what is common forms just as easily part of the evangelists' and their predecessors' experience as it does that of Jesus. It would be quite impossible, therefore, to establish why x must or probably recalls [sic] the historical Jesus, for the same could be said of everyone else as well. Regarding, however, what is peculiar, precisely because it is peculiar, it cannot be attributed to everyone and thus must be identified with someone, who could be

---

[28] Vaage, "Q¹ and the Historical Jesus," p. 163. The central main section of this paper, pp. 163–173, is presented in revised form in *Galilean Upstarts*, pp. 87–95.

[29] Vaage, "Q¹ and the Historical Jesus," pp. 160–161.

Jesus, if it proves less likely that what is said or depicted is the later or simultaneous perspective of others.

Now it is conceivable that this very peculiar material is the oldest and most authentic material in Q, especially if one postulated it derives from oral tradition behind the formative stratum that went as far back as the original followers of Jesus. Yet Vaage has already expressed a *caveat* about moving from concrete written sources to oral tradition (pp. 6–7):

> Regarding once more the tradition of New Testament scholarship, it is important to underscore the documentary bias of this book over against certain previous habits of historical description that have dominated scholarly work in the area. I have in mind specifically the analytical practices of form-criticism and tradition-history, both of which purport to be able to say something about the shape and transmission of early Christian materials at an "oral" stage of circulation before the texts at our disposal were first written down and subsequently transformed redactionally as early Christian literature. Unlike scholars who read the New Testament in this fashion, I do not presume in this book to know anything "beyond" or "behind" the text of Q's formative stratum: neither who the historical Jesus was or what he might have said,...

Indeed, in this specific instance he has been very explicit:[30] "Neither can it easily be argued that 7:33–34 ever existed independently of Q." In that case, the editor of the formative stratum who composed this pair of sayings must have meant by them what he took the formative stratum as such to be presenting as Jesus. It is no longer possible to conceive of them, as Vaage seems in theory to reject but in fact to do, as very primitive authentic traditions that diverge not only from our common view of Jesus, but also from that of the Gospels, and even from the formative stratum of Q—which however was the first to compose them!

Vaage seems to have come full circle. His archaeological model was explicitly designed as a corrective to what he designates the "growth and aggregation" method he associates primarily with Heinz Schürmann, whereby one somehow knows given sayings to be oldest tradition, and then postulates, from this

---

[30] Vaage, "The Son of Man Sayings in Q," p. 113, cited above.

invisible bottom of the tell, the successive layers added to it, until this mole-like action finally surfaces into the clear air and sunlight of the top of the tell as one's predetermined "historical Jesus." Yet Vaage himself says:[31]

> A stratigraphical analysis consistently applied cannot switch in mid-stream to a discourse based on metaphors of growth and aggregation.

The impression of Jesus one gets from the formative stratum of Q is no doubt as near to the "historical Jesus" as we can hope to get, in which regard Vaage is correct (p. 178, n. 1):

> I confess that I believe that the memory of Q's formative stratum is at least as reliable a source of information as any of the other early Christian textual traditions typically employed for the purposes of this distinctly modern (christological) undertaking.

But that historical Jesus of the formative stratum of Q was not the alcoholic Vaage presents. For serious people today, the Jesus of the formative stratum comes across less as a dismaying anti-clerical shock than as a radical human challenge.

3. The Cynical Disciples

Chapter One is entitled: "Ethos: 'Like Sheep among Wolves': The 'Mission' Instructions (10:3–6, 9–11, 16)." Putting "mission" in quotation marks not only warns that we are not to interpret the "mission" with the connotations that "foreign missions" have given that term in modern usage, but also suggests that one should question whether the instructions were intended for a "preaching mission" at all (p. 25):

> But the fact that money, a bag, footwear, and a staff were regularly taken on ancient trips does not mean that, therefore, not taking them reveals a completely new mode of travel. For not only travelers used these things. Hoffmann is still influenced by the unnecessary assumption that the persons whom Q represents were on a preaching mission.

---

[31] Vaage, "The Son of Man Sayings in Q," p. 113.

In fact Vaage seems to have intellectualized the whole concept of itinerancy (p. 185, n. 4):

> By "subversive wisdom," I mean to recall what I refer to in the title of my doctoral dissertation as an "itinerant intelligence."... The term "itinerant" was supposed to pick up and play off of [Gerd] Theissen's earliest proposal of "itinerant radicalism" (*Wanderradikalismus*) as the original *Sitz im Leben* of much of the traditional material in Q. Theissen's proposal has subsequently been subjected to a number of critiques, especially regarding the idea of "itinerants." I remain interested, nonetheless, in the possibility of describing Q's formative stratum as the discourse of an alternate "type" of "intelligence" characterized by its "itinerant" (or, in postmodern speak, disseminating) logic, comparable, e.g., to the account of *metis* or *Cunning Intelligence in Greek Culture and Society* by Détienne and Vernant.

Chapter Two is entitled: "Ethics. 'Love Your Enemies.' Strategies of Resistance (6:27–35)." The nomenclature may already be indicative: What is often designated as "non-retaliation" is now envisaged as "Strategies of Resistance." This chapter on ethics is limited to Q 6:27–35. Vaage explains why this text was selected (p. 158, n. 2):

> ...it appeared the most likely to resist accommodation to the characterization of the Q people advanced in the preceding chapter and thus a good test case, insofar as the usual interpretations of "love your enemies" did not seem to be especially compatible with my description of these persons.

Over against "the usual interpretation," Vaage launches upon a *tour de force* to show that the ethics of Q 6:27–35 are intended "not to register in practice merely an open invitation to repeated abuse by others and ultimately self-destruction" (pp. 40–41):

> I assume that the moral maxims gathered together in 6:27–35 were not initially proposed and subsequently appropriated by their first adherents simply to make life more miserable but, instead, to help these persons out by suggesting a better way of dealing with the various difficulties and displeasures facing them in life. In this regard, the language of the text has meaning only if and when it worked in practice. To state Theissen's question another way: What made the imperative to "love your enemies"

and the related recommendations in 6:27–35 more than just "lousy" advice?...

Certainly, the paradoxical effect felt for centuries by commentators on this passage of the combination in it of "love" and "enemies" should alert us to the possibility that a certain rhetorical craft—and craftiness—is here expressed rather than self-evidently a high "altruistic" moral ideal.

Thus Vaage's task becomes to make pragmatic sense of this "test case" as a non-altruistic text (p. 41):

What is the logic of this speech? How do its different parts fit together? What kind of concrete strategy is here developed? How persuasive is it as an ethical posture? Are the claims it makes believable, both those implied and those explicit? What are the odds that it would work, if put into practice? What "objective conditions" must be in place for it to have a chance to succeed?

Vaage rejects (p. 42) ascribing love of enemies to "the purity of... Jesus' concern for the welfare of the enemy." One is advised to love one's enemies "not for reasons of intrinsic merit, but in the hope that some other good might thereby be achieved," to obtain "specific benefits" such as "liberation" from "a simmering state of unresolved hostility and sporadic military repression, with personal enmity and the permanent threat of abuse as constant problems." One's goal was to attain "the highest degree possible of bodily happiness, to experience in the fullest available form the reign of blessedness, to attain a mode of existence in which the need constantly to defend oneself could be felt at last to have been overcome," "getting 'one up' on surrounding evil and misfortune." On this reading, love of enemies was indeed very self-centered!

The injunction "love your enemies" is (p. 43) "the secondary formulation: an effort to conceptualize in a more general way the diverse field of actions defined by the individual imperatives in 6:28–30." It was (p. 159, n. 16) "created by the editor of Q 6:27–35 in order to extend the significance of a number of peculiar acts to other situations as well." The nigh-universal ascription of this "oxymoron" (p. 43) of love of enemies to the historical Jesus is thus replaced by the ascription of it to the editor of the formative stratum of Q.

The non-altruistic point of the injunction to love one's enemies is clarified as a Cynic-like manipulative technique to evade hardship from one's enemies (p. 48):

> The Cynic parallels to 6:27–28 help us to appreciate the "agonistic" quality of these sayings. We are not here in the presence of an altruistic ethic of "selflessness" or even notable concern for the welfare of the other. Indeed, quite the opposite. The counsel to "love your enemies" and to "pray for those who revile you" belongs in Q, as also in the different statements by Diogenes, Epictetus, and Bion cited above, to the formation and exercise of a certain social character. One of its more salient features was precisely this ability to handle hostility with notable restraint and calculated inversion.

The same lack of altruism and focus on one's own needs is the Cynic context in which "turning the other cheek" (Q 6:29–30) is interpreted (p. 50):

> Rather, at stake is the procurement of the maximum available good for those who otherwise stand in danger of personal assault and battery as well as uninvited theft. The imperatives in 6:29—and 6:30, as we soon shall see—were originally prudential considerations provided for persons whose lives must wend their way through contexts of diverse insecurity. To turn the other cheek and give up both cloak and tunic were hardly expressions of "universal love," but just "smart moves" under the circumstances.

What seems to have been left out of consideration is the interpretation imbedded in the formative stratum of Q. For what is most problematic in this presentation is not the Cynic parallels to Q 6:27–35 that Vaage has presented. Rather it is the focus of attention on the suggestions Cynic texts contain for interpreting such deprivation: The self-serving cunning typical of Cynics for evading often violent social disapproval. This Cynic interpretation replaces the formative stratum of Q itself for interpreting Q 6:27–35, where sense is made of the Q people's counter-cultural conduct by appeal to trust in God for survival (Q 11:9–13; 12:22–30), since his reign is really happening (Q 10:9; 11:2; 12:31).

This dominant theological expression of the formative stratum, βασιλεία τοῦ θεοῦ (kingdom of God, God's reign or rule), is discussed in Chapter Three: "Ideology: 'The Kingdom of God Has Arrived': Symbolic Subversion (6:20B; 10:9; 11:2, 20; 12:31; 13:18–21)." This idiom for "symbolic subversion" is defined (p. 56) as "a form of social dissent":

> The Q people endeavored to imagine and construct an alternate reality to the dominant social institutions of their immediate context and its prevalent moral values.

Such talk was "merely a discursive instrument of ongoing socio-political destabilization." That is to say, the formative stratum of Q liked to use a political term ("kingdom") with a subversive, anti-establishment slant ("of God") to protest against and destabilize the given political and social establishment. This may well have been one effect of their talk and largely responsible for the political opposition they aroused. But did they mean no more than such a subversive manipulation of language for destabilizing purposes?

They apparently actually trusted in a God whom they thought knew them and cared to intervene in their actual lived experience. This becomes clearest when the formative stratum uses the coming of the kingdom of God to explain the healing of the sick (Q 10:9—Vaage prefers, p. 35 and *passim*, to translate "treat the weak"). There is a similar passage ascribed by Kloppenborg to the redactional stratum, but by Vaage to the formative stratum, involving a saying that has almost universally been ascribed to the historical Jesus, e.g. in the following comment by Robert W. Funk:[32]

> When asked for evidence that the creator's control of creation was being renewed, he referred to the defeat of demonic powers:
>> But if by God's finger I drive out demons, then for you God's imperial rule has arrived. —Luke 11:20

Vaage presents this saying as a close parallel to Q 10:9 (p. 35):

> Indeed, beyond the biblical pastiche in 7:22 that uses Isaianic phrases of physical recovery to answer affirmatively the christological inquiry of John whether or not Jesus is "the coming one,"

---

[32] Robert W. Funk, "The Gospel of Jesus and the Jesus of the Gospels: A celebration of *The Five Gospels*," *The Fourth R* 6,6 (1993), pp. 3–10, here p. 4.

there are only two "other" accounts of actual "miracle-working" in the document, namely, 7:1–10 and 11:14–20. It is noteworthy, therefore, that in the second of these passages (11:14–20) after the demon-possessed mute has been healed and the ensuing debate over "how'd he do that" draws to a close, the concluding statement is again that "the kingdom of God has appeared to you." The logical sequence is identical to that of 10:9.

But Q 10:9 is then interpreted by Vaage as the Cynic (or Stoic) bliss in living according to nature (p. 36):

> The kingdom of God in 10:9b explains the newly won ability dispensed by the Q people in 10:9a to enjoy freedom from debilitating woe in the midst of otherwise difficult circumstances, much as the Cynics promised *eudaimonia* to those who would join them in following the rule of "nature."

Some such interpretation, dispensing with God's actual intervention, may be all we today, like the ancient Cynics, can make of such traditions. But this is not even a demythologization of the text, but rather what Bultmann sought to replace—Nineteenth Century liberalism's elimination of the miraculous:[33]

> If we may say schematically that during the epoch of critical research the mythology of the New Testament was simply *eliminated*, the task today–also to speak schematically–is to *interpret* New Testament mythology....
> For the epoch of the older "liberal" theology, it is characteristic that mythological representations are simply eliminated as time conditioned and inessential while the great basic religious and moral ideas are explained to be essential. One thus distinguishes between husk and kernel.

In any case, Vaage's cynical interpretation cannot be consistently carried through the formative stratum of Q: Here Jesus is presented as calling upon his followers to pray a prayer he taught them, beginning "Father." This masculine form of address was not heard as male chauvinism, nor was God thus addressed understood as a threatening paternalistic figure. Rather the term

---

[33] Rudolf Bultmann, *New Testament and Mythology and Other Basic Writings*, ed. Schubert M. Ogden (Philadelphia 1984), p. 12.

was intended to suggest the protective, caring role of an ideal parent. This is made explicit in the commentary on the Prayer that follows it directly (Q 11:9–13): The initial call to pray (Q 11:2a) is here expanded—ask, seek, knock—and the promise of a positive response is appended: receive, find, be admitted. For a human parent will not give a snake when asked for a fish, or a stone when asked for a loaf of bread. Even more so the heavenly Father will give good things to those who ask. Not even a dirt-cheap sparrow falls without God being concerned, whereas you are worth much more (Q 12:6–7). Do not be anxious, since the God who feeds the ravens and clothes the wild flowers will feed and clothe you (Q 12:22–28). Your Father knows your needs before you ask (Q 12:30). So devote your attention to his rule, and your needs will be taken care of for you (Q 12:31). This, rather than Vaage's Cynic/cynical interpretation, is also the way Robert W. Funk interprets Jesus:[34]

> He advises those around him not to fret about food and cloth-ing. His Father looks after the sparrows, he says, and they are a dime a dozen. With typical hyperbole, he insists that God counts the hairs on human heads. Perhaps that is the reason Je-sus takes no thought for shelter...

This explicit interpretation of the practice of the Q communi-ty as turning from self-interest is quite the reverse of the "cunning," the "prudential considerations," the "craftiness," the "specific benefits," the "'smart moves' under the circumstances," the "ability to handle hostility with notable restraint and calculat-ed inversion," which Vaage derives from the Cynics and applies to the formative stratum of Q in replacement for the text's own interpretive sayings. Hence this deconstruction of the stated pur-pose of the formative stratum of Q has not been worked out in methodologically intelligible and defensible form. One must con-clude: It is less the Cynic parallels to selected texts in the formative stratum of Q than their cynical interpretation that forms a Procrustean bed into which the Q movement is forced.

---

[34] Funk, "The Gospel of Jesus and the Jesus of the Gospels," p. 5.

DIE RHETORISCHE FUNKTION
DER FASTENWARNUNG MK 2,20

Wolfgang Schenk
(Saarbrücken, Deutschland)

Die Frage, wie Mk 2,20 in seinem Zusammenhang zu verstehen sei, hat die Ausleger wenig beschäftigt.[1] Der herrschenden Traditionsgeschichte schien es in ihrem evolutionistischen Modell als ausgemacht, daß hier eine nachträgliche Einschaltung vorliege, die ein konzessives Fastengebot für ein (wöchentliches oder jährliches) Karfreitagsfasten eingebracht habe.[2] So hat wohl

---

[1] Tjitze habe ich immer wegen seiner Spürnase für mögliche und unmögliche Herrenworte vor, während und nach meiner, von ihm iniziierten Gastprofessur aus Anlaß des hundertjährigen Jubiläums der "Vrije Universiteit" (1979), bewundert. Auf den Spuren von Tatians βιβλίον προβλημάτων hat er selbst solche geschaffen. Seine immer wieder neu aufgenommene Frage nach Sinn und Funktion schwieriger Sentenzen war mir oft Anlaß, mich nicht mit eingebürgerten Antworten zufrieden zu geben, wenn begründeter Anlaß für Zweifel bestand.

[2] So (vom 19. Jh. her) in den Kommentaren gängig (H. J. Holtzmann, HC 1 [Tübingen 1901³], 122–123; J. Wellhausen, *Das Evangelium Marci* [Berlin 1909²], 18–19; J. Weiß/W. Bousset, SNT 1 [Göttingen 1917³ 1929⁴], 95–96; F. Hauck, ThHK 2 [Leipzig 1931], 38; E. Klostermann, HNT 3 [Tübingen 1936³], 27–28; E. Lohmeyer, KEK 2 [Göttingen 1937, 1967⁸], 59–60; E. Hirsch, *Frühgeschichte des Evangeliums* I: Das Werden des MkEv [Tübingen 1941] 12–14; J. Schmid, RNT 2 [Regensburg 1958⁵], 66–67; C. E. B. Cranfield, CGTC [Cambridge 1959, 1977⁶], 110–111; D. E. Nineham, PNTC [Harmondsworth 1963, 1977¹⁰], 102–103; E. Haenchen, *Der Weg Jesu* [Berlin 1966, 1968²], 118–119; E. Schweizer, NTD 2 [Göttingen 1967], 37–38; R. Pesch, HThK 2 [Freiburg 1976], 174–176; W. Grundmann, ThHK 2 [Berlin 1977⁶], 85–87; J. Gnilka, EKK 2 [Einsiedeln 1978], 112–115; W. Schmithals, ÖTK 2 [Gütersloh 1979, 1986²], 179–180; J. Ernst, RNT 2 [Regensburg 1981], 99; D. Lührmann, HNT 3 [Tübingen 1987], 63), weil verstärkt durch die synoptischen Formgeschichte: A. Jülicher, *Die Gleichnisreden Jesu* II (Tübingen 1910²), 178–188; M. Dibelius, *Die urchristliche Überlieferung von Johannes dem Täufer*, FRLANT 15 (Göttingen 1911), 41; ders., *Die Formgeschichte des Evangeliums*, (Tübingen 1933²), 62–63; R. Bultmann, *Die Geschichte der synoptischen Tradition*, FRLANT 29 (Göttingen 1931²), 17f.

Vgl. u.a. auch: H.-W. Kuhn, *Ältere Sammlungen im MkEv*, StUNT 8 (Göttingen 1971) 62–63; K. Berger, *Die Gesetzesauslegung Jesu* I, WMANT 40

(Neukirchen 1972) 576–578; G. Schille, *Offen für alle Menschen*: Redaktionsgeschichtliche Beobachtungen zur Theologie des MkEv, AVTR 61 (Berlin
1973), 28–32; J. B. Muddiman, "Jesus and Fasting: Mk 2,28–22," in: *Jésus aux
origines de la Christologie*, J. Dupont (hg.), BEThL 40 (Gembloux 1975), 283–301
(von Jesus selbst angeordnetes Fasten); H.-J. Klauck, *Allegorie und Allegorese in
synoptischen Gleichnistexten*, NTA 15 (Münster 1978), 160–166; W. Stegemann,
"Von Kritik zur Feindschaft: Eine Auslegung von Mk 2,1–3,6," in: W.
Schottroff/Ders. (hg.), *Der Gott der kleinen Leute* II (München 1979²), 39–57, hier
46–47; P. J. Maartens, "Mk 2,18–22: An Exercise in Theoretically-founded
Exegesis," *Scriptura (Journal of Biblical Studies)* 2 (1980), 1–54; ders.,
"Interpretation and Meaning in a Conflict Parable. A Study of Semiotic
Relations in Mk 2,18–22," *LingBibl* 67 (1992), 61–82, bes. 67–68; J. Zmijewski,
s.v., *EWNT* II (1981), 1144–1147; J. Kiilunen, *Die Vollmacht im Widerstreit:
Untersuchungen zum Werdegang von Mk 2,1–3,6*, AASF 40 (Helsinki 1985), 80–81;
W. Stenger, "Die Grundlegung des Evangeliums von Jesus Christus: Zur
kompositionellen Struktur des MkEv," *LingBibl* 61 (1988), 7–56, hier 45–46 (=
ders., *Strukturale Beobachtungen zum NT*, NTTS 12 [Leiden 1990], 1–38, hier 30–
31); W. Weiss, *Eine neue Lehre in Vollmacht: Die Streit- und Schulgespräche des
MkEv*, BZNW 52 (Berlin 1989), 97–99; D. Correns, *Taʿanijot: Text, Übersetzung
und Erklärung*, Mischna II/7 (Berlin 1989), 10–11; J. Sauer, *Rückkehr und
Vollendung des Heils: Eine Untersuchung zum Problem der "ethischen Radikalismen" des
historischen Jesus* (Regensburg 1991), 350–353, hier 797–803; B. van Iersel,
"Concentric Structures in Mk 1,14–3,35(4,1)," *BiblInt* 3 (1995) 75–98, der das
schließlich von 2,20 her auch noch auf 2,21f überträgt: "Perhaps the loss of the
wine is a metaphor for the way the bridegroom is taken away (2,20), for his
stand on this and related matters is, in the first instance, his undoing" (96). Das
dabei verfolgte Anliegen der Kohärenz ist beachtlich, doch dürfte die Lösung
eher in umgekehrter Richtung zu vollziehen sein.

Das hängt auch (wie besonders die letzten Beispiele zeigen) damit
zusammen, daß man für Mk eine wie auch immer bestimmte "*theologia crucis*"
voraussetzte und hier dann eine erste "Leidensweissagung" fand (wiewohl es bei
Mk sonst nirgends isolierte "Leidensweissagungen" gibt: W.S., Art. "Leidensge-
schichte Jesu," *TRE* 20 [1990], 714–721), so daß die Anwendung dieser
Kategorie auf seinen Text nur irreführend sein kann. Daß man unter der
Voraussetzung eines Todesbezuges auch zu ganz anderen Rückschlüssen
kommen kann, demonstriert J. C. O'Neill, "The Source of the Parables of the
Bridegroom and the Wicked Husbandmen," *JThS* 39 (1988), 485–489 (W.S.
IZBG 36:1044), der (unter Voraussetzung einer Priorität des mt Wortlauts und
der entsprechenden Auslassung bei Mk [D W 28 1424 pc; *b i q* bo^ms] bzw. mt
mit Tatian, M*, 34 "und *er* sagt zu ihnen") den Täufer Johannes als Autor für die
Antwort Mk 2,19f auf die Frage seiner Schüler erweisen will.

Eine nicht unbeträchliche Rolle spielt bei dieser Dekomposition auch das Postulat einer vor-mk "Sammlung" (für "Stoffgruppen" inauguriert von C. Weizäcker, *Das apostolische Zeitalter* [Tübingen 1902], 400; dann über J. Weiß, *Das älteste Evangelium* [Göttingen 1903], 363–365 und G. Heinrici, *Der literarische Charakter der ntl. Schriften* [Berlin 1908], 39 an die "Formgeschichtler" vermittelt, wie W. Schmithals, "J. Weiß als Wegbereiter der Formgeschichte," *ZThK* 80 [1983], 389–410, spez. 396.406.409 gezeigt hat): M. Albertz, *Die synoptischen Streitgespräche* (Berlin 1921), 5–32; Kuhn, *Sammlungen*, 53–98; W. Thissen, *Erzählung der Befreiung: Eine exegetische Untersuchung zu Mk 2,1–3,6*, fzb 21 (Würzburg 1976), 192–223; M. J. Cook, *Mk's Treatment of the Jewish Leaders*, NovT.Supp 51 (Leiden 1978), 34–51; A. Hultgren, *Jesus and his Adversaries* (Minneapolis 1979), 151–174; vgl. als Nachzügler auch Sauer, *Rückkehr*, 350–351. Daß angeblich prä-mk "Sammlungen," die von gleichartigen "Gattungen" (Gleichnisse, Wundergeschichten, Streitgespräche) her postuliert werden, einen Gipfel des Deduktivismus der synoptischen Formgeschichte darstellen (da sie ja in den "Gattungen" die determinierende Kraftquelle ihrer Evolution der "Tradition" sah; vgl. Dibelius, *Formgeschichte*, 219–234), ist als unbrauchbares, ja absurdes Postulat spätestens seit der Annahme einer Vorlage "Offenbarungs-reden" aus gleichartigem Material für 1Joh (aber analog auch für JohEv) offenkundig: Bultmann (analog H. Braun) fand in 32 der 195 Verse des 1Joh eine aus Antithesen bestehende "Offenbarungsquelle," zu der schon E. Haenchen ("Neue Literatur zu den Johannesbriefen," in: ders., *Die Bibel und wir* [Tübingen 1968], 235–311 = *ThR* 1960) m.R. anmerkte: "Man lese einmal ein aus lauter Antithesen bestehendes längeres Stück laut, und man wird es unerträglich finden... Keine Hausfrau wird einen Kuchen backen wollen, der aus lauter Rosinen besteht" (245–246). Seit dem literaturwissenschaftlichen Paradigmenwechsel (N. Petersen, *Literary Criticism for NT Critics*, GBS.NTS [Philadelphia 1978] 11–20) wird darum für Mk 2,1–3,6 m.R. (übrigens schon von Dibelius, *Formgeschichte*, 220) eine prä-mk "Sammlung" als unbegründet abgewiesen: J. Dewey, *Mk in Public Debate: Literary Technique, Concentric Struc-ture, and Theology in Mk 2,1–3,6*, SBL.DS 48 (Chico [California] 1980) passim; Kiilunen, *Vollmacht*, 1–20; W.Weiss, *Lehre*, 20–25; S. H. Smith, "The Role of Jesus' Opponents in the Markan Drama," *NTS* 35 (1989), 161–182, spez. 164.

Skepsis gegen die Bestimmung als Fasten-Ätiologie hat sich immer wieder gemeldet: H.-J. Ebeling, "Die Fastenfrage (Mk 2,18–22)," *ThStK* 108 (1937/8), 387–396 wollte es auf die Abwesenheit während der "messianischen Wehen" beziehen (dgg. J. Roloff, *Das Kerygma und der irdische Jesus* [Göttingen 1970, 1973²], 225); V. Taylor, *The Gospel According to St. Mark* (London 1952, 1966² = 1977), 211–212; K. T. Schäfer, ""Und dann werden sie fasten, an jenem Tag" (Mk 2,20)," in: *Synoptische Studien für A. Wikenhauser* (München 1953) 124–147; Roloff, *Kerygma*, 229–234, spez. 231: "Wäre Mk 2,20 eine Fastenregel, so würde sie zu beidem in Widerspruch stehen: denn erstens würde hier, entgegen Mt

schon Lk den mk Text verstanden oder aber wohl eher umge-
deutet:

(a) Der Einschnitt Lk 5,36 hat die bei Mk verbundenen
Segmente der Argumentation voneinander abgesetzt;
(b) auch Lk 5,33 macht einen klaren Einschnitt;
(c) ein lk Fastengebot Lk 5,33 ist von 2,37 her in seinem
Gesamtkonzept sinnvoll (wie es andererseits bei Mk völlig un-
vorbereitet wäre);
(d) die in der Apg (13,2f; 14,23; 27,9) fortgesetzten
Fastenaussagen belegen ein solches Konzept (das davon bestimmt ist, daß das Christentum der wahre Pharisäismus sei).

Doch weder eine für Mk gemutmaßte Vorgeschichte noch die
früheste Rezeption in der Nachgeschichte bei Lk können für die
Bestimmung des mk Aussagegehalts einen eindeutigen Aufschluß
geben. Wie sehr man jedes Textsegment in seinem Kotext analysieren muß (was rezeptionstheoretisch ohnehin selbstverständ
lich ist),[3] zeigt auch die Rezeption in ThomEv 104.[4]

6,16ff, das Fasten aus der *Trauer* über das Hinweggenommensein des
Bräutigams begründet, zweitens aber würde, wenn der Tag des Hinweg-
genommenseins auf einen *bestimmten Wochentag*, nämlich den Freitag zu deuten
wäre, hier entgegen Did 8,1 nur *ein* wöchentlicher Fasttag vorausgesetzt sein,"
daher 233: nur "metaphorischer Ausdruck für Trauern"; Thissen, *Befreiung*, 165–
166 (gleichzeitige Funktion einer Abgrenzung "von enthusiastischem
Eschatologismus"). Die von ihnen vorgeschlagenen Alternativen haben aber
m.R. keine Überzeugung, sondern Widerspruch gefunden (vgl. Sauer, *Rückkehr*,
800.802f.809). Dennoch bleiben die ihre Skepsis begründenden Beobachtungen
weiterhin wichtig.
[3] G. Grimm, *Rezeptionsgeschichte: Grundlegung einer Theorie*, UTB 691 (München
1977) 31–34; N. Groeben, *Rezeptionsforschung als empirische Literaturwissenschaft*,
ELW 1 (Tübingen 1980) 133–138.
[4] "Wenn der Bräutigam aus der Kammer kommt, dann läßt er sie fasten und
beten." Die Deutung, die der wahre Gnostiker daraus entnehmen soll, ergibt
sich deutlich daraus, daß in der Textabfolge Spruch 6 + 14 vorausgehen, wo
Fasten + Beten (und Almosengeben) als Lüge und Sünde bestimmt wurde: "Der
wahre Gnostiker wird die Brautkammer nicht mehr verlassen. Er hat die
angestrebte Einheit erreicht (ThomEv 106)": Klauck, *Allegorie*, 169 mit W.
Schrage, *Das Verhältnis des ThomEv zur synoptischen Tradition und zur koptischen
Evangelienüberlieferung*, BZNW 29 (Berlin 1964) 193; E. Haenchen, "Die
Anthropologie des ThomEv.," in: *NT und christliche Existenz*, FS H. Braun
(Tübingen 1973), 207–227, spez. 212–215.

1. Die Logik der Zeitbestimmungen

Da es eine Aufgabe der elementaren Aussagenlogik ist, die Wahrheitsbedingungen für komplexe Sätze festzulegen, die logische Konstanten *(nicht, und, oder* u.a.) enthalten, so ist es die Aufgabe der philosophischen Logik der Zeit, diejenigen Synsemantika zu analysieren, die Zeitverhältnisse beschreiben. Es geht (wie bei unserer Frage) um temporale Relativa, die Ordnung zwischen den Ereignissen herstellen.[5] Die Syntax dieser Relation ist es, die in unserem Zusammenhang in Frage steht: "Doch-Fasten-(Sollen?)" versus "Nicht-Fasten-Können"? Geht es um eine Konzession oder um eine Warnung?

1.1 Zunächst einmal ist zu fragen, ob schon in der *propositio* der rhetorischen Frage Mk 2,19b eine Zeitbestimmung gemacht wird: In den Kommentaren wird das eingeschobene Relativ-Syntagma ἐν ᾧ (bei Mk nur hier verwendet) meist diskussionslos selbstverständlich temporal aufgelöst: "während." Doch zunächst bezieht sich das Relativpronomen auf das voranstehende Nomen τοῦ νυμφῶνος ("Hochzeitssaal")[6] zurück und ist demnach lokal zu verstehen, womit ein typisch mk *Doppelausdruck* mit explikativem Relativum gebildet wird.[7] Der Doppelausdruck besteht aber nicht zwischen dem Relativ-Syntagma (ἐν ᾧ) und dem nachfolgenden Präpositional-Syntagma (ὁ νυμφίος μετ᾽ αὐτῶν ἐστιν), weil damit nur eine Tautologie entstünde. Nur so, lokal kodiert, gibt die Propositio auch ihren Sinn als Antwort auf den Torheitsvorwurf der Opponenten: Es geht um den *Ort*, durch den eine personale Gemeinsamkeit bestimmt ist, was hier zutreffend ist, da es ja darum geht, die jesuanische Nicht–Fasten–Schülerschaft von

---

[5] A. Sinowjew/H. Wessel, *Logische Sprachregeln* (Berlin 1975), 511–518; vgl. W. Nöth, *Chronemics: The Semiotics of Time*, in: Ders., *Handbook of Semiotics* (Bloomington [Indiana] 1990), 415–418 (vgl. Rez.: W. S., *LingBibl* 66 [1992], 114–122).

[6] W. Bauer/K. Aland/B. Aland, *Griechisch-deutsches Wörterbuch zu den Schriften des NT* (Berlin 1988), 1103.

[7] Vgl. zur Doppelung durch Wiederholung der gleichen Motive: F. Neirynck, *Duality in Mk,* BEThL 31 (Leuven 1972, 1988²), 98–102 (Nr. 12 "Double Statement: Repetition of the Motiv") bzw. 102–107 (Nr. 13 "Synonymous Expression") verweist (ohne schon 2,19 einzubeziehen) auf die relativischen Anschlüsse in direkter Rede: Mk 1,7 (Stärkerer); 10,14f (Kinder); 13,2 (Stein); 13,19 (Schöpfung); 13,20 (Erwählte).

anderen Schülerschaften zu unterscheiden.[8] Bei der Konfron-
tation zwischen den *Gruppen* geht es eher lokal um ihren Ort als
temporal um "Heilszeit," da ja auch die Opponenten in der
gleichen "Zeit" (also Heils-Zeit) leben, was die Zurückweisung

---

[8] Von "Jüngern Jesu" hat man bis dato nichts gewußt. Sie werden erst Mk
2,15f.18.23 unvermittelt literarisch eingeführt. Sogar Mk hatte den Ausdruck,
der bisher weder in LXX noch in frühchristlichen Schriften vorkommt, bis
dahin nicht verwendet. Es stammt aus der griechischen Sphäre der Schülerschaft
eines Philosophen und bezeichnet die in Lerngemeinschaft zu einem
διδάσκαλος stehenden Anhänger (R. Schütz, *Apostel und Jünger: Eine quellen-
kritische und geschichtliche Untersuchung über die Entstehung des Christentum* [Gießen
1921], 14.77–79; V. K. Robbins, *Jesus the Teacher: A Socio-Rhetorical Interpretation of Mk* [Philadelphia 1984, 1989[2]], 87–94). Sie dient Mk dazu, um im
Unterschied zur "Philosophen-Biographie" Q (G. Downing, "A Genre for Q and
a Socio-Cultural Context for Q. Comparing Sets of Similarities with Sets of
Differences," *JSNT* 55 [1994], 3–26) seinen Jesus-Bios erweiternd als "Lehrer/
Schüler-Biographie" zu gestalten. Wo immer er den Ausdruck einführt, geht es
darum, die betreffenden als Lerngruppe (quasi verschiedene "Seminargruppen")
zu markieren.

Was Mk dazu inspiriert hat, geht aus Mk 2,18 klar hervor: Q 7,18 kannte
nur "Schüler des Johannes." Indem Mk diese hier übernahm, hat er als Kontrast
dazu nun auch "Schüler Jesu" kreiert (sie V.15.23 und dann weiter multipliziert)
und zur Verstärkung des Kontrasts auch noch in historisch unmöglicher Konstruktion (die nur seinen Abstand zu den wirklichen Verhältnissen und seine
Nicht-Vertrautheit damit beweisend) "Schüler der Pharisäer" konstruiert. Doch
sind eben nicht nur diese, sondern auch die "Jünger Jesu" sein redaktionelles
Konstrukt. Daß hier nur die "Pharisäer" (auch sie von Q 11,42.43 her) erst von
Mk eingebracht seien, ist schon darum unwahrscheinlich, weil er sie eben Mk
2,16 erstmalig untergeordnet zu den γραμματεῖς ("*Rechtsentscheider*") eingeführt
hatte, dem Häufigkeitswort (21 : Mt 22 : Lk 14+4 : Joh 0; allein wie in
Gruppierung mit anderen als mk Stilmerkmale; P. Dschulnigg, *Sprache,
Redaktion und Intention des MkEv*, SBB 11 [Stuttgart 1984, 1986[2]], 102–103.120–
121.127, Nr. 32.64.76), das bei Mk die eigentlichen Opponenten bezeichnet
(während dgg. "Pharisäer" seltener erscheint: 12 : Mt 29 : Lk 27+9 : Joh 19): vgl.
D. Lührmann, "Die Pharisäer und Schriftgelehrten im MkEv," *ZNW* 78 (1987),
169–185 (vor allem gg. Fehlangaben wie bei Gnilka, *Mk*, 107–109, der im ersten
Teil ein sachliches Referat von R. Meyer/H. F. Weiß, s.v., *ThWbNT* IX 11–51,
bringt, aber im zweiten Teil eine sich an W. Grundmanns Antijudaismus
anlehnende Bewertung, die im Widerspruch dazu steht); Smith, "Opponents,"
NTS 35 (1989); J. D. Kingsbury, "The Religious Authorities in the Gospel of
Mk," *NTS* 36 (1990), 42–65 (schon mk Klischée einer kollektiven Einheitsfront).

nicht einleuchtend begründen würde.[9] Die Relativ-Wendung expliziert also synonym das "Söhne-des-Hochzeitssaals"-Syntagma in nicht-temporaler Kodierung. Im antithetischen Parallelismus Mk 2,19.20 geht es primär um Anwesenheit vs. Abwesenheit des entscheidenden Faktors bei der durch ihn determinierten Gruppe.[10]

1.2 Auch die begründende Antithese Mk 2,21 ist nicht primär durch die Logik der Zeit bestimmt, sondern durch die kontradiktorische Unverträglichkeit, wobei die mk "Neuheit" durch ihre eigene Dynamik (mk Dämonenvertreibungen) definiert ist: "The expression ἐπίβλημα ῥάκους ἀγνάφου in verse 21 is a replacement metaphor leading to διδαχὴ καινή in Mk 1:22 and 27 as the proper term... This imagery depicts the Gospel which Jesus preached as a dynamic force. Such creative new teaching stands in contrast with the ἱμάτιον παλαιόν... It is significant that the author uses παλαῖον and not ἀρχαῖον to qualify ἱμάτιον. The word ἀρχαῖον means 'old in respect of time.' The contrast which the author draws between the new patch of cloth and the old garment is not a contrast in point of time (= ἀρχαῖον), but a *contrast in point of use* (= παλαιόν). The old garment is 'worn out,'...obsolete."[11] Eine fastende Jesus-Schüler-schaft im Rahmen

---

[9] Bauer/Aland, *Wörterbuch*, 527 s.v. IV.6 klassifiziert die Stelle unter (b), die temporalen Kodierungen (mit Lk 5,34; 19,13; 24,44D; Joh 5,7—doch die lk Kodierung ist nicht *eo ipso* auf Mk zu übertragen), erwähnt aber im Zusammenhang auch (a) die lokalen ("*worin*": Röm 2,1; 14,22; 2Kor 11,12—also die bei Paulus häufigsten; auch sonst dürfte Mk von paulinischer Sprache beeinflußt sein: W. S., *Sekundäre Jesuanisierungen von primären Paulus-Aussagen bei Mk.*, in: *The Four Gospels 1992*, F. Van Segbroeck [u.a. hg.], FS F. Neirynck, BEThL 100 [Leuven 1992], 877–904), ferner (c) die instrumentalen ("*wodurch*": Röm 14,21) und (d) die kausalen ("*darum, weil—auf Grund dessen, daß*": Röm 8,3; Hebr 2,18; 6,17), die man neben der lokalen und vor der temporalen Mk 2,19 ebenfalls veranschlagen könnte.

[10] Maartens, *Interpretation*, 67.

[11] Maartens, *Interpretation*, 68 vgl. 73. Vgl. zum Status des "Abgenutzten," "Unbrauchbar-Gewordenen" Soph OedR 290; Lys fr. 6; DiodSic 3,46,4 (Bauer/Aland, *Wörterbuch*, 1225). In diesem Sinne ist es Mk (wie Kol 3,9; Eph 4,22) wiederum von Paulus (1Kor 5,7f; 2Kor 3,14; Röm 6,6; 7,6) her vorgegeben, während später 1Joh 2,7 wie R-Mt 13,52 und R-Lk 5,39 den Ausdruck dann im Gegensatz dazu positiv kodiert verwenden. Daß Mk 2,21 unter dem "neuen Flicken" den Neologismus "der Fastenform des Täufers und der Pharisäer eine nicht genügend radikale Erneuerung der alten Religion gesehen" habe (so F. Bovon, *Das Evangelium nach Lk*, EKK III/1 [Neukirchen,

eines pharisäisch fastenden Judentums würde auch den Untergang ihres Tempels und ihrer zentralen Tempelstadt Jerusalem nicht aufhalten, sondern in diesen Untergang hineingezogen werden.

1.3 Da die *propositio* Mk 2,19b aus einer rhetorischen (besser: argumentativen) Frage besteht, deren Antwort der intendierte Leser eindeutig selbst gibt ("das ist unmöglich"),[12] wird sie hier dennoch 2,19c redundant auch noch beantwortet, obwohl sich diese Antwort von selbst versteht. Diese bei Mk mehrfach wiederholte Praxis[13] dient seinem didaktischen Anliegen, auch den einfachsten Hörer zu erfassen ("Elementarunterricht," wie Hebr 2,3–4; 5,11–6,3 wohl genau dieses Buch direkt verstanden hat). Erst mit dieser redundanten Antwort wird eine Temporalbestimmung in die Argumentation eingebracht.[14] Dabei ist wichtig,

---

1989] 262–263), entspricht nicht den angeführten Beobachtungen. Es geht um die dynamische "Gefährlichkeit des Neuen" (Klostermann, *Mk*, 28), das die Brüchigkeit und Überholtheit des "Alten" erweist (F. Hahn, "Das Bildwort vom neuen Flicken und jungen Wein," *EvTh* 31 [1971] 357–375.370; G. Steinhauser, "Neuer Wein braucht neue Schläuche," in: *Biblische Randbemerkungen*, FS J. Schnackenburg [Würzburg 1974²], 113–123; Klauck, *Allegorie*, 172; R. T. Beckwith, "The Feast of New Wine and the Question of Fasting," *ET* 95 [1984], 334–335). Es kann auch keine Rede davon sein, daß Mk 2,21 eher vor dem Aufgeben des Alten warnt und damit der angebliche neue Fasttag "Freitag" gerechtfertigt sei (gg. Kuhn, *Sammlungen*, 72.109 mit Schweizer, *Mk*, 37).

[12] Aristot *Top* 8,1,156; *Rhet* 3,18; vgl. B/D/R, 496; H. Lausberg, *Elemente der literarischen Rhetorik* (München 1963, 1976⁵) § 445,2; 2,3; 398,1; D. F. Watson, "James 2 in Light of Greco-Roman Schemes of Argumentation," *NTS* 39 (1993) 94–121, spez. 103–104 zu Jak 2,4.5–7 und 108 zu Jak 2,13, wo wie hier sogar schon eine *propositio* in Gestalt der rhetorischen Frage gegeben wird.

[13] Vgl. auch Mk 3,23b.26—dabei ist gerade in der jetzigen Anordnung V.26 von Q vorgegeben und die rhetorische Frage als *propositio* V.23b erst redaktionell gebildet. Analog folgen redundante Ergänzungen auf rhetorische Fragen in 3,33b → 34b + 35b; 9,50a → b; 12,9a → b; 12,26 → 27 (vgl. Neirynck, *Duality*, 127–131, Nr. 26 "Correspondence in Discourse," wo noch nicht alle Beispiele unserer speziellen Gruppe erfaßt sind). Die Auslassung dieser redundanten Antwort in D W *f*⁷ 33 700 it vg^mss (sy^p) ist Angleichung an die schon von Mt und Lk vorgenommenen Auslassungen, wobei Mt aber das Relativum gelesen und in die Frage selbst versetzt hat, wenngleich unter Ausschaltung des temporalen Aspekts.

[14] Dabei ist das verwendete Syntagma der Zeitdauer (Bauer/Aland, *Wörterbuch*, 1770) wieder ein typischer Nachklang der Pauluslektüre des Autors (vgl. Gal 4,1; 1Kor 7,39; Röm 7,1—NT sonst nie).

daß ein Subjektwechsel eintritt (ὁ νυμφίος μετ' αὐτῶν ἐστιν →
ἔχουσιν τὸν νυμφίον μετ' αὐτῶν).

Es geht absolut nicht um eine Zeit der Anwesenheit Jesu bei
ihnen (so 9,21, aber nicht hier), sondern um ihre möglichst
dauernde Gruppenzugehörigkeit zu ihm, da die mögliche Grenze
als Warnung in den Blick kommt: nicht Jesus ist es, der die
Zeitdauer begrenzen würde, sondern sie sind es gegebenenfalls;
solange sie an ihm festhalten, ist Fasten für sie eine Un-
möglichkeit.[15] Die Logik der Zeit würde hier also mißdeutet,
wenn man Jesus zu ihrem Subjekt macht, während es um die
Gruppe als Subjekt geht.

1.4 Es besteht im Gebrauch von ὅταν[16] ein Unterschied zwischen Mk 2,20 einerseits, wo ἡμέραι ὅταν ("*Tage, wo*") zusammen-
gehört und τότε mit καί[17] angeknüpft ist, und der davon zu
unterscheidenden Konstruktion andererseits, wo ὅταν mit direkt
folgendem τότε steht, wie Lk 5,35 abändert, '*wenn (etwas geschehen
ist), dann*' bedeutet (wie Mk 13,14; Mt 24,15f; 25,31; Sir 18,7; Jos
Bell 6,287; Ant 10,213), wo also die Handlung des Nebensatzes
der des Hauptsatzes vorangeht.[18] Die Parallele zu Mk 2,20 liegt

---

[15] Das δύνασθαι (+ *Inf.* eine Häufigkeitswendung) ist ein mk Häufigkeitswort
(33 : Mt 26 : Lk 26 + 21 : Joh 36; R. Morgenthaler, *Statistik des ntl. Wortschatzes*,
[Zürich 1958, 1982³], 90, das Dschulnigg, *Sprache*, 234 mit seiner Kategorie "D"
statistisch knapp aus dem Bereich mk Stilmerkmale ausschließen wollte. Doch
ist dafür das Lexem nicht isoliert zu veranschlagen, sondern auch in seinen
makro-syntaktischen Einbindungen wie hier, wo nicht nur eine Repetition
vorliegt, sondern die Position auch noch durch eine ringkompositorische
Inclusio ausgezeichnet ist; bei Neirynck, *Duality*, 132–134.244, Nr. 27 "Inclusion," als solche noch nicht registriert).

[16] Im Prinzip gilt: "ὅταν is indefinite": I. H. Marshall, *The Gospel of Luke*,
NIGTC (Exeter 1978), 252 zu Lk 6,22.

[17] Das adverbiale καί bei τότε unterstreicht die Gleichzeitigkeit: So findet sich
auch nach Zeit- und Bedingungssätzen, "besonders häufig bei den Epikern καί
zu Anfang des Nachsatzes, wo es der deutschen Übersetzung nach zum Vorder-
satz gehört und dazu dient, das unmittelbar gleichzeitige Eintreten der beiden
Ereignisse anzudeuten (Hom Il 1,494f: 24,31f)": F. Passow, *Handwörterbuch der
griechischen Sprache* I (Darmstadt 1983), 1539a.

[18] Bauer/Aland, *Wörterbuch,* 1190; B/D/R 382,2. Es steht hier auch nicht
ἐλεύσονται ἡμέραι ὅτε wie Lk 17,22 bzw. eine Konstruktion wie 19,42. Wegen
des kausalen Aspekt ist auch der Hinweis von G. Delling, *ThWbNT* II, 950 "vgl.
auch Jer 16,1; 23,5.74. usw." irreführend; denn die offenbar von Jeremias geschaffene prophetische Einleitungsformel "siehe, es kommen Tage" erscheint
immer für ein Eingreifen JHWHs als direkte Gottesrede (E. Jenni, *THAT* I, 266–

also nicht in 13,14, wo eine kausale Folge vorliegt, sondern (besonders für den Nachsatz) in 13,11, wo eine analoge Gleichzeitigkeit ausgesprochen ist (ὅταν → ἐν ἐκείνῃ τῇ ὥρᾳ). Ginge es Mk hier um eine kausale Geschehensabfolge, dann hätte er es nicht mit folgendem καὶ τότε aufgenommen, sondern diese mit seiner Vorzugsverbindung ὅταν → εὐθύς (4,15.16.29)[19] angegeben. Das ὅταν + Konjunktiv meint entweder einen Eventualis (was den Warncharakter hervorhebt) oder steht iterativ für häufiger Wiederkehrendes.[20] Der Plural von Mk 2,20a kann auf den iterativen Aspekt weisen: "Es wird immer wieder mögliche Fälle (Tage) geben, an denen ihnen das Pneuma (der Bräutigam) weggenommen wird—und an einem solchen Tage fangen sie an zu fasten." Also nur, wenn ὅταν in Mk 2,20b mit Indikativ stünde (wie Mk 11,25 vgl. 3,11; 11,19),[21] läge eine mögliche Todesvorhersage vor. Nun aber steht ὅταν als eingebettete Hypotaxe mit dem Obersatz ἐλεύσονται δὲ ἡμέραι, die den Hauptton trägt, und darum nicht so stark von 2,19c abzuheben ist.[22]

267.721; H. Preuß, *ThWbAT* I, 552–554.556; G. von Rad, *ThWbNT* II, 949): "Die Präsentativ/*jamim*/Pt.-Formel ist Am 4,2; 9,13 red. Abgesehen von Prophetenlegenden 1Sam 2,31; 2Kön 10,17 (= Jes 39,6) wird die Formel 15mal in Jer verwendet... Angekündigt wird also mit *jamim boim* ein Zeitraum anderer Qualität als die Gegenwart, "Tage, welche die Möglichkeit/Nötigung in sich bergen, daß..." Insofern wird nicht bloß ein ungewisses Datum umrissen, sondern ein Einsatz zu präsentativischer Weissagung gegeben" (K. Koch, *Amos* II, AOAT 30 [Neukirchen 1976], 54).

[19] Dschulnigg, *Sprache*, 165–166 (mk Merkmal Nr. 154 als 107. der zweiten Kategorie B).

[20] B/D/R, 382,3. Auch Mk 14,25 (ἡμέρα + ὅταν "*bis zu*") liegt ein anderer Fall vor, da es hier als Umschreibung für ein attisches πρὶν ἄν erscheint (ebd. n. 4).

[21] Das ist ebenfalls ein mk Stilmerkmal: Dschulnigg, *Sprache*, 165 (Nr. 153 als 106. in der zweiten Kategorie B); NT sonst nur Apk 4,9; 8,1.

[22] Mk 2,20 wird leider zu oft lukanisierend interpretiert, wie etwa bei E. Grässer, *Das Problem der Parusieverzögerung in den synoptischen Evangelien und in der Apg*, BZNW 22 (Berlin 1957, 1977³) 44–46; J. Schreiber, *Theologie des Vertrauens: Eine redaktionsgeschichtliche Untersuchung des MkEv* (Hamburg 1967), 123–125.

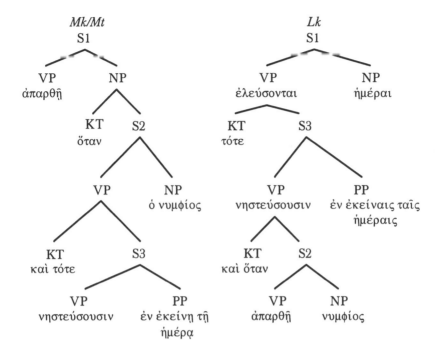

2. Zur Logik des Argumentationsgefüges

2.1 Das in seiner Kodierung infrage stehende Kompositum von
Mk 2,20b (ἀπαρθῇ NT und LXX nur hier und in den Parallelen)[23]

---

[23] H. Dunkerley, "The Bridegroom Passage," *ET* 64 (1952/53), 303–304
erinnerte dafür (wie Taylor, *Mk*, 211, neben A. T. Cadoux, *The Parables of Jesus*
[London 1930], 72–74) an A. H. McNeile, *The Gospel according to St. Mt* (London
1915 = 1955⁶), 121 z.St.: ἀ. "could not signify violent death or removal because
it is never used in LXX"; Bauer/Aland, *Wörterbuch*, 159 übersetzt "wenn ihnen
der Bräutigam entrissen ist" und merkt an: "doch braucht dabei keine Gewaltsamkeit im Spiele zu sein Apg 1,9 D" (dort für ἐπήρθη; Grundmann, *Mk*,
85.87, will es hier von Lk 9,51 ἀνάλημψις her auf eine "Entrückungs"–Erhöhung
bezogen sehen, was, zwar seinem, von seinem Jesus-Konzept her deduzierten
Osterkonzept entspricht, aber erst recht einen logischen Widerspruch ergibt:
vgl. dgg. W.S., *Der Jenaer Jesus*, forthcoming). Ausrottendes ἐξαίρειν steht im NT
nur 1Kor 5,13; vgl. Dt 24,7.
    Das Sem der "gewaltsamen Trennung" fehlt noch in Vulgata mit ihrer
Wiedergabe "*cum auferatur*" (Lohmeyer, *Mk*, 60 n. 4 wünschte hier von seinem
Sinnimplikat des "Gewaltsamen" her "eher: *cum ablatus fuerit*" zu finden!). Wenn
Smith, "Opponents," 165 das Verb dennoch wieder als "forceful removal"

findet in der Fortsetzung Mk 2,21b durch das Simplex (αἴρει) mit
nachgestellter gleicher Präposition (ἀπ') eine überraschende
Wiederaufnahme.[24] Dazu hat man weiter zu beachten, daß Mk
4,25 genau dieses Syntagma als die einzig vorgegebene Verb-
Stelle mit dieser Präposition (von seinem Quellort Q 19,24.26
her) wiederholt, d.h. daß 2,21 (und damit auch das Kompositum
2,20) eine Duplizierung der Q-Vorlage darstellt: "Wer dagegen

---

verstehen will, dann weil er Mk 2,20 (ohne rhetorische Argumentationsanalyse)
als "pivot" des Segments verstehen will, um auch hier "Jesus' passion clearly
anticipated" zu sehen. Folgende Mischung von Unlogik und Gewaltsamkeit
kann man nicht mehr Exegese nennen, weil sie deutlich aus der Not eine
Tugend im Interesse des eigenen Vorurteils macht: "ἀπάρθη spielt eindeutig [?!]
auf Passion und Tod Jesu an, "auch wenn[?!] das Wort sonst in dieser Bedeutung
nicht belegt ist. Gerade weil [?!] es sonst im NT nicht vorkommt, aber an Jes
53,8 erinnert [?!], macht es eine Anspielung an den Tod Jesu wahrscheinlich [?!].
Was sonst [?!] sollte die Gemeinde unter "Hinwegnahme des Bräutigams"
verstehen, wenn nicht [?!] seine durch den Tod vollzogene Abwesenheit?"
(Thissen, *Befreiung*, 173)" (Sauer, *Rückkehr*, 351; die rhetorische Schlußfrage
macht den Zirkelschluß offenkundig, indem sie auf einen bestehenden *common
sense* rekurriert. Den von Thissen als scheinbar empirisches Element (wie
Lohmeyer, *Mk*, 60; Taylor, *Mk*, 211) ohne eingehende Begründung
eingebrachten angeblichen Bezug auf Jes 53 (ein früher oft gezogener Yoker) hat
schon Roloff, *Kerygma*, 232 n. 105 zurückgewiesen: "das hat wenig Wahrscheinlichkeit für sich," da Jes 53 mk wie vor-mk keine erkennbare Rolle spielt. Die
Wendung LXX-Jes 53,8c αἴρεται ἀπὸ τῆς γῆς ἡ ζωὴ αὐτοῦ, wo der Bezug auf das
Lebensende explizit gegeben ist (aber nicht im Verb als solchem liegt; denn
außerdem geht hier 53,8a eine andere Verb-Verwendung voraus: ἐν τῇ
ταπεινώσει ἡ κρίσις αὐτοῦ ἤρθη), steht zunächst einmal weiter von Mk 2,20
entfernt als die primären mk Kotextparallelen selbst.
[24] Solche "Stichwortanschlüsse" hat man früher vorschnell diachron als Indiz
für eine Zusammenfügung ursprünglich selbständiger Einheiten gewertet (z.B.
hier J. Sundwall, *Die Zusammensetzung des MkEv*, AAA.H 9/2 [Abo 1934], 16–17
und seine Adepten), während man sie primär synchron als Repetitionen im
Blick auf den Leser stilisiert ansehen muß in ihrer Funktion als Rezeptions-
dispositionen (J. Dewey, "Oral Methods of Structuring Narrative in Mk," *Int.* 43
[1989], 32–44; dies., "Mk as Interwoven Tapestry: Forecasts and Echoes for a
Listening Audience," *CBQ* 53 [1991], 221–236; dies., "Mk as Aural Narrative:
Structures as Clues to Understanding," *Sewanee Theological Review* 36 [1992], 45–
56; dies., "The Gospel of Mk as an Oral-Aural Event," *JSNT.S* 109 [1994], 145–
163; vgl. Rez.: W. S., *ThLZ* 120 [1995], 625–628); das tritt hier ganz eindeutig in
Erscheinung, wenn man den Blick nicht auf das engere Segment begrenzt,
sondern Mk 4 einbezieht.

nicht (Wurzeln 4,6.15 bzw. Frucht 4,8f.20.23 entwickelt) hat, dem wird selbst das, was er (von mir gehört) hat, künftig weggenommen werden (ἀρθήσεται ἀπ᾽)." Damit es für den implizierten Leser unüberhörbar bleibt, hat der Autor Mk 4,15 den Satan zum Subjekt dieses "Wegnehmens" gemacht und ihn so in das von ihm gestaltete Wortfeld eingebracht.

Die ausgearbeitete Argumentation der Antwort auf die Torheitsfrage von 2,18 im Munde des mk Jesu läuft also von Mk 2,19 bis 2,22 kontinuierlich fort, so daß eine fortlaufende Sequenz von begründenden Argumenten gegeben scheint. In diesem Rahmen ist nicht zu erwarten, daß statt der Begründung in Mk 2,20 eine abweichende Konzession parenthetisch eingesprengt ist, und zwar um so weniger als 2,21b das entscheidende verbale Stichwort der temporalen Protasis von 2,20b aufgenommen ist. Dafür sprechen auch weitere Beobachtungen:

2.2 Diese Fortsetzung Mk 2,21f ist ohne jede Unterbrechung, also ohne eine dazwischengeschaltete Anreihungsformel (wie etwa in der folgenden Chreia 2,27a) weitergeführt; diese Weiterführung ist vielmehr asyndetisch, was klar im mk Sinne eines kausalen Asyndetons zu verstehen ist. Während Mk kausale Partikeln in Begründungssätzen gewöhnlich nur für Weisungen, die an Schüler gerichtet sind, verwendet, ist kausales Asyndeton "a major part of Markan style"[25] gegenüber Opponenten. Ein kausales Asyndeton ist außerdem rhetorisch kennzeichnend dafür, daß es die entscheidende Begründung einführt und das durch diese Art eines komprimierenden Anschlusses kennzeichnet.[26]

---

[25] R. B. Vinson, *A Comparative Study of the Use of Enthymemes in the Synoptic Gospels*, in: D.F. Watson (hg.), *Persuasive Artistry*, FS G. A. Kennedy, JSNT.S 50 (Sheffield 1991), 119–141, spez. 119.123–124. Es steht besonders Opponenten gegenüber zur Hervorhebung der Autoriät des mk Jesus (vgl. auch 2,9.17; 5,39; 12,9.27.31.36.36): V. Taylor, *Mark*, 49–50.58 mit M.-J. Lagrange, *Evangile selon St. Marc* (Paris 1929) LXX–LXXI; vgl. weniger funktionsspezifisch im Interesse eines angeblichen Semitismus: C. H. Turner, "Markan Usage," *JThS* 28 (1929), 15–19; M. Black, *An Aramaic Approach to the Gospels and Acts* (Oxford 1967³), 55–61; N. Turner, *Style*, in: J. H. Moulton, *A Grammar of NT Greek*, IV (Edinburgh 1976 = 1986), 12.31.

[26] Lausberg, *Elemente*, § 327–328: "Komprimierende *detractio*." Von daher ist nicht von vornherein davon auszugehen, daß Mk 2,21 in einem Widerspruch zu 2,20 formuliert ist (so Wellhausen, *Mc*, 19 "widerspricht ihm innerlich"—wobei immer schon eine (oberflächliche) semantische Vorentscheidung über 2,20 getroffen ist, ohne vorher die syntaktisch-logische Struktur auf ihre text-

pragmatische Struktur hin zu erfragen. Aus dem gleichen Grunde entfällt die in den Kommentaren häufig vorgenommene Schlußfolgerung, daß das Asyndeton belege, daß Mk 2,21f eine vor-mk eigene und isolierte Sprucheinheit gewesen sein müsse. Schon das Überwiegen des Wortfeldes "Textilien" mit der Schneiderei-Metaphorik bei Mk deutet eher auf seine redaktionelle Bildung von 2,21 (und weist auf seine besondere Vertrautheit mit diesem sozio-kulturellen Umfeld hin—etwa im Unterschied zum Überwiegen des monetären Wortfeldes bei Mt: W.S., *Die Sprache des Mt* [Göttingen 1987], 153–155 : 44–47). Der zweite Vergleich ist offenbar sprichwörtlich in Rom zeitgenössisch vorgegeben, wie Seneca Ep. 83,16 zeigt (Klostermann, *Mk*, 29): "*quem ad modum musto dolia ipsa rumpuntur* (wie vom jungen Most die Fässer selbst gesprengt werden)" (L. Annaeus Seneca, *Philosophische Schriften* IV, hg. M. Rosenbach [Darmstadt 1984], 212–213). Veranlaßt ist die mk Bildung dieser Sentenz 2,22 mit dem viermalig betontem οἶνος von Q 7,34 (also demselben Q-Segment, aus dem er analog dazu rahmend das einleitend viermalige μαθηταί rezipiert und quantitativ entsprechend multipliziert hatte—wie sogar schon 2,15.16a.b daraus das "Essen mit Zöllnern und Sündern," wobei das Leitwort des Segments "Sünder" mit V.17 ebenfalls auf viermal multipliziert wurde). Die Analogie dazu in seiner Schneiderei-Metaphorik dürfte der Autor hier 2,21 ebenso selbst zur Verstärkung geschaffen haben, wozu deren Schlußwendung wiederum Q 11,26 aufnimmt.

Was Mk 2,21f nicht aus Q stammt, ist stark mk stilisiert: Beide bilden nicht nur einen synonymen Parallelismus (Neirynck, *Duality*, 134, Nr. 29), sondern sind auch analog mit negativer Protasis + positiver Apodosis dual strukturiert (Neirynck, *Duality*, 90, Nr.9A; dabei ist εἰ δὲ μή nach negativer Protasis ein starker Gräzismus, der so nicht auf ein semitisches Original rückführbar ist: K. Beyer, *Semitische Syntax im NT* I/1, StUNT 1 [Göttingen 1962, 1968[2]], 100); 2,21a Komposita mit gleichem Präfix (ἐπί-βλημα: ἐπι-ράπτει) und Wiederholung der Präposition ἐπί nach dem Kompositum (Neirynck, *Duality*, 76, Nr. 1); 2,21b Simplex (mk Häufigkeitswort) nach Kompositum von V.20 (Neirynck, *Duality*, 78, Nr. 4); die Repetitionen von παλαιός 2,21a.b.22a wie von οἶνον νέον 2,22a.d, zugleich als Inclusio für doppeltes ὁ οἶνος 2,22b.c (Neirynck, *Duality*, 86, Nr. 7); 2,22 οὐδείς: ἀλλά (Neirynck, *Duality*, 91, Nr. 9B; die Negation als mk Vorzugswort [26 : Mt 19 : Lk 33+25] zählt Hauck, *Mk*, 176 zum mk Stil, was erst recht für ἀλλά gilt: 43 : Mt 37 : Lk 35 + 30; Morgenthaler, *Statistik*, 181).

Dabei hat νέος noch eine besondere zeitgenössische Affinität zum "Wein": Der ptolemäische Herrscherkult war dionysisch geprägt. Schon Ptolemaios IV. (Philopater; 220–204 v.Chr.) hatte den inoffiziellen Beinamen Νέος Διόνυσος, den Ptolemäios XII. (80–50 v.Chr.) dann als offiziellen Beinamen trug. Sowohl Antonius als auch Caesar traten in Ägypten in diese Funktion ein, wie auch Caesar in Rom den Dionysos-Kult legitimierte (G. Hölbl, *Geschichte des Ptolemäerreiches* [Darmstadt 1994], 145–152.256–259.264–268).

2.3 Daß auch hier die Argumentation einer ausgearbeiteten Chreia (als genuin hellenistischer Gattung) vorliegt,[27] zeigt auch der programmatische Abschluß Mk 2,22d: Die elliptische Formulier- ung ohne ein Verb ist kennzeichnend für eine *conclusio* und demonstriert damit diese Funktion.[28] Hiermit ist nicht nur die *conclusio* zur Prämisse der Unvereinbarkeit, die 2,19 aufstellte, gegeben, sondern als Bekräftigung von Mk 1,27 zugleich der Verweis auf das Buchkonzept selbst als endgültige Lehre. Als abschließende *complexio* hat sie wie so oft (als peroratio) einen exhortativen Charakter.[29] Statt sie aber primär auf die *propositio* 2,19b zu beziehen, wurde sie oft auf das in V.20 angeblich ge- fundene neue "christliche Fasten" bezogen.[30] Man kann die Stelle auf 2,20b nur in Konkordanz mit V.19b beziehen, d.h. dann aber als Warnung vor einem Fasten. Wenn die *conclusio* Mk 2,22d wie die Küfer-Regel insgesamt eine Warnung impliziert (als generelle "Ethik des Gottesreiches"),[31] dann ist diese schon V.20 expliziert.

Diese Fortsetzung 2,21f ist wichtig, denn wer Mk 2,20 als eine Konzession versteht, tut so, als wäre das schon der Schluß der entgegnenden Antwort auf die Torheitsfrage.[32] Diese aber liegt

---

[27] B. L. Mack/V. K. Robbins, *Patterns of Persuasion in the Gospels* (Sonoma [California] 1989), 207; vgl. K. Berger, *Formgeschichte des NT* (Heidelberg 1984), 80–93; ders., "Hellenistische Gattungen im NT," *ANRW* II/23 (1984), 1031– 1432, spez. 1092–1110.

[28] F. Siegert, *Argumentation bei Paulus*, gezeigt an Röm 9–11, WUNT 34; (Tübingen 1985); Lausberg, *Elemente*, § 319: "Die eigentlich rhetorische Suspen- sion ist ein Ausdrucksmittel der Gedanken-Emphase, und zwar als syntaktische Realisierung der Gedanken-Aposiopese."

[29] Lausberg, *Elemente*, § 45,4; 271–273.

[30] Von Hirsch, *Mk*, 13 her bei Haenchen, *Weg*,118 n.7; Pesch, *Mk*, 177; Gnilka, *Mk*, 116 ("neue Fastenpraxis der Gemeinde"); Kiilunen, *Vollmacht*, 72. Eine noch weniger überzeugende Variante lieferte J. A. Ziesler, "The Removal of the Bridegroom: A Note on Mk 2,18–22 and Parallels," *NTS* 19 (1973), 190–194, der 2,20 nicht auf ein kirchliche, sondern ein pharisäisches Trauerfasten abhob, weil den Juden der Messias genommen sei.

[31] Maartens, *Interpretation*, 69.

[32] Eine ätiologische Deutung von Mk 2,20 wäre nur möglich, wenn damit (a) nicht ein Argument im Gesamtzusammenhang der Argumentation gegeben wäre, und wenn man (b) darin einen Abschluß sehen dürfte, den die Fortsetzung 2,21f dann wiederum negierte (wie man es immer für eine ältere "Traditionsstufe" reklamiert). Aber selbst wenn man zur Begründung dafür auf die zweigliedrige Argumentation von Mk 2,17.27f verweist, so müßte man kon- sequenterweise sagen, daß dort zwei Argumente für die zu begründende

erst in der *conclusio* 2,22d am Ende: "also neuer Wein in neue
Schläuche." Dann muß sich auch 2,20 in das Argumentations-
gefüge einfügen und darf nicht vorschnell als daraus her-
ausfallend angesehen werden: 2,20 scheint eher als *"argumentum e
contrario"* zu dienen. Dann aber gibt Mk 2,20b nicht einen
Realgrund, sondern einen Erkenntnisgrund für 2,20a an.

2.4 Daß besonders der Singular am Ende von Mk 2,20 ("an
jenem Tag") auf einen wöchentlichen Fasttag hinweisen müsse,
dürfte auch deshalb eine wenig überzeugende Inferenz-Folgerung
sein, weil dieser Singular hier als wiederaufnehmende Folge des
Plurals von 2,20a ("Tage aber werden kommen")[33] nicht gerade
auf einen bestimmten Wochentag weist, sondern synonym steht,
wie auch gleich anschließend der doppelte Plural "Sabbat"
2,23.24 vom doppelten Singular 2,27–28 rahmend aufgenommen
wird.

2.5 Neben der Plural/Singular-Identität wird man auch noch
makrosyntaktisch veranschlagen, wie dieser Autor ἔρχεσθαι in
direkter Rede verwendet: Mk 1,7 machte die Täufervorhersage
des "Kommenden." Dieser Ausdruck wird zunächst positiv und
bestätigend aufgenommen im Munde der Dämonen 1,27 wie als
Selbstaussage 2,17 im Munde Jesu selbst (beidemale mit dem
Infinitiv des Zwecks seiner Sendung). Diese wird wieder aufgenommen und fortgesetzt in den beiden Selbstaussagen 4,21 (hier
betont, indem Mk gegen die Vorgabe Q 11,33 betont den Bild-
bruch vom "Kommen" der Lampe in jesulogischer Absicht einführt, wiederum mit einer analogen Angabe des Zwecks) wie unmittelbar anschließend 4,22 (von Q 12,2 her in die Zweckansage

---

Entscheidung gegeben werden, nicht aber eine widersprechende Aufhebung der
ersten Begründung durch die zweite (gg. Klauck, *Allegorie*, 169). Das kausale
Asyndeton ist aber die entscheidende Gegeninstanz gegen eine solche
Argumentation. Außerdem wird bei der ätiologischen Deutung von Mk 2,20
immer unterstellt, daß es sich um ein "Fasten aus Trauer" handele, während
man vorher von der richtigen Voraussetzung ausgeht, daß sowohl bei den Phari-
säern als auch beim Täuferkreis das Fasten eben nicht als Ausdruck der Trauer
zu sehen ist (Klostermann, *Mk*, 28, ohne zu bemerken, daß er damit in einen
Widerspruch zu seiner vorherigen, richtigen Feststellung von S.27 gerät).

[33] So ein "gnomisches Futur" für "das *unter Umständen* zu erwartende" (B/D/R
349,1) ist in Mk 2,20a nach 2,19 als dessen Umkehrung und Komplettierung gut
verständlich. Auch der Charakter des bloßen Eventualis widerstreitet der
Annahme eines Fastentages und damit der Funktion einer Korrektur der
Fastenfreiheit. Das Syntagma ist auch lateinisch im temporalen Gebrauch
möglich (Passow, *Wörterbuch* I, 3403).

selbst hineingenommen. Mit der paarweisen Explikation des Zweckes der bejahten Sendung ist deutlich eine *Inclusio* hergestellt

Dazwischen steht ein Block mit zwei deutlich negativen Verwendungen des Verbs (vgl. später auch 13,6: viele werden "kommen"),[34] die aufeinander bezogen sind: 4,4 (Vögel "kamen" und fraßen das Gesäte weg) = 4,15 (sogleich "kommt" der Satan...). Dem ist Mk 2,20a vor- und zugeordnet als negative Verwendung ("Kommen" werden aber Tage...) zumal das folgende Kompositum-Verb nicht nur 2,21 im Simplex wieder aufgenommen ist, sondern dann auch nur noch 4,15 als das Werk des Satans. Diese Abfolge beider Verben (Kommen + Wegnehmen) ist also die gleiche, sodaß 4,15 für den Leser eine wiederholende und bestätigende Erläuterung der 2,20 gemachten Aussage darstellt. Diese Zuordnung von 2,20 zum negativen Block von 4,4.15 wird durch den Anschluß in der Abfolge wie durch die abhebende Rahmung durch das 1,24; 2,17 voranstehende wie 4,21.22 nachfolgende positive Paar betont als deutliche Antithese gegenüber dem "Kommen" Jesu bestimmt.

2.6 Wenn man die Aussagen über das Fasten in Mk 2,19–20 vergleicht, so fehlt in V.20 im Unterschied zu V.19d.c das typisch mk δύνασθαι, das auch noch durch seine doppelte negierte Verwendung als eine *Inclusio* hervorgehoben war; d.h. pointiert: "sie *werden* fasten, nicht: sie *können* fasten."[35] Es geht also nur um eine bloße Möglichkeit, die auch noch als düsteres Orakel erscheint, so daß Vorsicht geboten ist, den Satz als "Konzession" zu bestimmen. Eine solche hätte Mk mit δύνασθαι ausgedrückt. Ein solches δύνασθαι darf man aber nicht in Mk 2,20 hineinschmuggeln. Dagegen wird durch die, gerade auch in dieser Hinsicht mit V.19b.c (Α μὴ δύνανται : Α' οὐ δύνανται) kontrastierende, expliziten Zeitbestimmungen als hier wiederum rahmende *Inclusio* (A ἡμέραι : A' ἡμέρᾳ) der primär temporale Charakter dieser Weissagung und die Differenz zu einer nichtgedachten "Möglichkeit"/"Erlaubnis" noch unterstrichen.

---

[34] Auch hier geht es um Warnung vor "Irreführung," also dem Verlassen des richtigen, von Mk gelehrten Weges, wie der Nachsatz ausdrücklich sagt und 13,22 analog bestätigt (Futurum hier ἐγερθήσονται + δώσουσιν → πρὸς τὸ ἀποπλανᾶν als Zweckangabe). Gerade auch diese Vorhersagen haben Warnfunktion wie dann auch 13,23 zusammenfassend der Warncharakter der Vorhersagen generell eingeschärft wird (ὑμεῖς δὲ βλέπετε — προείρηκα ὑμῖν πάντα).

[35] So richtig beobachtet von Wellhausen, *Mc*, 18; trotz dieser Einsicht spricht er aber S.19 dann doch von einer "Erlaubnis."

3. Die elaborierte Chreia

Fest steht, daß Mk 2,18–20 das von zwei *Inclusiones* um-
schlossene Zentrum der Ringkomposition Mk 2,1–3,6 ist[36] und
damit über den konkreten Fall weit hinausgehende grundsätzli-
che Bedeutung hat, was noch dadurch unterstrichen wird, daß
dem Segment eine lokale und temporale Eingrenzung fehlt. Der
innere Argumentationszusammenhang wurde als für alle mk
Kontroversen (Mk 2,16f.18–22.23–28; 3,1–4; 7,1–12; 10,1–12;
12,13–17, der sich noch auf weitere Parallelen übertragen läßt)
typischer Begründungsgang herausgestellt: Eine Torheitsfrage
wird beantwortet mit einer Sentenz, der ein Kommentar folgt
(und evtl. ein antijüdisch gemeinter Schriftbeweis).[37] Das kann
man von der rhetorischen Chreia-Forschung her inzwischen
präziser strukturieren:[38]

A Mk 2,18a *Quaestio*: Situativ einleitende Verortung (ohne
    konkreten Orts- und Zeitbezug).

B Mk 2,18b *Propositio*: Torheitsfrage (zu widerlegende These)
    von Un- (bzw. der Zuvor-) genannten.

C Mk 2,19–22 Argumentative *Refutatio* durch den maß-
    gebenden Lehrer (V.19a):

---

[36] Seit J. Dewey, "The Literary Structure of of the Controversy Stories in Mk
2,1–3,6," *JBL* 92 [1973], 394–401; dies., *Debate*, 29–32.122–123; D. Rhodes/D.
Michie, *Mk as Story* [Philadelphia, 1982, 1985⁴], 51–53; Kiilunen, *Vollmacht*, 80–
81; Stenger, *Struktur*, 43–45; Van Iersel, *Concentric*, 91–92.

[37] K. Berger, *Gesetzesauslegung*, 576–584. Die dafür zementierte Kategorie
"Streitgespräche" (inauguriert von J. Weiß, *Evangelium*, 365; vgl. dazu
Schmithals, *Wegbereiter*, 397–399; M. Albertz, *Die synoptischen Streitgespräche*
[Berlin 1921]; Bultmann, *Tradition*, 39–56 + G. Theißen, *Ergänzungsheft*, 1979,
31–32) ist nicht beschreibungsadäquat, sondern irreführend, da es nur um
Widerlegung und ein Zum-Schweigen-Bringen einer Einstellung geht, die von
vornherein als abwegige Torheit eingeführt ist, wo "der kollektiv eingeführte
Gegner nur das Stichwort bringen" muß (so schon M. Dibelius, *Formgeschichte*,
64–65; ders., "Zur Formgeschichte des Evangeliums," *ThR* 1 [1929], 185–216,
bes. 195: Nur "die evangelische Versuchungsgeschichte stellt ein solches
Streitgespräch dar"). Die Replik Bultmanns (*Tradition*, 18, n.1), "Dibelius ver-
kennt m.E. den Stil [?!] des Streitgesprächs," ist typisch deduktivistisch, weil sie
voraussetzt, was erst zu erweisen wäre.

[38] Hermogenes 7,10–8,14 (vgl. Mack/Robbins, *Patterns*, 39.51.57f; Watson,
James 2, 97–102).

C1 Mk 2,19b *Ratio* (Sprichwort-Sentenz als argumentative Frage, die zum Analogieschluß auffordert): In einer Hochzeits-Gesellschaft kann man wegen der Gemeinschaft mit[39] dem Bräutigam nicht fasten (Enthymem als verkürzte deduktive Schlußfolgerung):

(a) Primäre Prämisse: Ein Bräutigam ist ein Essender und Trinkender

(b) Sekundäre Prämisse: Hochzeitsgäste sind Mitesser und -trinker

(c) Conclusio: Folglich ist Nichtessen und -trinken ausgeschlossen.

C2 Mk 2,19c–22c Amplifizierende *Elaboratio*:

C2.1 Mk 2,19c–d *Confirmatio* (argumentative Verstärkung) durch redundante Antwort auf die argumentative Frage.

C2.2 Mk 2,20 *Argumentatio e contrario*[40] (*reductio ad absurdum*: Ironie[41] der ausgeschlossenen Möglichkeit) als reduktiver Schlußfolgerung:[42]

(wenn nicht [a]): Nichtessen und -trinken findet nur ausserhalb der Bräutigamsgemeinschaft statt (dann also [b]): Die Gemeinsamkeit mit dem die Gruppe Definierenden ist aufgegeben.

C2.3 Mk 2,21a–b *Exornatio*[43] durch Analogieschluß-Argument vom exemplum der Klugheitsregel der Schneiderin her als induktive Schlußfolgerung.

---

[39] Wegen μετά nicht "in der Freudenzeit" (so Schille, *Offen*, 29), sondern personal. Auch hier gilt mit Quint 9,2,7: "The purpose is not to get information but to emphasize the point" (Watson, *James 2*, 104).

[40] Mack/Robbins, *Pattern*, 172–173 (wie Mk 3,22–27): ἐξ ἐναντίου komplementär zu ἀπὸ τοῦ ἴσου.

[41] Ironie ist ein literarisches Mittel des Kontrasts als Rezeptionsdisposition für den Leser, zu dem auch das Mittel der Prolepse (αἴρειν ἀπό im weiterlaufenden Erzähltext) gehört: J. Camery-Hoggatt, *Irony in Mk's Gospel: Text and Subtexts*, SNTS.MS 72 (Cambridge 1992), 86.

[42] Also nicht "Korrektur der Fastenfreiheit" (so Schille, *Offen*, 30), weil dann der Erkenntnisgrund zum Realgrund gemacht würde (eine auch sonst häufige Verwechslung, z.B. bei 1Kor 15,13.16; vgl. W. S., *Die Korintherbriefe*, BiAuPr 22, [Stuttgart 1980²], 94–95; ders., Art. Korinthertbriefe, *TRE* 19 [1989], 620–640, spez. 628).

[43] Vgl. zur *Exornatio*, die ein schon begründetes Argument weiter verstärkt: Hermogenes 2,18,28; 2,29,40; 4,13,56 (Mack/Robbins, *Patterns*, 54–57). Das Argument von der Nützlichkeit (ὄφελος) her ("niemand tut...") vs. Nutzlosigkeit [ἄχρηστον]/Schaden) ist kennzeichnend für die deliberative Rede (Berger,

C2.4 Mk 2,21c–d Vorläufige *Conclusio* als anwendende Parenthese, mit der der Autor sich direkt an den Leser wendet (primäre, metanarrative Kommunikationsebene).

C2.5 Mk 2,22a–c *Exornatio* durch Analogieschluß-Argument (ἐκ παραβολῶν) vom *Exemplum* der Klugheitsregel des Küfers als induktive Schlußfolgerung.

C3 Mk 2,22d Programmatische *Conclusio* (= bestätigte *Propositio*) zugleich als Buchprogramm des Autors überhaupt mittels einer parenthetisch abgesetzten Schlußfolgerung, mit der sich der Autor direkt an die Leser wendet.

4. Die Konsequenzen

4.1 Die Diskussion um diese Stelle ist zu stark von einer zu formalen Klassifikations-Diastase "öffentliches" vs. "privates" Fasten bestimmt gewesen.[44] Eine Annäherung an das richtige Verständnis hat von zwei primären Eckdaten auszugehen:

(a) "In the written Law Yom Kippurim ist the *only regular* day of fasting" (Lev 16,29f; 11QT 25,20–27,20; mYom 8). "The term for this fasting is not the usual Hebrew root *swm*, but *'nh nfš*, "to

---

Formgeschichte, 45–46, 91). Da es in dieser Chreia von vornherein nicht um wahre oder falsche Sachverhalte geht, sondern um richtiges oder falsches Verhalten, ist der Horizont von vornherein nicht der judiziale, sondern der symbuleutische. Es wird darum eben auch nicht legalistisch, sondern rational argumentiert (Hermogenes 3,7,20) und zwar mit dem Konzept des "Gleichen" (Hermogenes 8,9,16 ἀπὸ τοῦ ἴσου). Das ist der Wahrheitskern der ansonsten textpragmatisch falsch verorteten Funktion als Bekehrungsparänese bei A. Kee, "The Old Coat and the New Wine: A Parable of Repentance," *NovT* 12 (1970), 13–21; vgl. ders., "The Question about Fasting," *NovT* 11 (1969) 161–173. Die Einsicht in Vertrautheit des Autors mit der rhetorischen Elementarausbildung läßt uns heute die symbuleutischen Funktionen der Argumente präziser verorten.

[44] Zu unspezifisch bleiben J. Behm s.v., *ThWbNT* V, 928–932; (H. Strack/) P. Billerbeck, *Kommentar zum NT aus Talmud und Midrasch* IV/1 (München 1928, 1965⁴), 77–114 (ein Gemischtwarenladen); S. Safrai/M. Stern (hg.), *The Jewish People in the First Century* II, CRI I/2 (Assen 1976), 814–816; E. Schürer/G. Vermes, *The History of the Jewish People in the Age of Jesus Christ* II (Edinburgh 1979), 483–484; H. Mantel, *Fasten/Fastentage* II (Judentum), *TRE* 11 (1981), 45–48; C. C. Mitchell, "The Practice of Fasting in the NT," *BS* 147 (1990), 455–469 (*IZBG* 37: 1938); Sauer, *Rückkehr,* 355–359. Zum antiken Fasten überhaupt vgl. R Arbesmann, *Das Fasten bei Griechen und Römern*, RVV 21 (Gießen 1929); ders., s.v., *RAC* VII, 447–493; L. Ziehen, s.v., *PRE* XVII/1, 88–107.

humble or afflict one's soul or oneself," ταπεινοῦν τὴν ψυχήν in Greek."[45] Die nachexilische Verwendung dieses speziellen Ausdrucks der "freiwilligen Selbstminderung" setzt Esr 8,21 ein und geht über Trito-Jes 58,3; Ps 35,13; Sir 31,21; CD A1 6,19; PsSal 3,8 weiter und mündet in der Bezeichnung der entsprechenden Rechtssammlung, dem Mischna-Traktat II/9 *mTaʿanijot,* "Fastentage."[46]

(b) "As far as we know regular fasting had been characteristic of *one* group of Judaism *only,* the Pharisees, twice in the week, as the Pharisee of Lk 18,12 says, perhaps on Monday and Thursday (cf. Did 8,1)... PsSol 3 helps us to understand what fasting meant for the Pharisees: atonement for the inevitable sins of ignorance."[47]

---

[45]D. Lührmann, "Paul and the Pharisaic Tradition," *JSNT* 36 (1989), 75–94, spez. 83; R. Martin-Achard, s.v., *THAT* II (1976), 342; H. A. Brongers, "Fasting in Israel in Biblical and Post-Biblical Times," *OTS* 20 (1977) 1–21; E. Gerstenberger, s.v., *ThWbAT* VI (1989), 247–270, bes. 253–255. Der in der endgültigen essenischen Gemeindeordnung CD A1 (um 100 v.Chr.) 6,19 als *jom ha-taanit* benannte "Entsühnungstag" (mit eindeutigem Rückverweis auf die Halacha von Jub und CD A2: "entsprechend der Festlegung der Mitglieder des "Neuen Bund im Lande Damaskus") heißt 50 Jahre später in der jüngsten bekannten essenischen Schrift 1QpHab 11,6–8 in mehrfacher Synonymie "zur Zeit des Festtermins der Ruhe des Tags der Entsühnungen," "am Tag des Fastens (hier als *jwm swm*) ihrer Arbeitsruhe" (als dem Tag des Mordanschlags des Frevelhohenpriesters auf den "Anweiser zur Gerechtigkeit"); vgl. J. Maier, *Die Qumran-Essener. Die Texte vom Toten Meer I,* UTB 1862 (München 1995), 17.163–164.

[46] Vgl. Ed. Correns (1989). Hier erscheint Yom Kippur nur gelegentlich gegen Ende 4,1.8a (S. 96–98 n. 11. 124–126 n. 110), wie andererseits das Fasten in mYom (Mischna II/5; ed. J. Meinhold, [Gießen 1913]) auch nur am Ende 8,1–9 erscheint (S. 68–73).

[47] Lührmann, *Tradition,* 84f; F. Böhl, "Das Fasten an Montagen und Donnerstagen: Zur Geschichte einer pharisäischen Praxis (Lk 18.12)," *BZ* 31 (1987), 247–250: Nach dem Solarkalender der betont hebräischen Programmschrift der Damaskus-Exilierten, der Apokalypse "Buch der Einteilung der Zeiten" (K. Berger, Das Buch der Jubiläen, *JSHRZ* II/3 [1981], 271–575; H. Stegemann, *Die Essener, Qumran, Johannes der Täufer und Jesus* [Freiburg 1994³], 131–132.168.172 zur Frühdatierung noch ins 3. Jh. v.Chr.) können Festtage nur auf Sonntag, Mittwoch und Freitag fallen. Wenn die Pharisäer Montag und Donnerstag auswählten, dann wird das darin seinen Ursprung haben und damit ihr Fasten als Bußfasten zu verstehen sein. In der abschließenden Sabbat-Halacha, auf das die ganze Apokalypse zuläuft, wird Jub 50,10 begründet: "Denn groß ist die *kbwd* (*"Wichtigkeit": * C. Westermann, *THAT* I [1971], 794–

4.2 "Fasten" schien gerade in Rom (neben dem Sabbat) als ein typisches Kennzeichen des Judentums schlechthin empfunden zu sein, und zwar als der übrigen Welt völlig zuwiderlaufenden Bräuche:[48]

> (a) Tac Hist 5,4: "Von ihrer langen Hungersnot (in der Wüste) legen sie jetzt noch durch häufiges Fasten Bekenntnis ab (*adhuc ieuniis fatentur*)."
>
> (b) Suet Aug 76,2: "Kein Jude hält sein Fasten (*ieunium servat*) am Sabbat strenger, als ich es heute gehalten" (mit der üblichen Verwechslung mit dem Sabbat durch Fernstehende).

Für eine mögliche römische Provenienz des Autors der Lehrer/Schüler-Biographie Jesu ergäbe sich so ein sozio-kultureller Hintergrund für seine Warnung: Wer zu fasten beginnt (also Jude wird), beweist damit, daß er nicht mehr den

---

812; M. Weinfeld, *ThWbAT* IV [1984], 23–40), die der Herr Israel gegeben hat, zu essen und zu trinken und satt zu werden an diesem Tag-des-Festes und zu ruhen an ihm von aller Arbeit, sofern sie aus der Arbeit der gewöhnlichen (= nichtpriesterlichen) Menschen ist." Unter die Sabbat-Verbote (Jub 50,12) wird "auch der, der fastet" gestellt, tut er es dennoch, dann steht auch darauf die Todesstrafe (50,13).

Der früh-pharisäische und möglicherweise anti-hasmonäische Judit-Roman (mit Judit als Witwe Typos von Jerusalem/Zion) zeigt die spätere (um 100 v.Chr.) Geltung dieses Programms: "Sie fastete, seit sie Witwe war, alle Tage, außer am Vortag des Sabbat und am Sabbat, am Vortag des Neumonds und am Neumond, an den Fest- und Freudentagen des Hauses Israel" (Jdt 8,6 vgl. 4,13; E. Zenger, Das Buch Judit, *JSHRZ* I/6 [1981], 425–534, bes. 486; auch M. Hengel/R. Deines, "E. P. Sanders' 'Common Judaism,' Jesus, and the Pharisees," *JThS* 46 [1995], 1–70, spez. 48–49 reklamieren Jdt daneben von der Reinheitsvorsorge 11,13 her m.R. als "early Pharisaic"). Ein Weiterwirken zeigt auch noch eine beim Erstdruck der Mischna erscheinende Baraita zu mTaan 4,3 über das "Fasten des Laiendienstes": "Und die Männer des Laiendienstes fasteten vier Tage in der Woche, vom zweiten bis zum fünften. Aber sie fasteten nicht am Vorsabbat (= Freitag) wegen der *kbwd* (stärker: "Wichtigkeit" als die gängige Übersetzung "Würde") des Sabbats und nicht am ersten (Tag) nach dem Sabbat, damit sie nicht von Ruhe und Freude (des Sabbats zu plötzlich) übergingen zu Arbeit und Fasten und (womöglich) stürben" (Correns, *Taan*, 103–104). Egeria 27,9 bezeugt den Brauch eines fünftägigen Fastens, das der Großkirche wohl von Judenchristen her zugewachsen ist (F. Manns, "Une tradition judéo-chrétienne mentionée par Egérie," *Hen* 10 [1988], 283–290).

[48] J. Behm, s.v., *ThWbNT* IV 929–930.

"Bräutigam mit sich hat." Eine besondere Ironie kann in der als Orakel stilisierten mk Warnung Mk 2,20 auch noch darin liegen, daß Fasten als (nicht auf Apollon beschränkte; vgl. 4Esr 5,13; 2Bar 9,2) übliche Vorbereitung für die Erlangung einer Orakelerteilung eine geltende Voraussetzung war.[49] Hier erlangen die Fastenden das Orakel mit einer Negation ihres Fastens.

4.3 In dem fromme Neugier unterhaltenden Bekehrungsroman ägyptischer Juden (offenbar vor dem jüdischen Aufstand unter Trajan 115–117 n.Chr. entstanden), JosAs, wo der Heirats-Übertritt zum Judentum als Übergang von Finsternis/Irrtum/Tod zu Licht/Wahrheit/Leben erscheint, trennt sich die Satrapen-tochter Aseneth (die Mutter aller Proselyten) mit einem sieben-tägigen[50] Reinigungsfasten, das wie PsSal 3,8 gut pharisäisch als

---

[49] R. Muth, *Einführung in die griechische und römische Religion* (Darmstadt 1988), 150.

[50] Es wird sich um eine runde Zahl handeln, die die Woche beschreibt, da nicht denkbar ist, daß das Fasten auch den Sabbat umfaßt. Auf diesen wird wohl das folgende festliche Essen und Trinken fallen.

Auch das (nach der Zerstörung Jerusalems entstandene) *LibAnt* 30,4f spricht in seiner Nacherzählung von Ri 4 vom Entschluß eines wöchentlichen Buß-fastens: "Und jetzt kommt, laßt uns fasten sieben Tage lang vom Mann bis zur Frau und vom Kleinsten bis zum Säugling. Und wer weiß, ob nicht der Herr sich wieder mit seinem Erbe versöhnen wird, daß er die Pflanzung seines Weinbergs nicht zerstöre" (C. Dietzfelbinger, Pseudo-Philo: Antiquitates Biblicae, *JSHRZ* 2 [1979²], 87–271, bes. 189; vgl. den Kommentar von F. J. Murphy, *Pseudo-Philo: Rewriting the Bible* [Oxford 1994], z.St.). Denn Debora erscheint am 7. Tag und verkündet: "Siehe, jetzt wird sich der HERR euer erbarmen, am heutigen Tag" (30,7).

Hinter der runden Zahlenangabe für die Woche kann als Vorgabe die ägyptische 10-Tage-Woche stehen, die im Isisbuch von Apul Met 11 eine entsprechende Rolle als Fastenfrist spielt (vgl. D. Sänger, *Antikes Judentum und Mysterien*: Religionsgeschichtliche Untersuchungen zu JosAs, WUNT 2/5 [Tübingen 1980], 128–130; J. G. Griffiths, *Apuleius of Madaura: The Isis-Book* EPRO 39 [Leiden 1975], 290.355–356): "Ich solle 10 Tage hintereinander den Genuß im Essen einschränken, kein Fleisch verzehren und ohne Wein leben. Nachdem ich dies in ehrfurchtsvoller Enthaltsamkeit richtig innegehalten hatte, war schon der Tag da, der mir durch den göttlichen Termin bestimmt war" (11,23,3–4)—d.h. die Initiation, bei der er mit dem "Gewand" der Isis "aus feinem Linnen," der "Olympischen Stola," bekleidet wird (24,2f; "und es gab einen lieblichen Schmaus und ein heiteres Gelage. Auch der 3. Tag wurde mit der gleichen Form von Feierlichkeiten begangen, und ein religiöses Essen fand statt und die regelrechte Vollendung der Einweihung" (24,5; Apuleius, *Meta-*

"Selbsterniedrigung" definiert ist, von ihrer götzendienerischen Vergangenheit: "Und so tat Aseneth die sieben Tage; und Brot aß sie nicht und Wasser trank sie nicht in jenen sieben Tagen ihrer (Selbst)erniedrigung" (10,17 = 11,2.6.12.17; 13,1; 15,3).[51] Vom Tage danach an ißt, trinkt und salbt (= generell: Hygiene) sie sich (= innere und äußere Körperpflege wie Ps 23)[52] nur in

---

morphosen: Lateinisch und Deutsch [hg. R. Helm, SQAW 1 [Berlin 1970[6]] 382–385); vgl. analog auch für die 2. und 3. Weihe; 28,4 : "10 Tage wieder mit fleischlosen Speisen" (ebd. 388–389) und 30,1: "dann nehme ich sofort wieder das Joch der Enthaltsamkeit durch fleischlose Nahrung auf mich, vervielfache die durch ein dauerndes Gesetz vorgeschriebenen 10 Tage durch freiwillige Nüchternheit" (ebd. 390–391).

Auch das kann für Mk lebendiger Anschauungsunterricht sein: "Der Staatstempel der Isis und des Serapis auf dem Marsfeld wird im Jahr 71 beim Triumph des Vespasian und Titus zum ersten Mal erwähnt und ist wenige Jahrzehnte vorher erbaut, nachdem noch im Jahre 19 Tiberius gegen ägyptische Kulte eingeschritten war" (ebd. 420). Vgl. zum Text auch W. Burkert, *Ancient Mystery Cults* [Cambridge Ms, 1987] = *Antike Mysterien: Funktion und Gehalt* [München 1994[3]], 23–24 ("das religiöse Hobby wirkt als Ausgleich gegen beruflichen Streß; der Mysteriengott erweist sich als Psychiater").43–45.82 ("parodistisch" und "spielerisch-ironisch").84 (die Isis-Weihe ist nicht zu verallgemeinern).

[51] C. Burchard, "Joseph und Aseneth," *JSHRZ* II/4 (1983), 575–735, bes. 657–662.668.675 = "Joseph and Aseneth," *OTP* II (New York 1985), 177–247 (entgegen der Edition der ein Drittel kürzeren Fassung nach Textfamilie "d" durch M. Philonenko, *Joseph et Aséneth*, SPB 13 [Leiden 1968]); ders., "The Importance of Joseph and Aseneth for the Study of the NT," *NTS* 33 (1987), 102–134. Wenn Burchard, *JosAs*, 614; "Importance," 104 durchaus zuzustimmen ist, daß weder Essener noch Therapeuten oder gar "Mysterien" als spezielle Ausformungen eines Judentums dahinter stehen (gg. das theologische Mißverständnis und den Mißbrauch der Kategorie "Mysterien" von der "religionsgeschichtlichen Schule" her; vgl. jetzt grundlegend: Burkert, *Mysterien*, 9–12.19–34: primär durch Gelübde bestimmte, ergänzende "Votiv-Religion"), sondern eine sehr normale Form jüdischen Lebens, so wäre doch von Jub (Engelgemeinschaft, prophetische Rolle Levis) und PsSal her zu bedenken, daß diese Ausgestaltung primär pharisäisch bestimmt erscheint, was auch die Vertrautheit des Damaszener Pharisäers Paulus mit der Terminologie, der ja offenbar auch mit Jub als Programmschrift sehr vertraut ist (G. Sass, "Noch einmal 2Kor 6,14–7,1," *ZNW* 84 [1993], 36–64, bes. 44–47.61), näher erklären dürfte.

[52] Auf den Zusammenhang mit den konstitutiven Elementen von Ps 23 (m.E. ein Konversions-Psalm für Proselyten) hat besonders B. Lindars, "'Joseph and Aseneth' and the Eucharist," in *Scripture: Meaning and Method*, B. P. Thompson

Verbindung mit jüdischen Berakot, trennt sich damit von einer nicht-jüdischen Gestaltung des familiär alltäglichen Lebens und hat so teil an der engelgleichen Ewigkeit des jüdischen Volkes (8,5; 15,5f; 16,16): "Siehe doch, von dem (Tage) heute (an) wirst du wiedererneuert und wiedergeformt und wiederlebendigge-macht werden, wirst essen jüdisch "berakiertes" (mit Lob-sprüchen zum Gott Josephs genossenes)[53] Brot, das Leben gibt (finaler Genitiv),[54] und trinken jüdisch "berakierten" Becher, der Unsterblichkeit gibt, und dich salben mit jüdisch "berakierter" Salbe, die Unverweslichkeit gibt" (15,5). Dieses das Fasten ablösende Essen und Trinken mit jüdischer Danksagungs/ Beraka-Formel nimmt sie hinein in die Ewigkeit des jüdischen Volkes.

Wie Mk 2,19f ist auch hier in diesem Zusammenhang des beendeten Fastens die Metapher des *"Bräutigams"* verwendet:[55] "Sei getrost Aseneth, die keusche Jungfrau! Siehe, ich habe

---

(hg.), FS A. T. Hanson (Hull 1987), 181–199.188 aufmerksam gemacht (W. S., *IZBG* 34:1622).

[53] Burchard, "Importance," 130 n. 57: "The German Translation 'Segens-becher' (e.g. Luther, revision of 1975) is inappropriate, Bauer's 'Weihebecher' is also inadequate"; vgl. so schon betont W. S., *Der Segen im NT*, ThA 25 (Berlin 1967), 125–130.

[54] Burchard, "Importance," 111: "It is generally agreed that the genitive attributes after bread, cup, and ointment designate the effect caused by eating, drinking, and ointing. ἄρτος ζωῆς is not a metaphor for something which is not really bread; it designates bread which gives life."

[55] Der ständige Verweis der Ausleger darauf, daß "Bräutigam" keine vorge-gebene jüdische "Messias"—Bezeichnung sei (J. Jeremias, *ThWbNT* IV [1942], 1094–1096) verschiebt das Problem von falschen Prämissen her; denn abgesehen davon, daß es "den" Messias" als von christlichen Ansätzen retrospektiv definiert so gar nicht gibt (A. S. van der Woude/M. de Jonge, *ThWbNT* IX, 501–12; W.S., *Das biographische Ich-Idiom "Menschensohn" in den frühen Jesus-Biographien*, FRLANT), könnte man einwenden: "The Bridegroom is the Messiah in Ps 45 (explicitly Davididic in LXX A superscription); in the Song of Songs (or how else did this book eventually achieve canonical status?); in Isa 51,5 (Qumran) taken with 62,11, and so also Zech 9,9; in Rev 19 and 21; in 2Cor 11; in Eph 5,25–7; as well as in rabbinic passages like Pesikta Rabbati 149a referring to Isa 61,10" (O'Neill, *Bridegroom*, 485). JosAs bietet eine näherliegende Parallele für die Sachverhalte von Mk 2,19f.

gegeben dich heute (zur) Braut dem Joseph, und er (selbst) wird sein deiner (der) *Bräutigam* in die Ewigkeits-Zeit" (15,6).[56]

Nicht weniger überrascht es, daß dazu auch ein Gewandwechsel zu einem betont *neuen* Gewand gehört, so daß auch Mk 2,21 im Gefolge von 2,19f nicht zufällig erscheint, sondern auf ein zusammenhängendes Wortfeld der Konversion verweist: Aseneth erhält vom Engelfürsten (der dem Mann Joseph gleicht, 14,9) den Auftrag: "Lege ab den Leibrock den schwarzen deines Leides und das Sack(tuch)…und zieh an ein Gewand, linnen, *neu*, unberührt und ausgezeichnet" (14,12; 14–15 Vollzug). Mk 2,19– 22 adoptiert also eine ganze Reihe der Elemente einer Konversion zum Judentum und polt sie zu einer Warnung vor einer Konversion zum Judentum um. Mk "Fasten" signalisiert die Aufgabe der Tischgemeinschaft mit dem mk Jesu, wie er dadurch illustriert, daß er Gethsemane (als Versagen der besonders gründlich instruierten "Lerngruppe," faktisch seines "Oberseminars") und eine "Flucht" aller Schüler (Mk 14,26–27.50 als *Inclusio*) nach dem letzten gemeinsamen Mahl (Mk 14,17–25) in seiner erzählten Welt stattfinden läßt. Wer fastet (oder andere jüdische Sitten übernimmt), trennt sich damit von seinem Herrn: Mk 2,20 setzt einen *status confessionis*.

---

[56] Burchard, *JosAs*, 675. "Beraka" ist nicht mit einem Schlußkonsonanten zu transskribieren, da "h" am Wortende Vokalbuchstabe ist (J. Körner, *Hebräische Studiengrammatik* [Leipzig 1990[4]], 27–28).

DAS AGRAPHON "SEID KUNDIGE GELDWECHSLER!" BEI ORIGENES

Johan S. Vos
Vrije Universiteit Amsterdam
(Amsterdam, the Netherlands)

1. Das Agraphon und das antike Bild des Geldwechslers

Die Metapher des Bankiers oder Geldwechslers, der die Fähigkeit hat, wahre und falsche Münzen voneinander zu unterscheiden, begegnet wiederholt in der antiken Literatur. Sie wird verwendet, wenn es darum geht, Wahres und Falsches, Gutes und Böses auseinanderzuhalten, namentlich auf dem Gebiet der Philosophie oder der Jurisprudenz.[1] Die Kunst des Wechslers-Prüfers wird beschrieben als eine Kunst, bei der die Erfahrung eine entscheidende Rolle spielt. Plastisch beschreibt Epiktet, wie der Wechsler zur Prüfung sämtliche Sinne—Sehsinn, Tastsinn, Geruch und Gehör—verwendet und wie es dabei auf Aufmerksamkeit und wiederholte Übung ankommt.[2] Während bei dem auch im Alten Testament begegnenden Bild der Feuerprobe von Edelmetallen das Subjekt dessen, der die Feuerprobe vornimmt, völlig zurücktritt gegenüber dem gleichsam objektiven Prozeß im Feuerofen oder im Schmelztiegel,[3] liegt bei der Metapher des Wechslers der Akzent gerade auf der subjektiven Fähigkeit des Prüfers.

Das außerkanonische, zumeist dem Herrn, gelegentlich aber auch dem Apostel Paulus zugeschriebene Wort "γίνεσθε δόκιμοι τραπεζῖται" ("seid kundige Geldwechsler!") ist eine spezifische Form dieser Metapher. Das Wort war in der alten Kirche weit-

---

[1] (Ps)Plat., *De virt.* 378d–e; Arist., *Rhet.* I,15,7 (1375b); Epikt., *Diss.* I,20,7–11; II,3,1–5; Lukian, *Hist.conscr.* 10; ders., *Paras.* 4; ders., *Hermot.* 68; Max.Tyr., *Diss.* 31,2; Philo, *Spec.Leg.* IV,77; ders., *Sobr.* 20; vgl. R. Bogaert, "Changeurs et banquiers chez les pères de l'église", *AncSoc* 4 (1973), 239–270: 246.

[2] *Diss.* I,20,7–11.

[3] Z.B. Plato, *Politikos*, 303e; Ps 12(11):7; Prov 27:21; Jer 6:29–30; vgl. das Material bei J. Hangard, *Monetaire en daarmee verwante metaforen* (Groningen 1963), 61–68.

verbreitet.[4] Im Vergleich mit dem in der nicht-christlichen Literatur geläufigen Bild sind drei Merkmale kennzeichnend für die Gestalt des Agraphons:

1) Die Form des Imperativs. Obwohl auch in der nicht-christlichen Literatur das Bild des Wechslers den Lesern als ein Ideal vor Augen gestellt werden kann, begegnet hier nie die Aufforderung in der direkten Form des Imperativs.

2) Das Adjektiv δόκιμος als Epitheton des Wechslers. Während in der nicht-christlichen Literatur der Wechsler-Prüfer δοκιμασ- τής und seine Tätigkeit δοκιμάζειν bzw. ἀποδοκιμάζειν heißen kann und die Objekte der Prüfung als δόκιμος bzw. ἀδοκίμασ- τος qualifiziert werden können, fehlen Stellen, in denen δόκιμος als Epitheton des Wechslers verwendet wird. Philo verwendet einmal das Adjektiv ἀγαθός.[5]

3) Mit einem gewissen Vorbehalt auch der Begriff τραπεζίτης. Während der Begriff τραπεζίτης sehr geläufig ist zur Bezeich- nung des Bankiers und Wechslers, werden in der nicht-christ-

---

[4] Vgl. F. M. A. Hänsel, "Ueber die richtige Auffassung der Worte Pauli 1 Thess. 5,21f. durch Berücksichtigung eines Ausspruchs, der unserm Herrn zuge- schrieben wird: γίνεσθε δόκιμοι τραπεζῖται", *ThStKr* (1836), 170–184; A. Resch, "Miscellen zur neutestamentlichen Schriftforschung. V", *ZKWL* 9 (1888), 177– 186; A. Resch, *Agrapha. Aussercanonische Schriftfragmente*, TU N.F. 15.3–4 (Leipzig 1906²), 112–128; J. H. Ropes, *Die Sprüche Jesu, die in den kanonischen Evangelien nicht überliefert sind*, TU 14.2 (Leipzig 1896), 141–143; A. v. Harnack, *Der kirchen- geschichtliche Ertrag der exegetischen Arbeiten des Origenes*, Teil I, TU 42.3 (Leipzig 1918), 19–20; Teil II, TU 42.4 (Leipzig 1919), 39–40; W. Bauer, *Das Leben Jesu im Zeitalter der neutestamentlichen Apokryphen* (Tübingen 1909), 400–401; H. J. Vogels, "Zum Agraphon γίνεσθε δόκιμοι τραπεζῖται", *BZ* 8 (1910), 390; L. Vaganay, "Agrapha", *DBS* I (Paris 1928), 159–198: 187; J. Ruwet, "Les 'agrapha' dans les oeuvres de Clément d'Alexandrie", *Bib.* 30 (1949), 133–160: 146–148; H. Rahner, "'Werdet kundige Geldwechsler!' Zur Geschichte des hl. Ignatius von der Unterscheidung der Geister", *Gr* 37 (1956), 444–483: 475–483; ders., *Ignatius von Loyola als Mensch und Theologe* (Freiburg/Basel/Wien 1964), 312–343; J. Jeremias, *Unbekannte Jesusworte* (Gütersloh 1963³), 95–98; R. Bogaert, *AncSoc* 4 (1973), 239–270: 247–252; L. L. Kline, *The Sayings of Jesus in the Pseudo-Clementine Homilies*, SBL.DS 14 (Missoula [Montana] 1975), 158–159; O. Hofius, "Unbe- kannte Jesusworte", in: P. Stuhlmacher (Hg.), *Das Evangelium und die Evangelien*, WUNT 28 (Tübingen 1983), 355–382: 375–376; ders., "Versprengte Herren- worte" in: W. Schneemelcher (Hg.), *Neutestamentliche Apokryphen in deutscher Übersetzung*, Bd. I (Tübingen 1987⁵), 76–79: 78.

[5] *Spec. Leg.* IV,77.

lichen Literatur, wenn der Begriff metaphorisch verwendet wird, im allgemeinen die Begriffe ἀργυρογνώμων, ἀργυραμοιβός und δοκιμαστής verwendet.[6] Zugleich gilt aber, daß die Grenzen fließend sind. So kann Epiktet sagen, daß der Bankier (τραπεζίτης) oder der Gemüsehändler eine Münze, die das Bild des Kaisers trägt, nicht ablehnen darf. Hier ist zwar die prüfende Tätigkeit des τραπεζίτης im Blick, aber nicht als eine spezifische Fähigkeit, denn der Bankier unterscheidet sich in dieser Hinsicht nicht von jedem beliebigen Händler.[7]

Origenes hatte eine besondere Vorliebe für dieses Agraphon. Im folgenden untersuche ich, in welcher Form er es verwendet, welche Autorität es für ihn hatte und wie er es anwendet.

2. Der Wortlaut

2.1 Der Wortlaut ohne Berücksichtigung von I Thess 5:21-22

Resch hat zehn Stellen aus den Schriften des Origenes zusammengestellt,[8] von Harnack zählte insgesamt zwölf Stellen,

---

[6] Vgl. R. Bogaert, *Les origines antiques de la banque de dépôt* (Leiden 1966), 143–144; ders., *Banques et banquiers dans les cités grecques* (Leiden 1968), 39–41; ders., *AncSoc* 4, 249, Anm. 60.

[7] In Cebes, *Tab.* 31,3, ist mit τραπεζίτης in der Aufforderung des Daimons μηδὲ γίνεσθαι ὁμοίους τοῖς κακοῖς τραπεζίταις der Bankier gemeint, der das Geld von den Leuten annimmt, aber es nicht zurückgeben will. Die prüfende Tätigkeit ist hier nicht im Blick. Der Befund bei Clemens von Alexandrien fordert jedoch dazu auf, die Grenzen nicht zu scharf zu ziehen. Nach Bogaert, *AncSoc* 4, 249, Anm. 60, verwendet Clemens, wenn er das Bild des Wechslers ohne Bezugnahme auf das Agraphon benützt, nicht den Begriff τραπεζίτης, sondern ἀργυραμοιβός. Das ist jedoch nicht richtig. In *Strom.* II,15,4 (GCS Clem. 2, 120, 19-25) unterscheidet Clemens zwar beide Begriffe, indem er den ἀργυραμοιβός, den Wechsler-Prüfer, als Schüler des τραπεζίτης, des Bankiers, betrachtet, aber in der Rolle des Schülers oder in der des Lehrers kommt es bei beiden auf die gleiche Fähigkeit, das Falsche vom Wahren zu unterscheiden, an. In *Strom.* VI,81,2 (GCS Clem. 2, 472,7-11) scheint Clemens beide Begriffe als völlig identisch zu verwenden. An keiner dieser Stellen ist eine Bezugnahme auf das Agraphon ersichtlich.

[8] *Agrapha*, 112-122; nr. 2: *MtCom* 17,31 (GCS 10, 673,32-674,5); nr. 3: *MtCommSer* 33 (GCS 11, 60,16-18); nr. 27=47: *JohCom* 19,44 (GCS 4, 307,2-7); nr. 28=50: *LevHom* 3,8,83-85 (SC 286, 156-158); nr. 29=51: *MtCommSer* 28 (GCS 11, 51,16-22); nr. 44: *JerHom* 12,7 (GCS 3, 94,6); nr. 45: *JerHom* 20(19),9

indem er drei weitere hinzufügte[9] und eine von Resch schon zitierte übersah.[10] Einerseits ist dieses Material noch um wenigstens vier Stellen zu erweitern,[11] andererseits ist es zu reduzieren, weil sowohl Resch als von Harnack sämtliche Stellen bei Origenes, an denen sich der Wechslervergleich findet, als ein Zitat des Agraphons oder eine Bezugnahme darauf betrachten.[12] Man sollte jedoch genauer unterscheiden zwischen (1) expliziten Zitaten des Agraphons, (2) eindeutigen Anspielungen darauf, (3) möglichen Anspielungen und (4) der Verwendung der Metapher ohne Bezugnahme auf das Agraphon.

2.1.1 Explizite Zitate

Dreimal verwendet Origenes das Wort als ein explizites Zitat, zweimal in vollständiger und einmal in unvollständiger Form. Im *Johanneskommentar* zitiert er als ein "Gebot Jesu" das Wort: Γίνεσθε δόκιμοι τραπεζῖται,[13] in der *Commentariorum Series zu Matthäus* beruft er sich auf "jenes Gebot", das besagt: *Estote prudentes nummularii*,[14] und im griechisch erhaltenen Teil des *Matthäuskommentars* weist er auf denjenigen hin, der "nach der Schrift" ein δόκιμος τραπεζίτης genannt wird.[15]

(GCS 3, 193, 22–23); nr. 46: *MtCom* 12,2 (GCS 10, 71,5); nr. 48: *JohCom* 20,286 (GCS 4, 369, 33); nr. 49: *JohCom* 32, 215 (GCS 4, 454,31).

[9] *Ertrag* II, 39–40: *LucHom* 1 (GCS 9, 3,13[lat.] & 16–17[gr.]); *EphCom* §19,60–62 (J. A. F. Gregg, "The Commentary of Origen upon the Epistle to the Ephesians", *JThS* 3 (1902), 233–244, 398–420, 554–576: 419 (v. Harnack zitierte nach Cramer, *Catenae* VI, 182); *EzHom* 2,2 (SC 352, 104,47–48).

[10] *LevHom* 3,8 (Resch nr. 28=50).

[11] *MtCommSer* 68 (GCS 11, 161,20–23); diese Stelle wird auch von Bogaert, *AncSoc* 4, 248, Anm 53, genannt; die anderen von ihm neu gegenüber Resch aufgeführten Stellen finden sich schon bei von Harnack; *EphCom* §22, 37–39 (*JThS* 3, 557); *EphCom* §25,47 (*JThS* 3, 562); *Frg in Mt* 341 (GCS 12.1, 147); dieses Fragment berührt sich zwar eng mit *MtCom* 12,2 (Resch, nr. 46), ist aber damit keineswegs identisch: während in *MtCom* 12,2 die Wechsler die Aufgabe haben, "die wirkenden Geister" zu unterscheiden, werden sie im genannten Fragment "kundige Wechsler der Schriften" genannt.

[12] Resch (*Agrapha*, 112–122) unterscheidet zwischen Zitaten und Bezugnahmen auf das Logion; von Harnack (*Ertrag* II, 40) bezeichnet sämtliche Stellen als Zitate.

[13] *JohCom* 19,44 (GCS 4, 307,2–7).

[14] *MtCommSer* 33 (GCS 11, 60,16–18).

[15] *MtCom* 17,31 (GCS 10, 673,32–674,5).

2.1.2 Eindeutige Anspielungen

An zehn Stellen kann man mit Sicherheit annehmen, daß
Origenes auf das Herren- oder Schriftwort anspielt, ohne daß er
es explizit als ein Zitat bezeichnet. Die Variabelen sind nur das
Verb und der Numerus. Einmal ist die Anspielung dreigliedrig:
δόκιμοι γενόμενοι τραπεζῖται,[16] in den anderen Fällen zweiglie-
drig und redet er entweder im Singular vom δόκιμος τραπεζίτης[17]
oder im Plural von den δόκιμοι τραπεζῖται.[18] In den lateinischen
Übersetzungen steht dafür: *probati trapezitae*,[19] *probabiles trapezitae*[20] oder *exercitatissimi trapezitae*.[21] Da die Kombination dieses
Substantivs mit diesem Adjektiv in nicht-christlichen Texten
nicht begegnet, hat man guten Grund, anzunehmen, daß hier
eine Anspielung auf das Agraphon vorliegt. An einer Stelle
macht Origenes diese Verbindung explizit: zunächst redet er
allgemein von der spezifischen Fähigkeit des δόκιμος τραπεζίτης
und fügt sodann hinzu, daß diejenigen, die diese Fähigkeit
besitzen, das Gebot Jesu Γίνεσθε δόκιμοι τραπεζῖται befolgen.[22]

2.1.3 Mögliche Anspielungen

An drei Stellen kann man nicht mit Sicherheit sagen, ob
Origenes auf das Agraphon anspielt, darf man aber die
Möglichkeit auch nicht ausschließen. Im *Kommentar zum Johannesevangelium* verwendet er einmal die Verbindung καλοὶ
τραπεζῖται.[23] In der lateinischen Übersetzung des *Matthäuskommentars* steht zweimal nur das Substantiv: *trapezitae*[24] bzw.
nummularii.[25] *Nummularius* kan an sich sowohl für τραπεζίτης wie
für ἀργυραμοιβός stehen, das parallele griechische Fragment im
Scholienkommentar des "Petrus von Laodicea" hat hier jedoch
τραπεζῖται.[26] Dieser Begriff könnte ein Indiz dafür sein, daß

---

[16] *JerHom* 12,7 (GCS 3, 193,22–23).

[17] *EphCom* §22,37–39 (*JThS* 3, 557); *EphComm* §19,60–62 (*JThS* 3, 419); *JohCom*
20,286 (GCS 4, 369,33).

[18] *MtCom* 12,2 (GCS 10, 71,5); *Frg in Mt* 341,4 (GCS 12.1, 147); *LucHom* 1gr
(GCS 9, 3,16–17); *EphCom* §25,47 (*JThS* 3, 562).

[19] *EzHom* 2,2 (SC 352, 104, 47–48).

[20] *LevHom* 3,8,83–85 (SC 286, 156, 158).

[21] *LucHom* 1lat (GCS 9, 3,13).

[22] *JohCom* 19,44 (GCS 4, 307,2–7).

[23] *JohCom* 32,215 (GCS 4, 451,31).

[24] *MtCommSer* 28 (GCS 11, 51,18).

[25] *MtCommSer* 68 (GCS 11, 161,20).

[26] 293,17 (GCS 11, 161,20).

Origenes hier an das Agraphon denkt, aber ein durchschlagendes
Argument ist das nicht, weil, wie oben gesagt, die Grenzen
zwischen dem Sprachgebrauch bei den nicht-christlichen Schrift-
stellern und dem Wortlaut des Agraphons fließend sind. Einen
anderen Hinweis auf eine mögliche Anspielung auf das Agraphon könnte man in den beiden letzten Fällen darin sehen, daß
das Bild der *trapezitae* bzw. *nummularii* eng mit dem Pauluswort I
Thess 5:21–22 verbunden ist. Wie wir im folgenden Paragraph
sehen werden, zitiert Origenes das Agraphon und das Pauluswort
oft als engstens zusammengehörig. Aber auch dieses Argument
ist nicht stichhaltig, weil die Gefahr eines Zirkelschlusses droht.

2.1.4 Das Bild des Wechslers ohne Anspielung auf das Agraphon

An zwei Stellen, an denen der Wechslervergleich begegnet,
kann man mit an Sicherheit grenzender Wahrscheinlichkeit
sagen, daß Origenes keine Anspielung auf das Agraphon macht.
In seiner Auslegung von Jer 20;12—wo der Herr vorgestellt wird
als derjenige, "der das Gerechte billigt, der Nieren und Herzen
kennt"—bezeichnet er den Herrn als τραπεζίτης δικαίων καὶ
ἀδίκων.[27] In diesem Falle liegt es nicht nahe, an das Agraphon zu
denken, weil die für dieses Wort kennzeichnende Aufforderung
schwerlich auf Gott anwendbar ist.

In einem Fragment aus der *Prophetenkatene*[28] vergleicht
Origenes denjenigen, der das Charisma der Unterscheidung der
Geister besitzt, mit einem ἀργυραμοιβός, der die echten und die
gefälschten Münzen unterscheiden kann. An dieser Stelle liegt
keine einzige Reminiszenz an das Agraphon vor. Origenes
verwendet das Bild mit genau derselben Begrifflichkeit wie die
nicht-christlichen Schriftsteller.

2.2 Das Agraphon in Verbindung mit I Thess 5:21–22

An sieben Stellen bei Origenes begegnet das Agraphon bzw. der
Wechslervergleich in engster Verbindung mit I Thess 5:21–22:
"Prüft aber alles, behaltet das Gute; haltet euch fern von jeder
Gestalt des Bösen." Die Art der Verbindung ist jedoch jeweils
von verschiedener Art:

> 1. Einmal zitiert Origenes das Agraphon und die Mahnung des
> Apostels explizit als Worte aus zwei verschiedenen Quellen;

---

[27] *JerHom* 20(19),9 (GCS 3, 193,22–23).

[28] *Frg in Jer* 19 (GCS 3, 207,13–14); diese Stelle wurde mit Recht weder von
Resch noch von v.Harnack aufgeführt.

ersteres nennt er "ein Gebot Jesu" und letzteres "die Lehre des Paulus."[29]

2. Ein anderes Mal leitet er die beiden Worte als zwei verschiedene Gebote ein: "jenes Gebot, das besagt..., und jenes (andere), das besagt..."[30]

3. Einmal zitiert er das Agraphon und I Thess 5:21–22 in einem Atemzug als "Schrift", so daß der Eindruck entsteht, es handle sich um ein und dasselbe Wort: "...der nach der Schrift kundiger Wechsler genannt wird, der alles zu prüfen und das Gute zu behalten, von jeder Gestalt des Bösen aber sich fernzuhalten versteht."[31]

4. Zweimal verknüpft er, ohne explizit eine Quelle oder Autorität anzugeben, das Bild des Geldwechslers bzw. eine Bezugnahme auf das Agraphon so eng mit einem buchstäblichen Zitat aus I Thess 5:21–22, daß beide gleichsam eine Einheit bilden: "Wer ist nun in solcher Weise ein kundiger Geldwechsler, daß er alles zu prüfen versteht...?"[32]; "denn es ist notwendig, ein kundiger Wechsler zu sein und die Fähigkeit zu besitzen, alles zu prüfen..."[33]

5. Einmal begegnet das Bild des Geldwechslers in einem Atemzug mit einer eigenen Variante auf I Thess 5:21–22: "...den Geldwechslern, die alles versuchen und prüfen, um die gute und wahre Lehre zu behalten, die verworfene und falsche dagegen zurückzuweisen."[34]

6. Einmal verwendet Origenes den Wechslervergleich als Epexegese von I Thess 5:21: "Deswegen sagt der Apostel gleichsam zu den kundigen Geldwechslern: prüft aber alles, behaltet das Gute."[35] Mit dem Adverb "gleichsam (*velut*)" dürfte er angeben, daß das Bild eine Interpretation des Pauluswortes ist.

---

[29] *JohCom* 19,44 (GCS 4, 307,4–7).

[30] *MtCommSer* 33 (GCS 11, 60,16–18).

[31] *MtCom* 17,31 (GCS 10, 673,32–674,5).

[32] *EphCom* §22,37–39 (*JThS* 3, 557).

[33] *EphComm* §19, 60–62 (*JThS* 3, 419).

[34] *MtCommSer* 68 (GCS 11, 161,20–23): "...*nummulariis qui omnia tentant et probant, ut bonum quidem dogma et verum teneant, reprobum autem et falsum repellant.*" Anklänge an I Thess 5,21–22 sind: "*omnia...probant*" und "*bonum... teneant.*" Das parallele griechische Scholienfragment liest: τραπεζῖται δὲ οἱ ἀκροαταί, οἱ τὰ μὲν καλὰ κατέχοντες δόγματα, τῶν δὲ φαύλων ἀπεχόμενοι.

[35] *LevHom* 3,8,83–85 (SC 3, 286,156.158).

Im Anschluß an Hänsel[36] nahm Resch[37] an, daß die ursprüng-
liche Form des Herrenwortes den Wortlaut von I Thess 5:21–22
mitumfaßte, daß Paulus dort also einen Teil des Herrenwortes
zitierte und daß die Form "seid kundige Wechsler!" eine
sekundäre und abgekürzte Form sei. Diese These ist mit Recht
von der Mehrheit der Forscher abgelehnt worden.[38] Die wichtigsten Argumente für diese Ablehnung sind:

1. Zweimal macht Origenes explizit klar, daß die Texte ausein-
ander zu halten sind.[39]
2. Origenes verwendet das Agraphon auch in einem Atemzug
mit einer Anspielung auf ein anderes Schriftwort wie I Kor
12:10, obwohl er sehr genau weiß, daß es sich um verschiedene
Worte handelt.[40] Aus der Tatsache, daß er zwei Texte kombiniert, darf man also nicht schließen, daß Origenes beide Worte
einer einzigen Quelle entnahm.
3. Nicht nur I Thess 5:21–22, sondern auch andere Texte, in
denen die Worte δοκιμάζειν und δόκιμος begegnen wie Eph
5:10 und Jer 20:12 rufen bei Origenes den Wechslervergleich
hervor.[41] Das dürfte damit zu erklären sein, daß diese Begriffe
auch in der nicht-christlichen Literatur häufig mit Bezug auf das
Prüfen von Geld und Edelmetallen verwendet werden.[42]
4. Es gibt vor Origenes keine Belege, in denen das Agraphon
eindeutig in der von Resch postulierten ursprünglichen Form

---

[36] *ThStKr* 1836, 170–184.

[37] *ZKWL* 9, 177–186; *Agrapha*, 112–128.

[38] Z.B. Ropes, *Sprüche*, 142–143; E. von Dobschütz, *Die Thessalonicher-Briefe*,
KEK 10 (Göttingen 1909⁷), 226.

[39] *JohCom* 19,44 (GCS 4, 307,2–7); *MtCommSer* 33 (GCS 11, 60,16–18).

[40] *MtCom* 12,2 (GCS 10, 71,5): "...μὴ δόκιμοι τραπεζῖται, μηδὲ ἐπιστάμενοι
διακρίνειν πνεύματα ἐνεργοῦντα..."

[41] *EphCom* §25,47 (*JThS* 3, 562); *JerHom* 20,9 (GCS 3, 193,220–23).

[42] Hangard, *metaforen*, 25–26, 35–36; Bogaert, *AncSoc* 4, 249, Anm 59.

erscheint. Das Wort erscheint in den frühen Quellen entweder ohne Bezug auf I Thess 5:21–22[43] oder höchstens mit einer Anspielung darauf.[44]

Am wahrscheinlichsten ist also, daß an den Stellen, an denen Origenes das Agraphon bzw. das Bild des Wechslers in einem Atemzug mit I Thess 5:21–22 anführt, eine sekundäre Kombination vorliegt.

3. Die Autorität des Wortes für Origenes

Daß Origenes das Wort so eindeutig als "Gebot", "Gebot Jesu" und als "Schriftwort" bezeichnet,[45] is bemerkenswert, weil er mit Nachdruck von der ganzen Überlieferung der Worte Jesu nur die Evangelien nach Matthäus, Markus, Lukas und Johannes als autoritativ und inspiriert anerkennt.[46] Ein Kenner der Schriften wie Origenes wird sich dessen bewußt gewesen sein, daß das Wort in diesen Schriften nicht zu finden war. Wenn er aus anderen ihm bekannten Quellen der Jesusüberlieferung, wie dem *Petrusevangelium*, dem *Buch des Jakobus* oder dem *Evangelium nach den Hebräern* zitiert und mit deren Inhalt sympathisiert, macht er zumeist einen Vorbehalt wie: "wenn man es denn annehmen mag…", oder: "wenn aber jemand annimt…"[47] Für die Weise, in der Origenes beim Wort von den kundigen Wechslern unein-

---

[43] Apelles bei Epiphanius, *Pan.* 44,2,6 (GCS Epiph. 2, 192,17); vgl. auch PsClemens, *Hom.* 2,51,1 (GCS 42², 55,17); 3,50,2 (GCS 42², 75,20); 18,20,4 (GCS 42², 250,13); *Didasc.* 2,36,9 (Funk, Band I, 123,17–18).

[44] Clem. Alex., *Strom.* I,177,2 (GCS Clem. 1, 109,12–14): γίνεσθε δὲ δόκιμοι τραπεζῖται τὰ μὲν ἀποδοκιμάζοντες, τὸ δὲ καλὸν κατέχοντες; *Pistis Sophia* 134 (GCS Kopt.-Gnost., 228,10–12): "Werdet wie die klugen Geldwechsler, das Gute nehmet, das Schlechte werfet weg." Resch rechnet erstere Stelle zum paulinischen und letztere zum nicht-paulinischen Typus. In Wirklichkeit aber dürfte nur der dritte Teil des Zitates bei Clemens aus I Thess 5:21 stammen.

[45] *MtCommSer* 33 (GCS 11, 60,16–18); *JohCom* 19,44 (GCS 4, 307,2–7); *LevHom* 3,8,83–85 (SC 286,156.158).

[46] *LucHom* 1 (GCS 9, 3–5); *MtCom* 1 nach Eus., *h.e.* VI,25.

[47] Z.B. *JerHom* 15,4 (GCS 3, 128,26–29); *JohCom* 2,87 (GCS 4, 67,19–23); *MtCom* 15,14 (GCS 10, 389,15–21); vgl. A. van den Hoek, "Clement and Origen as Sources on 'Noncanonical' Scriptural Traditions during the Late Second and Earlier Third Centuries", in: G. Dorival/A. Le Boulluec (Hg.), *Origeniana sexta*, BEThL 118 (Leuven 1996), 93–113: 103–104.

geschränkt die Autorität eines sich nicht in den anerkannten Schriften begegnenden Herrenwort anerkennt, gibt es, soweit ich sehe, in seinen Schriften nur teilweise Parallelen. Das als Herrenwort angeführte: "Bittet um das Große und das Kleine wird euch hinzugetan werden; bittet um das Himmlische und das Irdische wird euch hinzugetan werden" ist nicht ganz vergleichbar, weil man es als eine freie Wiedergabe vom Mt 6:33 betrachten kann.[48] Am ehesten vergleichbar is das Wort: "Wer mir nahe ist, ist dem Feuer nahe; wer mir ferne ist, ist dem Königreiche fern." An einer Stelle zitiert Origenes dieses Wort ohne Vorbehalt als ein Schriftwort.[49] An einer anderen Stelle macht er jedoch klar, daß er das Wort zwar als Herrenwort irgendwo gelesen hat, daß er aber nicht weiß, "ob jemand die Rolle des Heilandes angenommen oder gedächtnismäßig zitiert hat, oder aber, ob es wahr ist, was gesagt ist."[50] In diesem Falle dürfte die Quelle das von Origenes an anderer Stelle abgelehnte *Thomasevangelium* sein.[51] Die bei diesem Wort zum Ausdruck gebrachte Spannung zwischen vorbehaltsloser Anerkennung als "Schriftwort" und größter Zurückhaltung in der Frage der Authentizität fehlt beim Wort von den kundigen Geldwechslern.

4. Die Anwendung des Wortes bzw. des Metaphers

Nach H. Rahner[52] gehört das Wort von den "klugen Geldwechslern" in die Geschichte der διάκρισις oder der "Discretio" hinein. Er unterscheidet fünf Zusammenhänge, in denen das Wort auftaucht: (1) die Unterscheidung von Wahrem und Falschem innerhalb der Schrift (Apelles und die *pseudo-klementinischen Homilien*), (2) die Unterscheidung von kanonischen und unkanonischen Evangelien (Origenes und Ambrosius), (3) die biblisch-exegetische Diskretion (Victor von Capua), (4) die dogmatische Diskretion: die Unterscheidung von Wahrheit und Irrtum in der Lehre (z.B. Origenes und Athanasius), (5) die aszetische Diskretion: die Unterscheidung der Wirkungen des

---

[48] Z.B. *MtComm* 16,28 (GCS 10, 571,18–22); weiteres bei Resch, *Agrapha*, 111–112; Ropes, *Sprüche*, 140; Jeremias, *Jesusworte*, 93–95.

[49] *JosueHom* 4,3 (SC 71, 154): "*quod scriptum est.*"

[50] *JerHom*(lat) 3,3 (GCS 8, 312,23–26).

[51] *ThomEv* 82; vgl. *LucHom* 1 (GCS 9, 5,9–10); dazu: R. M. Grant/D. N. Freedman, *The Secret Sayings of Jesus* (London/Glasgow 1960), 85–86; Jeremias, *Jesusworte*, 65.

[52] *Gr* 37, 476–482.

guten und des bösen Geistes im seelisch-innerlichen Bereich (von Clemens und Origenes an über die *Vita Syncleticae* des Ps. Athanasius und Cassian bis in die Exerzitiendeutung der Jesuiten des 16. Jahrhunderts). Nach Rahner ist das Agraphon bei Origenes namentlich mit dem zweiten, dem vierten und dem fünften Komplex verbunden. Meiner Meinung nach sind damit jedoch die Akzente nicht ganz richtig gesetzt. Im Folgenden bespreche ich die Zusammenhänge, in denen Origenes das Agraphon bzw. das Bild des Geldwechslers verwendet, und frage dabei jeweils, wie er die Aufforderung "seid kundige Wechsler!" konkretisiert.

4.1 Die anerkannten und die nicht-anerkannten Bücher der Schrift

Zweimal verwendet Origenes die Metapher der kundigen Geldwechsler im Zusammenhang mit der Frage, welche Bücher als inspirierte Schrift anzuerkennen sind, und welche nicht. Einmal handelt es sich dabei um die Schriften des Alten und einmal um die des Neuen Bundes.

4.1.1 Die Schriften des Alten Bundes

In seinem Kommentar zu Mt 23:37–39[53] stellt Origenes fest, daß weder die sich bei Jesus, Stephanus, Paulus und dem Verfasser des Hebräerbriefes findende Behauptung, die Juden hätten die Propheten getötet, noch die Geschichte des Jannes und Mambres in II Tim 3:8 noch das Zitat I Kor 2:9 in den öffentlich bekannten Schriften des Alten Bundes hinlänglich bezeugt ist, daß sie aber in den "Apokryphen" (*secreta*), die bei den Juden in Umlauf sind. Einerseits gilt es, klar zu unterscheiden zwischen den "öffentlich bekannten Schriften"—oder, wie der Übersetzer unter Verwendung einer ihm geläufigen Kategorie sagt, den "kanonisierten Büchern"[54]—und den "Apokryphen, die bei den Juden in Umlauf sind", weil vieles darin erdichtet ist. Andererseits darf man letztere auch nicht völlig verwerfen, weil sie manches enthalten, was zum Beweis der Schriften des Neuen Bundes gehört. Um wie Geldwechsler zwischen den Worten unterscheiden zu können, muß man nach Origenes das Vermögen "eines großen Mannes" haben, der I Thess 5:21 zu hören und zu erfüllen versteht. Wegen derer aber, die diese Fähigkeit nicht besitzen, darf niemand zur Bekräftigung der Lehren Bücher benützen, die nicht zu den "kanonisierten Schriften" gehören. Kennzeichnend für Origenes ist, wie er eine

---

[53] *MtCommSer* 28 (GCS 11, 49,19–51,22).

[54] Dazu Harnack, *Ertrag* II, 43–44, Anm. 1; Hanson, *Doctrine*, 138, 143.

Entscheidung darüber, wer diese Fähigkeit besitzt, in der Schwebe läßt. Mit der Formulierung "eines großen Mannes also ist es..." deutet er eher auf ein Ideal als auf eine konkrete Wirklichkeit hin. In seinem *Kommentar zum Hohenlied*[55] gibt er jedoch konkretere Auskünfte darüber, wer zur Kategorie eines solchen "großen Mannes" zu zählen sei: "Denn vielleicht wußten die Apostel oder Evangelisten, die erfüllt waren vom Heiligen Geist, was aus jenen (apokryphen) Schriften anzunehmen und was zu verwerfen sei. Für uns aber, die nicht solchen Überfluß des Geistes haben, ist es nicht ohne Gefahr, solches zu wagen." Sogar bei idealen Gestalten der Vergangenheit, den Aposteln und Evangelisten, fügt Origenes noch ein verunsicherndes "vielleicht" hinzu. In dem "Wir", die nicht das erforderliche Maß an Geistbesitz haben, schließt Origenes sich selbst an dieser Stelle mit ein. Im *Matthäuskommentar* jedoch redet er—oder der lateinische Bearbeiter des Kommentars—über die Leute, die nicht das Vermögen zur Unterscheidung haben, in der dritten Person. Der Grund dafür, daß niemand zur Bekräftigung der Lehren apokryphe Bücher verwenden darf, liegt eher in der mangelnden Fähigkeit anderer als in dem eigenen Unvermögen. Die konkrete Weise, in der Origenes an mehreren Stellen[56] mit Argumenten aus den anerkannten Schriften zu unterscheiden versucht, inwieweit die Apokryphen für wahr oder für falsch zu halten sind, zeigt ebenfalls, daß er sich selbst das Vermögen nicht ganz abgesprochen hat. Der Tatsache jedoch, daß er diese Fähigkeit, zu unterscheiden, einmal der besonderen pneumatischen Fähigkeit der Apostel und Evangelisten zuschreibt und das andere Mal dem Vermögen eines idealen großen Mannes, kann man entnehmen, daß er an diesem Punkt ein wirkliches Problem erfahren hat, wofür er keine fertige Lösung hatte.

4.1.2 Die Schriften des Neuen Bundes

Anders ist der Ton des Origenes in der ersten *Homilie zum Lukasevangelium*,[57] wo es um die Schriften des Neuen Bundes geht. Wie es im alten Volke wahre und falsche Propheten gab, so sagt er, jedoch mittels der dem Volke verliehenen Gabe der Unterscheidung der Geister erstere angenommen und letztere

---

[55] *CantCom*, Prolog 4, 34 (SC 375, 170).

[56] Z.B. *Ep ad Afr*, passim (SC 302, 522–573); *MtCom* 10,18 (GCS 10, 24,6–13); *MtCommSer* 46–47 (GCS 11, 94,17–95,31); 61 (GCS 11, 140,9–20); 117 (GCS 11, 249,16–250,12).

[57] GCS 9, 3,1–5,24.

verworfen wurden, so haben jetzt im Neuen Bund viele versucht, Evangelien zu schreiben, "die kundigen Wechsler" haben daraus jedoch nur vier—Matthäus, Markus, Lukas und Johannes aufgenommen und die anderen verworfen. Während die "vielen" nach dem Wortlaut des Lukasprologs nur "versucht haben", ein Evangelium zu schreiben, wurden die vier Evangelisten vom Heiligen Geiste dazu angeleitet. Weil Origenes die Fähigkeit der Wechsler auf eine Linie mit der dem Volke des Alten Bundes verliehenen Gabe der Unterscheidung der Geister stellt, dürfte er bei den "kundigen Wechslern" weniger an eine besondere Gruppe, als vielmehr an die Kirche als Ganze[58] bzw. den für sie maßgebenden Teil[59] gedacht haben. Indem er die Fähigkeit der Wechsler mit der Gabe der Unterscheidung der Geister identifiziert,[60] unterstreicht er deren pneumatischen Charakter. Der Zusammenhang zwischen der Gabe der Unterscheidung der Geister im Alten Bunde und dem Kanon begegnet man auch sonst bei Origenes. So bemerkt er in seinem Kommentar zu I Kor 14:31,[61] daß er sich wiederholt die Frage gestellt hat, wie es möglich war, daß die falschen Propheten bei den Herrschenden zwar oft in höherem Ansehen standen als die wahren, daß aber nur die Bücher der letzteren veröffentlicht und anerkannt sind. Die Lösung dieser Frage fand er in den Aussagen des Apostels Paulus über die Gabe der Unterscheidung der Geister. Dieses Charisma gab es schon im Alten Bunde. Gemeinsam ist beiden Stellen, daß Origenes nicht von Kriterien redet, sondern von der pneumatischen Gabe und deren im nachhinein feststellbaren Effektivität. Der Bezug auf diese Gabe hat in beiden Fällen eine legitimierende Funktion.

Anders als im oben genannten Text über die Schriften des Alten Bundes findet man in der ersten *Homilie zum Lukasevangelium* keine Spur von Unsicherheit. Origenes zieht eine klare

---

[58] Man kann als parallele Sätze lesen: "...ἀλλ' οἱ δόκιμοι τραπεζῖται οὐ πάντα ἐνέκριναν, ἀλλά τινα αὐτῶν ἐξελέξαντο" und: "...τὰ δὲ τέσσαρα μόνα προκρίνει ἡ τοῦ θεοῦ ἐκκλησία" (GCS 9, 3,16–18 und 9, 5,16–17).

[59] So H. J. Vogt, *Das Kirchenverständnis des Origenes*, BoBKG 4 (Köln/Wien 1974), 109; Hanson, *Doctrine*, 137, Anm. 1 denkt dagegen an die Evangelisten.

[60] Im griechischen Text steht die Gabe der Unterscheidung der Geister im alten Volk auf einer Linie mit der Fähigkeit der kundigen Wechsler im Neuen Bund, in der Übersetzung des Hieronymus wird der Wechslervergleich auf die Gabe der Unterscheidung der Geister im Volk der Juden angewandt.

[61] *Frg in I Cor*, § 73 (C. Jenkins, "Origen on I Corinthians", *JThS* 9 [1908], 231–247. 353–372.500–514; 10 [1909], 29–51: 10,41).

Trennungslinie zwischen Kirche und Häresie bzw. zwischen den anerkannten und den verworfenen Schriften[62] und betrachtet die Fähigkeit der Geldwechsler nicht als ein Ideal oder als eine Möglichkeit einer besonders begabten Gruppe, sondern als ein der Kirche ohne Einschränkung eigenes Vermögen. Das ist um so auffälliger als Origenes an anderen Stellen in dieser Hinsicht ein größeres Problembewußtsein zeigt und den Eindruck erweckt, die Grenzen zwischen den anzuerkennenden und den zu verwerfenden Evangelien seien fließender. So kann er nicht nur, wie oben gezeigt, Agrapha oder ein Wort aus dem Thomasevangelium als Schrift anführen, sondern auch die Akzeptation des *Hebräerevangeliums*, des *Petrusevangeliums* und des *Buches des Jakobus* durch andere tolerieren und eine Entscheidung über das *Kerygma Petrou* in einer bestimmten Situation offen lassen.[63] Das alles steht zur in der ersten *Lukashomilie* postulierten Klarheit in einem Spannungsverhältnis. Bei den verschiedenen Stellungnahmen zu dieser Frage dürften die verschiedenen Rollen des Origenes als Mann der Kirche,[64] als Wissenschaftler mit einem großen Problembewußtsein und als Theologe mit seinen besonderen Vorlieben mitspielen. In der *Lukashomilie* ist er nur an einer klaren Abgrenzung nach außen hin interessiert und blendet er die kritischen Fragen völlig aus.

---

[62] Nur der lateinische Text hat den expliziten Gegensatz zwischen "Kirche" und "Häresie." Weil Origenes aber auch im griechischen Text Basilides als einen der Autoren der verworfenen Evangelien nennt, ist der Gegensatz hier wenigstens impliziert, wenn er auch nicht jedes der aufgeführten Evangelien im gleichen Maße für häretisch gehalten haben dürfte. Vgl. J. Ruwet, "Les Apocryphes dans les oeuvres d'Origène", *Bib.* 25 (1945), 143–166. 311–334: 161–163.

[63] Z.B. *MtCom* 10,17 (GCS 10, 21,26–22,3); 15,14 (GCS 10, 389,13–390,17); *JohCom* 2,87 (GCS 4, 67,19–23); 13,104 (GCS 4, 241,12–22); *JerHom* 15,4 (GCS 3, 128,26–29); dazu Harnack, *Ertrag* II, 37–38; Hanson, *Doctrine*, 137–139; B. M. Metzger, *The Canon of the New Testament* (Oxford 1987), 137. 141; Van den Hoek, *Origeniana sexta*, 103–107.

[64] Dazu J. W. Trigg, "Origen Man of the Church", in: R. J. Daly (Hg.), *Origeniana quinta*, BEThL 105 (Leuven 1992), 51–56.

4.2 Die Erfüllung der Schrift des Alten Bundes in den Taten Jesu

Nicht nur bei der Unterscheidung der Schriften, sondern auch bei deren Interpretation ist die Funktion des Geldwechslers entscheidend. Zunächst kommt es darauf an, das Wirken Jesu im Lichte der Schriften des Alten Bundes zu verstehen. Darüber handelt Origenes im *Matthäuskommentar* anläßlich der Forderung eines Zeichens vom Himmel durch die Sadduzäer und Pharisäer (Mt 16:1–4).[65] Er vermutet, daß sie ein solches Zeichen deshalb forderten, weil sie die Zeichen auf Erden verdächtigten, sie könnten auch von einem anderen als von Gott bewirkt worden sein—sie warfen ja Jesus vor, er treibe die Dämonen auf Erden aus in der Kraft des Beelsebul—und weil sie meinten, ein Zeichen vom Himmel könne nicht von einer bösen Kraft bewirkt werden. Nach Origenes gingen sie jedoch in dieser Annahme fehl, weil sie weder kundige Wechsler waren, noch die wirkenden Geister zu unterscheiden vermochten, nämlich welche von Gott stammen und welche von ihm abgefallen sind. Origenes verbindet hier das Bild des Wechslers mit einer Anspielung auf I Kor 12:10. An den anderen Stellen, an denen er das tut, ist die Fähigkeit der Wechsler identisch mit der der Unterscheidung der Geister,[66] an dieser Stelle jedoch dürfte er mit beiden jeweils einen verschiedenen Aspekt bezeichnen. Während die Fähigkeit der Unterscheidung der Geister sich hier auf die Unterscheidung der göttlichen und dämonischen Zeichen bezieht, besteht die der kundigen Wechsler in der richtigen Interpretation der Schrift. In einem überlieferten *Katenenfragment*, das sich sehr eng mit dieser Stelle berührt, redet Origenes denn auch von "kundigen Wechslern der Schriften" (δόκιμοι τραπεζῖται τῶν γραφῶν).[67] Hier wie dort liegt der Akzent darauf, daß die Pharisäer und Sadduzäer die Schriften nicht richtig verstanden haben. Origenes bringt insofern Verständnis für ihr Mißtrauen auf, als er mit der Möglichkeit rechnet, daß sie aufgrund der Schriftstellen, nach denen Zauberer und Beschwörer manche Zeichen und Wunder der Wahrheit nachahmten, die Zeichen Jesu verdächtigten. Aber ihre Annahme, daß ein Zeichen vom Himmel im Gegensatz zu einem Zeichen auf Erden ein Beweis göttlicher Herkunft sei, ist seiner Meinung nach keineswegs schriftgemäß. Sie hätten zum Beispiel

---

[65] *MtComm* 12,2 (GCS 10, 70,23–72,20).

[66] *LucHom* 1 (GSC 9, 3,3–18); *EzHom* 2,2 (SC 352, 104,46–49); *Frg in Jer* 19 (GCS 3, 207,9–14).

[67] *Frg in Mt* 341,4 (GCS 12,1, 147).

wissen müssen, daß einerseits die Wunder, die unter Moses gegen Ägypten geschahen, und die nicht vom Himmel waren, eindeutig von Gott stammten, und daß andererseits das Feuer, welches vom Himmel auf die Schafe des Job fiel, nicht von Gott war. Zugleich bemerkten sie nicht, daß die Worte der Propheten in den Taten Jesu in Erfüllung gingen. Die Fähigkeit der kundigen Wechsler besteht nach dieser Stelle also darin, daß man Schrift mit Schrift vergleichen und die Wirksamkeit Jesu im Lichte der Schriften richtig interpretieren kann.

4.3 Der buchstäbliche und der tiefere Sinn der Schrift

Die Fähigkeit der kundigen Wechsler mit Bezug auf die Interpretation der Schrift geht aber noch weiter und bezieht sich auch auf die Unterscheidung zwischen dem buchstäblichen und dem tieferen Sinne der Schrift. In der Aufforderung Jer 13:15—"Hört zu und tut die Ohren auf!"—handelt es sich nach Origenes[68] um zwei Arten der Schriftauslegung: "Tut die Ohren auf!" bezieht sich auf das Vordergründige, dasjenige, was dem Hörer ohne Auslegung eine Hilfe sein kann. Man braucht das Gesagte nur "in die Ohren hinein aufzunehmen." "Hört zu!" dagegen bezieht sich auf den tieferen Sinn der Schrift, auf das Geheimere und Mystischere; man soll das nicht nur "in die Ohren", sondern auch "in das Denken hinein aufnehmen." Die Ausleger sollen zu kundigen Geldwechslern werden, indem sie die ganze Schrift untersuchen und dabei fähig werden zu sagen: Dies ist ein "Hört zu!", dies aber ein "Tut die Ohren auf!" Bei der Fähigkeit des Geldwechslers handelt es sich an dieser Stelle also um das Vermögen der Ausleger zwischen dem vordergründigen und dem tieferen Sinn zu unterscheiden. Man kann dieses Vermögen erwerben durch das Studium der ganzen Schrift. Daß es sich bei der Entdeckung des tieferen Sinnes jedoch nicht um etwas selbstverständliches handelt, drückt Origenes dadurch aus, daß er bei der Möglichkeit, den Sinn des Schriftwortes in das Denken hinein aufzunehmen, ein verunsicherndes "vielleicht ist es möglich" hinzufügt.[69]

Die bei der Auslegung von Jer 13:15 nur gestreifte Frage nach der Möglichkeit einer geistigen Auslegung bekommt an einer

---

[68] *JerHom* 12,7 (GCS 3, 93,17–94,7).

[69] Dazu E. Schadel in: Origenes, *Die griechisch erhaltenen Jeremiahomilien*, eingeleitet, übersetzt und mit Erklärungen versehen von E. Schadel, BGrL 10 (Stuttgart 1980), 295.

Stelle im *Matthäuskommentar* mehr Profil.[70] Anläßlich der Frage
der Sadduzäer über die Konsequenzen der Schwiegerehe für die
Auferstehung der Toten führt Origenes zunächst den Wortlaut
von Deut 25:5–10 an und fragt sodann nach der Absicht des
Textes, also nach dem tieferen Sinn. Bevor er zur konkreten
Auslegung übergeht, sagt er zunächst einige Sätze zum Grundsätzlichen dieser Auslegungsmethode: Jedes Gesetz, welches sich
als Gesetz Gottes zu erkennen gibt, ist etwas Ehrwürdiges und
Ehrfurchtgebietendes. "Ob wir aber das, was an diesem Gesetz
ehrwürdig und ehrfurchtgebietend ist, finden oder nicht, das
dürfte zuerst Gott wissen und sein Christus, sodann aber auch
der, der nach der Schrift kundiger Wechsler genannt wird, der
alles zu prüfen und das Gute zu behalten, von jeder Gestalt des
Bösen aber sich fernzuhalten versteht."[71] Im bezug auf seine
eigene Fähigkeit, den tieferen Sinn zu finden, ist Origenes hier
und im Folgenden äußerst zurückhaltend: er betet, daß er die
tiefere Einsicht empfängt, schließt aber die Möglichkeit, daß er
nur seine persönliche Interpretation vorbringt, nicht aus und fügt
hinzu: "Urteilen wird, wer unsere Worte in die Hände bekommt."[72] Der kundige Wechsler ist an dieser Stelle also nicht
der Ausleger selbst, der zwischen dem buchstäblichen und dem
tieferen Sinn unterscheiden kann, sondern der Hörer oder Leser
der Auslegung. Das Urteil über die Richtigkeit der Auslegung ist
in erster Linie eine Angelegenheit Gottes und Christi, sodann
aber auch des irdischen kundigen Wechslers und schließlich
sämtlicher Hörer und Leser seiner Auslegung. Zwischen den
beiden letzten Kategorien besteht eine gewisse Spannung: die
kundigen Wechsler stellt Origenes an die Seite Gottes und
Christi. Daraus geht hervor, daß das Urteil nicht jedermanns
Sache ist, sondern eine besondere pneumatische Einsicht fordert,
eine Einsicht, die Origenes an anderer Stelle nur den Vollkommenen zuschreibt.[73] Andererseits ist das Urteil eine Sache aller
seiner Hörer und Leser. Es ist nicht anzunehmen, daß er sie alle
für kundige Wechsler hält. So steht das Urteil über die Richtigkeit seiner Auslegung im Spannungsfeld von vier Instanzen:
(1) des Auslegers, (2) Gottes und Christi, (3) des besonders

---

[70] *MtComm* 17,31 (GCS 10, 672,31–674,14).

[71] Übersetzung H. J. Vogt in, Origenes, *Der Kommentar zum Evangelium nach
Mattäus*, BGrL 18.30.38 (Stuttgart 1983–1993), Teil II, 285.

[72] Zu dieser Zurückhaltung vgl. E. R. Redepenning, *Origenes* I (Bonn 1841),
316–318; H. Crouzel, *Origène* (Paris/Namur 1984), 109.

[73] *JohComm* 20, 286 (GCS 4, 369,32–370,2).

befähigten kundigen Wechslers und (4) sämtlicher Hörer und Leser. Da das Urteil Gottes und Christi dem Menschen in der Gegenwart nur beschränkt zugänglich ist und somit auch der Unterschied zwischen dem kundigen Wechsler, der das Urteil Gottes und Christi vertritt, und dem Hörer, der sein eigenes Urteil verkündigt, nicht von vornherein klar ist, bleibt die Entscheidung einstweilen offen. Ausdruck dieser Offenheit sind die sehr allgemein gehaltenen Formulierungen des Origenes.

4.4 Die wahren und die falschen Ausleger und Lehrer

An zwei Stellen geht Origenes unter Verwendung der Metapher von den kundigen Geldwechslern konkreter auf die Frage ein, wie die wahren und die falschen Ausleger oder Lehrer voneinander zu unterscheiden sind. Da ein Lehrer für ihn immer auch ein Ausleger der Schrift ist, sind beide Kategorien nicht voneinander zu trennen.

In der zweiten *Homilie zu Ezechiel*[74] nimmt er die Rede gegen die falschen Propheten (13:1–19) zum Anlaß für eine Ausführung über die Unterscheidung der wahren und falschen Propheten im wahren Israel, der Lehrer der Kirche und der Ausleger der Schriften. Sein Ausgangspunkt ist, daß die Ausleger, die die verborgene Bedeutung der Schrift explizieren wollen, denselben Geist brauchen wie die Propheten. Der falsche Prophet und der Häretiker redet "aus seinem eigenen Herzen" und verwechselt seinen eigenen Sinn mit dem des Evangeliums, der wahre Prophet dagegen redet "aus dem Heiligen Geiste" oder "aus dem Sinne Gottes."[75] Aus dem Heiligen Geiste redet der Ausleger, der die Worte Jesu "so versteht, wie der Herr sie gesprochen hat"[76] und "übereinstimmt mit der Absicht des Geistes, der durch die Apostel gesprochen hat."[77] Die wahren Ausleger können mit Paulus sagen: "wir aber haben den Sinn Christi" (I Kor 2:16). Origenes weiß, daß manche Leute meinen, er gehöre zu den falschen Propheten und der Herr rede nicht durch ihn.[78] Angesichts dieser Tatsache lädt er seine Hörer ein, aufmerksam

---

[74] SC 352,100–120.

[75] "*de sensu Dei*", EzHom 2,2 (SC 252, 102,13–23).

[76] "*...intelligens ut dominus locutus est*" (SC 352, 104,34–35). Die parallele Formulierung lautet: "*Si quis enim ea quae Iesus Christus Dominus locutus est et intellexit in eo loco loquitur quo locutus est ipse qui docuit*" (SC 352, 103,26–104,28).

[77] "*Si consentit sancti Spiritus voluntati, eius qui in Apostolis locutus est*" (SC 352, 104,29–30).

[78] 2,5 (SC 352, 118,38–40).

zuzuhören, und bittet er, daß sie die Gabe der Unterscheidungen
der Geister empfangen, so daß sie kundige Wechsler werden und
beurteilen können, wann er ein falscher Lehrer sei und wann er
die Wahrheit predige.[79] In diesem Zusammenhang nennt er
nochmals das Kriterium, jetzt aber zugespitzt auf die Auslegung
der Schriften des Alten Bundes: "Wenn ich in Moses und den
Propheten den Sinn Christi finde, rede ich nicht aus meinem
eigenen Herzen, sondern aus dem Heiligen Geiste. Wenn ich
aber nichts finde, was (mit diesem Sinne) übereinstimmt, sondern
meine Rede selbst erdichte, hin- und herschwankend zwischen
Wörtern, die Gott fremd sind, dann rede ich aus meinem eigenen
Herzen und nicht in Übereinstimmung mit den Gedanken
Gottes."[80] Wer wissen möchte, wie man konkret die Vermi-
schung von eigenen und Gottes Gedanken vermeiden kann,
bekommt in diesen Sätzen kaum eine Antwort. Auch Origenes
ist sich dessen bewußt, daß die Häretiker die gleichen Kriterien
verwenden. Auch sie sagen, "sie hätten die Tradition der
Apostel", "ihre Lehre sei die Lehre des Herrn", "ihr Sinn sei in
Übereinstimmung mit dem Sinne der Propheten." Obwohl sie
sagen "so spricht der Herr", hat der Herr sie jedoch nicht
gesandt.[81]

Origenes ist weit davon entfernt, das Paulinische Bild des
Pneumatikers, der jetzt schon den Sinn Christi hat und deshalb
nicht von anderen beurteilt werden kann (I Kor 2:15–16) für sich
zu beanspruchen.[82] Indem er seine Hörer auffordert, die Fähigkeit der kundigen Wechsler mit Bezug auf ihn auszuüben, erweckt er den Eindruck, er lege ihrem Urteil viel Gewicht bei. Im
gleichen Abschnitt wertet er jedoch das Urteil seiner Hörer ab
mit der Behauptung, es sei nicht entscheidend, wie Menschen
urteilen, es komme ausschließlich darauf an, was das Wort Gottes
zu ihm sage und wie Gott selbst urteilen werde. Dem Urteil
Gottes sehe er zuversichtlich entgegen.[83] Die Gegner des
Origenes werden über ihre eigene Fähigkeit, zu urteilen, gewiß
anders gedacht haben. Was Pamphilus später in seiner Apologie
für Origenes schreibt, daß es gerade die Gegner des Origenes

---

[79] 2,2 (SC 352, 104,43–50).

[80] 2,2 (SC 352, 104,50–106,55).

[81] *EzHom* 2,5 (SC 352, 116,25–118,1).

[82] Vgl. auch *JohCom* 10,172–173 (GCS 4, 201,11–22); *MtCom* 14,11 (GCS 10,
303,14–26); *MtCom* 15,30–31 (GCS 10, 440,23–442,21); *LevHom* 5,6 (SC 286,
232,16–23).

[83] 2,2 (SC 352, 102,6–12); 2,5 (SC 352, 118,40–49).

sind, die die Fähigkeit, kundige Wechsler zu sein, ausschließlich
sich selbst zuschreiben und es denen, die die Bücher des
Origenes lesen, absprechen,[84] wird man auch für die Lebenszeit
des Origenes annehmen dürfen.

Auf das hier offen bleibende Problem, wie man Hörer, die die
Gabe der Unterscheidung der Geister empfangen haben, von
denen unterscheiden kann, die vorgeben, im Namen Gottes zu
reden, in Wirklichkeit aber nur ihr menschliches Urteil vorbrin-
gen, geht Origenes ausführlich im *Matthäuskommentar* ein, und
zwar anläßlich der Ankündigung Jesu: "viele werden kommen
unter meinem Namen und sagen 'Ich bin der Christus'" (Mt
24:4–5).[85] Bei dieser Ankündigung, so erklärt er, sei weniger an
konkrete Personen zu denken als vielmehr an jede falsche Auslegung der Schrift. Die Ausleger der Schrift stoßen oft auf ein
Verständnis, "das sich für wahr ausgibt, obwohl es nicht wahr
ist", und manchmal werden sie "von anderen der Wahrheit
ähnlichen verfärbten Reden" angezogen.[86] Jeder, der jenes Gebot
"Seid kundige Wechsler!" und jenes andere "Prüft alles, behaltet
das Gute..." erfüllt, wird sehen, daß viele sich von einem
falschen Verständnis führen lassen. In dieser Allgemeinheit kann
Origenes das voller Zuversicht sagen. Er fügt aber sofort hinzu,
daß es leicht wäre, dieses Gebot zu erfüllen, wenn die Verführten
sich nur außerhalb der Kirche befinden würden. In Wirklichkeit
aber befinden sie sich auch unter denen, die sich als Männer der
Kirche bekennen. Neben denen, die das gerade Gegenteil der
Wahrheit denken—wie die Markioniten, Basilidianer, Valentini-
aner, Apellianer und die Ophiten—gibt es auch manche, die in
den "öffentlichen und offenkundigen Kapiteln"—z.B. in der
Lehre vom einen Gott, der das Gesetz und das Evangelium gegeben hat, oder in der Lehre von der Fleischwerdung Christi—
die kirchliche Meinung vertreten, aber über weniger bedeutende
Punkte neue Lehren vorlegen. Auch auf diese letzten kommt es
nach Origenes aber an, denn in dogmatischen Punkten abzuirren
ist schlimmer als in ethischen; wenn nämlich ein guter Lebens-
wandel für das Heil ausreiche, würden auch viele heidnische
Philosophen und Häretiker gerettet werden. Während Origenes
in diesem Abschnitt die großen Irrtümer namentlich nennt und
er von den "öffentlichen und offenkundigen Kapiteln"—haupt-
sächlich antignostisch ausgerichtete—Beispiele gibt, wird er in

---

[84] Lommatzsch 24,293–294.

[85] *MtCommSer* 33 (GCS 11, 59,9–64,9).

[86] Übersetzung nach H. J. Vogt, *Kommentar* (s. Anm. 71), Teil III, 95.

bezug auf die weniger bedeutenden Lehren nicht konkret.[87] Es geht ihm anscheinend an dieser Stelle mehr um das Problem als solches als um eine konkrete Auseinandersetzung. Konkreter wird er, wenn er im folgenden zeigt, wie schwierig es in der Praxis ist, Wahrheit und Irrtum auseinanderzuhalten. Der Antichrist täuscht ja in jeder Hinsicht Christus vor: nicht nur gibt es vorgetäuschte Lehre, Wahrheit und Weisheit, sondern auch vorgetäuschte Tugenden: Gerechtigkeit, Keuschheit, Barmherzigkeit und Geduld. Auch bei den Häretikern gibt es Leute, die in Keuschheit leben, die Almosen geben, die für Christus leiden und sogar ihr Leben geben. Ja, auch vorgetäuschte Wunderkraft gibt es, wie aus Mt 7:22–23 hervorgeht. Weil die Betätigungen Christi und die des Antichrist sich in jeder Hinsicht ähnlich sind, so fügt er hinzu, brauchen wir Gott und den in uns lebenden Christus als Helfer, um mit geöffneten Augen zu schauen und die verführerischen Reden und Taten zu unterscheiden.

Klar und zuversichtlich ist der Ton des Origenes in bezug auf die Fähigkeit des kundigen Wechslers an dieser Stelle also nur, wenn er allgemein redet oder wenn er bestimmte gnostische Lehren im Auge hat. An allen anderen Punkten, den weniger bedeutenden Lehren, den Tugenden und der Wunderkraft, weist er nur auf die Schwierigkeiten hin und betont er die Notwendigkeit der göttlichen Hilfe. Origenes verweist innerhalb seiner Argumentation auf seine Auslegung von Ps 23:3–4,[88] wo er ausführlicher von der Notwendigkeit der reinen Lehre in der Seele neben dem untadeligen Leben gehandelt hat. Er bezeichnet jene Ausführungen als eine Selbstbelehrung und dieser Aspekt sollte auch bei seiner Auslegung von Mt 24:4–5 mitberücksichtigt werden: aus der oben besprochenen zweiten *Homilie zu Ezechiel* geht hervor, wie Origenes damit gerungen hat, selbst nicht zu den falschen Lehrern gerechnet zu werden.

An fünf weiteren Stellen bezieht Origenes die Fähigkeit der kundigen Wechsler auf die Unterscheidung der wahren und falschen Lehre, ohne tief auf das damit verbundene Problem einzugehen.[89] Er unterstreicht, daß das Reden der Wahrheit und das

---

[87] Zu den Irrlehren, die er im Auge habe könnte, vgl. Crouzel, *Origène*, 205–206; A. Le Boulluec, *La notion d'hérésie dans la littérature grecque IIe–IIIe siècles* II (Paris 1985), 521–522.

[88] Oder die von Spr 20:9; aus dem Zusammenhang geht das nicht klar hervor.

[89] *JohCom* 20,286 (GCS 4, 369,30–370,2); 32,215 (GCS 4, 454,30–32); *EphCom* §19,60–62 (*JThS* 3, 419); §22,37–39 (*JThS* 3, 562); *LevHom* 3,8,83–85 (SC 286, 156, 158). Ich übergehe *Frg in Jer* 19 (GCS 3, 207,9–17), einmal weil, wie oben

Ablegen der Lüge "nicht ein beliebiges Werk" ist,[90] daß das Vermögen, zwischen den verschiedenen Lehren zu unterscheiden und einzig und allein der Wahrheit zu glauben, nach Hebr 5:14 eine Fähigkeit der "Vollkommenen" und deshalb ein "vollkommenes" Werk ist,[91] und daß allein der Herr diese Kunst lehren kann.[92] Soweit Origenes von dieser Kunst als einer Gabe redet, identifiziert er sie nicht nur mit dem Charisma der Unterscheidung der Geister (I Kor 12:10),[93] sondern auch mit dem Charisma des Glaubens (I Kor 12:9), weil es darauf ankommt, einzig der Wahrheit zu glauben.[94] Diese Betonung des besonderen Charakters dieser Fähigkeit hängt zusammen mit der an fast allen Stellen erwähnten Tatsache, daß falsche Lehrer immer im Gewande der Lehrer der Wahrheit auftreten.

4.5 Die Unterscheidung der den Gläubigen anvertrauten Worte

Die Tätigkeit der kundigen Wechsler soll sich nach Origenes nicht nur auf den Stand der Lehrer ausatrecken, sondern zu allen Gläubigen. Jeder Gläubige liefert seinen Beitrag zum geistlichen Schatz der Kirche und die Wechsler sollen deren Echtheit prüfen. In einer komplizierten Argumentation erörtert er diese Sicht in seinem *Kommentar zu Johannes* 8:20, wo davon die Rede ist, daß Jesus seine Worte "bei der Schatzkammer" sprach.[95] Den Sinn dieser Ortsbezeichnung findet er in der Erzählung vom Heller der armen Witwe (Lk 21:1-4; Mk 12:41-44): Die Schatzkammer im Tempel soll man im geistigen Sinne verstehen. Es ist die Stätte, wo die Münzen zur Ehre Gottes und zum Gemeinwohl geopfert werden. Die Münzen sind die göttlichen Worte, die das Bild des großen Königs aufgeprägt tragen, die von den kundigen Wechslern angeschaut werden, die das Gebot Jesu befolgen: "Seid kundige Wechsler!", sowie die Lehre des Paulus in I Thess 5:21-22. Zugrunde liegt der Gedanke, daß in der Kirche jedes Mitglied aktiv zur Erkenntnis der gesamten Gemeinde beitragen soll.[96] Daß solche Beiträge der Prüfung bedürfen, mag für sich

---

gezeigt, kaum eine Anspielung auf das Agraphon vorliegen dürfte, und sodann, weil der Text zu fragmentarisch ist, um daraus Schlüsse ziehen zu können.

[90] *EphCom* §19,59-60 (*JThS* 3, 419).

[91] *JohCom* 20,286 (GCS 4, 369,32-370,2).

[92] *LevHom* 3,8,85-88 (SC 286, 158).

[93] Z.B. *EzHom* 2,2 (SC 352, 104,47-48).

[94] *JohCom* 20, 285-286 (GCS 4, 369,26-370,2).

[95] *JohCom* 19,40-63 (GCS 4, 306,1-310,9).

[96] Vgl. H. J. Vogt, *Kirchenverständnis*, 105-107.

sprechen. Auffällig ist jedoch, wie beiläufig Origenes diesen Gedanken erwähnt. Weder erwähnt er einen konkreten Anlaß, noch geht er auf die Frage ein, wer die Fähigkeit des kundigen Wechslers besitzt oder welche Kriterien bei einer solchen Prüfung gelten. Man bekommt den Eindruck, daß er hier mehr oder weniger mechanisch der Assoziationskette: Schatzkammer—Münzen—Wechsler—Prüfen folgt.

Das wird bestätigt durch die Tatsache, daß er im folgenden Abschnitt zunächst einer anderen Spur folgt, indem er die Heller der Witwe auf die Quantität der Erkenntnis und des Handelns der Gläubigen bezieht und die Frage nach der Qualität oder Authentizität völlig außer acht läßt.[97] Unter einem anderen Gesichtspunkt bringt er sodann doch den Aspekt des Prüfens wieder hinein, wenn er ausführt, daß Jesus mit seinen Worten des ewigen Lebens mehr als alle anderen in die Schatzkammer gebracht hat. Diese Worte sind—mit dem Bild der Feuerprobe aus Ps 12(11):7—"reine Worte des Herrn, siebenfach im Feuer geprüft, gereinigt und als echt befunden." Im Vergleich mit der Weisheit dieser Worte ist die Weisheit dieser Welt, die man für Gold hält—mit den Worten von SapSal 7:9—nur "ein wenig Sand" und wird die glänzende und gewinnende Rede der vielen, die man für Silber hält, als Kot betrachtet. Zusammenfassend ermahnt Origenes seine Leser: Wenn einer ein Nachfolger Christi ist, soll er die geprüften Münzen, die Worte des ewigen Lebens und die denen entsprechenden Werke in den geistigen Tempel Gottes bringen.[98] Auch wenn Origenes hier den Gedanken des Prüfens wieder aufnimmt, so tut er es doch in einer anderen Weise als am Anfang: Er verwendet nicht das Bild der Geldwechsler, sondern das der Feuerprobe und das des Vergleichs der Edelmetalle. Die Worte Jesu sind von Anfang an schon als echt befunden worden. Die Gläubigen sollen solche schon geprüften Münzen in den Tempel bringen. Der am Anfang zum Ausdruck gebrachte Gedanke, daß die von den Gläubigen eingebrachten Worte jeweils geprüft werden müssen, spielt in der weiteren Erörterung keine Rolle mehr. Das bestätigt die Vermutung, daß Origenes an dieser Stelle eher mechanisch assoziiert, als daß er etwas konkretes zur Gemeindepraxis sagen will.

Das Verhältnis zwischen den empfangenen Herrenworten und dem eigenen Beitrag der Gläubigen und die damit zusammenhängende Notwendigkeit der Prüfung erörtert Origenes

---

[97] 19,45–52 (GCS 4, 307,10–308,22).
[98] 19, 53–57 (GCS 4, 308,22–309,21).

klarer im *Matthäuskommentar* bei der Auslegung des Gleichnisses
von den anvertrauten Talenten (Mt 25:24–27).[99] Auch hier
bezieht er die Münzen auf die Herrenworte, die jeder Gläubige
empfängt und bezeichnet er als Objekt der Tätigkeit der Geldwechsler den geistlichen Beitrag jedes Gemeindegliedes. Das
Gleichnis von den anvertrauten Talenten bezieht er auf die Interpretation der Schrift. Manche haben den erhabeneren Sinn der
Schrift empfangen, andere sind nur wenig über den Buchstaben
hinaus emporgestiegen und eine dritte Gruppe ist beim Buchstaben steckengeblieben. Der Knecht, der sein Talent in der Erde
verborgen hatte, wird deswegen als böse verurteilt, weil er mit
dem empfangenen "erprobten Geld der Herrenworte" kein
Handel getrieben hat. Die Gläubigen haben die Aufgabe, die
empfangenen christlichen Worte zu erörtern, um tiefere Geheim-
nisse der Güte Gottes zu erwerben und so das eigene und der
anderen Heil zu erwirken. Die Hörer haben die doppelte
Funktion des Bankiers: Einmal müssen sie in der Funktion der
Wechsler die Worte prüfen, um so die wahre und gute Lehre zu
behalten, die verworfene und falsche dagegen zurückzuweisen.
Sodann zahlen sie, indem die gute Lehre zu ihrem Heile wirkt, in
der Funktion der Geldverleiher das Geld mit Zinsen denen, die
es ihnen anvertraut haben, zurück. Die Geldwechsler werden
hier also ausdrücklich mit allen Hörern identifiziert. Origenes
schreibt ihnen ohne weiteres die Fähigkeit zu prüfen zu. Die
Prüfung ist notwendig, weil die Gläubigen die empfangenen
Herrenworte in einer eigenen Interpretation—entsprechend der
ihnen verliehenen Einsicht—weitergeben. Als Kriterium für die
Echtheit nennt Origenes nur allgemein, daß die Worte die könig-
liche Gestalt Gottes und das Bild seines Wortes an sich tragen
müssen.

4.6 Gerechtes und Ungerechtes

Zweimal verwendet Origenes das Bild der Wechsler für die
Fähigkeit, gerechte und ungerechte Taten zu unterscheiden. Zu
Jer 20:12 "Herr, der das Gerechte billigt, der Nieren und Herzen
kennt" kommentiert er: "Der Herr billigt (δοκιμάζει) das Gerechte, doch er mißbilligt (ἀποδοκιμάζει) das Ungerechte. Und
er ist, um es so auszudrücken, der Wechsler des Gerechten und
Ungerechten."[100] Nur an dieser Stelle wendet Origenes das Bild

---

[99] *MtCommSer* 68 (GCS 11, 158,33–162,5).

[100] *JerHom* 20 (19),9 (GCS 3, 193,21–23; Übersetzung nach E. Schadel, *Jeremiahomilien*, 234).

auf die göttliche Tätigkeit an. Wie schon gesagt, liegt hier kaum eine Anspielung auf das Agraphon vor.

An einer Stelle im *Kommentar zum Epheserbrief* [101] sind die Gläubigen das Subjekt. Zu Eph 5:10—"Prüft (δοκιμάζοντες), was dem Herrn wohlgefällig ist"—bemerkt er, daß es notwendig ist, die Taten zu prüfen und "wie kundige Wechsler das Bewährte und Gott Wohlgefällige anzunehmen, das Unbewährte und das ihm nicht Gefällige von sich zu schütteln."

In beiden Fällen hat sich Origenes zu dem Wechslervergleich durch das Wort δοκιμάζειν der Bibelstelle anregen lassen und bleibt es bei dieser kurzen Bemerkung.

4.7 Zusammenfassung

Origenes verwendet das Agraphon bzw. das Bild der kundigen Wechsler in der überwiegenden Mehrzahl der Fälle mit Bezug auf die Schriften des Alten und Neuen Bundes und deren Auslegung. Die Unterscheidung der wahren und falschen Lehre hängt damit zusammen. Völlig am Rande begegnet das Bild auch im Zusammenhang mit der ethischen Diskretion. Anders als H. Rahner sehe ich keinen Zusammenhang zwischen dem Agraphon und der aszetischen Diskretion. Die drei Stellen, die Rahner zur Begründung seiner These—"Hier beginnt schon die Diktion der kommenden Mönchsaskese zu sprechen"—anführt, gehören m.E. in einen anderen Zusammenhang und enthalten nichts, das für das Phänomen der asketischen Diskretion, wie man es z.B. bei Johannes Cassianus findet, typisch ist. [102]

Soweit Origenes dem Wortlaut des Agraphons entsprechend imperativisch redet, gilt die Aufforderung, kundige Wechsler zu sein, jedem Kirchenglied. Anders als z.B. in der *Didaskalie* [103] ist sie nicht auf einen bestimmten hierarchischen Stand beschränkt. Soweit Origenes von dieser Fähigkeit als einem Charisma redet, gibt es jedoch wohl verschiedene Begabungen: Nur die Vollkommenen, die erfüllt sind mit dem Heiligen Geist oder die das

---

[101] *EphCom* § 25,45–48 (*JThS* 3, 562).

[102] In *JohCom* 19,44 sagt Origenes nicht, wie Rahner meint, daß der vollkommene Christ die echten Münzen "im Schatzkasten seines Herzens" bergen muß. Der geistliche Schatzkasten ist hier nicht das Herz, sondern die Kirche. *JohCom* 32,215 handelt allgemein von Dienern der Wahrheit und Dienern der Lüge. *JerHom* 20,9 kann man kaum eine Anspielung auf das Agraphon nennen; die Stelle handelt zudem allgemein vom Gerechten und Ungerechten. Vgl. Rahner, *Gr* 37, 478.

[103] II,36,9–10 (Funk, Band I, 123,16–20).

Charisma der Unterscheidung der Geister empfangen haben, haben im eigentlichen Sinne das Vermögen, zu urteilen. Soweit Origenes von dieser Gabe als einer konkreten Realität spricht, nennt er nur die Kirche als Gesamtheit oder mit einem gewissen Vorbehalt Autoritäten aus einer vergangenen Epoche wie die Apostel und Evangelisten als deren Empfänger. In beiden Fällen geht es dabei um die Feststellung der anerkannten Schriften. Sonst redet Origenes von der Fähigkeit der kundigen Wechsler ausschließlich als von einem Ideal oder einer virtuellen Größe. Entweder redet er allgemein von der Möglichkeit und Notwendigkeit dieser Gabe, oder er betet, daß seine Hörer sie empfangen. Nie weist er in seiner Gegenwart Personen oder Gruppen an, die diese Gabe konkret besitzen. Was von dieser spezifischen Fähigkeit gilt, kann man auf die Charismata im allgemeinen ausweiten: Wenn Origenes von den Gaben des Geistes redet, denkt er oft mehr an ideale oder virtuelle Größen als an konkrete und in der Gegenwart sichtbare Fähigkeiten.[104] Dem entspricht, daß er an einer Stelle sagen kann, daß sich in der Gegenwart der wahre Weise nach Gottes Maßstab nicht finden läßt und daß die meisten der besonderen Charismen erloschen sind.[105]

Und damit macht Origenes es mir schwer, meine Absicht für diesen Aufsatz zu verwirklichen: Ich hatte dieses Thema gewählt, weil ich Tjitze Baarda über viele Jahre hinweg kennengelernt habe als einen *exercitatissimus trapezites* in wissenschaftlichen, kirchlichen und menschlichen Fragen. Nach der Lektüre des Origenes getraue ich mich jedoch kaum noch, es auszusprechen.

---

[104] Vgl. H. Crouzel, *Origène et la "connaissance mystique"*, ML.T 56, (Paris/Bruges 1961), 483.486–491; ders., *Origène*, 159: "Quand Origène fait le portrait du spirituel et du parfait, il regarde en fait son idéal jamais vraiment réalisé en cette vie."

[105] *Frg in Prov* 1:6 (PG 13, col. 25A); nach A. Le Boulluec, *La notion d'hérésie*, Vol. II, 462, Anm. 109, denkt Origenes in diesem Kontext insbesondere an die Gabe der Unterscheidung der Geister.

INDEX LOCORUM

I. BIBLICAL CITATIONS

A. Hebrew Bible (OT)

Genesis
- 6:10: 187
- 6:15: 97
- 9:21: 125
- 11:27: 187
- 15:8 LXX: 182 n. 14
- 22:1-2: 188
- 22:11: 180, 184, 188
- 35:11: 158
- 46:2: 180, 184

Exodus
- 3:4: 180, 184, 188
- 7-8: 102
- 8: 93
- 12:11: 158
- 8:12-15 (16-19): 90
- 8:15 (19): 90, 91, 93, 95, 97, 102
- 12:2: 96-97 *bis*
- 14:31: 95
- 23:20: 146
- 29:38: 96, 97
- 30:13: 98
- 31:18: 90, 91, 93
- 34:6: 181

Leviticus
- 11:29: 96, 97 *bis*
- 16:29-30: 270

Numbers
- 6:4: 125
- 8:4: 96, 97, 97 n. 24

Deuteronomy
- 3:5: 14 n. 29

- 3:24: 181 n. 13
- 9:10: 90, 91, 91 n. 8
- 9:26: 181 n. 13
- 24:7: 261
- 25:5-10: 293

Judges
- 4: 273 n. 50
- 6:22 (A): 181 n. 13
- 6:28 (A): 181 n. 13
- 13:14: 125

1 Samuel (1 Kingdoms LXX)
- 2:31: 260 n. 18
- 3:4-10: 184
- 3:4: 180
- 3:6 MT: 180
- 3:10 LXX: 180

2 Samuel (2 Kingdoms LXX)
- 7:18: 182 n. 13
- 7:19 *bis*: 182 n. 13
- 7:20: 182 n. 13
- 7:25: 182 n. 13
- 7:28: 182 n. 13
- 7:29: 182 n. 13
- 19:1: 180
- 19:5: 180

1 Kings (3 Kingdoms LXX)
- 8:53 LXX: 181 n. 13
- 13:2: 180, 183

2 Kings (4 Kingdoms LXX)
- 1:8: 235
- 2:12: 180, 184, 184 n. 24
- 10:17: 260 n. 18

B. New Testament

John (*cont'd.*)
7:53–8:11: 191–221
  Armenian: 196, 198, 208,
    218, 220
  Diatessaron: 195
  Georgian: 196
  Latin Vulgate: 195
  Old Latin: 194
  Syriac: 195
8:2–11: 195 n. 20, 200
8:2: 195 n. 20
8:3–4 (D, 1071): 197 n. 27
8:11: 191–221
8:20: 298
8:51: 84
11:43: 187
12:14: 44
12:21: 189 n. 30
13:38: 128 n. 18
17:3: 44
18:4: 178
19:15: 175
19:16: 175
19:17: 35
20:15: 189 n. 30
20:16: 182 n. 15
20:25: 212, 213 n. 75, 220
20:28: 213
21:23: 128 n. 18
21:25: 193 n. 8, 194 n. 13

Acts
1:9 (D): 261
2:30: 158
3:17: 32 n. 23, 35
4:19: 110
4:29: 39
4:31: 39
5:1–11: 109 n. 13
7:42: 44
7:55–60: 35
7:60: 31, 34, 35 n. 32
8:25: 39
9:4: 179, 184, 184 n. 24
9:10: 184 n. 24
9:32–43: 109 n. 13
11:19: 39

13:2–3: 254
13:27: 32 n. 23, 35
13:46: 39
14:23: 254
16:30: 189 n. 30
17:34: 109 n. 13
19:34 (B): 175
22:7: 179
26:14: 179
27:9: 254

Romans
1:17: 44
2:1: 257 n. 9
6:3–11: 84
6:6: 257 n. 11
7:1: 258 n. 14
7:6: 257 n. 11
8:3: 257 n. 9
8:34: 108

1 Corinthians
1:31: 44
2:7: 139 n. 12
2:9: 287
2:15–16: 294, 295
3:13: 164 n. 41, 165 n. 45
5:7–8: 257 n. 11
5:13: 261
6:9: 131
7:39: 258 n. 14
9:12: 41
11:23–26: 124, 127
11:25: 129
11:26: 127
12:9: 298
12:10: 291, 198
14:31: 289
15: 171
15:13, 16: 269 n. 42
15:20–28: 132
15:50: 131
15:52: 167
16:22: 127

II. "Q" CITATIONS

III. CLASSICAL, QUMRAN, PSEUDEPIGRAPHIC, APOCRYPHAL, RABBINIC, AND PATRISTIC CITATIONS

IV. PAPYRI (NON-CHRISTIAN AND CHRISTIAN)

INDEX AUCTORUM

(*post 1500 C.E.*)

INDEX RERUM

SUPPLEMENTS TO NOVUM TESTAMENTUM

ISSN 0167-9732

2. STROBEL, A. *Untersuchungen zum eschatologischen Verzögerungsproblem auf Grund der spätjüdische-urchristlichen Geschichte von Habakuk 2,2 ff.* 1961. ISBN 90 04 01582 5

6. *Neotestamentica et Patristica.* Eine Freundesgabe Herrn Professor Dr. Oscar Cullmann zu seinem 60. Geburtstag überreicht. 1962. ISBN 90 04 01586 8

8. DE MARCO, A.A. *The Tomb of Saint Peter.* A Representative and Annotated Bibliography of the Excavations. 1964. ISBN 90 04 01588 4

10. BORGEN, P. *Bread from Heaven.* An Exegetical Study of the Concept of Manna in the Gospel of John and the Writings of Philo. Photomech. Reprint of the first (1965) edition. 1981. ISBN 90 04 06419 2

13. MOORE, A.L. *The Parousia in the New Testament.* 1966. ISBN 90 04 01593 0

15. QUISPEL, G. *Makarius, das Thomasevangelium und das Lied von der Perle.* 1967. ISBN 90 04 01595 7

16. PFITZNER, V.C. *Paul and the Agon Motif.* 1967. ISBN 90 04 01596 5

17. BELLINZONI, A. *The Sayings of Jesus in the Writings of Justin Martyr.* 1967. ISBN 90 04 01597 3

18. GUNDRY, R.H. *The Use of the Old Testament in St. Matthew's Gospel.* With Special Reference to the Messianistic Hope. Reprint of the first (1967) edition. 1975. ISBN 90 04 04278 4

19. SEVENSTER, J.N. *Do You Know Greek?* How Much Greek Could the first Jewish Christians Have Known? 1968. ISBN 90 04 03090 5

20. BUCHANAN, G.W. *The Consequences of the Covenant.* 1970. ISBN 90 04 01600 7

21. KLIJN, A.F.J. *A Survey of the Researches into the Western Text of the Gospels and Acts.* Part 2: 1949-1969. 1969. ISBN 90 04 01601 5

22. GABOURY, A. *La Stucture des Évangiles synoptiques.* La structure-type à l'origine des synoptiques. 1970. ISBN 90 04 01602 3

23. GASTON, L. *No Stone on Another.* Studies in the Significance of the Fall of Jerusalem in the Synoptic Gospels. 1970. ISBN 90 04 01603 1

24. *Studies in John.* Presented to Professor Dr. J.N. Sevenster on the Occasion of His Seventieth Birthday. 1970. ISBN 90 04 03091 3

25. STORY, C.I.K. *The Nature of Truth in the 'Gospel of Truth', and in the Writings of Justin Martyr.* A Study of the Pattern of Orthodoxy in the Middle of the Second Christian Century. 1970. ISBN 90 04 01605 8

26. GIBBS, J.G. *Creation and Redemption.* A Study in Pauline Theology. 1971. ISBN 90 04 01606 6

27. MUSSIES, G. *The Morphology of Koine Greek As Used in the Apocalypse of St. John.* A Study in Bilingualism. 1971. ISBN 90 04 02656 8

28. AUNE, D.E. *The Cultic Setting of Realized Eschatology in Early Christianity.* 1972. ISBN 90 04 03341 6

29. UNNIK, W.C. VAN. *Sparsa Collecta.* The Collected Essays of W.C. van Unnik Part 1. Evangelia, Paulina, Acta. 1973. ISBN 90 04 03660 1

30. UNNIK, W.C. VAN. *Sparsa Collecta.* The Collected Essays of W.C. van Unnik Part 2. I Peter, Canon, Corpus Hellenisticum, Generalia. 1980. ISBN 90 04 06261 0

31. UNNIK, W.C. VAN. *Sparsa Collecta.* The Collected Essays of W.C. van Unnik Part 3. Patristica, Gnostica, Liturgica. 1983. ISBN 90 04 06262 9
33. AUNE D.E. (ed.) *Studies in New Testament and Early Christian Literature.* Essays in Honor of Allen P. Wikgren. 1972. ISBN 90 04 03504 4
34. HAGNER, D.A. *The Use of the Old and New Testaments in Clement of Rome.* 1973. ISBN 90 04 03636 9
35. GUNTHER, J.J. *St. Paul's Opponents and Their Background.* A Study of Apocalyptic and Jewish Sectarian Teachings. 1973. ISBN 90 04 03738 1
36. KLIJN, A.F.J. & G.J. REININK (eds.) *Patristic Evidence for Jewish-Christian Sects.* 1973. ISBN 90 04 03763 2
37. REILING, J. *Hermas and Christian Prophecy.* A Study of The Eleventh Mandate. 1973. ISBN 90 04 03771 3
38. DONFRIED, K.P. *The Setting of Second Clement in Early Christianity.* 1974. ISBN 90 04 03895 7
39. ROON, A. VAN. *The Authenticity of Ephesians.* 1974. ISBN 90 04 03971 6
40. KEMMLER, D.W. *Faith and Human Reason.* A Study of Paul's Method of Preaching as Illustrated by 1-2 Thessalonians and Acts 17, 2-4. 1975. ISBN 90 04 04209 1
42. PANCARO, S. *The Law in the Fourth Gospel.* The Torah and the Gospel, Moses and Jesus, Judaism and Christianity According to John. 1975. ISBN 90 04 04309 8
43. CLAVIER, H. *Les variétés de la pensée biblique et le problème de son unité.* Esquisse d'une théologie de la Bible sur les textes originaux et dans leur contexte historique. 1976. ISBN 90 04 04465 5
44. ELLIOTT, J.K.E. (ed.) *Studies in New Testament Language and Text.* Essays in Honour of George D. Kilpatrick on the Occasion of His Sixty-fifth Birthday. 1976. ISBN 90 04 04386 1
45. PANAGOPOULOS, J. (ed.) *Prophetic Vocation in the New Testament and Today.* 1977. ISBN 90 04 04923 1
46. KLIJN, A.F.J. *Seth in Jewish, Christian and Gnostic Literature.* 1977. ISBN 90 04 05245 3
47. BAARDA, T., A.F.J. KLIJN & W.C. VAN UNNIK (eds.) *Miscellanea Neotestamentica.* I. Studia ad Novum Testamentum Praesertim Pertinentia a Sociis Sodalicii Batavi c.n. Studiosorum Novi Testamenti Conventus Anno MCMLXXVI Quintum Lustrum Feliciter Complentis Suscepta. 1978. ISBN 90 04 05685 8
48. BAARDA, T., A.F.J. KLIJN & W.C. VAN UNNIK (eds.) *Miscellanea Neotestamentica.* II. 1978. ISBN 90 04 05686 6
49. O'BRIEN, P.T. *Introductory Thanksgivings in the Letters of Paul.* 1977. ISBN 90 04 05265 8
50. BOUSSET, D.W. *Religionsgeschichtliche Studien.* Aufsätze zur Religionsgeschichte des hellenistischen Zeitalters. Hrsg. von A.F. Verheule. 1979. ISBN 90 04 05845 1
51. COOK, M.J. *Mark's Treatment of the Jewish Leaders.* 1978. ISBN 90 04 05785 4
52. GARLAND, D.E. *The Intention of Matthew 23.* 1979. ISBN 90 04 05912 1
53. MOXNES, H. *Theology in Conflict.* Studies in Paul's Understanding of God in Romans. 1980. ISBN 90 04 06140 1
55. MENKEN, M.J.J. *Numerical Literary Techniques in John.* The Fourth Evangelist's Use of Numbers of Words and Syllables. 1985. ISBN 90 04 07427 9
56. SKARSAUNE, O. *The Proof From Prophecy.* A Study in Justin Martyr's Proof-Text Tradition: Text-type, Provenance, Theological Profile. 1987. ISBN 90 04 07468 6

59. WILKINS, M.J. *The Concept of Disciple in Matthew's Gospel, as Reflected in the Use of the Term 'Mathetes'.* 1988. ISBN 90 04 08689 7

60. MILLER, E.L. *Salvation-History in the Prologue of John.* The Significance of John 1:3-4. 1989. ISBN 90 04 08692 7

61. THIELMAN, F. *From Plight to Solution.* A Jewish Framework for Understanding Paul's View of the Law in Galatians and Romans. 1989. ISBN 90 04 09176 9

64. STERLING, G.E. *Historiography and Self-Definition.* Josephos, Luke-Acts and Apologetic Historiography. 1992. ISBN 90 04 09501 2

65. BOTHA, J.E. *Jesus and the Samaritan Woman.* A Speech Act Reading of John 4:1-42. 1991. ISBN 90 04 09505 5

66. KUCK, D.W. *Judgment and Community Conflict.* Paul's Use of Apologetic Judgment Language in 1 Corinthians 3:5-4:5. 1992. ISBN 90 04 09510 1

67. SCHNEIDER, G. *Jesusüberlieferung und Christologie.* Neutestamentliche Aufsätze 1970-1990. 1992. ISBN 90 04 09555 1

68. SEIFRID, M.A. *Justification by Faith.* The Origin and Development of a Central Pauline Theme. 1992. ISBN 90 04 09521 7

69. NEWMAN, C.C. *Paul's Glory-Christology.* Tradition and Rhetoric. 1992. ISBN 90 04 09463 6

70. IRELAND, D.J. *Stewardship and the Kingdom of God.* An Historical, Exegetical, and Contextual Study of the Parable of the Unjust Steward in Luke 16: 1-13. 1992. ISBN 90 04 09600 0

71. ELLIOTT, J.K. *The Language and Style of the Gospel of Mark.* An Edition of C.H. Turner's "Notes on Marcan Usage" together with other comparable studies. 1993. ISBN 90 04 09767 8

72. CHILTON, B. *A Feast of Meanings.* Eucharistic Theologies from Jesus through Johannine Circles. 1994. ISBN 90 04 09949 2

73. GUTHRIE, G.H. *The Structure of Hebrews.* A Text-Linguistic Analysis. 1994. ISBN 90 04 09866 6

74. BORMANN, L., K. DEL TREDICI & A. STANDHARTINGER (eds.) *Religious Propaganda and Missionary Competition in the New Testament World.* Essays Honoring DIETER GEORGI. 1994. ISBN 90 04 10049 0

75. PIPER, R.A. (ed.) *The Gospel Behind the Gospels.* Current Studies on Q. 1995. ISBN 90 04 09737 6

76. PEDERSEN, S. (ed.) *New Directions in Biblical Theology.* Papers of the Aarhus Conference, 16-19 September 1992. 1994. ISBN 90 04 10120 9

77. JEFFORD, C.N. (ed.) *The* Didache *in Context.* Essays on Its Text, History and Transmission. 1995. ISBN 90 04 10045 8

78. BORMANN, L. *Philippi – Stadt und Christengemeinde zur Zeit des Paulus.* 1995. ISBN 90 04 10232 9

79. PETERLIN, D. *Paul's Letter to the Philippians in the Light of Disunity in the Church.* 1995. ISBN 90 04 10305 8

80. JONES, I.H. *The Matthean Parables.* A Literary and Historical Commentary. 1995 ISBN 90 04 10181 0

81. GLAD, C.E. *Paul and Philodemus.* Adaptability in Epicurean and Early Christian Psychagogy. 1995 ISBN 90 04 10067 9

82. FITZGERALD, J.T. (ed.) *Friendship, Flattery, and Frankness of Speech.* Studies on Friendship in the New Testament World. 1996. ISBN 90 04 10454 2

83. VAN TILBORG, S. *Reading John in Ephesus.* 1996. 90 04 10530 1

84. HOLLEMAN, J. *Resurrection and Parousia.* A Traditio-Historical Study of Paul's Eschatology in 1 Corinthians 15. 1996. ISBN 90 04 10597 2

85. MORITZ, T. *A Profound Mystery.* The Use of the Old Testament in Ephesians. 1996. ISBN 90 04 10556 5

86. BORGEN, P. *Philo of Alexandria - An Exegete for his Time.* 1997. ISBN 90 04 10388 0 (In preparation)

87. ZWIEP, A.W. *The Ascension of the Messiah in Lukan Christology.* 1997. ISBN 90 04 10897 1

88. WILSON, W.T. *The Hope of Glory.* Education and Exhortation in the Epistle to the Colossians. 1997. ISBN 90 04 10937 4 (In preparation)

89. PETERSEN, W.L., J.S. VOS & H.J. DE JONGE (eds.). *Sayings of Jesus: Canonical and Non-Canonical.* Essays in Honour of TJITZE BAARDA. 1997. ISBN 90 04 10380 5